THE ISLAMIC UTOPIA
The Illusion of Reform in Saudi Arabia

Andrew Hammond

PlutoPress
www.plutobooks.com

First published 2012 by Pluto Press
345 Archway Road, London N6 5AA

www.plutobooks.com

Distributed in the United States of America exclusively by
Palgrave Macmillan, a division of St. Martin's Press LLC,
175 Fifth Avenue, New York, NY 10010

British Library Cataloguing in Publication Data
A catalogue record for this book is available from the British Library

ISBN   978 0 7453 3270 3   Hardback
ISBN   978 0 7453 3269 7   Paperback
ISBN   978 1 8496 4737 3   PDF eBook
ISBN   978 1 8496 4739 7   Kindle eBook
ISBN   978 1 8496 4738 0   EPUB eBook

Library of Congress Cataloging in Publication Data applied for

This book is printed on paper suitable for recycling and made from fully managed
and sustained forest sources. Logging, pulping and manufacturing processes are
expected to conform to the environmental standards of the country of origin.

10   9   8   7   6   5   4   3   2   1

Designed and produced for Pluto Press by Chase Publishing Services Ltd
Typeset from disk by Stanford DTP Services, Northampton, England
Simultaneously printed digitally by CPI Antony Rowe, Chippenham, UK and
Edwards Bros in the United States of America

The Islamic Utopia

Contents

Glossary

abaya	A black cape with hood worn by women.
Abbasid	The name of the second major dynasty of Islam, which established itself in Iraq in 750 and lasted until the Mongols sacked Baghdad in 1258.
Al-Azhar	A religious seminary and university based in Cairo, with branches around the Islamic world.
al-Fi'a al-Daalla	Term meaning the deviant group or sector of society, used to refer to al-Qa'ida militants.
al-Quds	The Arabic term for Jerusalem, with an inherent religious connotation for Muslims: the word means 'the sacred' or 'the holy' and is only used to refer to the city.
al-'Uruba	Post-colonial political notion of 'Arabness' and the sense of Arab identity (also *al-qawmiyya al-arabiyya*, or Arab nationalism).
al-wasatiyya	Term meaning 'the middle way', often used to suggest 'moderate Islam' and contrast with religious positions deemed extreme or overly zealous.
'awra	Something shameful.
bid'a	Un-Islamic innovation.
caliph	The term used to describe the ruler of the Arab-Islamic state after the Arab conquests.
da'wa	Term meaning 'preaching' or 'calling'. Wahhabism is often referred to as the 'Wahhabi calling'.
dustour	Constitution.
Eid al-Adha	The festival during the hajj pilgrimage that marks Abraham's willingness to sacrifice his son for God.
Eid al-Fitr	The festival that marks the end of the fasting month of Ramadan.
fatwas	Authoritative opinions issued by religious scholars as guidance for believers; they can be solicited by individuals or a cleric may issue a fatwa voluntarily.
fiqh	Islamic jurisprudence.

fitna   Civil strife in the political sense, but also used for forms of social disorder.

ghuluww   Excessive observance of religion.

ghutra   The headdress worn by men in the Arabian Peninsula and other Arab regions.

hadiths   Sayings of the Prophet or his close family and companions which have been passed on from generation to generation and collected by hadith scholars some 200–300 years later.

hajj   The pilgrimage to Mecca that falls during the Islamic lunar month of Dhulhijja.

haram   Acts proscribed in Islamic law.

Haroun   One of the most famous of the early Abbasid al-Rashid   caliphs.

Hashemites   The ruling family in Jordan, which was forced out of the Hejaz by Abdulaziz in 1925.

Hejaz   The coastal region of the Arabian Peninsula on the Red Sea, from Jeddah to Aqaba.

hijab   The veil which covers the hair.

hijra   The Prophet's move from Mecca to Medina where he founded a new state.

hisba   The maintenance or concept of maintaining Islamic public morals.

hudud   Punishments mentioned in the Quran such as stoning for adulterers.

ihram   The pilgrim's state of ritual purity during hajj, also refers to the simple garments the pilgrim then wears.

ijtihad   Islamic legal concept of independent intellectual endeavour to arrive at just decisions in the absence of clear guidance in the Quran or the hadiths.

imam   Prayer leader, also the title of the early Shi'ite leaders and sometimes used by Sunni rulers (Abdulaziz used it for a time).

intifada   The Palestinian uprisings against Israeli occupation.

islah   Reform.

'isma   Infallibility.

jihad   Holy war.

jizya   The Islamic tax on non-Muslims.

jumhuriyya   Republic.

Kaaba	The cube-like wood and brick structure that houses an ancient black stone in Mecca.
kafala	The sponsorship system that allows Saudi nationals to charge money to hire foreigners for employment.
keffiya	Head covering often used by men in Arab countries; usually it is checkered in black and white or red and white, though there are more colourful versions.
khawaga	Well-known colloquial Egyptian term for a foreigner or educated Westerner.
khilafa	The institution of the caliphate.
khususiyya	Cultural specificity or particularism.
Levant	The geographical area comprising Israel, Palestinian territories, Jordan, Syria and Lebanon.
Malik/maleek	Terms for 'king' in Arabic.
Mashreq	The Arabic term for the eastern part of the Arab world.
Maghreb	The Arabic term for the western part of the Arab world, as well as for Morocco specifically. It also refers to the setting of the sun and prayers that take place at that time.
majallah	The Ottoman regulations institutionalising the Hanafi legal school as the main source of law in Sharia courts.
mas'a	An area in the Grand Mosque in Mecca that pilgrims must visit during hajj.
mihna	An inquisition over Islamic theology implemented by some Abbasid caliphs.
mufti	A Sunni Muslim religious scholar charged with issuing religious opinions, or fatwas.
Mujahideen	Term for those fighting jihad. It is used to describe the Arabs who fought in Afghanistan, and Islamist insurgents in Iraq describe themselves in the same manner.
Muslim Brotherhood	The first group in modern 'political Islam' in the Arab world, set up in Egypt in 1928 after the Islamic caliphate was officially abolished with the end of the Ottoman empire.
mutawwa'	Religious volunteers (plural, *mutawwa'een*) who work for the Commission for the Promotion of Virtue and Prevention of Vice.

nasiha	Advice to rulers on governance.
niqab	The full face-covering veil.
Prophet	Islam posits that God's final revelation, completing the message of the prophets of Christians and Jews, came through his final prophet Mohammad.
Quran	In Islam, God's final revelation came in a text referred to as *al-Qur'an*, meaning 'the reading' or 'the recitation'. At some stage in early Islam this oral text was codified in book form.
Ramadan	The month of the Islamic lunar calendar when Muslims fast from dawn to dusk.
sahn	The inner courtyard of the Grand Mosque in Mecca where the Kaaba stands.
Sahwa	A movement of reformers in Wahhabi Islam that emerged in the 1980s.
Salafists	Fundamentalists who advocate returning to the ways of the early Muslims who witnessed the lived example of the Prophet.
sa'wada	The effort to replace foreign workers in Saudi Arabia with Saudi nationals.
sha'wadha	Sorcery or black magic.
sheikh	Term of respect for older men (fem. sheikha), people of wisdom or religious knowledge. Sometimes a formal title.
shirk	Polytheism or attributing the qualities of God to other beings. Covers pre-Islamic worshippers of idols such as stones, trees or talismans, the Hindu pantheon or the Christian Trinity.
Sunna	The example of the Prophet's life through his words and actions on correct Islamic thought and practice.
tafra	The 'jump' or oil boom that Saudi Arabia witnessed in the 1970s and again in the early years of the twenty-first century.
takfir	The declaration of others as no longer Muslim, or infidel (*kafir*).
talbiya	Chant used by pilgrims when approaching Mecca or during various stages of pilgrimage.
Tanzimat	Series of Ottoman regulations that limited Sharia justice, ended inequality between Muslims and non-Muslims and introduced European legal codes.

tashri'	Legislation.
tawaf	Circumambulation of the Kaaba in Mecca.
tawhid	Proclaiming the oneness of God, a central principle of Wahhabi Islam.
thobe	The robe worn by Arab men in the Arabian Peninsula.
ulama	Generic term for the class of religious scholars in Arab societies (sing. *'aalim*). The name derives from the word 'knowledge' (*'ilm*), which also designates science.
Umayyad	The first dynasty in early Islam, named after the Bani Umayya family and based in Damascus, Syria, from 661 to 750.
umma	Arabic term meaning a community or nation, normally used with reference to Islam but also in recent decades to the Arab world.
'umra	*Pilgrimage to Mecca and Medina made at any time of year outside the prescribed dates of hajj.*
velayat-e fagih	The theory developed by Ayatollah Khomeini of 'rule of the jurisprudent'.
Wahhabism	Refers to the Sunni legal tradition and religious teachings prevalent in Saudi Arabia which are derived from the eighteenth-century preacher Mohammed ibn Abdulwahhab.
wali al-'asr	Shi'ite term meaning 'ruler of the age', referring to the twelfth imam who went into occultation.
waliyy al-amr	The Saudi rulers are regarded as the legal 'guardian', or *waliyy al-amr*, of the Islamic state.
wilaya	The concept of guardianship. The Saudi king possesses *wilaya* as guardian or custodian of his subjects, while fathers have *wilaya* over their daughters and husbands over their wives.

Introduction

On the eve of the Arab Spring, Saudi Arabia was a country that stood at a crossroads. After the 9/11 attacks in 2001, Crown Prince Abdullah seized the initiative to push ahead within the ruling family with policies of modernisation that were the subject of dispute with his conservative and powerful half-brothers and the class of religious scholars, who had no desire and saw no need for change. When Abdullah became king in 2005, ordinary Saudis, many of whom could only remember the long years of King Fahd's reign, hoped it would be the beginning of a new era where the grip of religious extremism on society would relax, the country would open up to the world and political reforms would final return the country to the path it was on the early 1960s when there was hope of popular participation in political life. Five years later when the Arab uprisings broke out, there was little to show for Abdullah's years in power and a sense of disillusion had set in among the educated middle class who hoped that Saudi Arabia's self-appointed status as the true, purist Islamic state could find accommodation with modern ideas of governance and a more open concept of social relations.

In 2010, Saudi Arabia was more relaxed than it had been under Fahd when the morality police run by the religious scholars had a free hand to interfere in as many aspects of life as they saw fit. The country had joined the World Trade Organisation (WTO), foreign investment in the country had grown significantly and Saudi Arabia's investments in Asia in particular had advanced with ties to China, Malaysia, India and Pakistan. But political reforms – the great hope that Al Saud would change itself voluntarily – had gone nowhere. Saudis were no more players in the political and economic policies of their country than they were in 2005, when window-dressing municipal elections were held that allowed Saudi men to vote for half of the councils' seats in a sop to American pressure that obviated giving real powers to the Shura Assembly, a quasi-parliament of royal appointees who offer recommendations on legislation whose activation lies ultimately with cabinet and the king, or allowing commoners to vote for its members. Political parties were banned, and those who had campaigned for any changes to this situation had been imprisoned for various periods of time on fraudulent charges or simply without charge at all.

The state was in any case embroiled in the high drama of a barely-concealed succession crisis. In 2008 Abdullah's half-brother Prince Sultan was taken ill with intestinal cancer and left the country for months of treatment and recovery. Overweight and in his early eighties, Sultan's prospects of a recovery looked bleak. In 2009 Abdullah, at least 85 years old at the time, appointed the interior minister Prince Nayef as 'second deputy prime minister', a move which suggested two things: (1) that Abdullah did not want Nayef to succeed to the throne (why not simply make him deputy crown prince, as Sultan was under King Fahd?); (2) that he may well not be able to stop him. Nayef, who finally assumed the position two years later upon Sultan's death, was highly unpopular among various minority or marginalised groups in Saudi Arabia's complex society: rights activists, independent women with a public voice, Shi'ites in the Eastern Province and Najran in the south, political activists of various ideological persuasions (Islamist, Arab nationalist, leftist, liberal), not to mention al-Qa'ida sympathisers. The Saudi family rules of government state that only one of the sons or grandsons of the founder of modern Saudi Arabia Abdulaziz bin Saud can inherit the throne. Nayef's insistence on pressing his claim was seen by many of those groups as bound to delay change. Nayef died in 2012 at the age of 78 without fulfilling his ambition, leaving many to ponder whether long-awaited changes would still be possible under Abdullah.

When Abdullah returned from months of convalescence abroad in February 2011 – descending from a special elevator on the tarmac at Riyadh airport – he returned to a region in turmoil. Mubarak had been forced out of office by the army after street protesters successfully pressed their case during three weeks of a tense and violent confrontation with the various apparatuses of Mubarak's police state. Zain al-Abideen Ben Ali, the Tunisian president, fled the country to exile in Saudi Arabia in January after the army told him it would not allow his security forces to crush a protest movement that started in December when a young man disillusioned with corruption and repression set himself on fire in the remote town of Sidi Bou Zaid in the Tunisian interior. The Saudi shock was that the United States could allow its trusted ally Mubarak to go down in the face of what it viewed as a street rabble fired up by the provocative and stirring coverage of Qatar's pan-Arab news channel Al-Jazeera.

The Saudi response exposed the fallacy of the reform discourse that Saudi Arabia had sold domestically and internationally with some success throughout the previous decade. The government announced firstly $37 billion in public spending – pay rises and bonuses for public sector employees – then several weeks later, after Saudis were cowed into staying at home and ignoring a call for mass protests on 11 March, the king decreed another $93 billion in handouts, including housing for the low-income earners and new health facilities, which this time extended to more funding for the police, army and religious establishment – keeping key pillars of the regime happy in order to obviate the need for any changes to Saudi family rule. 'I am so proud of you. Words are not enough to describe you', the king said in a rare televised address that appeared to thank his 'sons' for not taking to the streets after a series of warnings from princes, government and the clerics. 'You are the safety valve of this nation and you struck at that which is wrong with the truth and at treachery with loyalty.' A few days later the government said municipal elections that had been delayed in 2009 would be held in 2011, and in September of that year the king announced that women could take part in the next round in 2015; he would also now consider placing women in the advisory Shura Assembly – the concessions of the reformer king.[1]

Saudi Arabia's response did not stop at its own borders. Abdullah had returned to find Bahrain dangerously close to instituting reforms that threatened to create the first real democracy in the Gulf, the first Gulf country where the ruling dynasty gives up its monopoly on decision-making via an elected parliament with full legislative powers, if not the ability to form cabinets. Saudi anger that Bahrain's rulers had not nipped the protest movement in the bud was extreme. What made it worse was that the majority of the protesters were Shi'ites with long-standing frustration over political and economic marginalisation by the ruling elite. As demonstrators escalated civil disobedience and sectarian violence began to flare, Saudi Arabia and the United Arab Emirates (UAE) sent in troops to back the monarchy under the aegis of an obscure Gulf Cooperation Council defence pact. Saudi tanks drove over the Bahrain causeway linking the island to the peninsula mainland in what was taken by many observers to be a Saudi-ordered operation to force the democracy movement off the streets; a period of martial law followed that saw thousands detained and hundreds tortured in prison. Saudi media smeared the protests as Iranian-inspired acts of treachery against Gulf Arab values; Al-Jazeera Arabic ignored them. Al-Jazeera's cameras moved like guns from Tunisia, to Egypt, to Yemen and on to Libya and Syria, but they bypassed Bahrain, gave scant mention to protests in Oman, and Shi'ite mobilisations in the Eastern Province were no more than a footnote in the ticker line at the bottom of the screen.

Saudi counter-revolutionary actions intensified with financial help to Jordan and a proposal for Jordan and Morocco – as the remaining Arab monarchies – to join the Gulf Cooperation Council, offers of financial aid to Egypt's ruling military council, suspected support for Egyptian Salafists, and pressure to avoid the Mubarak trial, which the military was ultimately unable to avoid. Despite its distaste for Syrian leader Bashar al-Assad because of his close ties to Iran and Hizbullah, Saudi Arabia did not move until the United States requested more action from its Arab allies several months after the protests began. Saudi Arabia's contribution was a statement calling on Bashar to stop the 'killing machine' – language that sounded as if it began life in English on a desk of the State Department – and withdrawing its ambassador from Damascus. The Saudi intervention which was to blossom in the following months was a chance to outfox Iran and promote its vision of conservative, Western-friendly Arab foreign policy. Those two themes in fact explain much of Saudi diplomacy throughout the decade since the 9/11 attacks in 2001: appeasing America and confronting Iran.

9/11

When I first visited Saudi Arabia, the country stood accused by Americans and most Westerners of a role in the first act of a new era of global warfare. It was 2003 and the Bush administration and a small group of hangers-on, including most prominently the British government, were on the point of invading Iraq. But the fear was very real that the US administration could expand its circle of targets to the country where most of the 19 men who carried out the attacks hailed from, and which cradled the ideology that partly inspired their movement. The fear in March 2003 in Riyadh that 'Saudi Arabia was next' was palpable.

Osama bin Laden had effectively drawn out the latent contradictions underpinning the political marriage of convenience stretching back to the 1940s between the House of Saud and successive US administrations seeking advantageous access to oil, investment contracts and compliant foreign policy. The United States has typically sought to promote political and economic liberalisation as the international norm for post-colonial global relations, based on a concept of rights presented as universal. US governments consistently failed to challenge the resistance of Saudi Arabia's rulers to this model. Neither the ruling Al Saud family nor the class of religious scholars (*ulama*), who have been their allies in governing the country since its inception, were interested in importing the political or cultural models developed in the West. Saudi Arabia shielded itself not only from the political and economic liberalism of the United States, but from the rival ideology of communism as well as the ideologies of the immediate surrounds such as pan-Arabism, Baathism, and 'political Islam' as it became a threat to the regime in the 1980s (after Egypt's Muslim Brotherhood made its historical decision to take part in parliamentary politics).

The worldview of Saudi Arabia's Wahhabi ideology is located simultaneously in the eighteenth century when the Wahhabi *ulama* first allied with the Saudi family, and in the early period of Islam when God manifested His laws and guidelines for the ordering of human society through the revelation of the Quran and example of the Prophet's life. The Saudi-Wahhabi pact involves a division of power between clerics administering Sharia law in society and a dynasty sitting above managing the higher affairs of state with the advice of the *ulama*. In this arrangement subjects are not intended to be active forces independent of the ruler; the masses, rather, are viewed as disorderly and requiring the leadership of the ruler. Thus, protest movements such as those witnessed in 2011 and which threatened to spread to the kingdom are alien to the conceptual framework of both the king and the priestly class. In this, the royal family, in its conduct and its claims to legitimacy, is heir to a long tradition of kingship that of course predates Islam, but one which should also be interpreted in light of the discourse over the prerogatives of the ruler and the priests, their role in facilitating the divine will on earth, and their relationship to the Quran and the Prophet. Many of the Umayyad and Abbasid caliphs claimed their own direct relationship with God 'unmediated by the Prophet', as historian Aziz Al-Azmeh puts it, and held that their own *sunna*, or example, was worthy of following.[2] By the time of the Abbasid caliphate's demise, the Sunni Muslim schools of law had replaced this caliphal charisma with the supremacy of Sharia, such that the *ulama* had established themselves as the guardians and interpreters of the divine plan. The caliph was reduced to a temporal ruler who was as liable to be judged by the standards of the Quran and the Prophet as anyone else. These ideas were still evolving; the famed jurist Ibn Taimiyya took them further in an era after the caliphate as an institution in Baghdad had been destroyed. Modern iterations of the Sharia state of the Sunni jurists such as Saudi Arabia are highly stripped-down versions of a long and colourful tradition of Islamic statecraft.

Such polities stand quite apart from the nation-state model that emerged in Europe in the nineteenth century, and whose formal structure most countries in the post-colonial Middle East, in their Nasserist, Baathist, communist, nationalist, Islamist guises, inherited, internalised and adapted. In the pre-modern Sharia state, the *ulama* were not only guardians of divine law, they were guardians for society against the absolutism of the caliphate. Wael Hallaq argues that the traditional role of the *ulama* as administrators of Sharia courts was to act as guardians for society from a tyrannical ruler capable of disposing his arbitrary power in only certain fields. In countries such as Egypt, Iraq and Syria the apparatus of surveillance and coercion that is characteristic of the modern nation-state swept aside the Sharia court and the *ulama*'s role as society's guardian. In the modern state, as Hallaq puts it, surveillance replaces the obedience to God of the pre-modern Sharia society.[3]

Since its recognition by the United Nations in 1932, Saudi Arabia has sought to remain an 'ante-state', ring-fencing itself from the nation-state structures around it and pressures to import, adopt and come to terms with features of the modern nation-state. Saudi Arabia not only shunned modern ideas of popular representation, it was reluctant to develop the apparatus of state coercion and interference in the individual's life, preferring to rely on the religious police, the Sharia courts and the moral authority of the *ulama* and their networks rather than developing a large, invasive, centralised bureaucracy. It was reluctant to develop the police-state model of its Arab neighbours and reluctant to establish a national army that could turn against the ruler (the Abbasid caliphs resolved this conundrum through Turkish slave soldiers); due to its oil wealth, it was not obliged to tax its populace and face calls for representation in return. In stages, the ante-state has been obliged to conform with the modern state. It developed a physical infrastructure and a full cabinet of government ministries with an organised state budget. It institutionalised a hierarchy of the Wahhabi *ulama* as state functionaries through the justice ministry, the Council of Senior Religious Scholars and the office of the mufti. By the 1970s this work was done. In establishing these mechanisms to more closely and directly administer society in the vast and disparate territories of the state, the Saudi regime risked provoking questions among various strata of its population concerning its legitimacy.

Political Islam perhaps had better chances of influencing the Saudi-Wahhabi realm in the twentieth century. Wahhabism as a prop for state-building and governance in Saudi Arabia is a highly depoliticised ideology advocating almost blind obedience to the ruler. But Saudi rulers found themselves employing Islam for political reasons in regional conflicts. King Faisal promoted Saudi Arabia as an Islamic power in the 1960s to counter Nasserism, and members of Egypt's Muslim Brotherhood, the seminal Arab movement of political Islam, were welcomed to Saudi Arabia as teachers and other professionals after first establishing a presence in 1954. The 1967 defeat for the Arabs in the war with Israel set the stage for the gradual ascendance of Islamic politics and the discrediting of secular ideologies. Saudi Arabia was a beneficiary, but political Islam came in time to present a challenge for Saudi rulers. Wahhabism was always conflicted by its relationship with the Saudi dynasty. Its senior *ulama* were engaged throughout the twentieth century in a perpetual tug-of-war with Saudi rulers over how far its ideological vision could be implemented in a country that could not avoid dealing with the world around. Its first problem had been the relations with infidel powers both near and far that state-building required, but its growing problem was the compromised foreign policy pursued by the Al Saud. They were unwilling to implement a foreign policy that reflected the will of its people, including the *ulama*, on a key issue such as the Israeli-Palestinian conflict, because that would endanger the dependency relationship with Washington and raise questions about the Saudi family's monopoly on power.[4] Saudi Arabia was happy to coordinate with the United States over the Islamic resistance movement in Afghanistan during the 1980s, to appease the clerics and export its politicised Islamists to distant lands.

Saudi Arabia's response to the challenge of 9/11 was the invention of a media-friendly discourse of 'reform'. Some senior princes felt a new dispensation was needed for the state to survive the aftermath and the questioning in the US of its support for a country so opposed to the values of democracy, freedom of expression and rule of law that the US espouses. A new policy of 'reform' was needed to appease the foreigners and revamp al-Wahhabiyya as a respectable ideological adjunct to Saudi rule. These reformers were vindicated by the campaign launched by al-Qa'ida in 2003 to topple the Saudi monarchy. The head of this reformist wing, Prince Abdullah bin

Abdulaziz, ascended the throne in 2005, though he had been in charge of many aspects of policy during King Fahd's final decade of illness. Saudi liberals had more ambitious aims. They hoped to loosen the control of clerics over society, in particular over women, and revive the promise of political participation that the ruling family managed to bury in the 1960s. They saw King Abdullah as their champion in the face of the alliance of *ulama* and conservative princes led by Nayef. Abdullah led a drive for a degree of economic liberalisation, taking the country into the WTO and opening it up to foreign investment. Many commentators believed he supported easing the clerics' system of social control and taking up the popular representation ditched in the 1960s in a brief experiment before Faisal consolidated power and deposed his half-brother Saud. But how much is this merely window-dressing for the West? What power does Abdullah have to effect such policies? What chances are there of a fundamental change in the structure of power in the kingdom, based as it is on a division of labour between the *ulama* and Al Saud?

AMERICAN CONNECTION

US-Saudi relations appear at face value to be the strangest in the world. One country claims to champion democracy and freedom of expression, the other combats and represses those at will. Perhaps the most relevant difference is that the United States, like other Western countries, is very much a country of law and institutions; Saudi Arabia is woefully lacking in that regard. Whether external or internal factors have been the decisive element in the survival of modern Middle East states such as Saudi Arabia forged in the era of Ottoman decline and British imperial ascendancy has been the subject of some debate among historians. Malcolm Yapp argued in his *The Near East since the First World War* that internal factors had been more important than they were generally given credit for. On the side of external factors, the role of the United States has if anything been overemphasised, and never reached the influence Britain and France enjoyed before 1945, Yapp writes. Moreover, the United States, and the Soviet Union, were often manipulated by their clients. There has certainly been a sense of this in political circles in the United States since 9/11. Since then, Saudi Arabia has cast a wide net in the search for friends, reaching out to China, Russia and India, while its wealthy businessmen and companies have invested abroad. But the United States and other Western powers have been a central element in the regime's calculations in more recent times on how to secure itself, and this backing, while occasionally embarrassing, has been sold to key domestic constituencies as a source of strength, vindication of their backing for Al Saud and a guarantee of the continuation of the Islamic state. And Robert Vitalis's *America's Kingdom* has revealed the massive American political and economic interventions of the 1950s and 1960s when oil company Aramco was the United States' largest single overseas private enterprise.

Abdel-Rahman Munif captured the ambivalent feelings felt by ordinary Saudis towards the Americans in *Mudun al-Malh* (*Cities of Salt*). The inhabitants of a desert valley in the 1930s wonder at three foreigners who have appeared in the area, claiming they are looking for water. 'What could they really want? What is there in this waterless desert other than hunger, sand and clouds of dust? … And they ask sly questions, like "have any foreigners been here, have you heard about any English or French who've come here, did they stay long?" … They said more of them would come, and they said "wait and be patient, every one of you will become rich!"'[5] The Bedouin mistake the Americans' early-morning exercises for a strange form of prayer. Like Munif's Mooran, Riyadh was transformed from a dusty desert town into an expanding city of foreigners with the accoutrements of modern, foreign culture. From the Americans' perspective, Saudi Arabia's otherworldliness offered excuses for overlooking its strange ways, which was something Al Saud was able to play up. The rulers of Egypt, for example, did not have the same concern. Sure of themselves as leaders of an ancient polity, they had plans for regional leadership that contrasted the insular fear of Al Saud over its future. One tried to challenge the West, the other solicited its help.

After confusion over how to handle the threat of Gamal Abdul-Nasser and Arab nationalism, Al Saud found a working model under King Faisal (1964–75): political repression at home, projection of an alternative Islamic politics abroad, closer ties with the United States. With the death of Nasser in 1970, Saudi Arabia emerged as a major regional player, and Saudi Arabia and Egypt were to become close allies as Egypt followed the Saudis into the American orbit. Saudi Arabia and the United States cooperated closely against the Soviet Union in Afghanistan in the 1980s, and the US government came to Saudi Arabia and Kuwait's aid when Saddam Hussein's Iraq threatened them in 1990. The threat of al-Qa'ida offered Saudi Arabia an opportunity to redeem itself in

American eyes after the nadir of 2001, and in subsequent years security cooperation between the two countries reached unparalleled levels. Throughout all this, democracy and human rights concerns were side issues that only occasionally got in the way, such as when the State Department made public statements about trials of activists or egregious cases such as the conviction of a raped woman in 2007.

Yet many Saudis wondered what had happened to them: oil had brought them American-tinged modernisation, American food, American TV, American cars, American foreign policy, American-approved rulers. Munif once wrote:

> The oil which was found by chance in parts of the Arab region became the basis on which the victorious countries in the First World War dealt with the region. It set the geographical and political form of the states they set up, the nature of the regimes that ruled them, the nature of the relations between them and between each state and the rest of the world. Thus, oil became an instrument of destruction and rivalry, a reason for controlling the region's peoples and even blocking the way to their future development.[6]

AN INDIGENOUS MODEL?

Given the brutal police states that some of the nation-state regimes in the Arab region became, Saudi Arabia could have been viewed as an indigenous model that survived colonialism: the Najd region where the Saudi-Wahhabi state first emerged in the mid eighteenth century was one of the few areas of the Arabian peninsula to avoid direct European control and imperial subjugation. Indeed, since the oil boom of the 1970s, white- and blue-collar labour from around the world clamoured to live in Saudi Arabia for a job, a better wage and a better living. Saudis are ensured education and welfare coverage in a relatively safe and clean environment; the Muslim is offered sanitised access to certain aspects of let's say modernity – fast-food restaurants, high-tech gadgetry, the internet, designer home furnishings. Only Westerners complain because there is no easy, regularised access to branded alcohol and corporatised nightlife.

Yet Saudi Arabia has not evolved in a manner that nationalists consider would have been possible in Algeria, Egypt or Iraq had the heavy hand of colonialism not intervened in their historical development. The Saudi-Wahhabi state tried to lock itself in time through the collusion of colonialism with Al Saud and the *ulama*, fearing that to import or accommodate the modernising political and social trends of the outside world would spell the downfall of both in a polity they idealised as an Islamic Utopia. The country's historical experience is intimately involved with Western imperial power. The consequence has been a country trapped within a pre-modern framework that perpetuates religious obscurantism, tribalism, misogyny, inequality and a notion of the citizen as little more than consumer, all in the name of a manufactured cultural particularism (*khususiyya*) that has become so pervasive that it is cited *ad nauseum* by many Saudis and Westerners, not least diplomats and government officials, as justification for maintaining the status quo. Ultimately the question is whether this hybrid Sharia/ nation-state is capable of producing what its people, in surveying all the political, economic, social and cultural aspects of their society as well as the alternatives available, would today in fairness describe as justice. The judicial reforms which have become a central plank of Abdullah's modernisations answer Western concerns about conducting business in Saudi Arabia and help synchronise the country with the global economy while formalising injustice through codifying the *ulama*'s contested replication of Sharia. They are also reforms that spring from a Najdi context, thus development itself is defined in Najdi terms: Abdulaziz unified the judicial system in 1927 under Hanbali Sharia courts, ending Ottoman judicial reforms that had applied in the Hejaz.[7]

The Saudi Arabia described in this book is one seen ultimately through the eyes of its author. After my initial trip in 2003, I was back in 2004 and 2005 as a member of the media invited to cover the hajj pilgrimage. In December 2005 I began a three-year stay and in 2009 I had to leave after finally pushing my luck – a story I relate in Chapter 8. Since my first visit I had wrestled with the question of how to define the country. Regular news copy applies words such as 'puritan', 'conservative', 'austere', 'Islamic', but Saudi Arabia's close ties with the United States and history of opposition to movements challenging Western hegemony in the Middle East mean it cannot be placed in the same bracket as Iran or Sudan, states that also utilise Islam as guiding ideology of government. Unlike both those countries, it has no elected parliament or participatory process for choosing those who run the country, if only nominally. Its ruling family does not claim descent from the Prophet, like the rulers of Jordan and Morocco. Once close to Egypt's Muslim Brotherhood, its rulers eschewed links to them post-9/11 and ponder now how to deal with them post-Mubarak. It says it applies Sharia law, but al-Qa'ida said that was not enough.

*   *   *

I have only in part relied on a journalistic approach to a limited degree to establish arguments. I didn't want to rely too much on the first-hand interview since I have always found something inherently manipulative in the process; interviewees craft their comments, consciously or otherwise, towards the question, the interviewer and the wider audience. For example, preacher Mohsen al-Awajy told me in 2008 that 'this country is founded on religious bases, it will never change'. He was speaking to me after an article I had published about new urban communities where the normal rules of gender segregation would not apply, which provoked an angry reaction from some Saudi commentators. One of the Sahwa generation of Islamists and clerics, Awajy was always a lively interlocutor. He fixed me in the eye, then declared baldly that some people – liberals, the king, Western media – may want to see certain things change in the country, but that won't happen. Despite that, I think the statement has value as a definition of the conservative position at this juncture. I also use official pronouncements on the state news agency, websites of public figures, blogs and forums where posters are often anonymous, the literary output of Saudi novelists, commentary in Saudi media, and the analysis of others who have written about the country. In the final chapter, which aims to examine the role that Saudi control of Mecca and Medina plays in establishing the regime's credentials for Muslims generally, I offer a large chunk of personal experience of pilgrimage as a journalist operating under the government's watch. I hope this pluralistic approach to sources will succeed in painting a vivid portrait of one of the world's more unusual and enigmatic countries in the most interesting of times. Finally, I am solely responsible for the work, while grateful to my employer at the time for the chance to live in Saudi Arabia.

1
The Religious Society

It was early evening in May 2007 when 28-year-old Salman al-Huraisy was sitting with relatives and friends enjoying homemade alcohol in his mudbrick home in the poor Uraija district of Riyadh. Suddenly they found themselves besieged as some 30 members of the vice squad – a force of religious zealouts called the Commission for the Promotion of Virtue and Prevention of Vice – stormed their home from all sides. The *mutawwa'een*, or the 'volunteers', as they are commonly referred to, were coming through the front door, jumping down into the back yard from the roof and the walls and climbing through the windows. They began beating the group with sticks then dragged twelve of them off to a nearby office of the Commission. The beatings continued, but it was Salman, 28 at the time, whom they accused of selling alcohol and drugs, who attracted their wrath. He was beaten to death over two hours in front of his family's eyes.

I managed to arrange a meeting with the family in Riyadh several weeks after the tragedy. What they described was abuse of an underclass that is easy prey to God's warriors on the streets of Saudi Arabia. Uraija is a district with a reputation for being a den of poverty and crime. There are many like this in Riyadh and Jeddah where the various layers of Saudi Arabia's underclass huddle together: pilgrim overstayers and other migrant labour, non-tribal Saudis referred to as *khudeiri* who have trouble obtaining passports or getting full access to health, education and other benefits accorded to 'pure-bred' Saudis and the dark-skinned Saudis of African origin who were officially emancipated from slavery in the 1960s. Deprived from enjoying the fruits of petrodollar wealth dispensed by the ruling family, many have turned to crime. Drugs and prostitution are rife in some districts of Jeddah, in particular, where police sometimes fear to tread.

The family talked of the hysteria of the army of zealots when they descended upon their home. I met the family in Riyadh several weeks after the tragedy. 'They called him black, "You black, you slave!" But we're not living in the age of slavery any more, slavery ended. These are people who I don't think have much awareness and they should not represent this body', said Ali, one of Salman's seven brothers.[1] 'They arrested, insulted, and then they gave their verdict about the person and implemented it. That's the result, that someone died.' Khaled al-Kaabi, a family friend who was also there, described their attackers' state of frenzy. 'They got into the house from the roofs of neighbours' houses, forced the door open and then handcuffed us all together. They were beating with sticks, and legs and fists, and stamping on us. They were in a frenzied state, hitting randomly, but mostly they were hitting Salman', he said. 'They said, "You're *mukhannatheen* ['homosexuals'], you're slaves, this is your level." They called us *fasaqa* ['depraved'], *fussaq al-ard* ['the depraved of the earth'], *kuffar* ['infidels'] – insulting stuff that you shouldn't say.' His father described the state of the body when it was finally released to the family for burial: 'He was so badly beaten it was hard for us to recognise him. There was a crack in his skull, his right eye was popped out, his jaw was broken, and there was another opening in his belly. His mother could not absorb the entire thing and she fainted in the washroom … I feel disturbed by what they did. They have no conscience, otherwise they wouldn't have done this. They could just have knocked on our door and asked me to hand anyone over.'[2]

The family raised legal action, leading to the first ever trial of Commission individuals. An autopsy report established severe head injuries as the cause of death, but still the two men charged in the murder walked free because the Sharia court judge said murder was a premeditated crime that in this case evidenced no sign of intent on the part of the *mutawwa'een* since the means used to cause violence to the victim – hands and various forms of stick or baton – are not lethal. The Commission defended itself, saying some of those involved in the raid were not proper members on its payroll. 'The verdict was based on the jurisprudential argument that [a blow to] the head cannot cause death and that the hand is not an instrument that can cause death, therefore it cannot be premeditated murder', lawyer Abdulrahman al-Lahem reported.[3] Such is the Saudi justice system, however, that no charges of manslaughter or even accidental killing were pressed against the men. The judge simply considered that in beating Huraisy up these defenders of the faith had no intention to kill him, therefore they were not legally culpable or responsible for his death. 'They say it was an unintended mistake – does an unintended mistake lead to someone's death? They didn't just incapacitate someone, they crushed a life', Ali says.

What struck me was how sanguine and composed the family were about such a tragic and senseless experience. 'If alcohol was the reason for coming and it was done in a legal manner, we wouldn't have a problem. The problem is the way they behaved. There were violations – the biggest one being beating someone to death', Ali said. 'I know my brother drinks alcohol. I can't deny it. But they say he promoted it and there's a difference between consuming and promoting. We don't object to the system, which is above everyone, and everyone must behave according to the system. But while the system has its obligations from us, it also guarantees us rights.' The religious police were implicated in the deaths of several others in 2007 and the subject of heavy criticism of liberals in the press who would love to get rid of it. It has been drummed into generations of Saudis in the central part of the country where the body has its historical origin that the religious police are their protection force from sin: the saying goes, 'Let there be a *mutawwa'* between you and God!' The state also employs the force as a key element in its social policing and its rhetoric allots it a lofty place in the structure of the Sharia state. For these reasons ordinary Saudis tend not to engage in easy abuse of the Commission. So Ali chose his words carefully, focusing on the language of rights that in practice doesn't work with people who see themselves doing God's work in a system they believe is God's model for human society. Its members should at the very least carry identification cards with them, Ali said: 'There should be regulation of their actions and appropriate guidelines, and they should deal with people on the basis of equality. It's a respected institution that serves society and helps people to do what's right. But the problem is individuals and I hope they are a minority – I'm sure they are a minority.'

The exhortations of the priestly class to adhere to Wahhabi orthopraxy dominate public space in Saudi Arabia. In the cities, large electronic billboards look down upon motorists, urging the faithful to remember God amidst advertisements for luxury cars, takeaway food and holiday destinations. Mosques number in the tens of thousands, since any room in any given building may be given over to daily worship with nothing more than a few carpets or rugs on the ground and space in front for a prayer leader, or imam, to stand. Loudspeakers broadcast the call to prayer to every corner of lived urban space, as they do in other Muslim countries. Imams have been known to use laptops to read their sermons. The various channels of the Saudi-owned pan-Arab news and entertainment network MBC carry ads that call on the modern young Gulf Muslim to perform his daily prayers. At every turn, technology is mobilised to maximise the reach of Saudi Arabia's religious orthodoxy. 'The modernizing – that is Westernizing – wealth has not led to Westernization of social structures and values. In fact, in some cases modern technologies such as closed circuit TVs, computer technologies, and telephones, enforce an already predominantly gender-segregated society, where men can communicate via various channels without actual human contact', one study of opposition movements that evolved in Saudi society in the 1990s observed.[4] The trend has continued, inexorably. Satellite television, the DVD, talkback radio, mobile phones, the internet, the webcam, blogs and chatrooms have all presented, each in their own way, a challenge of some nature or another to the imposing structure of morality constructed by and maintained by the Wahhabi clerics, who are at home with the putative postcolonial dichotomy thrown up between tradition/modernity because they are able to moderate it, and ensure their position.

More than just a reminder and an exhortation to remember Islam, religion in Saudi Arabia is a set of institutions which function in coordination to maintain moral order and social control. The religious police are only one element in this array of bodies that form the Wahhabi religious establishment – thousands of religious scholars who have studied at education institutions such as the Imam University in Riyadh. The clerics man the morality police, thousands of mosques, the judiciary, the Ministry of Justice, much of the Ministry of Education and Ministry of Higher Education, and a host of bodies such as the Council of Senior Religious Scholars, the World Muslim League, the World Assembly of Muslim Youth, charity organisations, and others. The religious police, or *mutawwa'een* (sometimes more ominously known simply as *al-hay'a*, 'the Commission'), drive around the streets with megaphones, exhorting men to pray during prayer times. They trawl the ubiquitous shopping malls to make sure shops stay shut at prayer time and check that men keep their distance from unrelated women. Their remit to interfere is extensive and, with the backing of the interior ministry, has increased with the development of the modern Saudi state. Abdulaziz set the body up the in 1902 immediately after his forces took Riyadh. His mufti Sheikh Abdulaziz bin Abdullatif Al al-Sheikh was tasked with gathering a volunteer force to maintain public morality, and the body was extended in time to all the Najd and the Eastern Province and furnished with its own administration. A separate body dealt with the Hejaz cities until 1976 when King Khaled unified them and raised the Commission's director to the level of cabinet minister.

Abdulaziz defined its functions in 1925 as ensuring men prayed the five prescribed prayers and closed their shops, encouraging people to acquire more knowledge about Islam and to pay Islamic alms, and keeping people away from 'usury, cheating and injustice'.[5] In 1980, following an attempt by disaffected Wahhabi activists to stir a revolt against Al Saud by seizing the Grand Mosque in Mecca, the Commission was given the green light to step up its monitoring of society; the Basic Law promulgated by King Fahd in 1992 referred to the work of the Commission in its list of the state's basic duties (which also included 'call people to God'). A cabinet regulation subsequently formalised the body as an apparatus of social control complementing the policing functions of the interior ministry, though it answers directly to the king and its director is an official of state at the level of minister. Eager to prove its worth, the Commission boasts on its website that it handles over 300,000 cases a year, which can involve anything from alcohol, to being together with an unrelated woman, to 'sorcery' (an anti-sorcery unit was established in 2009; the punishment can be death).[6]

Today, clerics are a constant presence on television, both state and private. They offer legal opinions and advice to the faithful on how to live the a proper Muslim life, in accordance with the Quran and the Sunna, or example of the Prophet Mohammad, codified in the schools of Islamic Sharia law and administered since then by the clerics who preside as judges in Sharia courts. The Islam of the clerics is highly legalistic, concerning itself with orthopraxy and the minutiae of daily life. They will be on hand during Ramadan to advise on the rules over the month of fasting. The faithful will enquire whether it is acceptable to swallow saliva during daylight hours, or whether the clerics prescribe performing special evening prayers called *witr*, an open-ended prayer time after the fifth Maghreb prayer. 'The *witr* prayers bring blessings from God, and the Prophet said they can be done any time between the evening and dawn prayer', Sheikh Saad bin Nasir al-Shathri explained to a caller.[7] But he said only one of the four schools of Sunni Islamic law deems *witr* obligatory and it is not the one followed in Saudi Arabia. The injunctions of clerics form the backdrop to every life; Saudis and Arabic-speaking Muslim residents may not follow every clerical ruling, and Saudis will pick and choose among them to find the sheikh that appeals to them the most, but the clerics are in essence an extension of the Sharia law they both safeguard and embody. Since Muslims gather around the television in the evening after breaking their fast at sunset, Ramadan is a key time for advertisers to win lucrative consumer spending. 'Brands use messages that portray them as reminding people that "this is what you should do", that this is the month of faith', a Lebanese advertising executive in Riyadh says.[8] The state-run Saudi Telecom, for example, airs ads instructing Saudis how to be better Muslims during the holy month and encourages viewers to send text messages of prayers to mark the two major religious festivals of Eid al-Fitr and Eid al-Adha. Malaysia's Proton car is touted to Saudis as 'the number one Islamic car in the market'.

While some Saudi scholars such as Salman al-Odah have spread their influence through television – televangelism has been a noted phenomenon throughout the Arab region since the 1970s – others have used literature. The publishers of popular cleric Ayedh al-Qarni's *La Tahzan* (*Don't Be Sad*) claim to have sold over 2 million copies. A self-help guide for the believer, it offers close-up details on how to live a happy life of faith. They should steer clear of romance and forbidden love, thank God after drinking cold water and clean their teeth with the *miswak* plant; they should avoid too much sleep, too much laughter and gaining weight; they should take the family out for a trip at least once a week but not clutter the desk with papers; they should avoid the poison of books by atheists. Sadness, Qarni says, is not something Sharia wants for you. Though life will come with some sadness, it will disappear in paradise; the Prophet's companions were happy because they knew him and his message; the duties of faith will keep the believer too busy to indulge in a deeper sadness. Depression is the lot of unbelievers. '... how sad life is without faith; what eternal curse afflicts those who are outside God's path on earth ... After the experience of centuries, the intellect has concluded that idols are superstition, infidelity is a curse and atheism is a lie; that the prophets were true and God is the truth ... with power over all.'[9]

Modern media has revolutionised the access that clerics have to the public, so that Saudis can find the view of their favourite sheikh on thousands of websites, as well as through television, radio and newspapers. The question of whose fatwas (clerical opinions) to listen to is a crucial one throughout the Muslim world. Modern Arab states have sought to control the clerical opinions flowing to the people through appointing a leading fatwa-giver, or state mufti. In Egypt there is a state-appointed fatwa-giver (the Grand Mufti), who heads a body of clerics involved in that task, as well as the nominally independent religious seminary and university Al-Azhar, an institution which Nasser essentially nationalised in

1961 by decreeing that its rector would be a presidential appointee. In Saudi Arabia a king-appointed mufti heads the Council of Senior Religious Scholars. In 2007 the mufti Sheikh Abdulaziz Al al-Sheikh launched his own website, www.alifta.com. The mufti inevitably offers opinions that suit the policies of the rulers, and this has created much tension in the modern state. Television, in particular, has had an enormous impact on Saudis. State television, although it is trying to be more open (employing women broadcasters post-9/11) devotes considerable space to the *ulama*. Satellite television has seen a plethora of religious channels spring up in recent years to counter the sweeping influence of Arabic music video channels and other entertainment coming from Lebanon and Egypt via Saudi-owned pan-Arab channels. 'Before, anyone who wanted a fatwa would find a sheikh in a mosque. Now he watches the satellite channels', says Hassan al-Buluwi, a former manager of Saudi religious channel al-Majd.[10] 'With a mosque sheikh, the fatwa was limited to no more than 500 people. On satellite television it reaches millions.' Clerics are looking to maximise their reach and impact through whatever means they can, be it television, internet or the mosque. King Abdullah made a belated attempt to control the fatwa market with a ruling in 2010 specifying only the clerics of the senior clerical body as those qualified to issue such religious opinions. The situation reminded me of an Egyptian music executive who once commented that music is such an obsession in the Arab world that it is virtually 'coming out of the taps': in Saudi Arabia, it is religion that flows like tap water.

Some areas, however, are out of bounds to the religious police. Diplomats within the diplomatic quarter and residents of some residential compounds have access to either imported alcohol or locally made versions, some of it drinkable. Princes in the port city of Jeddah are the patrons of a heavy party scene. A report compiled by US diplomats notes: 'Behind the facade of Wahhabi conservatism in the streets, the underground nightlife for Jeddah's elite youth is thriving and throbbing. The full range of worldly temptations and vices are available – alcohol, drugs, sex – but strictly behind closed doors. This freedom to indulge in carnal pursuits is possible merely because the religious police keep their distance when parties include the presence or patronage of a Saudi royal and his circle of loyal attendants.'[11] Often the prince will have a retinue of prostitutes available for *in situ* activities, as well as cocaine and hashish, which are easily smuggled in from Yemen and regarded as a major problem in Saudi society.[12] The report observed that 'It is not uncommon in

Jeddah for the more lavish private residences to include elaborate basement bars, discos, entertainment centers and clubs.'

The northern area of the city has many private beaches where foreigners and Saudis hang out at the weekend, as well as private residential compounds where Jeddah's wealthy families live. I found foreigners living normally in the streets of Jeddah, heading to the beach at the weekend, and hanging out till late at night at home with hashish and their Saudi girlfriends. It was a world away from the repressed atmosphere of the rest of the country and the capital where I had to work. It was strange what scenes of people you could suddenly fall in with though. Not long before I left Saudi Arabia I discovered a rave scene, taking place every few weeks in the desert outside Riyadh. I had befriended some people who lived in Kingdom compound, one of the more expensive for rents in Riyadh which was owned by Prince Alwaleed's Kingdom Holding and had a bar inside it. Whisky and hashish were easily accessible in the compound, which made it quite a popular destination at weekends for party-seekers in search of an event. One weekend there was word of an event in a desert area north of the city set aside as a recreation area where families or groups can rent a private chalet. We drove through numerous security points for miles along a track that weaved its way through sand dunes until eventually, after more than an hour, we came to an area enclosed by the sand on all sides where the music was blaring and people were dancing. They had all brought along their own drinks and drugs. In our rush to get there and fearing the police checks, we had brought nothing with us. After three years of living in Riyadh I had stumbled upon a community of people I never knew existed, which struck me as very typical of the atomised society Saudi Arabia is – islands of disconnected people negotiating their own space within the structures and constrictions of an oppressive state.

THE ORIGINS OF WAHHABISM

Saudi Arabia is governed through a division of power between the Saudi family which dominates the higher policies of state, including foreign policy, and the class of religious scholars, with a special position for the family which descends from the founder of the Wahhabi *da'wa* ('mission') Sheikh Mohammed Ibn Abdulwahhab. Saudi society is their Islamic Utopia. They enjoy control of the judiciary, the education system and the mosques as well as their own coercive apparatus (the religious police). The cleric-controlled judiciary is the key to the idea of an Islamic state. It has as its origin the model of government established in the early Islamic period during the Umayyad and Abbasid caliphates, Islamic empires based in Damascus and Baghdad. The *ulama*, with their monopoly on interpreting the Word of God in the Quran, governed society through control of Sharia courts, while the temporal ruler enjoyed an absolute monopoly on political power and state policy. The caliph was left 'sitting on top of society', to use Patricia Crone and Martin Hinds' phrase in *God's Caliph*, with no popular restraint on his freedom of manoeuvre.[13] It is not clear to historians how much of an innovation this Islamic structure was, or whether it rather perpetuated models of statehood already present in the Arabian Peninsula, the Levant or Mesopotamia before the Arab conquests. It may have resulted from the stretch on resources and control mechanisms that the ruling elite faced in asserting their power and establishing a stable polity. Aziz Al-Azmeh argues that memes of kingship present in Late Antiquity – that is, empires that only partially overlapped with the areas where the Hejazi Arabs established their new polity – were reworked in a Muslim context.[14] However, it also answered the problem of legitimacy that an absolutist ruler faced in a world where the egalitarian ideas of popular participation in governance were more or less absent: the *ulama* sanctified caliphal power in return for his protection of a realm in which *ulama* were free to apply God's law. Baghdad was designed as a circular walled city that reflected the cosmic order and radiated world dominion: it centred on the palace of the caliph who, in the strictly Sunni view, was the successor of the Prophet as leader of the community of Muslims.

Saudi Arabia today is the third incarnation of the Saudi-Wahhabi state; Abdulaziz bin Saud seized control of Riyadh in 1902 and 30 years later, through years of conquest, shrewd diplomacy with foreign powers and simple good fortune, the League of Nations (predecessor to the United Nations) offered its recognition. The story of the first Saudi-Wahhabi state begins in 1744 with a pact between Mohammed bin Saud, the ruler of small town called Dir'iyya (now part of the modern city of Riyadh) in the centre of the Najd region, and a local preacher called Ibn Abdulwahhab. The Wahhabi movement involved a rigorous application of the Hanbali school of Islamic law, much influenced by the ideas of Hanbali jurist Ibn Taimiyya (1268–1328), the Syrian scholar from Harran in what is now Turkey who advocated the strict Shari'ism of the *ulama*. Abdulwahhab, his clerical disciples and followers were given free rein by the Saudi rulers to impose their purist vision on Najdi society and to wage jihad, or holy war, on surrounding regions in implementation of their idea that non-Wahhabi Muslims were apostates. They held Shi'ites to be heretics on the edge of unbelief, as well as Sunnis who engaged in Sufi practices, venerated ancestors, built and visited shrines, and held religious festivals to celebrate such figures, including the family of the Prophet. The driving principle was *tawhid*, or the oneness of God, and in their view the people of the peninsula had succumbed to a popular Islam of idolatry and superstition and must return to the original pure Islam of the early Muslims who followed the Prophet's example, as adduced by the Sunni clerics – an environment that offered the Sharia project of followers of Ibn Taimiyya and the Hanbalis a new playground on which to apply their ideas, a novel canvas to implement their vision.[15]

Wahhabism is technically a school of law within the Hanbali legal school, the most conservative of four legal traditions in Sunni Islam. The Hanbali school that gave us Wahhabism was born of the period of philosophy and theological speculation that marked ninth-century Baghdad, trends which its founder, Ahmed bin Hanbal (d. 855), opposed. Wahhabis revere the works of Hanbali scholars, such as Ibn Taimiyya and his protégé Ibn Qayyim al-Jawziyya (d. 1350). Wahhabi ideological rigour helped lead to the demise of the first Saudi state in 1818 after Saudi forces attacked the cities of Mecca, Medina and Kerbala in Iraq, provoking the Ottoman authorities into retaliation. The second Saudi-Wahhabi state was back six years later, but came to an end in 1891 when the rival Rashid family of Hail in the northern part of the Najd defeated Saudi forces. The second state was marked by internal disputes among the Saudi rulers, civil war and debate among the clerics on the compromises they should make in their relationships with the Saudi leaders and foreign powers. The state during this period pragmatically limited itself to the Najd and kept away from Iraq and the Hejaz, and though it controlled the Gulf coast including today's UAE, Qatar and Bahrain, its jurisdiction stopped at British-protected Kuwait – from where the exiled Saudi family plotted their return in 1902.

The third state benefited from a fortuitous conjunction of circumstances and wise choices made by Abdulaziz in the knowledge of past mistakes. During the First World War, both Abdulaziz bin Saud and Sherif Hussein, ruler of the Hejaz cities, curried favour with the British to support their plans for expansion. Abdulaziz's vision was less ambitious than that of the Sherif, who cooperated with British army officer T.E. Lawrence against the Ottomans in Arabia in the hope that, in return, Britain would support a pan-Arab state under his rule. It did not, as the system of British and French 'mandates' awarded to the European powers by the League of Nations in 1920 demonstrated. Abdulaziz looked only to establish as wide a hegemony as possible within the peninsula, which meant Britain had no problem with the fall of the Hejaz to the Saudi state in 1925. A recipient of British subsidies until 1924, the Saudi state's victory in Mecca in 1925 secured possession of the prestigious Muslim holy sites and control of its pilgrim revenues without inciting the wrath of any power; it continued to extend its borders as far as possible until 1932 when the country was declared a kingdom under the name Saudi Arabia. Abdulaziz utilised the *ulama*, led by the descendants of Ibn Abdulwahhab, to create a Bedouin fighting force, known as the Ikhwan. Bedouin of the Najd were settled in sedentary communities called *hijra*s – a term implying they were mimicking the Prophet's *hijra*, or emigration, in 622 CE from Mecca to Medina to establish the first Islamic community – in one of Abdulaziz's early acts of state-building. In these settlements Bedouin were at the disposal of Wahhabi preachers and military leaders for effective use of a controlled campaign of Saudi expansion.

Oil transformed the kingdom's fortunes. Discovered in the Eastern Province in 1938, American oil companies were authorised to explore and drill. In February 1945, US President Franklin D. Roosevelt met Abdulaziz on a cruiser in the Suez Canal on his way back from the Yalta conference with Stalin and Churchill as the Second World War was nearing its end. In this famous incident, the USS *Murphy* picked up the Saudi monarchy from the port of Jeddah to the meeting two days later on board the USS *Quincy*. Reports of the meeting made much of the personal chemistry between the two men – Roosevelt bequeathed to the curious Saudi king an extra wheelchair he had – but the contrast between the two polities they represented could not have been starker. For his first trip abroad, Abdulaziz brought with him rice, watermelon and tomatoes, set up a Bedouin tent on the USS *Murphy* and ate slaughtered sheep cooked on the deck.[16] Roosevelt, who also received the Egyptian and Ethiopian monarchs, wanted an assurance on access to Saudi oil and was told America would 'never have to worry' about supplies.[17] But those warships were symbols of the extraordinary political, military and economic might the United States now wielded, and the Saudis, just as they had correctly banked on the British during the

First World War, realised that imperial power was shifting towards the Americans.

When the *ulama* survey the world of secular nation-states around them, the demotion of the clerical class to functionaries in the service of overarching nation-states and the reduction of their Sharia dominion to 'personal status' courts (from the French *statut personnel*), as well as the fate of post-colonial Arab nationalist regimes who have challenged Western supremacy, they conclude that the devil you know is better than the devil you don't. Or as Ibn Taimiyya put it: 'Sixty years with a tyrannical imam [leader] are better than one night without him.' Gulf states have not only dismantled the clerical monopoly over the courts; in the UAE for example, the modernisation project has reduced the indigenous Emiratis to around one-fifth of their own population, alcohol is freely available in bars and nightclubs, and the sexes are free to mix in public spaces. Only in Kuwait is alcohol not on sale at all, including five-star hotels, the neutral zone where profane foreign culture is often tolerated in the Gulf; yet young men and women are still free to mix together in coffee shops, shisha cafés and malls; women can drive cars, and there are no religious policemen patrolling the streets (social conservatism might challenge this, but not the courts).

Since the formalisation of clerical power and crushing of independent political activity by King Faisal, Saudi liberals have rallied around the Saudi royal family as supposed protectors and guarantors of what liberal space there is, in the hope it could expand. '[The] cooperative and consensual relationship has provided the kingdom with one of the most stable societies in the region and has allowed it to avoid the war and revolution that has wracked nearly every one of its neighbours', one defender of the system writes.[18] Defenders often point to the unifying role of the royal family in ending petty but deadly tribal vendettas that can last for decades or longer. 'The royal family is there with the people. They know where the people are going and they will always be at the centre', Abdulrahman Said, an advisor to then Crown Prince Abdullah, said in 2003.[19] Yet it is Al Saud who chose to employ the Wahhabi movement for their own purposes, promoting conservative attitudes among a populace which, under a different political system, could arguably have developed into something more progressive (witness the former South Yemeni state or the Dhofar revolutionary movement in south Oman that ended in 1975). At numerous points in Saudi history, promoting fanaticism has been in the rulers' interest. The clerics' role in society was given a boost after the 1979 rebellion in Mecca when Wahhabi zealots – moved over morality, modernisation, marginalisation and tyranny – seized control of the Grand Mosque, and the Saudi rulers, fearful of internal unrest, gave ground to the clerics, increasing the powers of the religious police to stamp out liberal tendencies in society. Promoting fanaticism once more was in the rulers' interest because they knew only to turn to the clerics for legitimacy and as allies in social control. This happened again after the 1990–91 Gulf crisis when, in return for justifying the presence of American troops on Saudi soil, the clerics won more funding for the religious police.[20] It happened again in 2011 when the king awarded money to the Council of Senior Religious Scholars and the religious police institution to build more branches, in an effort to shore up key pillars of support for the ruling family. It would be more appropriate to say that Al Saud promote conflict between different sections of society – liberals, tribes, Salafis, Shia, and so on – in order to pose as mediator and guarantor of stability.

With the financial reach of Saudi Arabia after the oil price hikes of the early 1970s and discrediting of Nasserism after 1967, Wahhabism, a once-marginalised movement outside the Sunni mainstream, began to acquire a certain prestige and reach that it had not previously known. Considerable debate developed in Arab intellectual circles over the nature of Ibn Abdulwahhab's preaching and his movement: was it 'reformist' in an Arabian context or a remobilisation of regressive theory and practice, a new challenge from the hinterland to the city? Saudi Arabia promotes the term *mujaddid* ('reformer'), for Ibn Abdulwahhab. Many of these 'liberal' defenders are of course in Saudi Arabia itself[21] – they do not hesitate to defend all key elements of Saudi Arabia, its rule by Al Saud, its iteration of the Sharia state, within the context of rolling back or ditching the religious police, elections to the Shura Assembly and allowing women to drive, and they are on the payroll one way or another of the princes. Some Arab liberals who have come under the sway of Saudi Arabia's political, financial and media influence in the Arab world publicly advance the view that Wahhabism was a reform movement. They include, for example, Syrian poet and essayist Adonis, the pen-name of Ali Ahmed Said. A former Arabic professor at the Sorbonne, Adonis is a pioneer in modern Arabic poetry and viewed as a leading Arab liberal. But he has made positive comments in recent years about Wahhabism, which he once criticised in his *Al-Thabit wa-l-Mutahawwil* (*The Constant and the Variable*). 'Saudis and Gulf Arabs are freer than we are',

Adonis told Lebanese satellite channel LBC in one of his corrective statements of recent years.[22] 'I have tried (to visit Saudi Arabia) in order to see the places where the companions (of the Prophet) were. It's the Muslims' right – even if they don't believe in Wahhabism – to visit these places. This hope has not been fulfilled, but I'm prepared to visit Saudi Arabia on condition that I can visit all of it.'

Saudi efforts to defend Wahhabism have extended to Western academia. US Department of Education records from 1995 to 2007 list massive funding of, for example, some $18 million to the University of Arkansas, $13 million to George Washington University and $10 million to MIT.[23] Natana Delong-Bas, a scholar at the Center for Muslim-Christian Understanding of Georgetown University, an institute set up and funded by the Saudi entrepreneur Prince Alwaleed bin Talal, argued in her 2004 book *Wahhabi Islam* that Ibn Abdulwahhab was a reformer and a strong proponent of women's rights who did not really advocate jihadist expansion.[24] The book should be seen as part of an attempt by Saudi Arabia to disassociate its form of Islam from the al-Qa'ida network, improve the country's image in the United States and advance a limited reform agenda inside Saudi Arabia that aims to polish some of Wahhabism's rougher edges. Ironically, when the King Abdulaziz Foundation for Research and Archives published the book in Arabic it was translated as *Fikr al-Sheikh (The Sheikh's Thought)* since there cannot in the Wahhabi view be anything called 'Wahhabi' Islam.

THE NEW MUSLIM

Wahhabism aims to create a new society of Muslims whose minds and actions have been cleansed of the extraneous beliefs and popular practices of an Islamic culture that has, over the centuries, deviated from the community of believers who lived by the will of God as manifested through the verses (*qur'an*) revealed through the vehicle of His final Prophet Mohammad and the example of the last Prophet's lifestyle (*sunna*). While other Sunni fundamentalist, or Salafi, movements have advocated this return to the ways of the *al-salaf al-saleh* ('the pious ancestors'), Wahhabism has made of this call a living reality thanks to the indulgence of the Saudi state. This new society is peopled by the new Muslim, who lives as if 1,000 years of nonsensical accretions never happened at all; this new Muslim is blessed with the chance to return every day to the purity with which God created him through following the instructions of the Wahhabi *ulama;* he should shun foreigners and heretics such as the Shia where possible, and textbooks famously exhort Muslims not to emulate, befriend or greet them on holy days.

Wahhabism wields power through a range of acts, from the 'spectacular performances'[25] of its public punishments – execution by beheading outside mosques in city squares – to a range of requirements of orthodoxy and orthopraxy whose reach into the mundane and the everyday extends to the sartorial, with modifications to the traditional dress. Standard dress in Saudi Arabia is a simple white tunic, the *thobe* with headdress, or *keffiya*; the truly pious will make sure to leave facial hair growing and ankles showing from beneath the *thobe* because that is how Sunni tradition says the Prophet did it. The new Muslim woman, in Wahhabi thinking, should wear a face veil revealing only the eyes, and black gloves. The religious scholar wears a simple headdress, preferably white, without a *ghutra*, or head-band, to fix the *keffiya*. White is the colour of choice in the Wahhabi state; the white of robes, headdresses and most mosques; the white of the Muslim man who enters the state of ritual purity when performing pilgrimage to Mecca. Deviations from these standards are for the soi-disant Muslims, tainted by centuries of superstition and syncretism, bad rulers and weak faith. Shirts, trousers, ties and suits are the attire of the infidel; Iran's jacket and tieless shirt buttoned to the collar is a pale imitation of the infidel. Saudis working in the government sector are required to wear the *thobe*; Saudi citizens would be refused entry to a courthouse if they did not. This Wahhabi homogeneity matches the state's desire to minimise regional differences, a drive that has focused on the Hejazis of Jeddah, Mecca, Medina, Taif and Yanbu, as well as Asir and Jizan further to the southwest. Mai Yamani notes that wearing Hejazi clothes like *jubba* (overcoat) and *umama* (headdress) would cause a Hejazi problems with institutions of the state: national dress is Najdi, though Yamani still adds that 'there are subtle differences that local people recognise ... at the level of the choice of fabric, pattern or decorative motif, as well as in the manner in which the dress is worn'.[26] The Shia of the Eastern Province – another group with a markedly different history and sense of self from the Najdi elite – take the chance to remove their robes during Shi'ite festivals such as the ten-day mourning period over the death of Hussein known as Ashoura, instead wearing black T-shirts, pullovers and trousers to lament the fate of Hussein. These choices of attire are also a statement of defiance against Wahhabism's totalitarian claims on the Muslim.[27] 'In Riyadh you have to wear the same as everybody else. There is no tolerance and diversity', an acquaintance in Qatif told me.

Urban space is no less subject to Wahhabi purification. The Shia are sectioned off in their Qatif zone, but elsewhere they face the animosity of the state over the dissonance they represent for the homogenising ambitions of the Saudi-Wahhabism. US diplomatic cables in 2008 and 2009 report a campaign to close mosques and prevent public and private Shi'ite celebrations in al-Ahsa and Khobar, mixed areas outside the Qatif Shi'ite-only district, as well as ongoing arrests for people who try to take part. Mosques are closed for permit violations and zoning issues, and electricity is cut off and owners threatened with arrest (Bahrain closed and demolished some Shi'ite mosques and places of worship after Saudi troops entered the country in March 2011). American diplomats have identified three Saudi officials as the masterminds behind a sectarian policy of discrimination: the interior minister Prince Nayef, Eastern Province governor Prince Mohammed bin Fahd (cited as corrupt for taking commissions from businesses), and al-Ahsa governor Badr bin Juluwi. 'Several contacts have said that the discrimination in al-Ahsa is alienating the Shia community, particularly the youth, and is compromising their sense of Saudi "national identity"', acting consul general Kevin Kreutner wrote in one report.[28] 'The authorities often used tactics similar to what is currently being done in al-Khobar to force the closures ... including cutting off electricity to the mosques and threatening the arrest of the property owner.' Bin Juluwi cites 'security' concerns in conversations with US diplomats by way of explanation, but the diplomats suspect that these three officials feel sectarian animus towards the Shia because they are Shia, which definitely mirrors the views I heard from Shia on many visits to the Eastern Province.

The quintessential Saudi mosque is ubiquitous, large and very white; its realm is the modern city. Saudi Arabia has many such modern cities, including Riyadh itself – the original fortress town of Dir'iyya is preserved on its outskirts for the purposes of tourism and fetishisation of tradition – and the cities of Dammam and Khobar. But in other parts Wahhabi ideology has battled with pre-existing traditions, especially in the Hejaz cities of Mecca, Medina and Jeddah. Large Sunni mosques are placed in the centre of Shi'ite zones as a statement of doctrinal superiority and machismo, mostly used by Sunni Muslim expatriates. Old buildings in Mecca have been and continue to be demolished in the never-ending quest to increase the city's capacity to absorb pilgrims during the hajj season, when some 3 million Muslims converge there. Previous renovations to expand the Grand Mosque have resulted in the demolition of Mecca's old district, though Wahhabism has had no problem with rampant consumerism and capitalism as American fast-food restaurants, commercial towers and luxury hotels take their place, which offsets the arguments that could be made that destruction of potential pilgrimage sites aims to avoid the commercialisation of religion that one observes at Lourdes (pilgrim flights take you directly there), for example, or that Chaucer parodied in *The Canterbury Tales*. The hajj itself is a bona fide money-earner for Saudi Arabia. The result, as Sufi religious thinker and architect Sami Angawi puts it, is that Mecca and Medina are the 'most disturbed cities in the world', having lost the sense of balance they had as communities that developed across the ages according to local needs and requirements.

Local authorities have been unable to do anything about this, because the religious establishment has an elevated and untouchable status in the kingdom which any ordinary Saudi – which is to say, someone who is part of neither the royal family nor their clerical allies – understands instinctively. When the morality police ordered Saudi banks in the summer of 2007 to segregate women from men in the workplace, the bank administrations simply caved to the pressure of this autonomous clerical body. The authorities have demolished places where Muslims believe the Prophet prayed, lived or visited in order to preclude Muslims, especially Shi'ites, from making shrines of the sites. What was a rabbit warren of old Hejazi housing in central Mecca has been flattened to make way for various Grand Mosque expansions since the 1970s when oil money changed the face of the country, and, in recent years, luxurious high-rises. An early Islamic school called Dar al-Arqam once stood near the Bab Ali entrance to the mosque. 'The birthplace of the Prophet is to make way for a car park and hotels', says Irfan Al Alawi, a Hejazi researcher who runs an Islamic Heritage Research Foundation in Britain.[29]

Devotion of one sort has been replaced with devotion of another. Wahhabism destroys for Saudi capitalism to build. The Jabal Omar Development, with its major shareholder Makkah Construction and Development, is developing a series of high-rises containing hotels, apartments, shops and restaurants (the Saudi Oger company owned by Lebanon's Hariri family and the Binladin Group are the main contractors hired by Jabal Omar). Homes have been demolished to make it happen and their residents relocated. Property owners got stakes in Jabal Omar and other financial incentives to give up their land. The luxurious towers in fact dwarf the Grand Mosque. Some $20 billion worth of projects are underway in Mecca alone, according to Banque Saudi Fransi; $120 billion if we include Medina. A square metre of land in Mecca costs some 50,000 riyals ($13,333).[30] Hoteliers in Mecca say the authorities give them instructions to avoid outward displays of luxury, by which they mean swimming pools. But hotels such as the Makkah Clock Royal Tower Hotel advertise health spas (www.fairmont.com/makkah). The hotel has a clockface at its top facing the mosque that is meant to resemble Big Ben in London but is in fact bigger. The clock face lights up and a laser lights flash around the sky during the call to prayer. Jabal Omar was the subject of a $537 million public sale of 30 per cent of its capital in 2007; the rest is held by the owners of a 23 hectare (56.8 acre) plot of land in Mecca near the Grand Mosque, including princes and connected wealthy businessman.

Five-star pilgrimage is a major drive behind the changes, which were made possible by the second *tafra* when oil prices began to rise in 2002 (peaking at $150 a barrel in 2008 before the global financial crisis knocked prices back to well below $100 a barrel). Billboards in Arab capitals and advertising slots on Saudi-owned pan-Arab television invite the wealthy to stay in exclusive hotels in high-rises around the Grand Mosque with stunning views from above of the Kaaba. Given the history of violent reaction to perceived iniquity and corruption among those who control the Kaaba (the Prophetic conquest of Mecca, the Qarmatian revolt against the Abbasids, the 1979 Wahhabi revolt against Al Saud, it is perhaps surprising that the Saudi regime would allow these developments. The clerics, however – the Saudi family's partner in power – have raised no significant objection. 'One cannot help but feel sad seeing the Kaaba so dot-small between all those glass and iron giants', says novelist Raja Alem, whose *Tawq al-Hamam* (*The Dove's Necklace*) dramatises destruction of historic areas, corruption and abuse in Mecca. 'Long before Islam, Arabs didn't dare live in the circle of what we call "al-haram", meaning the sacred area (of the mosque). They spent their days in the holy city and moved out with nightfall. They thought their human activities defile God's home.'[31]

Novelist Abdo Khal touches on this link between commercial interests and Wahhabi destruction in *Fusouq*. Published in 2005, it talks of the neglect and disdain for the graveyards of the poor in Jeddah through the character of a police officer who finds himself charged with the strange case of a woman's corpse that has disappeared from her grave. The woman's morality had been impugned because of an illicit relationship and Fawaz and others suspect her death and burial were an elaborate ruse to run off with a lover. Khal's satire of suffocating moral codes in the kingdom takes swipes at Wahhabism. Fawaz seeks solace from the boredom of life by visiting the cemeteries – an irony given tthat visiting the tombs of the dead is anathema to Wahhabism. One such cemetery is cemented and turned into a transport depot. 'The municipality arranged it so that the station gave no impression of having been a place for the dead, whose bones were crushed and whose hides were tarmacked. Out of their kindness, they allowed the dead the chance to enjoy the jokes and hopes of those who frequented the coffee shop for two years. I spent long nights with friends over the remains of those dead. We made vulgar jokes and shared raucous laughs', Fawaz says.[32] One graveyard, al-Asad, has held out against the steam-rolling totalitarianism of the state religion. Khal writes: 'The cemetery with its ancient walls had held out against the changes. It had not succumbed and given up the bones of its dead to crush and tarmac as the Sabban cemetery had done. With this endurance the dreams of many businessmen of turning it over to commercial enterprises had been quashed.'[33]

Medina has also been the focus of Wahhabi destruction. The first Saudi state which took Mecca in 1802 and Medina in 1806 destroyed many shrines around the Prophet's mosque in Medina which were viewed as innovations that took away from worship of the one God (*tawhid*). The Saudi authorities also prevented pilgrims from Iraq, Iran, Syria and Egypt from performing hajj because their practices were at variance with Wahhabi views. The second Saudi state's jurisdiction did not extend to the Hejaz cities, thus enabling the Ottoman sultans to oversee the rebuilding of the Medina shrines and mosques marking the graves of companions and relatives of the Prophet, including his wives. A new era of destruction began in 1925, however, when the third Saudi state took control of the Hejaz and has continued until today. Each new act of vandalism, smaller versions of the Taliban destruction of Buddhist statues at Bamiyan in 2001, is spurred by the fear among the religious police that pilgrims from abroad are venerating shrines outside the official list of sites mandated for visits in mainstream Sunni Islam. For example, the grave of the Prophet's mother was destroyed in 1998 and a pile of stones left to mark the spot; the mosque supposedly marking the burial site of al-Uraidhi bin Jaafar al-Sadeq, a son of the sixth Shi'ite imam, was dynamited on 13 August 2002, Al Alawi says. Al Alawi states that there were attempts to cover up calligraphic work that does not fit with the Wahhabi agenda of *tawhid*, such as the words 'Ya Mohammad' ('O Mohammad') altered by adding dots to letters to read instead 'Ya Majid' ('O Exalted One'), one of the 99 names of God in Islam. The veneration of Mohammad is frowned upon as in violation of *tawhid*, worship solely of God, though Wahhabism has not been above victimising those who dare criticise elements of the received tradition on his life and character; no surprise given the inherent tension between forbidding veneration of his person while elevating his Sunna to the level of national cult.[34] Knowledge of these changes to the sacred topography of these cities is largely suppressed in the wider Islamic world, since governments and media have little interest in provoking Saudi ire by talking about them. Saudi Arabia alone decides how many pilgrims each country may send to take part in the hajj pilgrimage, and those who offend may find their quota reduced.

Saudi religious scholars have defended the destruction of heritage (*turath*). The Council of Senior Religious Scholars issued a fatwa in 1994 ruling that preservation of historical buildings could lead to *shirk* (polytheism). One cleric stated: 'Islamic legal scholars never talked about "reviving monuments" in Mecca, except those God approved of: the Grand Mosque and others which are part of the pilgrimage rites. Neither the Prophet's companions, nor anyone who came after them used to visit the alleged birthplace of the Prophet, because the Prophet never told them to.'[35] The clerics prefer replicas of tradition to the real thing. In 2002 Saudi authorities pulled down an eighteenth-century Ottoman fort in Mecca, prompting a protest from the Turkish government comparing the act to the Bamiyan incident. Islamic affairs minister Saleh Al al-Shaikh responded that a reconstruction of the fort would be included as part of the site redevelopment. Saudi newspaper editorials attacked Turkey for its own 'destruction' of heritage through Ataturk's secular state and usurping of Sharia law.[36] Sami Angawi estimates that over 300 historical buildings have been levelled in Mecca and Medina in 50 years.

An uber-expansion of the mosque precinct is underway, funded outside the official budget so that there is no public oversight of the process. Though Abdullah formally inaugurated the construction of the project in 2011, the full scale of the plans for the mother of all expansions has not been made fully public. Aspects of the project concerning the mosque specifically were seen in footage shown on Al-Arabiya television in which Binladin Group contractors discuss the plans with Abdullah. The king is clearly put out on hearing it will take six years to implement, at which the contractors backtrack saying what they really meant was three.[37] *Architects' Journal* first reported in 2008 that a number of British architects including Norman Foster and Zara Hadid had been asked to present designs that would increase the mosque's capacity from 900,000 to at least 1.5 million people and expand Mecca's accommodation capacity to at least 3 million pilgrims, with easy access to the mosque.[38] Foster had already been commissioned to design train stations on a high-speed rail link from Medina to Mecca via the King Abdullah Economic City and Jeddah. These developments – the demolition of ancient structures deemed to have no value or meaning, renovation of the existing Grand Mosque and erection of luxury towers where religion meets consumerism – reflect an ahistorical view of society and religion typical of al-Wahhabiyya. There is no past, only the eternal truth revealed during the lifetime of the Prophet; since there is then no future to talk of, meaningless material accretions around the mosque are of no import, or if anything they are positive since they facilitate the flow of the faithful to Mecca.

As hajj has been transformed into a mass event, the government has engaged in various projects to ease the flow of pilgrims visiting Mecca and surrounding areas during the hajj – the movement to Arafat from Mecca, then through Muzdalifa to Mina where pilgrims camp out for three days in order to perform the stoning ritual. Hundreds of thousands of pilgrims congregate there to throw stones at three pillars, the Jamarat, which marks the spot where Abraham is said in Islamic tradition to have been tempted by Satan. First a bridge was built over the pillars to allow pilgrims to either pass over the bridge or go underneath it to throw stones, splitting the pilgrim traffic in two. After the death of 250 pilgrims in a stampede caused by overcrowding in 2004, the authorities turned the pillars into solid walls: a wall is easier to target with a stone than a pillar. In 2006 they began transforming the single bridge into a multi-storeyed structure where pilgrims have the choice of several levels to walk across to target the pillar/walls. All of this has been driven by the idea that Saudi Arabia's duty is the 'processing' through pilgrimage of as many Muslims as possible. In light of these efforts to bring the largest number to the 'house of God', helping them fulfil the duty of every able-bodied Muslim to perform hajj at least once in his lifetime, the clerics are hardly inclined to object to a little crass commercialism in Mecca. The special consideration given to the wealthy is balanced out by concern to increase access to as many Muslims as possible to appease the Wahhabi clerics as well as Muslim scholars abroad. Public dissent over the mosque expansions has been almost non-existent.

Yet there have been indications of misgivings on the transformation of Mecca. 'The clerics are describing Mecca real estate boom as Babylon; of course, there is opposition', a Western diplomat told me in 2008. The only element of criticism to bubble to the surface has been discontent over renovations to an area inside the mosque compound called Safa and Marwa, two rocky outcrops separated by a half-kilometre-long walkway (the *mas'a*) between which pilgrims must walk seven times at various points during hajj and *'umra* on the spot where Islamic tradition says Hagar, the Egyptian wife of Abraham, sought water for her son Ismail. The walkway is situated on the well of Zamzam, whose water pilgrims return home with in bottles. 'We ask God to guide *waliyy amrina* ('our guardian'; that is, the king) towards that which *ahl al-'ilm* ('the people of knowledge'; that is, the clerics) have decided upon in this country and that which the clerics of the Islamic nation have followed', wrote Abdulrahman al-Barrak in July 2008, attacking the government's plan to create more space around the two ends of the walkway and install an upper floor to walk the same route.[39] Barrak cited hadiths that talk of what areas can be considered Safwa and Marwa. With the renovations, the pilgrim on the upper floors performs the *sa'y* (run/fast walk) between the two prescribed points in air and not on the ground, as pilgrims have done for 1,400 years. Pilgrimage is about carrying out to the letter the instructions from the Prophet on where go to and when: the pilgrim is not asked to understand or question, simply to do. Barrak is famously outspoken and he was one of the few to say anything publicly. What was important to the government was that it had the approval of the state mufti and the council of senior *ulama* that he heads.

For the Saudi rulers there is a bonus in the destruction of buildings: it helps erase the separate regional identities that present a challenge to the unity of the state, and advances a narrative that suggests a natural Saudi family role in establishing the unified state with a specific identity that straddles the regionalism of the peninsula through the use of religion. The government established the King Abdulaziz Foundation for Research and Archives to document folk tales, songs and poems from the kingdom's various regions that have been maintained from generation to generation through oral transmission and memory. Rapid urbanisation, settling of the Bedouin and rural migration is threatening to erase much of the historical memory. The project of retention is being carried out within a specific Saudi framework that will airbrush out of the picture opposition to Saudi rule in the time of Abdulaziz's wars of expansion, and material is collected in a way that seeks to legitimise Saudi rule. The project becomes in effect another part of the Wahhabi effort to create the new Muslim and does not challenge the destruction of the old. The result is a deep sense of dislocation. In the words of Saudi anthropologist Saad al-Sowayan:

> This sort of interruption (to the community's sense of self and history) is not healthy, there is a loss of cultural and historical continuity. Everyone is rushing for development and everybody is rushing for contracts and not realising that they are destroying culture. It is like cutting off your limbs. It's a serious matter and I don't think they realise how much, and I don't think they have the intellectual capacity to realise what it means.[40]

It would be understandable if Saudi Arabia wanted to avoid the heritage industry of packaging historical buildings and districts for the sake of the foreigner who has assigned them value. Egypt's culture ministry follows a policy of 'employing the antiquities' (*tawzif al-athar*) for the sake of garnering more tourist revenue and staving off Western criticism, stemming from the colonial era, that Egypt is not a worthy guardian of its treasures. But Saudi Arabia engages in fetishisation of its own, with the same aim as the obliteration as those other elements has: bolstering the narrative of the third Saudi state. Dir'iyya is preserved as a tourist attraction and symbol of national unity on the edge of Riyadh. Others, such as the ancient oasis towns of Khaibar and al-Ula with their labyrinthine alleys and mudbrick, palm-roofed homes with inscriptions proving their origins date back 200–300 years, stand abandoned after residents moved to adjacent new communities in the 1970s during the first oil boom. Jeddah, the oldest city in Saudi Arabia, possesses an old district with distinctive Red Sea architecture that has suffered considerable neglect and deterioration since the 1970s when population growth began to take off in Saudi Arabia. The city's municipality hopes to preserve the old town through efforts to win a place for it on the United Nations' World Heritage List, whose 830 sites include eight in Oman and Yemen. The old city remains a bustling market area where Jeddans live and work, so its preservation would have an immediate and practical purpose to it; it would not be an Orientalist fantasy. More than that, however, maintaining the lived city is about love and respect for a community, urban space and shared history and culture stretching back centuries.

Sami Nawwar, the head of tourism and culture at Jeddah municipality, has been campaigning to save the old city's buildings from institutional neglect since the 1980s. 'Now we have made an agreement with the education department in Jeddah to lecture in schools on the cultural history of the city, to do tours and involve male and female students in cleaning old buildings, beaches and the cornice', he says.[41] 'I used only to get foreign tourists and bored housewives. Now Saudi families, schools and students come to study architecture and heritage. Everybody is starting to be proud of it.' In Jeddah's old city, buildings still lie in narrow alleys running north–south and east–west to utilise sea winds and designed to create shadows that lessen the effects of the intense summer heat and humidity. They are constructed with coral-stone slabs and blue wooden-lattice windows called *roshan*, which give a unique flavour to architecture in historical towns in Egypt, Sudan, Yemen and Saudi Arabia along the Red Sea littoral. 'See how mankind used available materials to build a habitat that gives a good atmosphere, natural air conditioning, and natural windows that match culture and religion. It was the best use of materials to fulfil human and cultural needs', Nawwar says. In the 1980s many residents of the old quarter moved out with their new money. In their place came overcrowding, poor foreign migrants, and haphazard sewage and wiring. Around 10 per cent of 570 traditional buildings have been lost to fire and many are abandoned and in a state of disrepair. New regulations say they cannot be demolished, extra storeys cannot be added beyond the maximum six, and banks can offer owners loans to restore them. At the same time Prince Alwaleed bin Talal's Kingdom Holdings plans to outdo Dubai with the tallest tower in the world along the corniche. 'I think they will build a high-rise city like Dubai', Nawwar says, though he adds that even if that is the case, 'Jeddah has all the elements to succeed – it has no fake elements, it's authentic.'

Riyadh has jumped from a sleepy town of 150,000 in 1960 to a desert sprawl of over 5 million, expanding horizontally at an uncontrolled pace that stretches water and electricity resources to the limit. Wahhabism has indulged a cultural preference for the villa rather than the apartment, since open streets of single-storey buildings are easier to patrol and high-rises create spatial possibilities for undermining the Wahhabi moral order ('girl from floor 6 meets boy on floor 7 in the lift, in the stairwell', sort of thing). Disdain for public space and its unlimited scope for moral corruption also explains the absence of a public transportation system (metro plans were announced in 2012); and yet Riyadh is the largest city in the Gulf and one of the largest cities in the entire Arab world. Industrial zones of the Riyadh area have seen power outages in the summer since 2006.[42] Construction of around 1.1 million square metres of office space was underway as part of a new King Abdullah Finance District, being touted by the Public Pension Fund directing the project as a 'New Riyadh'. Borrowing from the ideas of Dubai, the district was to include residential, retail and entertainment areas and a monorail system. But with no cinemas in Saudi Arabia (after a brief flowering in the 1970s) and the ban on gender mixing, the project will have major drawbacks when it comes to attracting foreigners. It is hard to imagine the religious police would agree to being kept out of the area, though diplomats have suggested some embassies could move there – diplomat-quarter status would limit visits by the religious police. The city's original centre is lost in a massive grid of highways and wide boulevards based on an American model and designed for large (gas-guzzling) American cars – a legacy of the long American political and economic involvement in the country. As a result, Riyadh is something of a dehumanising concrete jungle. Professor of literature Abdullah al-Ghaddami writes:

> There was a complete split between physical construction and the human being in that development became something to do with places and not the individual. The human element was totally uprooted to the extent that you feel that urban spaces are devoid of any humanity, such as our wide streets designed for traffic and idolised with all form of advertisements, signs, signs and high-rises. Look for the human being there, we will only find the screeching of cars and tyres, and anyone who tries to find space there will only feel loneliness.[43]

The urban space of post-*tafra* Saudi Arabia, in the speed in which it was born and the Wahhabism that informs it at every turn, offers an imitation of the American city with little organic link to the past bar tokenistic funparks, museums and the other odd building in an ersatz 'traditional' style. 'From mudbrick houses,' Ghaddami writes, 'with their natural culture and direct link to the land, where human and cultural resources come together in one fabric, to cement where a manufactured reality is based on a complete separation from the environment and historical memory.'[44]

OUT OF TIME

Saudi Arabia presents itself as an exceptional country and the state perpetuates the idea of exceptionalism through promoting Saudi Arabia's *khususiyya*, or 'special characteristics'. The main element in this *khususiyya* is Saudi Arabia's status as the host of the two holy shrines in Mecca and Medina. Indeed, to shore up the regime's credentials King Fahd styled himself the 'custodian of the two holy sites' when he ascended the throne in 1982. The Saudi-Wahhabi polity presents itself as a kind of neo-caliphate, a transnational supraterritorial caliphate of the mind for the rightly-guided Muslims of the world. The Saudi propaganda claim that it is and should remain 'different' is absorbed by the millions who pass through its territory each year in pilgrimage or as migrant labour (and foreign governments through diplomacy and media). Abdullah al-Ghaddami thinks this concept of exceptionalism, which touches many other societies too, not least the United States, has managed to acquire the status of orthodoxy among many Muslims around the world:

> There is no question that conservatism is the most prominent feature of Saudi society, indeed it is required of this society and expected of it in the wider Arab-Islamic world. There is no Arab or Muslim who does not consider that Saudi Arabia is the essence of conservatism and they can imagine 'modernity' anywhere but in Saudi Arabia. Even the biggest champion of modernity in the Arab world would fight to stop Saudi Arabia transforming into a modern society and there are examples of Arab intellectuals who have lived in Saudi Arabia and took part in the battle against modernization.[45]

When the Saudi mufti appears before over 2 million pilgrims at the Namura mosque on the plain of Arafat outside Mecca during the hajj, his sermon reaches not only his congregation but millions of television viewers around the Islamic world: the presentation suggests that as the nominal head of al-Wahhabiyya he is the spiritual leader of Islam itself. The king's initiative for 'interfaith dialogue' launched in 2008, a major diplomatic initiative promoting dialogue between different religious blocs for the sake of world peace, had similar undertones. A participant at one of the interfaith meetings held in Madrid remarked that Abdullah sought to project himself as the representative of Islam itself: 'What I heard from him is that "I represent Islam, and I am the voice of moderation".'[46] A highly reductionist exercise, it began with a meeting between the king and Pope Benedict at the Vatican in November 2007, as if the king was Islam and the pope was Christianity. The king has often played up a comparison between the Vatican and the Saudi state. In an interview in 2006, the king told American network ABC that allowing churches in Saudi Arabia would be as inappropriate as building mosques in the Vatican. Yet the only territories in Saudi Arabia that bear comparison to the Vatican are the sacred precincts in Mecca and Medina; Al Saud are promoting the idea that the entirety of the country is 'holy land' and that Saudi Arabia is the authoritative voice of Islam.[47] Even Saudi liberals (a term that embraces secularists, leftists and Arab nationalists, most of them making their accommodations with Wahhabism and the regime) succumb to this thinking. Jamal Khashoggi, leading liberal in the Saudi-Wahhabi context,[48] writes, after an attempt by the al-Qa'ida Islamist rebels to assassinate the deputy interior minister Mohammed bin Nayef in 2009, 'Let us smash this ideology that allowed the ignoramus of yesterday to kill himself and kill a Muslim on a Ramadan night. This ideology is not Islam – we are Islam, Mohammed bin Nayef is Islam; we are the sacred space [al-haram], we are Sharia, we are the Islamic state. As for them, they are outside the bounds of religion and state.'[49]

The regime and its supporters felt the need to be more direct about its legitimising ideologies once the protest movements began in 2011. Tareq al-Humayed, editor of the Saudi pan-Arab mouthpiece Asharq al-Awsat, attempted to create an ontological divide between the republics and the monarchies in a number of columns during the three weeks of protests that brought Mubarak's term in office to an end. 'The issue isn't President Mubarak or the rest of the Arab presidents as much as it is a crisis of all the Arab republics', he wrote on 31 January; 'have the republics understood that they cannot behave like monarchies?' he asked on 3 February; 'if our monarchies insist on being monarchies and their constitutions stipulate that the people are the source of authority, then it would be better to hold elections if the people have questioned the president's authority', he said on 14 February.[50] In more sophisticated terms, columnist Yousef Bin Othman al-Huzayem explained, in an article in the Saudi daily Al-Eqtisadiah, the Saudi theory of governance, a theory that, as he outlined it, could be described in Western terms as enlightened despotism with an Islamic cast:

The political system in Islam is based on two principles: the sovereignty of Islamic Sharia, which is the quantitative, philosophical and moral framework for the rulers and the ruled, and which is the absolute truth they have recourse to in arbitration and guarantor of all basic rights and freedoms the human being needs, and secondly justice, either through applying the fixed sacred principles that have been stipulated or via the endeavor [*ijtihad*] of the ruler, or whoever he deputises, to use the tools of discretionary jurisprudence or act in the public interest as the ruler sees fit, through the force of his political acumen.

He continued: 'The Saudi political system represents this political legitimacy and is the contemporary model of the Arab-Islamic political tradition [*turath*], as an extension of the Islamic state [*dawlat al-islam*] of the age of the rightly-guided caliphs, the Umayyads, the Abbasids and the Ottomans.'[51] That last element interestingly raises issues about Saudi claims to carry the torch of the early Islamic state and the limitation of its realm to the borders of Saudi Arabia – on which more later. Nayef also broached Saudi exceptionalism in an address to the Mecca Region Council, carried in Saudi newspapers:

We thank God during the circumstances around us and in the world that are shaking the stability, security and economy, thanks be to God we don't have this in our country ... Our rule is not the work of man, rather it is a divine mission that we were tasked with by God in his book and with which the Prophet, the path of the rightly-guided caliphs and their followers taught us right behavior. A country is in a good condition when its justice system is in a good condition, and we can raise our heads and rest assured that our justice is the justice of God.[52]

Here he is outlining the central role of the religious scholars as the jurists of Sharia courts in the conception of Saudi Arabia as the model Sunni Islamic state. His meaning is clear: Saudi rule is divine.

These messages continued in different forms involving various media. For example, during the fasting month of Ramadan in 2011, which fell in August, the first show that ran after sundown on the Saudi-owned pan-Arab channel MBC1 was *Khawatir* (*Thoughts*), a Ramadan staple in its seventh season where youthful preacher (in the loosest sense of the word) Ahmed al-Shuqairi travels different countries to show how Muslims can improve their societies. The theme of *Khatawir* shows that year dealt directly with the slogan 'the people want to bring down the regime' (*al-sha'b yurid isqat al-nizam*), the ingenious Tunisian invention that spread to Egypt and every Arab country where protests took off. *Khawatir* tried to co-opt the subversive slogan and transform it into something less threatening. Each episode began with the sounds of crowds chanting 'the people want', but the words stop there as the word *nizam* ('regime') appeared with a bold red cross over it on placards carried by a sketch of protesting crowds. Then a visual followed of another crowd with placards in Islamic green writing saying 'no corruption'. The closing song, in the Islamic pop style of British singer Sami Yousef, appeals to Muslims to endeavour their own personal revolution in behaviour and lifestyle before they think of revolution in the larger political sense. Each episode focused on some aspect of non-Arab societies that was compared markedly better to how things are done in Saudi Arabia, the Gulf or the Arab countries generally. In one, al-Shuqairi visited a prison in Copenhagen, observing the comfort in which prisoners lived and the ethic guiding prison life of making them better people who can contribute to society when they leave. In another he compared the harsh school bell in Saudi schools to softer versions in Finland and elsewhere, and he examined the thinking behind these alternatives. The overall message is that it is Arab-Muslim society that needs to be fixed, not the leadership, and it is a message aimed primarily at Saudi Arabia and the Gulf countries.

This effort to shift blame for socio-political dysfunction from rulers to ruled has been a feature of Saudi Arabia since the 9/11 attacks. It is the message that the 'liberal' wing of the royal family – King Abdullah, the Faisal princes, and their patronage circle among the liberal elite – has promoted internationally and domestically through the reform discourse. Organisations like the King Faisal Centre for Research and Islamic Studies, an arm of the King Faisal Foundation headed by Prince Turki al-Faisal and kitted out with its 'senior fellows' to give it the air of respectability, play their role in propagating this view. Another is the Al Mesbar Studies & Research Centre, a Dubai-based think tank that focuses on Islamic movements. Founded in 2007 by television presenter Turki al-Dakhil, the centre's sources of funding are not clear. But it has a team of some 30 full-time researchers analysing various Islamic movements as if they have nothing to do with Saudi Arabia. Two books on al-Qa'ida and Osama bin Laden, Steve Coll's *Ghost Wars* and Lawrence Wright's *The Looming Tower*, betray signs of Faisal and his circle feeding their line, exonerating the family from the sins of the nation. Saudi funding of Western academic institutions also plays a role in this, though the aims are perhaps wider, including defending Wahhabism and challenging Western scholarship on the early Islamic period in particular, since much of it is viewed as an attack on Islam itself.

In this depoliticised, Utopian zone where history is the mere passage of time, the king is presented as above the fray. Royal rhetoric continually carries the implicit idea of unchanging conservative values unique to the Wahhabi realm. 'Social progress that does spring from the special characteristics of peoples is of no use, therefore we are continuing with this progress but according to that which fits traditions, customs, the heritage of the Saudi citizen, and most importantly our Islamic tenets which we hold as an example and follow and where we find guidance', Abdullah once told the Kuwaiti daily *Al-Seyassah*. 'Islamic tenets are religion and the real world and we ask for it to be applied with the tolerance that our divine constitution the Holy Quran ordered us to have. There are those who also talk about political action and I believe that when there is justice, governance will be correct and comfortable for people, especially if you are dealing with special characteristics; you have to pay attention to this for your people.'[53]

Because Saudi Arabia has established itself as unique, sacred and different, its media can pontificate over issues of mainstream international media discussion such as democracy and human rights with no concern for the hypocrisy of keeping Saudi Arabia out of the discourse. Indeed keeping Saudi Arabia *hors question* is one of the main aims of the Saudi media empire. Because the country is unchanging and outside of history, columnists drafted into the vast Saudi machine controlling Arab media will have no compunction in attacking the latest best enemies for lack of democracy (Syria) or lack of women's rights (Iran). In 2009, for example, the various arms of the Saudi media empire, including Al-Arabiya and *Asharq al-Awsat*, enthusiastically pursued the story of Iran's disputed presidential election and the repression of dissent with the same tone of reproach found in Western media, though Iran's political system allowed for more popular participation than much of the Arab region at the time. After sending troops to Bahrain and warning Saudis not to dare protest at home, Saudi Arabia addressed the Syrian government as if it was above reproach and together with Qatar went on to lead an opportunistic charge against the Assad regime.

With no need for democracy or foreign governments to offer lectures on the need for it, Saudi Arabia has found a challenge to its cultural specificity argument on its own doorstep: Kuwait, an Arab, Islamic, indigenous example of that which the kingdom claims is a dangerous alien import. Kuwait has a vibrant and boisterous political system and parliament. Kuwait's democracy is far from perfect. Members of Parliament are not allowed to form formal political parties and do not form governments, something which remains the preserve of the Al Sabah dynasty. Parliament tries to use its limited powers to question ministers and hold them accountable, but the cabinet members who are from the ruling family, which is most of them, usually resist, forcing cabinet reshuffles or dissolution of parliament by the emir. The Kuwaiti parliament's challenge to the ruling family has been held up in Gulf media as rowdy and irresponsible, a reason not to institute democratic reforms and allow popular participation in governance. Abdullah hinted at this in his *Al-Seyassah* interview. 'The kingdom will continue in its tireless effort to protect its people and its [Gulf] brothers from any political interventions and ideas that are far from its specific character and way of seeing things, factors which have provided security and stability', he said.[54] Senior cleric Saleh al-Luhaidan, a member of the senior clerics council and former Sharia courts chief, may have had Kuwait, Iraq and others in mind when he said that the kingdom had stayed true to itself through 'a period of changes in neighbouring countries, of revolutions, disturbances and hesitancies'. '[This country] has remained firm in its path because it is on the right path, did not follow a vain cause and it attained the approval of God', he said.[55]

If Saudi Arabia is outside of time and its rulers not subject to normal standards of accountability, it follows that a say for the people in state policy, domestic or foreign, is equally off the cards (its legislative assembly is consultative and unelected). Citizens have no say over oil or any other state policy, despite the role that non-royal technocrats have had in fronting oil policy, such as Abdullah al-Tariki, Hashem Yamani and Ali al-Nuaimi. A Shura Assembly member tried to raise the issue of reducing production to save for the future in 2008 but, coming at a time of international pressure on the kingdom to help lower prices, the proposal was not even debated. The king made similar comments in a play for public opinion when he said in April 2008 that some oil reserves had been left deliberately untapped for future generations.[56] Saudis saw their economy boom as oil rose from $10 a barrel in 1998 to nearly $150 in 2008. The stock market rose to unsustainable levels on the back of the oil boom and then crash in 2006, causing a significant hit for some half a million Saudis while wiping out the savings of millions more; spending increased to 410 billion riyals ($109 million) in the budget of 2008 in an effort to improve schools, roads, hospitals and sewage for ordinary Saudis since equitable distribution of wealth remains an illusion in a country whose rulers and businessmen appear on the Forbes list of the world's most wealthy. Indeed, the line between the wealth of the key members of the ruling family and the state itself is a thin one, as it is with other Gulf dynasties preserved by the old colonialism of Britain and the new colonialism of America (and who have all dabbled in the cultural relativism argument).

Novelist Abdo Khal examines the distortions created in society by the second oil boom in *Tarmi bi-Sharar* (*Throwing Sparks*, a Quranic reference to hell), which won the International Prize for Arabic Fiction, or Arabic Booker, in 2010. An unnamed, faceless tycoon figure in Jeddah builds himself a palace in the vicinity of a poor neighbourhood which provides individuals desperate enough to work as virtual slaves performing acts of sexual torture on those who have had the misfortune to stand in the big man's way. In the words of Kuwaiti novelist Taleb Alrefai, 'it looks at the humiliation of the human being and suffering ... how an individual tries to escape the social and economic chains that are taking away from his dignity'.[57] Yousef al-Mohaimeed depicts a similarly merciless society in his 2003 work *Fikhakh al-Ra'iha* (translated into English as *Wolves of the Crescent Moon*; into French as *Loin de Cet Enfer*). Spanning the period back to the 1960s, when slavery was officially outlawed, it features three characters who feel little sense of place or worth in society's new realm, the city. Each of them has lost something vital to their sense of self – freed Sudanese slave Tawfiq is a eunuch, Nasir was a child abandoned at birth with a missing eye, Bedouin robber Turad has lost an ear. The central character, Turad, relates in a gripping climax how he came to lose the ear, when a caravan raid went wrong and in revenge he and a friend were buried in the ground to their heads, leaving them easy prey for night wolves. Turad survives but witnesses with terrifying proximity his companion's grisly end. It serves as a metaphor for the experience of the Saudi metropolis, Riyadh. 'This place hasn't changed. Decades ago, when this Bedouin man lived in the desert and suffered, he could see the enemy, fight him and face him. Now he can't see him in the cities. Everything in this city is conspiring against you and tries to keep you down', Mohaimeed told me.[58] 'What I write in the novels doesn't approach the reality. The reality is fiercer than what I as a writer can show.'

Saudi society resembles a vast laboratory for clerics administering their vision, their replica amid the detritus of modernity, of the Islamic state. Yet the Saudi Muslim is neither the Muslim who lived under the first four Rightly Guided caliphs, nor in Abbasid Baghdad, nor even in the Najd during the first Saudi realm. Citizens and residents are trapped in a kind of gilded cage where for some the consumption of food, water, religion, television, clothes and modern gadgets is guaranteed, along with 'freedom' from the burden of managing the politics of state. The citizen is free to dabble in some intellectual pursuits if he really must, though even access to the novel is troublesome (most novelists are forced to publish in Beirut, and translators usually rely on authors handing them copies personally). Wahhabism has helped to create a grand form of anti-intellectualism that finds justification in the writings of the movement's founder. The 'experts in eloquence, knowledge and arguments', as he calls them, are enemies of God. 'What you must do is learn from the religion of God that which becomes a weapon with which you battle these devils.'[59] The Wahhabi Muslim is directed to consume electronics, invest in the stock market, digest American fast food, follow a certain cult of the Prophet's Sunna; he is not ordered to think.

2
Government in the Sharia State

The clerics have a position in Saudi Arabia that is unique among the Arab and Islamic countries. As well as the mosques, clerics control the justice ministry, the education ministry, the Islamic affairs ministry and the religious police force. The king appoints religious scholars to the Council of Senior Religious Scholars headed by the Grand Mufti, with four of its members forming the Permanent Committee for Religious Research and Fatwas. In 2009 he expanded its number from 16 to 21, adding five figures from outside the Hanbali school. This was hailed by reformers at home and abroad as a great advance though the council already included non-Hanbalis, and one of the new members who was ejected some months later for publicly criticising gender mixing at the King Abdullah University of Science and Technology (KAUST) was in fact a Hanafi. By allowing the class of religious scholars such extensive influence, Saudi rulers have delivered them control of society. Much remains in the hands of the senior princes, however, such as foreign policy and domestic security. The higher affairs of state are controlled by the most powerful members of the Saudi royal family, while social issues are in the hands of clerics, and both parties supervise economic policy, where civilians are only nominally in charge. Defence spending and mosque expansion programmes are off-budget and subject to process, however superficial, of public accountability.[1]

The key royals in the Abdullah era were public figures in government for some three decades or more. They included interior minister Prince Nayef (his son runs day-to-day affairs),[2] foreign minister Prince Saud al-Faisal, intelligence chief Prince Mugrin, Riyadh governor 1963–2011 Salman bin Abdulaziz, who became defence minister in 2011 and then crown prince in 2012, and crown prince and veteran defence minister Prince Sultan, who died in 2011, allowing Nayef to briefly assume (before he died in 2012) the role of heir to the throne and deputy prime minister to the king/prime minister, Abdullah. Former ambassador to Washington Prince Bandar bin Sultan was appointed head of a new national security council in 2005, and replaced Mugrin as intelligence chief in 2012. What unites them is their commitment to the rule of Al Saud. Mugrin, Salman and Sultan are sons of the kingdom's founder, Abdul[...] Nayef, Salman and Sultan are full brothers, and Nayef and Sult[...] were viewed as conservatives and hawks within the inner circle of Saudi power with regard to political and social reforms, while Salman's position was less publicly discussed but as governor for many years of a city where the religious police operate at will, it would be hard to argue he was much of a reformer. As governor of Riyadh, Salman was also charged by the inner circle of Al Saud with overseeing family spending and mediating in family disputes (the British liked him: a British ambassador in Riyadh told me, 'I cannot imagine that Salman will not one day be king'). Nayef and Sultan were described by diplomats afforded regular audiences with senior princes as resenting some efforts by King Abdullah to rein in spending among the Saudi princes and they viewed his concern to improve relations with the West after 9/11 as overstated and carrying the risk of a Wahhabi backlash. Mugrin, viewed by diplomats as an ally of the king, masterminded the Saudi effort to dispense large sums of money to pro-Western allies in Lebanon to make sure they won elections in 2009. Saud al-Faisal and his brother Turki, former intelligence chief and ambassador, present a cosmopolitan image of the ruling family to the outside world. Bandar was close to both Bush administrations as Saudi ambassador to Washington, and he is the star of the corruption scandal surrounding the so-called Yamamah series of defence contracts awarded by Saudi Arabia to British Aerospace. Prince Sultan and his family were accused by dissidents of having enriched themselves more than most Saudi princes through their control of the defence ministry, where the huge sums dispensed on arms purchases offer the possibility of hefty commissions.

Some ministries, such as the information ministry, are nominally outside direct royal control. Since 2001, information ministers have displayed a modernising bent – allowing Saudi women to appear on television as newscasters and presenters – but interior ministry supervision limits their room for independent action. Economic policy is nominally in the hands of civilians, through the Minister of Finance, Minister of Economic Planning and central bank governor and labour minister. The influence of the state *ulama* is never far away – they continued to impose gender segregation on banks and other commercial interests, despite the opposition of late labour minister Ghazi al-Gosaibi, and economic policy and practice must remain in line with their interpretation of Sharia law. The clerics delayed Saudi Arabia's accession to the WTO (finally achieved in

ilisation of the insurance sector, and maintain
oards of Saudi banks to ensure that activities
it.

a Basic Law in 1992 that led to the establishment
sembly the following year – a response to domestic
p... ed by the Gulf war and Saudi Arabia's decision
to host Americal troops. This Shura Assembly (*majlis al-shura*) is
not a parliament or legislative body (*majlis tashri'i*), despite efforts
to tout it as such internationally. It is an appointed body which
advises the cabinet of ministers. Saudi-Wahhabi thinking posits
that parliament in a Sharia state cannot legislate, it should only
advise, according to the principle of shura ('consultation') used by
the first Islamic leaders who were companions of the Prophet. The
Sharia is a mass of legal opinions based on the Quran and Sunna
of the Prophet, or the example that he set, and which is preserved
in the hadiths, short narratives gathered by the early Islamist jurists
that record comments the Prophet made or things he did, which
had been passed on orally through several generations. The hadiths
were organised into schools of law in the early Islamic period and
they are considered to reflect God's organising plan for society and
thus without peer. The Shura Assembly does not approve 'laws' (the
Arabic *qanun* is viewed as a 'secular' term associated in the early
Islamic period with Roman civil law) and *nuzum* (regulations), a
term used to describe cabinet decisions and decrees (Jordan, by
comparison, had a Basic Law as early as 1928, employing the term
qanun for 'law'). This means that in Saudi Arabia there can be no
body legislating law today since the divine law of the Sharia already
exists. These are of course semantic games; the key element is that
laws are promulgated via royal decree, they come into effect at the
king's pleasure, not because a legislative body, elected or otherwise,
deems them into existence. Similarly, King Fahd's Basic Law of 1992
is not a constitution, since the Arabic word *dustour* ('constitution')
is associated with the secular nation-state whose constitutions are
regarded by the *ulama* as documents compromising the supremacy
of the Quran. The Basic Law states that the Quran and Sunna are
Saudi Arabia's constitution and, through the prism of the Hanbali
tradition of Islamic law, this means that the 'constitution' is a mass
of material distributed in historical time through a series of texts and
opinions stretching over some 1,100 years, interpreting and ordering
a body of material considered to represent God's plan for mankind.

Three works serve as main reference points: the *Kitab al-Tawhid*
(*The Book on Worshipping the One God*) and *Al-Usul al-Thalatha*

(*The Three Principles*) of Ibn Abdulwahhab (1702–1792), the puritanical religious scholar whose ideas found favour with the Saudi rulers in the eighteenth century and for whom Wahhabism is named, and the collected fatwas of Ibn Taimiyya (*Fatawa Ibn Taimiyya, The Fatwas of Ibn Taimiyya*), the key scholarly reference for Wahhabism (despite disagreements in some areas). In *Kitab al-Tawhid*, Ibn Abdulwahhab selects Quranic verses and hadiths that illustrate the idea of devotion to God alone and rejection of *shirk*, a term usually translated as polytheism, which includes the Egyptian gods and idols that the Prophet Moussa (Moses) told the Israelites to avoid, to the local deities or objects such as trees that became places of veneration and worship in Arabian societies before Islam or up to the day of Ibn Abdulwahhab himself. In *Al-Usul al-Thalatha* he fleshes this out with three principles, that the worshipper should have knowledge of God, His religion and Prophet, again using Quranic verses and hadiths to demonstrate God's instruction to worship Him alone and avoid *shirk*. Ibn Taimiyya's opinions were a main point of reference for Ibn Abdulwahhab and his followers (and today's 'fundamentalist Islam' generally among Sunni Muslims). He lived during the period of the Mongol invasions of the Middle East – turbulent times for all concerned, they put an end to Abbasid Baghdad – and called for a return to the principles of the Quran and Sunna of the Prophet. The Wahhabi fixation with *tawhid* (monotheism), *shirk*, rejection of Shi'ism and Sufism, and emphasis on jihad has in Ibn Taimiyya its precedent. It should be noted that Ibn Taimiyya's beliefs do not wholly match those of Wahhabism. He accepted, for example, celebrating the Prophet's birthday and the legitimacy of Sufism. Ironically, considering he is a poster child for Wahhabi quietism, Ibn Taimiyya has been cited as an inspiration by many of the Islamist rebel movements from Sayed Qutb, the seminal Egyptian thinker persecuted in Nasser's Egypt, to Sadat's assassins, largely on the basis of his fatwas against the Mongol rulers of his time.[3]

The Shura Assembly has been chaired by a succession of cleric speakers and a certain minority of its members come from the religious establishment. The Basic Law and Shura Assembly were an attempt to further codify the relationship between the dynasty and the clerics – not the people – in the wake of the Gulf crisis of 1990–91. King Fahd's controversial invitation to American troops to operate from Saudi soil – for fear that Iraqi leader Saddam Hussein had Saudi Arabia in his sights too – provoked a movement of public dissent headed by some of the more independently-minded and ambitious of the *ulama* who sought an increased role for the religious scholars in overseeing all aspects of policy, including the key area of foreign policy. The war had exposed the ruling family as incapable of defending the realm, despite its wealth, and reliant upon the infidel Americans for protection. The Basic Law confirmed in writing the position of the cleric-judges within the Sharia court system, though it allowed for some areas of the judiciary to remain outside their control: some ministries have their own commercial tribunals overseen by committees headed by technocrats, and there is a grievance court system directly answerable to the king that deals with commercial disputes and cases where the government is a party. In 2007, King Abdullah ordered an extensive restructuring of the archaic system – belated Ottoman-style Tanzimat, if you will – but there was no indication that the position of the cleric-judges will be diluted when the judiciary is expanded from its current low numbers; rather, the government wants to train them in additional areas of legal specialisation, beyond Wahhabi *fiqh* (jurisprudence). Before the reforms began, there were only some 1,000 Sharia court judges for a country of some 25 million people. By contrast, Morocco, with a population of over 30 million, had some 6,000 judges, and even that is considered too few. A new justice minister was appointed in February 2009 and the veteran head of the Sharia courts was removed by King Abdullah in a sign of the monarch's frustration at the slow pace of the reforms, which made Saudi Arabia's membership of the WTO and its hopes of attracting foreign investment to provide jobs for young Saudis more urgent.

THE ISLAMIC STATE

I describe Saudi Arabia as the 'Utopia' of the religious scholar despite the fact that many, Salafi or otherwise, would quibble with the application of the term here. The Utopian concept has its origins in Greek philosophy and did not fare well in its direct translation into Islamic political thought. The tenth-century philosopher Abu al-Nasr al-Farabi developed Plato's notion of the philosopher-king in his treatise *Al-Madina al-Fadila*, or *The Virtuous City*, but for his dabblings in neo-Platonic thought his reputation has suffered: few businesses, for example, carry the name Farabi, just one sign of the Wahhabism's disdain for him. An Arabised form of the English word 'Utopia' is commonly used in public discourse today. Saudi Arabia and other Gulf monarchies fare rather well against Plato's standard, but badly against the Utopia of Thomas More's book of the same name. In Plato's *Republic* a small elite was invited into a consultative process on governing by an enlightened leader. The Gulf ruling families involve trusted families in some level of consultation on policy and governance; Saudi Arabia's Shura Assembly falls into that category, and when the franchise is finally extended to some Saudis, it is quite likely to be along tribal, favoured-family lines. More's satire, published in 1516, portrayed an imaginary island where women were encouraged to study, foreign labour was well-treated and the ruling elite were subject to an election process. Moreover, while official propaganda presents the king as enlightened, it never goes beyond folksy Bedouin values, where his difficulty reading and speaking play well.

The idealisation of the Medinan state of the Prophet, however, expresses similar notions. Salafis tend to regard polities such as Saudi Arabia as imperfect approximations of the Medinan state, but differ over how to respond to it: to work with it to iron out the inconsistencies where possible or take more radical action. The *ulama* have argued with Saudi rulers over many aspects of policy and state at various points in the kingdom's history. Most notably, a generation of preachers and clerics, affected by the wider currents of political Islam in the region, complained vigorously in the 1980s and 1990s that Saudi Arabia was not living up to its Islamic ideals. This culminated in two letters of protest to King Fahd after the 1991 Gulf war. Known as the 'Sahwa' ('awakening') clerics, they disputed foreign policy that served Western interests, on one hand, and laws banning Saudi women from marrying Muslim foreigners, on the other. They viewed this latter issue as un-Islamic and unnecessarily nationalistic in a country that aspires to implement Sharia and replicate the earliest community of believers. They also complained that the justice ministry and not the senior clerics council was the body charged with appointing judges to the Sharia courts. For them, Saudi Arabia was not the Islamic Utopia it should be.

These criticisms should be seen as part of an ongoing discussion within the country on harmonising a range of modern institutions and practices in politics, economy and society with the Islamic moral order. As for the mainstream of Wahhabi clerics, the state is Islamic enough for them to keep their gripes about its imperfections private. As literature professor Abdullah al-Ghaddami says, '[The clergy] considers that the state or the nation has a project that is Islam, and if this project was not Islam then they would turn away from it.'[4] Or as Sahwa preacher Mohsin al-Awajy put it: 'This country was set up on religious bases and it will stay that way forever, it can never change.'[5] Wahhabism rejectionists spanned the Ikhwan who rebelled against Abdulaziz in 1929–30, the 1979 revolt of Juhaiman and his followers, and Osama bin Laden's al-Qa'ida movement. Others have tried to withdraw from the state's sphere: Buraida has a community known as Ikhwan of Buraida, and the town of Zulfi has its Muhajireen District where they seek to reduce interaction with the state to as little as possible and refuse to adopt modern technologies such as electricity, cars or telephones. Some veered between the two extremes: the Juhaiman-inspired Bayt Shubra group in the 1990s produced some al-Qa'ida militants as well as liberal writers.[6]

Wahhabi and other varieties of Salafi Islam imagine a Medinan Utopia. The Medinan state came into being in the town of Yathrib after the Prophet's *hijra*, or emigration from Mecca in 622, the foundation point of the Islamic *hijri* calendar. The town was at some stage in Islamic historiography named after the event that it represented: Yathrib became *al-madina*, 'the city'. During his rule in Medina until his death in 632, the Prophet governed via a document often referred to as the constitution of Medina and preserved in early Islamic historiographical material. It concerns the power relationships between tribes of the area, including some Jewish among them, and reflects legal customs prevalent among nomadic and sedentary tribes in Arabia, such as the payment of 'blood money' to the family of murder victims. The Arab conquests of the Middle East took place later, after the Arabian Peninsula had been united under his rule. The first four caliphs (successors to Mohammad) extended the realm to the Levant, Mesopotamia, Iran and central Asia, Libya and Anatolia, while during the Umayyad dynasty (661–750) the Arab empire spread to the rest of North Africa, the Iberian Peninsula, Afghanistan and modern-day Pakistan – taking in territories with an array of traditions on statecraft, kingship, religion and law.

The relationship between the sovereign and the priestly class appears to have been an area of contestation in the developing Islamic polities. Many scholars of Islamic history consider that it was not until the Abbasid period that the *ulama* firmly established themselves as the guardians of the religious law, which they tied as much as possible to the Quran and a vast body of oral traditions on behaviour, morals, governance and belief that were attributed in one way or another to the Prophet. The caliphs were reduced in time to temporal rulers whose duty was to ensure the clerics were free to administer Sharia law while they managed the army, bureaucracy and relations with foreign states with guidance from the religious scholars. One famous instance of this tussle between the clerics and the caliph came during the reign of Al-Ma'mun, a son of Haroun al-Rashid who instituted a *mihna*, or inquisition. Al-Ma'mun issued a directive establishing as official dogma the belief of a school of philosophers known as the Mu'tazila that as God's word, the Quran, was created by God in time and therefore not equal to God in itself. Jurists such as Ahmed bin Hanbal insisted that the Quran was the 'uncreated' equal of God and their view was to win out after the caliphs finally rescinded the obligation to believe the Mu'tazila line. Shi'ite jurists and theologians, on the other hand, maintained a unity of temporal and religious power; thus in Medina the Prophet was both lawgiver – his own *'alim* – and ruler.

Of course, Shi'ism also posits that Ali, the Prophet's cousin and husband of his daughter Fatima, was Mohammad's chosen successor who was deprived of his right by the first caliphs until assumed the office in 656 CE. Shi'ites believe that Mohammad imparted Ali with secret knowledge and some believe that his blood link to the Prophet was in itself reason for him to deserve special status, since the Prophet and his line have *'isma*, an 'infallibility' from sin and error: the bloodline of Mohammad is depicted in Shi'ite iconography as almost semi-divine. There are twelve imams, or direct descendants of the Prophet, who mainstream Shi'ite tradition says were the rightful leaders of the Islamic community (*umma*), beginning with Ali and then his son Hussein, who was cut down by the forces of the Umayyad caliph Yazid at Kerbala in Iraq. Ali was killed in obscure circumstances in 661 by a group of dissident Muslims, allowing the Bani Umayya, a branch of the Prophet's Quraysh tribe, to establish dynastic rule out of their capital in Damascus. The Abbasids moved the caliphate to their new city of Baghdad after overthrowing the Umayyads. They also claimed links to the Prophet, through his uncle, though this was never enough to trump the claims to power of the living line of direct descendants through Ali. The Abbasid caliphs often sought to appeal to popular sympathies for the Alid line of descendants of the Prophet, but the twelfth imam was to be the last, after Abulqasim Mohammed, born in 869 CE, apparently disappeared during a period of heightened persecution of Shi'ites under the caliph al-Mu'tamid. Twelver Shi'ism holds that he remains *wali al-'asr*, the ruler of the age who will return one day from his occultation. The Islamic Republic in Iran implemented the novel theories of Ayatollah Ruhollah Khomeini that the most senior Shi'ite jurist should rule as sovereign in the absence of the hidden imam.

Al Saud behave as caliphs in the Sunni tradition that crystallised during the Abbasid period. It is true that they lack Prophetic or Qurayshi lineage, and they employ the title 'king' which many deem un-Islamic (*mulk*, or power/governance, belongs only to God). They established a dynastic system of rule and their state is locked into specific borders that preclude the expansionist aims of the caliphate of classical Islam. Yet the Saudi realm considers itself the true successor to the Prophet's polity, where the injunctions of the Quran and example of his life are implemented to cultish levels, which is far more relevant in the Salafi worldview than the idea of caliphal leadership by a figure close to the Prophet. Caliphal charisma, mystique and pretension are ditched in the Saudi-Wahhabi Islamic state for the stark and exacting dominion of Sharia and God's *ulama*. Al Saud are the temporal rulers that classical Sunni Islam says they should be with little claim to Weberian 'charismatic leadership'.

Al Saud shun the term *khilafa* because of the expectation among Muslims that a caliph should claim blood descent from the Prophet's tribe. The Saudi-Wahhabi state has shown consistent enmity towards those who claim family links to the Prophet because of the greater claim to political power that their lineage implies, Sunni and Shi'ite alike. The Hejaz region of Saudi Arabia, including the cities of Mecca and Medina, was ruled by such a political class, the Hashemites, until the fledgling Saudi state overthrew them by stages throughout the 1920s. Saudi rulers engaged in geographical expansionism from an early stage, and in later decades when Saudi Arabia had huge reserves of petrodollars to dispose of, ideological expansion became possible. When Arabs and Muslims from the subcontinent moved en masse to work in the country in the 1970s, they were influenced by the Wahhabi outlook, while some Saudis including religious scholars became exposed to the ideas of the middle-class cadres of Egypt's Muslim Brotherhood, the Islamist movement established in Egypt in 1928 after Kemal Ataturk abolished the caliphate, who were welcomed in the kingdom as doctors and teachers. Egyptians, Palestinians, Syrians, Indians, Pakistanis and Bangladeshis flocked to Saudi Arabia for the employment opportunities made possible by the oil boom.

Thus, once seen as a radical fringe movement, Wahhabism has moved to the centre of the Sunni Muslim mainstream.[7] Since the 1970s it has come to define conservative Sunni Islam. In 1982, King Fahd sponsored a new edition of the Quran for mass distribution, the first such undertaking since Al-Azhar published its version in 1926 following Turkey's abolition of the caliphate. It was, as

Islamic historian Walid Saleh has pointed out, more or less just a reprinting of the Azhar version but it signified the shift in power from old centres of Islamic learning like Cairo and Istanbul to the new one: Saudi Arabia. Interpretation of the text had passed to al-Wahhabiyya.[8] The Muslim World League, originally established in 1962, became the nerve centre of a massive operation to produce and disseminate Wahhabi scholarship around the world that has moved beyond building mosques to penetration of Western academia, endowing chairs in universities and funding history and religion schools and departments. Saudi activities stepped up in this regard after the Salafi theatre of 9/11, when the reputation of the Saudi-Wahhabi project at all levels was under attack: Saudi money provided even more grants and chairs at Western academic institutions in an effort to control the narrative on al-Wahhabiyya and Saudi Arabia.[9] From the 1970s, Azhari scholars took financially rewarding sabbaticals in Saudi Arabia, producing Wahhabi-inflected scholarship. Egyptian preacher Sheikh Muhammad Galal Kishk, who once mocked what he saw as the ignorance of Wahhabi Islam, published the pro-Wahhabi *The Saudis and the Islamic Solution* after receiving the $200,000 King Faisal Award and the $850,000 King Fahd Award from the Saudi government in 1981, though some influential scholars continue to belittle al-Wahhabiyya or say it has become an aberration of Ibn Abdulwahhab's *da'wa*.[10] Saudi Arabia funds around 500 mosque preachers outside its territory, the Islamic affairs ministry says.[11] A new chapter in this battle was opened with the fall of Mubarak in the wave of protest movements that swept the region in 2011. Al-Azhar is positioned to regain some of the independence it lost in the early post-colonial era and is likely to attempt to reclaim the middle ground in Sunni Islam.[12] At the same time, Saudi Arabia continues its effort to eclipse Al-Azhar: the Imam Mohammed bin Saud Islamic University in Riyadh, the leading school in Saudi Arabia for training religious scholars and judges, is spending $300 million on a campus expansion for new departments offering degrees in linguistics, English language, science, computer science, management and economics, in addition to the traditional Islamic disciplines. The aim is transform the institution into a fully-fledged university with the global reach to rival Al-Azhar. The Imam University already has affiliates in the UAE, Mauritania, Djibouti, Indonesia and Japan, in addition to over 60 branches in Saudi Arabia.[13]

As to kingship, while the term is entirely devoid of the implication behind *khalifa* of jurisdiction over the entirety of Muslims, ultimately the realm of most caliphs involved only a fraction of the world's Muslims. The third Saudi state has struggled with its terminology. Abdulaziz's official title was imam, before he was sultan, before he was king. Saudi kings are referred to in Friday prayers as *imam al-muslimeen* ('leader of the Muslims'). King Fahd took the title 'custodian of the two holy sites' and Saudi media shifted towards the term *maleek*, an intensifier of the term *malik* ('king') in its references to the Fahd and Abdullah. The national anthem chosen in 1984 uses the word in its title. Libya under the rule of Muammar al-Gaddafi also had name trouble: Gaddafi ditched *jumhuriyya* ('republic') for *jamahiriyya* ('state of the masses'). Both cases bring to mind the mystifications that Frantz Fanon observed of post-colonial regimes which perpetuated the exploitative systems they had inherited in new forms and guises. The key point is that the dominion of cleric-mediated Sharia is more important than the person of the ruler himself in the Sunni Islamic tradition that the Saudi-Wahhabi state claims to embody. Saudi Arabia sees itself as the true heir of the Islamic Utopia of Medina under the leadership of the Prophet and the four 'Rightly-Guided' caliphs who succeeded him.

SHARIA FAKE-STATE?

From French Algeria to British India to Indonesia, codification of Sharia law was central to the colonial project to control the legal sphere and enable economic exploitation of colonies. Where the colonial hand was lighter, in the Ottoman empire or Egypt before 1882, the native administrations felt that to protect themselves they had to ape the 'modernity' of the Europeans in the judicial sphere. 'The law had to be opened up to the inspection and, thus, control and surveillance of the state, while the entire legal profession had to submit to the higher wisdom and knowledge of that state. This is perhaps the most powerful political and legal tradition that colonialism has bestowed on the colonies and their inhabitants', writes Wael Hallaq.[14] When Saudi Arabia obtained international recognition in 1932, there was no colonial power forced to withdraw after having effected such reforms of Sharia, thus there was no native elite to 'fill the gap' left by the colonials and continue their work in modernisation. The Ottoman Tanzimat, which produced new courts, laws and judicial process in late nineteenth century, relied on Westernised bureaucrats who stood firmly behind the sultan's moves. This is largely absent in Saudi Arabia. The Tanzimat created French-inspired criminal, commercial and maritime courts outside the shrinking Sharia court system where the weight of testimony was equal between religious confessions. A prison system was built to complement the legal reforms. The idea was to regulate and centralise and thus generate more revenue to pay state debts to European states.

Gradually the mechanisms of the modern state have seeped into the protective bubble of Saudi Arabia: commercial tribunals, an increasingly overbearing security apparatus, expatriates segregated in residential compounds, Western pop culture via TV, internet and the Saudi mall. Saudi legal and judicial reforms of the last decade aim to facilitate the further integration of Saudi Arabia into the global capitalism after joining the WTO in 2005, as well as show a modernising face to the neo-colonial power, the United States, and avoid international incidents over the status of women. The justice ministry during Abdullah's rule began work on a penal code to establish boundaries for the discretionary punishments of Sharia courts and encourage judges to refer to judicial records of previous rulings in an effort to introduce the idea of precedent, though this runs counter to the whole ethos of Sharia where the judge in each case is a seeker after God's will.[15] In 2007 the ministry said it was publishing certain rulings to facilitate greater transparency and develop Saudi jurisprudence, in accordance with a cabinet decree from August 2002, but they would not be binding on judges.[16] With the population pushing 30 million, the idea of a rulebook became more attractive: it would ease the task of overworked judges and lawyers, for one. But amid much foot-dragging, there were indications that officials were telling foreigners what they wanted to hear. In 2009, officials told US diplomats they had not yet decided which system of judicial review to use – one based on judicial precedent or on new law.[17] One has to ask, what kind of justice would Saudi Arabia be codifying? In *Islam and the Secular State*, Abdullahi Ahmed An-Na'im asks this question, with primarily Sudan and Somalia in mind. 'What is problematic is for Sharia principles to be enforced as a state law or policy on that basis alone, because once a principle or norm is officially identified as "decreed by God", it is extremely difficult for believers to resist or change its application in practice', he writes.[18] In the Saudi case, we are talking about a gender-obsessed system that extends the *hudud* (the 'fixed punishments' that Islamic jurisprudents read in the Quranic text), at will, beyond murder and adultery.[19]

In Hallaq's view, Sharia-based society and the modern nation-state are incompatible. Sharia was characterised by its diversity and its independence from the state bureaucracy; 'precedent' has no meaning.[20] Egypt and Saudi Arabia in the decolonisation period offer interesting comparisons: one sought to be a modern nation-state, the other sought to replicate the classical Islamic state. In one, the state engaged in extensive and arbitrary interference in all aspects of individual and institutional life through forms of surveillance and punishment that tended to exceed those found in the Western democracies where the nation-state evolve;, in the other, the state was obliged in stages to encroach upon the domain of the *ulama*, whose Wahhabism reduces Islam and Islamic law to something of a caricature.[21] In Saudi Arabia justice apes the classical model, yet equality in justice remains elusive. To take one example, a son of interior minister Prince Nayef was tried for murder in 2004 but pardoned at the last minute when the victim's family declared they would accept blood money in retribution for the crime and save the murderer's life. On the face of it, this denouement upheld the rules of Sharia but the melodramatics of how the case played out in public betrayed the fact that so powerful a prince was never going to allow his son to lose his life. In 2007 a young Shi'ite woman from Qatif was pardoned for the crime of meeting with an unrelated man in an incident that led to her rape by seven men, in a manner that also upheld the supremacy of Sharia.

Further, low-income Asian and African nationals form a dispro-portionately high percentage of those executed, possibly due to the fact that they do not understand Arabic and have no access to influential figures who are able to intercede on their behalf, and, underlying that, possibly due to racism. Saudis also form a high percentage of those beheaded but they often come from remote, impoverished regions. 'The process by which the death penalty is imposed and carried out is harsh, largely secretive and grossly unfair. Judges, all men, have wide discretion and can hand down death sentences for vaguely worded and non-violent offences', Amnesty International said in a study published in 2008.[22] Use of the death penalty also increased dramatically under Abdullah: for example, Amnesty counted 158 executions in 2008, compared to 36 the year before, which the government's Human Rights Commission suggested, discouragingly, was due to an administrative clearing out of a backlog of names waiting on death row.

Professor of Islamic Law Khaled Abou El Fadl argues in *Speaking in God's Name* that Wahhabism has reduced Islamic law today to a set of rules divorced from the methodological process of *fiqh*.[23] 'As a set of positive commandments, Islamic law is alive and well in the contemporary age ... But as an epistemology, process, and methodology of understanding and searching, as a *fiqh*, Islamic law, for the most part, is dead', he writes. While al-Wahhabiyya long resisted the legal codifications of the nation-state, Saudi Arabia's imposition of Hanbali Wahhabite doctrine throughout the country and suppression of other schools of *fiqh* smothered the diversity that lies at the heart of the Sharia state. Moreover, this state orthodoxy led to a reading of Sharia that is obsessively focused on demeaning women and the pedantry of orthopraxy, and contradicts the spirit of the religion.[24] A number of researchers have noted that Wahhabism's positions are highly reactive, contrary to its claims of dogmatic rigour. Abou El Fadl argues that the output of Sheikh Abdulaziz Bin Baz, the hugely influential Saudi mufti who died in 1999, and his peers bears signs of a resort to extremist positions on the chosen field of battle – women – *in response to* the threat of modernising trends in Islamic thinking and Western secularism. In other words, much of Wahhabism's edifice is modern in provenance and as liable to critique as any other modern intellectual product; contrary to its claims, it has not been plucked untouched from the classical realm of Sharia in history. El Fadl writes:

> Post-1970s Salafism adopted many of the premises of the apologetic discourse, but it also took these premises to their logical extreme. Instead of simple apologetics, Salafism responded to feelings of powerlessness and defeat with uncompromising and arrogant symbolic displays of power, not only against non-Muslims, but also against Muslim women. Fundamentally, Salafism, which by the 1970s had become a virulent puritan theology, further anchored itself in the confident security of texts. Nonetheless, contrary to the assertions of its proponents, Salafism did not necessarily pursue objective or balanced interpretations of Islamic texts, but primarily projected its own frustrations and aspirations upon the text.[25]

COMPARISON TO OTHER LEGAL SYSTEMS

The position of the clergy in other Arab and Islamic countries falls short of the influence they hold in Saudi Arabia. The Turkish republic established by Ataturk stands at the far end of the spectrum. Neither Islam nor Sharia law are even mentioned in Turkey's constitution, which states at the beginning that the state is a secular republic. Most Arab states are nominally secular democracies, republican or monarchical, where clerics do not serve as judges and Islamic law is in any case restricted to personal status courts adjudicating in issues of marriage, divorce, inheritance and other family issues. In neighbouring Qatar, which follows Saudi Wahhabism, reforms instituted after the 9/11 attacks have restricted clerics to serving in personal status courts. Education syllabuses in other Arab states follow nationalist rather than strictly religious lines, whereas Saudi schools until recent years promoted a Muslim rather than a specifically Saudi identity: pride was located in Islam, and only in the Saudi state in as far as it was a country that followed God's law to the letter. To secular Arab intellectuals, the Saudi *ulama* are 'the clerics of darkness'.[26] Saudi-influenced Salafis in Kuwait and Yemen have in recent years called for a religious police body along the lines of the Saudi model. Constitutional debates in Egypt and Iraq over the role of Islamic Sharia law in fact highlight how distant these countries are from the classic Islamic state model applied in Saudi Arabia. In 1971, when President Anwar Sadat sought to bolster his support among Islamist forces to counter the strength of Nasserists and leftists, the Egyptian constitution was amended to state that Sharia was one of the sources of legislation; the constitution was further amended in 1980 to say Sharia was 'the main' source of legislation. Subsequent debate centred on whether the amendment was aimed at the judiciary, which should then give rulings that reflect Sharia principles and implement Sharia through the bench, or parliament, which should enforce Islamic law through the laws it passes. Egypt does apply Sharia law in personal status issues, but there are no special courts for these affairs with sitting cleric-judges.

The most celebrated attempt to enforce Sharia principles through Egyptian courts was the 2005 forced divorce of Islamic history Professor Nasr Abu Zaid from his wife on the argument, made by Islamists, that his writings on the Quran proved he was an apostate. He and his wife left the country. His detractors were adopting a Wahhabi argument, that even the Quranic description of God as sitting on a throne must be read literally. Reflecting the conflict between the secular state and Islamisers within the judiciary, the state never enforced the divorce verdicts and continued to offer the couple protection when in Egypt. The plaintiffs used the Islamic concept of *hisba*, which allowed them to raise legal action in the name of the public good. Saudi Arabia's Commission is an apparatus that actively enforces *hisba*, whereas in Egypt it is enacted through the right to prosecute in the courts – both actions, of the Saudi Commission or the Egyptian plaintiff, are an effort to implement the Quranic injunction to 'uphold morals and prevent vice'. The use of *hisba* was subsequently limited in Egypt to the public prosecutor through an act of parliament, negating the concept of any Muslim's right to directly petition cleric-judges to uphold the Islamic public good. Muslim Brotherhood Members of Parliament from 1984 to Mubarak's removal in 2011 made little headway in furthering the remit of Sharia law or implementing Sharia principles through legislation. Egypt has one of the most influential judicial structures in the Arab world, one that has been a secular model for other Arab countries, but it has struggled to ward off Saudi-Wahhabi influence since oil wealth empowered Wahhabism.

Iraq's strongly secular constitution of 1970 under Baathist rule was replaced by an interim constitution of 2004, and finally a new constitution approved by referendum in 2005.[27] It followed much wrangling between Sunni and Shi'ite Arabs and Kurds (who are also mainly Sunni Muslim) over its wording on religion, federalism and distribution of oil revenues. The present Iraqi constitution follows the example of the secular nation-states in predominantly Sunni Arab countries such as Egypt, Algeria or Syria in citing Sharia as a source of legislation (Algeria's Family Code of 1984 specified Sharia as the source of law). The final text says that Islam is the 'official religion of the state and a basic source of legislation', 'no law can be passed that contradicts the undisputed rules of Islam', and 'experts in Islamic jurisprudence' – meaning clerics – have a place alongside judges and other 'legal experts' on the Federal Supreme Court (a constitutional court). It also allows regional legislative bodies large scope to prevail over federal law, which allows Sharia courts to operate in areas such as family and criminal law. The constitution, then, generally imagines a secular judiciary, as before, but with considerable room for Sunni and Shi'ite clerics to administer Sharia in some areas of law. Both the Sunni Arab minority and the Shi'ite majority were happy with this; it was Muslim Kurds, Christians, other non-Muslims, and secular liberals who feared these concessions to Sharia could be used to enact legislation against their interests. The Baath constitution simply stated that 'Islam is the religion of the state' and did not mention Sharia by name, though the word 'secular' was avoided.

Pakistan has seen several constitutional amendments since its foundation in 1947 that have gradually increased the role of Islam. The current 1973 constitution says Pakistan is an Islamic republic where the executive and legislature are expected to make sure laws conform with Islam. It states that the presidency and prime minister's job are only for Muslims and attempts a definition of who is a Muslim that specifically rules some groups out. The court system, however, essentially follows the secular nation-state model, with the addition of a Federal Shariat [sic] Court where only three of eight sitting judges are required to be '*ulama* who are well-versed in Islamic law'.[28] The court allows citizens and organs of the state to question whether any laws are un-Islamic ('repugnant to the injunctions of Islam, as laid down in the Koran and Sunna of the Prophet'). The Supreme Court contains two cleric-judges to hear any appeals of Federal Shariat (Sharia) Court decisions, and the high courts also contain a bench of Shariat Court judges; that is, as in many countries where Sharia law is applied in some areas, the judges administering it are not necessarily religious scholars. Like Egypt, Pakistan offers the example of a country where judges and legislators have sought to Islamise society in a state set up along secular nation-state principles. In *The Role of Islam in the Legal System of Pakistan*, Martin Lau shows in a case study of legal rulings from 1947 to 2001 that parliament's efforts since 1977 to legislate more Islamic law have given succour to judges in their determined attempt to introduce Islamic law into judicial reasoning.[29] But what is relevant for our purposes here is to note that these efforts took place within and because of the state's essentially secular, non-classical Islamic state framework. Politicians, judges and parliamentarians are pushing Sharia because Pakistan is not a Sharia state.

Indeed, one of the few countries where the primacy of Islamic law and the clergy bears comparison to Saudi Arabia is Iran since 1979, an irony given Wahhabism's distaste for Shi'ism. Prior to the revolution, Iran kept clerics and Sharia law at a distance. Now Iran's constitution defines the country as an Islamic republic, authorises a council of guardians to ensure that the constitution and laws are based on Islamic principles, and makes explicit reference to the Supreme Leader's right to rule in the absence of the twelfth imam. Iran's constitution outlines a state of both political Islam and of Islamic law. It talks of Iranian society's development according to 'Islamic principles and norms' and the 'continuous leadership of holy persons'. It says 'all civil, penal, financial, economic, administrative, cultural, military, political and other laws and regulations must be based on Islamic criteria ... the wise persons of the Council of Guardians are judges in this matter'. And referring to the Supreme Leader, 'during the occultation of the *wali al-'asr* – may God hasten his reappearance – the leadership of the nation (*umma*) devolves upon the just and pious person'; that is, the supreme jurisprudent, or cleric-judge.[30] While the constitution specifies that the elected president must be Iranian, the office of Supreme Leader requires only jurisprudential knowledge and political wisdom, promoting the Islamic republic's claims to global Islamic leadership. The previous constitution of 1906 made considerable concessions to the clerics, citing the official religion of the country as Islam according to the Twelver Shi'ite doctrine and school of law. It also said laws must be approved by a committee of clerics (the term 'Shi'ite' does not appear).

The other modern state which was close to the Saudi model is Afghanistan under the Taliban, a group of Sunni Muslim Pashtuns who established an Islamic emirate there from 1996 to 2001. The Taliban state had all the key features of Saudi Arabia's Islamic state, including the fullest possible use of Sharia courts with Sharia cleric-judges and a morality force that patrolled the streets to enforce Islamic rules on behaviour. The Taliban arguably went further than Saudi Arabia in forbidding women from employment or education and carrying out the *hudud* punishment of stoning for adultery, though Saudi clerics are still arguing about women at work and doing their best to restrict it. Saudi Arabia was one of only three countries in the world to extend diplomatic recognition to the Taliban, including Pakistan and the UAE. The United Nations never recognised their rule as legitimate. The Taliban's beliefs differed from Wahhabism in that they did not frown upon the practice of visiting graves and shrines, and on some doctrinal issues they disagree, but they did match the Wahhabi hatred for Shi'ites and the belief that the application of Sharia obviates the need for political parties and legislative elections. The Taliban project in fact involved a mixture of Wahhabism, Pashtun tribal codes and the ideas of the Deobandi movement that formed in reaction to British colonial India that spawned many of the Islamist groups present today in the subcontinent.

POLITICAL ISLAM AND SAUDI ARABIA

The distinction between political Islam, on the one hand, and Islamic states where cleric-judges apply Sharia, on the other, is an important one. Egypt's Brotherhood is for the most part a party of laymen who want religious scholars, via Al-Azhar, to have an advisory role to government: they do not seek to bring clerical rule, or install a cleric as supreme leader as in Iran, or even a caliph, who in any case in

Sunni Islam is a temporal figure. Neither has the Brotherhood or its political party indicated they want to overhaul the judiciary along Saudi lines in a parallel attempt to recreate the early Islamic state. Saudi Arabia, on the other hand, says it has no need of political parties, and especially not Islamist parties, because it rules by Sharia, which is divine in origin. Sunni Islamist movements seek two goals: to ensure laws conform to Sharia and that rulers apply foreign policies that serve nationalist-Islamist interests. Salafis espouse obedience to the ruler to whom they have happy to provide advice; Islamists seek an executive role in governing itself. Wahhabism provides the religious-ideological cover for the absence of public politics and a foreign policy so closely linked with the United States. Sheikh Abdulrahman al-Mozainy, a member of the Council of Senior Religious Scholars, attacks even sending Saudi students abroad on study scholarships because political activism is among the infidel ideas they will return with. Not only will they 'stop praying, drink alcohol and befriend the infidels', they will also 'import deviant ideas and rowdy behaviour such as striking, demonstrating, following political parties and rebellion'.[31] After the 9/11 attacks, Prince Nayef openly accused the Muslim Brotherhood of having politicised Sunni Islam, seeking to lay the blame for al-Qa'ida's actions at the door of the Brotherhood's political activism rather than with Saudi Arabia's traditionally quietist Wahhabism.

Sudan under the Islamist regime that General Omar Hassan al-Bashir brought to power with an army coup in 1989 offers an interesting contrast: an Islamist state versus Saudi Arabia's Islamic state. Under the guidance of Islamist ideologue Hassan al-Turabi, whose background was in the Sudanese branch of the Muslim Brotherhood, Sudan was similarly an experiment, but one directed by politicians from the top of the system with the aim of rearranging and realigning the institutions of state and society to conform to a revolutionary model designed for export around the region. The question of whether to work through society and recreate the Medinan Utopia from the bottom up, rather than focus on overt political activity and action through the existing political system in a given state, has wracked the Brotherhood for decades. Turabi represented the activist extreme. Sudanese political scientist Abdullahi Gallab writes:

> The primary function of the state-directed regime, according to the Islamists model, is to operate in a manner that attempts to demolish or converge in their system other autonomous

institutions that normally act independently within the spheres of the civil, religious and the political societies. This is an important representation as the totalitarian setting attempts to deploy the state power to eliminate and demolish all civil and political societies, spheres and institutions. Within this approach to power, the Islamists in the Sudan, their strategists and allies tried very hard to establish such a state.[32]

However, in Sudan the effort to fashion the individual and society along specific lines is directed from the top by the regime. The regime's interest in the traditional *ulama*, the guardians of religious knowledge, is only passing. Turabi is typical of the Islamists who have emerged since the 1970s. As Wael Hallaq notes, they are for the most part not trained in traditional disciplines, do not read classical sources with the same perspective as the *ulama*, they are trained in modern disciplines (engineers, lawyers, doctors) and they are not bound by an established reading of the Quran and Sunna. '[T]he Islamists do not feel bound by the cultural and epistemic systems developed throughout Islamic intellectual and legal history', he writes.[33] Some *ulama*, however, flirt with the Islamist camp (for example, Egyptian cleric Yousef al-Qaradawi's Brotherhood links), but most stand apart. Turabi wanted to reorder society in a manner influenced by the colonial experience and he was perfectly prepared to find a place for the elected legislative chamber in this vision. 'The British colonial administration (1898–1956) provided the Sudanese [Islamist] project with the means to construct and essentialize the social, economic and cultural structures of a new state', Gallab says.[34] The Saudi rulers have no need for such inventions if the *ulama* play their role as guardians of the moral society, leaving them a free hand to deal with the higher issues of state. But they have often clashed as the ambitions of the *ulama* waxed and waned, which the next chapter looks at in more detail.

3
The Warrior King and His Priests

The *ulama* have often challenged temporal power during the modern Saudi state, in foreign policy as well as a range of domestic social and political issues where they argued and delayed but ultimately succumbed to the arguments of the Saudi rulers and force of events on the ground. The clerics saw the zealot Ikhwan army they had helped establish with the kingdom's founder subsequently cut down to size in a showdown with Al Saud in 1929/30. They watched with alarm as Americans began drilling for oil in the 1930s and then to exert huge influence over the developing state through the Aramco oil company and the American diplomatic presence, but ultimately oil came to replace plunder and open new vistas for al-Wahhabiyya. Though they agree with most of the causes championed by the zealots who seized control of the Grand Mosque in 2009, they denounced the group as the government used military force to crush them. Though they abhorred the idea of American troops on Saudi soil, they gave their blessing to the proposal after Saddam Hussein's occupation of Kuwait in 1990. They sought to obstruct the introduction of almost every consumer item of modern culture imaginable, including radio, television, satellite dishes and, most recently, mobile camera-phones. They resisted education for girls and dug their heels in over half-hearted attempts by liberals to roll back the powers of the religious police force and end the gender segregation that lies at the heart of the clerics' vision of a moral society.

Tensions between the two erupted in violence after the Ikhwan movement had done its work. In the Ikhwan settlements, of around 150,000 people by 1926, Wahhabi scholars preached observance of rituals and obedience to the Saudi ruler. Their cause was jihad to return the peninsula and beyond to the true Islam of the Prophet. The movement felt Abdulaziz should allow them to do more to spread Wahhabi values among the Hejazis and Shia; they resented his sending his son Saud to Egypt to study (controlled by Christian power, populated by pseudo-Muslims); they did not like the introduction of foreign innovations such as the telegraph system; they opposed his assumption of the title 'king'; they felt he was too deferential to the British; they wanted freedom to prevent pilgrim practices that Wahhabis frowned upon; they questioned the exclusive right of the Saudi family to govern. In Turki al-Hamad's novel *Sharq al-Wadi* (*East of the Valley*), the Ikhwan are portrayed as Bedouin who look down on sedentary urban dwellers and resent the restrictions placed on them by a profligate king. They clearly perceive the *hijra* settlements for what they were: an attempt to tame them. The Ikhwan and Al Saud are shocked by their victory over the Hashemites; a victory that they impute to divine favour. An Ikhwan rebellion finally broke out in 1929. Wahhabi allegiance to the Saudi ruler had been a subject of contention in the recent past. The leading Wahhabi cleric, Abdullah Bin Abdullatif Al al-Sheikh, switched allegiance between Saudi brothers fighting for control of the state in the 1870s. Sheikh Abdullah gave allegiance to the Rashidis of Hail after they defeated the Saudis in 1891 and backed the Rashidi ruler in 1900 when Abdulaziz made a first, abortive attempt to wrest back Riyadh from the Rashidis. The *ulama* then swore allegiance to Abdulaziz when he took control in 1902, and reluctantly accepted his treaty with Britain in 1915 which made the Najdi–Eastern Province realm a British protectorate on the imperial payroll, helping stymie the unification plans of another Arabian potentate, the Sherif of Mecca. The scholars were split during the Ikhwan revolt. Those who openly sided with the Ikhwan are known to have been lower-ranking *ulama*, from poorer social backgrounds who studied in the Najdi town of Buraida. Abdulaziz called the the Riyadh-based *ulama* to a meeting to hear them out on the Ikhwan's complaints. They acquiesced in his argument that taxes and decisions of war and peace were the ruler's prerogative alone. Then Abdulaziz turned on the Ikhwan with British airforce support.

The outlines of the modern Saudi state had been established: a balance of power between cleric and king that limited the *ulama* to religion and society, leaving Al Saud a free hand over the politics of state with a grey area in-between where clerics could advise the rulers on the Islamic correctness of various aspects of policy, especially technical innovations. Legal scholar Abdulaziz Al-Fahad argues that the Ikhwan revolt marks a turning point in the evolution of the Wahhabi clergy and their transformation, on the eve of the state's international recognition, into a partner in power that understood the practical limits of doctrine and the impossibility of permanent religious revolution (until the petrodollar era). During the nineteenth century the Wahhabi *ulama* had debated the legitimacy of dealing with infidel forces such as the Ottomans, Egypt, and the Rashidis in Hail and Kuwait. In the 1870s the Ottomans became involved in the internecine strife between leading members of the ruling Saudi clan. Some leading Wahhabi clerics at that time felt that relying on the Ottomans to regain and maintain power was an infringement of God's law – a stark contrast to 1990, Al-Fahad notes, when the clerics concluded that 'the assistance of non-Muslim U.S. forces was in conformity with that law'.[1] Al-Fahad notes that in the view of many in the Rashidi state to the north, the Wahhabis were dangerous extremists. The *ulama* appear to have gone silent as Abdulaziz re-established the Saudi realm after 1902. Al-Fahad notes there are no known fatwas or pronouncements by the religious scholars with respect to the Anglo-Saudi treaty of 1915, wherein Abdulaziz ceded powers to the British in exchange for material support, though some were energetic in their censure of the Rashidis' alliance with the Ottomans. Though some were not undecided as to whether Kuwait was in the zone of unbelief or not, there was no objection to the Saudi family taking refuge in Kuwait after the Rashidis seized Riyadh in 1891.

Conflict with a new, quite different group was to emerge in the 1950s – leftist and Arab nationalist politicians who sought influence over policy and seats in cabinet – but again the royal family won out. There were subsequently two major attempts to limit the absolutism of the Saudi rulers through a consultative assembly: one in the 1990s led by the Wahhabi clerics alarmed by Al Saud foreign policies and un-Islamic personal behaviour, and another after 2001 led by liberals who perceived the regime's weakness internationally and domestically following the 9/11 attacks. The clergy wanted to strengthen the role of Islamic institutions and enter the political sphere, and the liberals wanted to roll back the societal power of the clerics. There was some limited overlap between the two blocs: liberals took part in the Islamist mobilisation of the early 1990s and some clerics and Islamist intellectuals joined the campaigns of the early 2000s to create more participatory government. What united the scholars and the liberals was the desire to limit the monopoly on power of Al Saud.

EARLY TENSIONS IN THE OIL ERA

The sudden presence of foreigners in significant numbers in Najd and the Eastern Province was a culture shock to ordinary Saudis and a challenge to the religious establishment. Americans began exploring for oil in 1933 and drilling in 1938. The company became known as Aramco in 1944 as its headquarters in Dhahran expanded into two towns, a barbed-wire-protected all-American one with all mod-cons for the Americans and a squalid one next to it for the Saudis, other Arabs and Asians – and later, Italians. This iniquitous situation led to a decade of protest activity from 1945 to 1956 and led to the rise of a new breed of indigenous leftist, Arab nationalist politician, contemporaneous with the rise of the post-colonial Arab nationalist and leftist movements in the wider region. In Saudi Arabia they included Nasser al-Said, Abdullah al-Tariki, Abdullah Suleiman and Abdulaziz Bin Muammar, and they posed a challenge to the royal family as well as to American interests. As long as the infidels kept to themselves and there was no mixing of populations and cultures, the Americans were welcome, but it remained an uneasy relationship. Trouble threatened when American engineers moved into the town of Kharj, just south of Riyadh, in 1941 to manage a farming project and a young, ambitious cleric named Abdulaziz Bin Baz (1912–1999) objected. Bin Baz was summoned to Riyadh where he told Abdulaziz that selling land to infidels in this manner was contrary to his role as ruler of an Islamic society. The other clerics accepted Abdulaziz's argument that he was employing foreigners to do work on his behalf and that the Prophet had done the same, but Bin Baz said while he accepted the king's right to decide, he did not agree with the decision, at which he was imprisoned. He was released after apparently coming round during a private pep talk with the king. Bin Baz went on to become the official Grand Mufti and the most influential cleric in modern Saudi history.[2]

The period of the rule of King Saud from 1953 to 1964 was a particularly tumultuous time. It was a period of large-scale American intervention through Aramco's involvement in public works and infrastructure building and influence with the government, in coordination with the US embassy in Jeddah and the State Department, to ensure the best terms for Aramco's oil operations, labour relations and the oil rent to the Saudi government. It was a time when Egypt under Nasser took its revolutionary message of challenge to Western imperialism to every corner of the Arab world. The expectation was very real around the region that the Saudi state would collapse. Six years after finance minister Abdullah Suleiman was sacked because of pressure from Aramco, King Saud created in 1960 the most progressive cabinet ever seen in Saudi Arabia, with Prince Talal as finance minister, Abdullah Tariki as the first oil minister and Abdulaziz Bin Muammar as labour minister.

Foreign governments and Saud's half-brothers feared a democratic, nationalist takeover of the country. Under the influence of these ministers Saud promised a consultative assembly and some local elections were held. Saud's concessions to civilian politicians were deeply troubling to the other senior princes as well as the United States. The cabinet lasted only months, and in 1964 Saud's brother Faisal became king after Saud was forced from power with the approval of the *ulama* who declared that Faisal had mental problems that made him unfit to rule. The American hostility towards leftist and Arab nationalist politicians that Robert Vitalis notes in *America's Kingdom* surfaces in a US diplomatic cable on the subject of Abdullah's effort to revamp Saud's public image in 2006. The report glides over Saud's willingness to take on board commoners in government as 'incompetence' and argues his brothers feared he would try to install his eldest son as king.[3]

In his memoir-cum-novel *Qalb Min Banqalan*, a son of King Saud, Prince Saif al-Islam, offers memories and thoughts on this era through conversations with his mother, a concubine kidnapped by slave-traders from Baluchistan. The novel puts up a spirited defence of Saud's rule against his brothers, the clerics and the nationalists, as well as of the Saudi state itself in the face of those who would have turned it towards pan-Arabism or the left. The book raises the issue of whether it would not have been better for Saud to negotiate a transformation of Saudi Arabia into a constitutional monarchy and parliamentary democracy. Saif tells his mother: 'Some people imagine history as shining white and that it isn't possible to imagine the Arab and Islamic nations without (Saudi Arabia), while others say the future of these nations could have been much better if Abdulaziz's journey had failed and the efforts of the conquerors came to nothing.'[4] He says Saudi Arabia has 'the most conservative and ideological-leaning of all forms of leadership in the world', which was able to create a bureaucracy through the integration of the Hejaz but then faced the demands of its intellectual class for constitutional monarchy, parliaments and elections.[5] Though there were charges against Saud of profligate spending on palaces – ironic given how royal spending shaped up after the oil boom – his son concurs in his novel that it was Saud's readiness to make compromises with leftist and Nasserist commoners and princes that pushed the senior princes and religious scholars to depose him. Government finances were a shambles and Saud lacked the charisma of his father, but it was the danger that he would be unable to maintain the 'Saudi' in Saudi Arabia that ultimately ensured his downfall. Saif's mother relates: 'When the religious establishment felt that the Saudi state – the last citadel of Islam – could be "stolen" by a wayward prince, or a leftist military officer, or even a secular intellectual, they announced their position clearly that Saud, who was thought to favour opening the country – heresy in the religious lexicon at the time – must be deposed in the interests of the country and its people.'[6]

After the end of the kingdom's flirtation with civilian politics, the clerics were to face a number of challenges concerned with modern state-building and technical innovations in the era of King Faisal – his opponents had been equally concerned with modernisation, indeed even more so, but Gulf Arab neo-colonial powers such as Al Saud were as determined as the old colonial powers that progress should only come from them. Getting the Saudi house in order, Faisal decided to champion a pan-Islamic foreign policy to combat Nasser's pan-Arabism and the accusation that Saudi Arabia was an American client. This policy, which presented him as a devout modern Muslim, a precursor to Sadat's 'believer president', also gave him the capital to override clerical objections to his efforts to modernise. The *ulama* were more formally brought into the framework of the state bureaucracy, with the creation of the Ministry of Justice in 1970, offering clerics and their followers the incentive of a state salary, and the Al al-Sheikh – descendants of Mohammed ibn Abdulwahhab – were regularly given two or three ministerial posts. The position of mufti was left as a separate entity outside the justice ministry and kitted out with its own institutional framework through the Council of Senior Religious Scholars, headed by the mufti. These moves were made after the death of mufti Mohammed bin Ibrahim in 1969, who had resisted attempts to tame the clerics. Abdulaziz set up a new training institution for cleric-judges in 1953, the Sharia College in Mecca where scholars from Al-Azhar in Egypt were to form the teaching cadre – an attempt to temper Wahhabism's objections to modernity. Mohammed bin Ibrahim's response was to set up a separate Sharia College at the Imam University in Riyadh, which was under his control. The clerics were acutely aware of the fact that their collusion had been necessary for the removal of Saud. For Faisal, bringing the *ulama* to heel was not only imperative for certain modernisations, it was a crucial act of survival. Faisal had only managed to win their support for education for girls by creating a separate Ministry of Education for Girls under their control. In 1965, clerics and their followers protested in the streets against television broadcasting. A nephew of the king was shot by police, and it was the nephew's brother who assassinated Faisal in 1975.

By the late 1970s Saudi Arabia had witnessed a remarkable turnaround. The oil price hike effected by OPEC (the Organisation of the Petroleum Exporting Countries) in 1973 transformed the country's finances and ordinary Saudis, foreign hangers-on and princes, including those outside the state political machinery as well as those in it with cabinet posts, were able to obtain vast commissions or hidden payments on contracts for development projects. The country with its disparate regions and growing cities was more cohesive and the royal family more entrenched in the political and economic framework of the state. 'Democracy' signified the right of Saudis to study to become a member of the class of religious scholars who patrolled society for Al Saud, not the right to a role in governance.

1979: A NEW WAHHABI REVOLT

The seizure of the Grand Mosque in 1979 by a group of Wahhabi zealouts, though it was a messianic movement, was in many ways the sequel to the Ikhwan revolt of 1929 and the last scream of traditional Wahhabism in its objections to many aspects of modernisation. Its consequence was that the Saudi rulers bolstered the role of the religious establishment at a time when Wahhabism itself was going through a transformation partly in response to the example of political activism of the Egyptian Muslim Brotherhood, many of whose middle-class professional cadres worked in Saudi Arabia in the 1970s in education, medicine and other fields. A new form of Wahhabism was in the making, a neo-Wahhabism that matched the puritanism of al-Wahhabiyya with the political concerns of Islamists in the urban Arab context. The movement came to be known in Saudi Arabia as *al-sahwa*, 'the awakening'.[7] Scholars have differed on terminology and definitions: Stephane Lacroix suggests Juhaiman's movement represented a new movement of what he calls 'neo-Salafis', less interested in the political debates that interested the Sahwa movement.[8] They inspired others who attacked video stores and women's groups in the early 1990s. There does not appear to be much 'neo' about them; they were traditionalists disappointed with the realities of the Saudi-Wahhabi state, like the Ikhwan before them and those who opposed the modernisations of the 1960s. They were not politicised in the manner of the Sahwa and the Brotherhood, which has affiliates today that are well-established organisationally in Kuwait and Bahrain and is influential through Yousef al-Qaradawi in Qatar. Lacroix seems to be using the term 'Salafism' to refer specifically to people who rejected the legitimacy of the state and refused to work in government institutions. Salafism is often used to refer to non-political Islamist movements in countries such as Egypt and Algeria who have been influenced by Wahhabism, but who have begun to move into the political mainstream.

On 20 November 1979, the first day of the new Islamic year 1400, a group of rebels led by a former Bedouin National Guardsman Juhaiman al-'Utaybi stormed the mosque in Mecca, initially trapping thousands inside its large precinct. They promptly seized the mosque microphone from the Imam leading dawn prayers and began broadcasting at length around Mecca about the iniquity of the Saudi rulers, and proclaimed that the coming of the Mahdi, a messianic figure in Islamic tradition, was nigh in the person of a companion of Juhaiman's called Mohammed bin Abdullah al-Qahtani.[9] Qahtani's brother Sayed took the podium and announced what the revolt was all about. The list of grievances against the Saudi rulers centred on Western innovations introduced to the country and subservience to the infidel. They included television, women in the workplace, and even soccer. Particular opprobrium was spared for Prince Fawaz, the governor of Mecca with a liberal reputation for tolerating alcohol and mixing of the sexes in some public areas. Sayed then proclaimed the coming of the Mahdi, at which his brother walked forward and the group of rebels took an oath of allegiance (the interior ministry claimed in 2007 that it had uncovered a similar plot where militants took an oath of allegiance to a rebel figure inside the Grand Mosque). One day later the government acknowledged the revolt, attacking the group as Kharijites – early puritanical Muslims who refused to recognise the legitimacy of the caliph – and a group of 30 senior clerics, led by the Grand Mufti Bin Baz, publicly denounced them.

The incident strikingly laid bare the archaic and pre-modern nature of government in the country. It was not to his cabinet that the king turned, it was not to his parliament since there was not one: it was to the *ulama*, the Muslim scholars who collectively conferred legitimacy on the regime and in return for which they had extensive powers over the ordering of society. The clerics were sympathetic to the rebels' cause, but from the outset this cause was not helped by the fact that they shed blood in the holy precinct and halted the circumambulation of the Kaaba – the black stone at the centre of the mosque's inner courtyard. The Messianic movement had made the decision to take weapons into the mosque partly to make real the prophecies of hadith literature on the Mahdi that talked of the enemies armies' being swallowed into the earth.[10] From there the clerics were able to argue that the conditions for the return of the Mahdi were not in any case in place, ergo he was a fraud. So they decided to give the king his fatwa condemning the rebellion and affirming the Saudi ruler as the legitimate head of the Islamic state to which all Muslims owe their allegiance, but they avoided denouncing the rebels as deviants or apostates and offering any authorisation for military intervention to eradicate them.

Juhaiman's father fought at the battle of Sabala that ended the Ikhwan revolt in 1929, and the Juhaiman was born in the Bedouin *hijra* of Sajir, north of Riyadh. In the 1970s Juhaiman and some of his followers studied in Medina under Bin Baz, who had a raft of radical fatwas that were never implemented, forbidding smoking, clapping, barber shops, television for the foreign films where men and women mixed and kissed, radio stations where men and women were clearly broadcasting from the same studio room, and portraits of the royal rulers in government buildings. Gradually convinced that the theory of the Islamic Utopia did not match the practice, Juhaiman began to recruit students, tribesmen and people who had passed through the National Guard, many of them disaffected Bedouin scandalised by the 'modernisms' of the capital Riyadh and who cherished the memory of the Ikhwan revolt 50 years before. As Bedouin and Saudis from humble backgrounds, they were the Saudis who had been left out of the great boondoggle of oil wealth and royal largesse in the lottery that was the Saudi state. In 1978 Juhaiman managed to publish a book in Kuwait called *The Seven Epistles* in which he attacked the Al Saud as the lackeys of foreign powers and Bin Baz as their loyal servant. Twenty-five of his followers were arrested that year, but Bin Baz himself had requested that interior minister Prince Nayef let them go.

Relying on British and American air pilots and French commandos, the Saudi authorities managed to overcome the revolt in Mecca within two weeks.[11] But what followed in subsequent years, as Prince Khaled al-Faisal said in 2003, was that after executing him the royal family proceeded to implement Juhaiman's programme.[12] Tension had been evident between the conservatism championed by the *ulama* and the modernity being pushed by the ruling family throughout the 1970s (there were cinemas in Jeddah at the time – there are none today, except inside Al Saud palaces and foreign embassies). Now the *ulama* drove a hard bargain for their backing of Al Saud in the face of puritan revolt: the clerics wanted Utopia back on the agenda and the royal family, in their fear and confusion, acquiesced. The religious universities in Riyadh, Mecca and Medina were now generously funded by government, and in the early 1990s around a quarter of all students in the kingdom were enrolled in one of them.[13] The religious police also received more funding and leeway to impose their vision of purity on the streets, becoming notably more severe in their treatment of the population. Intermarriage between Sunnis and Shi'ites came to be frowned up on in both communities. 'We all lost freedom, my mother, grandmother all had more. Since the Iranian revolution and religious movement started, we ended up having nothing. We used to travel without permission. Women used to manage homes and work in farms, but money harmed this society and they decided we don't need women to run it', says Wajiha al-Huweidar, a teacher who works at Aramco and a rights activist. 'People said *al-hamdulillah* and *inshallah* in every sentence. Names become more religious, like Abdullah and Abdulaziz; Shi'ites used names of imams and Sunnis had Abu Bakr and Omar. It was as if Saudis woke up one day and decided we are too far from Islam.'[14] With strict monitoring of girls' dress and comportment, schools became a 'locked box', writes education professor Fawziah al-Bakr.[15]

The royal family and its supporters were sent into paroxysms of panic by the twin circumstances of the revolt and the overthrow of the Shah in Iran earlier that year by Shi'ite cleric Ayatollah Khomeini in a revolution.[16] The revolution in Iran was worrying because it chimed with that part of the rebels' rhetoric which attacked the rulers over foreign policy and their unwillingness or inability to challenge Western hegemony in the region. Wahhabism was finally being channelled into the wider region's Arab nationalist and Islamist currents that the Saudi rulers had been so desperate to shut out of the country, currents that Faisal thought he had banished with his palace coup of 1964. The Iranian revolution also provoked the Shia in the Eastern Province to take to the streets in an uprising in 1979 and 1980 against the institutionalised discrimination they faced through the state's promotion of al-Wahhabiyya. The Soviet invasion of Afghanistan in 1979, while initially disturbing, was then to provide a welcome chance for the regime to showcase its Islamic credentials by supporting the Mujahideen. Mosques encouraged ordinary people to give cash, equipment and clothes to the Afghans fighting the infidels or to volunteer to fight or work as medics, and an estimated 35,000 to 40,000 were given visas to Pakistan in the late 1980s.[17]

THE 1990–91 GULF CRISIS

When Iraq invaded Kuwait in 1990, the fear that Saddam Hussein's forces could move on to overthrow the Saudis or seize the Eastern Province was real. The regime turned to foreigners to protect itself and there was no hiding this fact from the public or from the clerics, who were called upon to justify it. The government had spent billions of dollars on military hardware in the 1980s, so King Fahd's decision within a week of the Kuwait invasion of 2 August to invite US troops exposed the regime to charges of fiscal incompetence, lying to the public about the exact nature of its relations with an infidel power and making a mockery of the legitimacy the *ulama* had bestowed upon the *waliyy al-amr*, the Islamic state's legal guardian. Military imports totalled $52.4 billion from 1985 to 1992 and represented 20 per cent of gross domestic product (GDP) throughout the 1980s.[18] During this crisis Osama bin Laden made two offers to the royal family of fighting off the Iraqis himself. In 1989, the Afghan jihad over, bin Laden tried to relocate his Afghan Arabs in South Yemen where he wanted to overthrow the socialist regime. But the 1990 unification of north and south, which the United States backed, scuppered his plans. In 1989 bin Laden sent a letter to King Fahd exhorting him to implement Sharia more effectively and warning him that Saddam Hussein had designs on the country and its oil wealth. In a second letter after the invasion, he offered his Arab fighters to defend the country against the Iraqis as well as the communists in South Yemen, who united with the north in 1990, and offered to train Saudi volunteers. The offer was rejected out of hand.[19] The leading clerics were at first appalled and refused to provide a fatwa approving King Fahd's decision to turn to the United States. On 13 August Bin Baz gave the king what he wanted and eventually 500,000 US troops were to amass on Saudi territory. Bin Baz produced a second fatwa in January 1991, when the troops were about to go into action, authorising jihad against the Iraqis, even if through the agency of non-Muslims.[20]

The debacle unleashed forces of opposition in society that were to mark most of the 1990s. Two middle-ranking clerics emerged as the leaders of this opposition during the 1990–91 Gulf crisis, Safar al-Hawali and Salman al-Odah. Hawali was dean of the Islamic College at the Umm al-Qura University in Mecca and known outside

Saudi Arabia as an Islamic intellectual who had made a name for himself criticising secularism as the ideological arm of a wholesale Western attack on Islam, including the state of Israel – neo-Wahhabi arguments of the first order, heavily influenced by the political Islam of the Muslim Brotherhood and its offshoots in the 1960s and 1970s which in turn influenced bin Laden.[21] The Gulf crisis clearly fitted this pattern, and Hawali was sure the American troops would not leave once the fighting was over. Al-Odah, a teacher at the Imam Muhammad bin Saud University in Riyadh, similarly talked about the imperfection of the moral order in Saudi Arabia through the rulers' allowing their realm to slip into the hands of the foreigner. The sermons of both were widely distributed on cassette tape from 1990 onwards.[22] It was not until 1994 that they and dozens of other clerics were finally arrested, after a tense period of public petitions to the royal family demanding reforms. This era of political activism came to define the Sahwa sheikhs who emerged in the 1980s.[23]

In 1991 two petitions were put together, one by clerics and other Islamist figures and another by public intellectuals whose demands included rolling back the power of the clerics. Both wanted 'reform' and limits on the absolute power on the royal family, but within radically different frames of reference. That of the liberals appealed to Westerners and the liberal democrat discourse of the outside world, the other more in language the Saudi royals could understand, since effectively it demanded re-establishment of the traditional relationship between the *ulama* and the rulers that strengthened the role of the religious scholars and allowed them to encroach on the temporal turf of the royals and rulers in Islamic states since the caliphs of Baghdad, that of foreign policy. The liberals wanted the municipal councils revived, a consultative council, a greater role for women in public life, 'reform' of the religious police and 'total equality' between citizens. The clerics also demanded a consultative council and listed ten areas of public life where they should be allowed oversight powers or a direct presence to ensure correct Islamic practice as they defined it (in media to stop scandalous Western films, for example, or to make sure women were not employed). It was the clerics whose campaign was to dominate, metamorphosing into the infamous Memorandum of Advice (*nasiha*) presented to Bin Baz in September 1992.

The memorandum exposed the Saudi regime on numerous fronts that struck at the heart of the contradiction between the monarchy's use of the scholars for legitimacy while relying on the military and political support of the United States. The regime stood accused of not carrying out its part of the historic bargain with al-Wahhabiyya, and it was attacked for bad governance through corruption and inefficiency, attacked as a human rights abuser that detained and tortured at will, and exposed as following a foreign policy contrary to its stated principles. The government demanded an apology; Bin Baz's middle way was to uphold the concept of *nasiha* but not its publication in the public sphere where it could generate *fitna*, or civil strife. The regime offered concessions, but concessions which involved a stronger affirmation than ever of the Saudi family's exclusive right to governance. The Basic Law of Government announced in March 1992 described the country as a monarchy with succession passing between the sons then grandsons of Abdulaziz, and it demands submission and obedience of citizens to his rule. A second Basic Law set up a consultative council, the Shura Assembly, whose members are chosen by the king. It has powers to interpret and suggest laws, advice which is decided upon by the king. Its speakers have always been clerics, while a preponderance of its members have been Najdi technocrats, in fact bolstering Saudi family rule.[24] A third reform codified the power structure of local government, defining the duties of governors and dividing the 14 provinces into various subgroups. When *ulama* and others continued to speak out of line, over 100 Islamic dissidents were arrested in a crackdown in 1994 that kept Hawali and Odah in jail until 1999. By 2003 all had been released. In 1993 some clerics and Islamist activists established the Committee for the Defence of Legitimate Rights in Saudi Arabia. Seen as an attempt to set up a kind of political party, the group was banned and the Council of Senior Religious Scholars denounced it as illegitimate. In 2004 its leading figures moved the group's operations to London where it became a vocal opposition group that annoyed the British government as much as its Saudi ally but received a fair amount of media coverage that made its leaders, Saad al-Fagih and Mohammed al-Mas'ari, the face of dissent in the West for a time.

CLERICS AFTER 9/11

Sheikh Abdulaziz Bin Baz died two years before the attacks of 9/11. A critical figure in preserving and updating Wahhabi orthodoxy in the key latter decades of the twentieth century when Saudi Arabia became the country it is today, he was succeeded by a figure seen as relatively weak by comparison, Sheikh Abdulaziz Al al-Sheikh. After the debacle of 9/11, where 15 of the 19 attackers were Saudi, acting in the name of an organisation led by a Saudi dissident, the *ulama* under the mufti were disposed to follow the policy of the government, under Crown Prince Abdullah's guidance, of acquiescing to the demands of their angry American ally. A range of shifts have taken place in domestic and foreign policy to mollify the Americans and ensure the continuation of the Saudi-Wahhabi state in the face of a hostile world. School textbooks have been reviewed, state control has been extended over Friday sermons and many imams sacked, the National Dialogue was instituted in 2003, a human rights organisation was set up in 2004, the international media were invited to set up offices in the country, local media was liberalised with larger scope for debate over issues once considered taboo, interfaith dialogue with non- and wayward Muslims was promoted in 2008, the government sponsored an Arab-Israeli peace proposal in 2002, renewed in 2007, and led campaigns by the Arab clients of the United States against Iran and its Arab allies and Shi'ism itself. The American-led invasion of Iraq in 2003, while worrying in many aspects for Saudi Arabia, was an opportunity to be rid of Saddam Hussein, and the outbreak of an al-Qa'ida insurgency against the royal family in 2003 strengthened Abdullah in his drive to smooth the rougher edges of al-Wahhabiyya. The al-Qa'ida militants lost some credibility with the public because Saudis, Arabs and Muslims died in suicide-bomb attacks on foreign housing compounds in Riyadh in 2003.

In the Saudi arena post-9/11 there were a number of opposition trends in Saudi politics – hardline Salafis, the Sahwa sheikhs and non-clerical Islamist democrats (Lacroix's 'Islamo-liberals') and secular-liberal democrats. The Islamists sought to bring the Sahwa sheikhs and the secular liberals together through another round of petitions in 2003, the 'Vision for the Present and Future of the Nation' in January and in December the 'National Call to the Leadership and People – Constitutional Reform First', often referred to as the Constitutional Monarchy petition.[25] They called for elected regional and national parliaments and appealed to Sharia law, pitching themselves as reformers of Wahhabi Islam as well as of Saudi governance. The first petition talked of an end to all sectarian discrimination, ensuring a large number of Shi'ite signatories, but it failed to attract major Sahwa names other than Salman al-Odah. The second, issued just before Crown Prince Abdullah's much-touted National Dialogue conference, went further than before in specifically calling for a three-year time-frame for establishing a real parliament – a provocation for Al Saud. It also had notably more religious language and drew a link between the al-Qa'ida violence that hit the country in May 2003 and US foreign policy in the region. This ensured the signature of a number of Sahwa Islamist figures such as Mohsen al-Awajy – though Odah sufficed with placing it on his website (www.islamtoday.com), because of warnings from the interior ministry, it seems – but it drove away a number of liberals.[26] The day after Crown Prince Abdullah's announcement in a speech in January 2004 that he favoured 'gradual and well thought-out reform', twelve reform activists were arrested, leading to the trial of three of them in 2004 and 2005. Sentenced to varying prison terms in 2005, they were pardoned after Abdullah became king in August of that year. The rebel clerics' concern in the 1990s had been liberals gaining privileged access to key royals and influencing education, as Fandy wrote in his study of the period – 'competition to win favours with the ruling family seems to be at the heart of the conflict between the secular trend in Saudi Arabia and the religious one' – and this remained the overriding concern of the *ulama* under Abdullah.[27]

There was another major round of petitions in 2011 following the protests that ended the rule of Zain al-Abideen Ben Ali and Hosni Mubarak. They will have confirmed the suspicions of the senior *ulama* that the 'reform' movement is a liberal project and raised only limited concerns for Al Saud of liberals and Islamists managing to coordinate their positions; both appeared to dismiss the efforts as lightweight compared to earlier mobilisations. All three were shorter than the Vision and Constitutional Monarchy petitions. Possibly in an attempt to hit a neutral note that attracts as many as possible from both the Islamist and liberal sides of the political divide, they were absent of words such as 'democracy' or even of Sharia. But two of them make explicit calls for women's participation in political life, one states the liberal demand of codifying law, all make appeals to the concerns of young people, and the spirit of the language generally is that of modern concepts of political and civic rights, not of Wahhabism or even the neo-Wahhabism of the Sahwa.

One, issued by around 50 journalists and internet activists, said 'youth elites from both sexes' should be among those invited to a National Dialogue to plan for democratic reform, suggested an average age of 40 for cabinet ministers and 45 for Shura Assembly members, and called for a 'renewal of religious discourse'.[28] The most detailed came in another liberal-dominated petition, with the title 'A Declaration for National Reform', which was dominated by liberals and rights activists: it also talked of general elections to the Shura Assembly with full women's participation. It stated that 'the people are the source of power, a full partner in deciding public policy', called for the right to form political and professional associations, codification of law to limit discretionary powers in judicial sentencing, legislation against sectarian, tribal and regional discrimination, full public access to use of public funds, an end to the interior ministry's use of the travel ban, monitoring of media, and indefinite detentions.[29]

The shortest was perhaps the most troubling for the regime. The 'State of Rights and Institutions' was signed by some 1,500 people within two weeks, including Sheikh Salman al-Odah, and garnered thousands more online signatures in the following months. Invoking the 'youth revolutions', it warned of 'serious consequences' for Arab rulers who do not 'listen to their people' on reform, development, freedom, dignity, ending injustice, fighting corruption and 'fundamental reform'. Unlike the others, it specified that an elected Shura Assembly should have 'absolute authority to enact laws and monitor the executive branches'. It also said the post of prime minister should not be occupied by the monarch and demanded an end to indefinite detention by the state security apparatus; it made no mention of women. In other words, like the Vision and Constitutional Monarchy documents there was an attempt to appeal to as many political trends as possible: Odah's punishment for putting his name to it was the cancellation of his weekly show on MBC. Perhaps the most interesting development with these three petitions was the use of the internet for publicising and gathering support for them.[30]

The clerics' relationship with the princes was strained over three issues after 9/11: the invasion of Iraq and ensuing Sunni Islamist violence against the new order, the outbreak of the al-Qa'ida insurgency inside Saudi Arabia itself, and Abdullah's efforts to rebuild the country's global image and relations with the United States through smoothing the edges of al-Wahhabiyya. The fighting in Iraq and the Islamist revolt in Saudi Arabia were closely connected. When the Iraq war broke out Odah and other middle-ground scholars argued to the populace that it was not worth a jihad since the situation in Iraq was too complex with shifting alliances and it was impossible to know who to support and who to oppose. That changed in November 2004 when American forces besieged the Sunni Muslim town of Falluja, which occurred at a point when it had become clear in the Arab world that Iraq had fallen under the sway of Shi'ite clerics and Islamist politicians. A letter addressed to the Iraqi people described the act of challenging the 'occupiers' as jihad, 'resistance' and a legitimate right. It was signed by 26 scholars including Odah, Hawali, Awad al-Qarni and Nasser al-Omar, all prominent Sahwa sheikhs. Hundreds of Saudis were thought to have gone to Iraq to fight with the jihadist group headed by the Jordanian Abu Musab al-Zarqawi and which became an al-Qa'ida affiliate through Zarqawi's contacts with Osama bin Laden and Ayman al-Zawahiri. Reports from the London dissidents said the Saudi authorities were telling some militant suspects in detention that they were fighting the wrong war in the wrong place – why not go to Iraq where the real jihad was to be found? By 2006 when the al-Qa'ida campaign in Saudi Arabia appeared to have peaked and begun to wane, officials talked publicly of their concern over 'returnees' from Iraq, like the al-Qa'ida returnees from Afghanistan in 2003–04. The government-allied traditional *ulama* continue to accuse the Sahwa clerics of introducing Muslim Brotherhood-style politicisation to the kingdom, which they imply produced the Islamist, al-Qa'ida violence against the state (while they also have differences over doctrine and relations with Shi'ism and Iran).[31]

Saudi funding for Islamist causes, after encouraging Saudis to fight in Afghanistan in the 1980s, approving of funding and fighting in Bosnia and Chechnya in the 1990s, and equivocating on Saudis heading to Iraq after 2003, became a media embarrassment in 2007 when the Lebanese army fought from May to September to evict the Fatah al-Islam group from the Nahr al-Barid Palestinian refugee camp. Lebanese officials indicated during the fighting that there were dozens of Saudis among Fatah al-Islam fighters. Saudi media said these numbers were exaggerated, but no final tally of those present and those who died was ever made public. Saudi researcher Faris bin Houzam wrote later that there were up to 300 Saudis operating in Nahr al-Barid, and Palestine Liberation Organisation (PLO) chief in Beirut Sultan Abul-Ainayn said the PLO believed 23 Saudis died.[32] Many of those Saudis may have found their way to Lebanon after spending time in Iraq. By July 2007 Iraq said it had tried 160 Saudis for involvement in violent acts.[33] There was much speculation during the Nahr al-Barid stand-off that Saudi money had found its way to Fatah al-Islam through the wider programme of Saudi funding for Sunni groups in Lebanon, paramilitary and otherwise, as a counterweight to Hizbullah. American journalist Seymour Hersh made the most prominent of these allegations, two months before the fighting broke out in May, arguing that Saudi Arabia was working with the United States to bolster the paramilitary capabilities of Sunni Muslim groups vis-à-vis Hizbullah.[34] US diplomatic cables confirm that during Abdullah's rule Saudi Arabia and the US government tried to strengthen the Lebanese army as a balance to Hizbullah. One cable written by then Secretary of State Condoleezza Rice in November 2008 indicates that Saudi Arabia paid the Lebanese army to complete the Nahr al-Barid operation. 'Saudi Arabia has been a strong political and financial backer of the LAF since mid-2007 when it quietly provided $100M to support LAF operations against Fatah al-Islam militants in Lebanon's Nahr al-Barid refugee camp', Rice wrote in November 2008, requesting that the Riyadh embassy win Saudi consent to help provide weaponry, including two $60 million grants for tanks and helicopter gunships.[35] Nearly 400 people are thought to have died by the time the Lebanese army retook control of Nahr al-Barid on 2 September. Saudi Arabia donated $25 million to UNRWA (the United Nations Relief and Works Agency) for the camp's reconstruction after its destruction left 31,000 refugees homeless. In other words, Saudi Arabia appears to have given the Lebanese army the money – 'quietly' – to destroy a refugee camp harbouring its own nationals, whose ideological zeal had outlived whatever use it had had, to become a stain on the Saudi government's reputation.[36]

In the same year the interior minister was unusually blunt with religious scholars, at a time when the United States was expressing public anger at the numbers of Saudi militants in Iraq. 'Do you know that your sons who go to Iraq are used only for blowing themselves up? Iraqi officials told me that themselves', Nayef told a large clerical gathering.[37] Some months later he told *Okaz* newspaper that the effort made by clerics was still not enough. In one indication of how conflicted the *ulama* were by Islamist violence in Iraq, it was not until 2007 that the mufti spoke out forcefully about the phenomenon. Saudi youth had become a 'commodity, bought and sold', he said. 'I decided to say this after it was clear that over several years Saudis have been leaving for jihad. They did this because they were passionate about their religion, yet not wise enough to know right from wrong', he said.[38] Odah announced his own break with bin Laden too, in an 'open letter' arguing that his jihad efforts had brought only suffering to Muslims.[39] The cables praise Saudi efforts to stop cash flows to Islamist groups but say that Saudi Arabia remains a major source of funds for al-Qa'ida, the Taliban, Lashkar e-Taiba and Hamas. One from Clinton's office to embassies in the Gulf and Pakistan in December 2009 states: 'While the Kingdom of Saudi Arabia (KSA) takes seriously the threat of terrorism within Saudi Arabia, it has been an ongoing challenge to persuade Saudi officials to treat terrorist financing emanating from Saudi Arabia as a strategic priority ... donors in Saudi Arabia constitute the most significant source of funding to Sunni terrorist groups worldwide.'[40]

More critical for Saudi authorities was the position of the clerics on jihad inside Saudi Arabia itself, and in this they had some success. The mufti repeated to Saudis in 2003 the old Wahhabi refrain that Muslims of the model Islamic state should obey their rulers 'even if they are unjust'. But the deaths of Arabs and Muslims in the attacks of May and November 2003 (killing 35 and 18 people respectively) gave the government valuable propaganda material against Saudis who joined what the state termed *al-fi'a al-dalla* ('the deviant group'). This term reflects a sense of them as merely wayward, a bit too enthusiastic about their religion. Indeed, this is Wahhabism's only possible view of them since they act on the principles of jihad and *takfir* (denouncing other Muslims as infidels/ unbelievers) that lie at its core; the problem with them is the target of their jihad and *takfir* and their freelancing without a cue from the clerics or the ruler on when to act. The government clerics accuse them of 'extremism in religion', succumbing to evil temptation, or having been duped. When the rhetoric of al-Qa'ida leaders concerns issues of general agreement such as Palestine, Afghanistan, Iraq, Chechnya, Pakistan, Israel, America, and so on, it is difficult for the *ulama* to demonise them. The mufti made only timid efforts to challenge the use of *takfir* by militant groups. In his strongest attack on al-Qa'ida activity, a statement issued in 2008, the mufti's focus was two-fold: that ordinary Muslims are the victims of their actions and that the Saudi state is sacred territory where God's law has dominion thus it cannot be a theatre of operations. He did not denounce *takfir* at all.

As oil prices rose from 2002, the power of the government to placate the clerics with lavish spending on religion increased significantly. With the situation in Iraq worsening amidst sectarian fighting between Sunnis and Shi'ites, it was easy for the *ulama* to occupy their minds with seemingly bigger issues than the probity and legitimacy of Al Saud. When the uprisings threatened in 2011, more funding was promised for the Council of Senior Religious Scholars and the religious police, while new regulations punished criticism of the senior clerics. The uprisings of 2011 caused some confusion in clerical ranks. A number made public statements supporting actions against Gaddafi in particular because Libya's political rift with Saudi Arabia made him fair game and he had previously been denounced by clerics as a heretic. Some backtracked on their comments, including Saleh al-Luhaidan, a member of the council gathering senior clerics. Salman al-Odah was the most outspoken, suggesting that the neglect and corruption Jeddans had witnessed during floods in 2008 was the kind of thing that brought Tunisians and Egyptians to revolt. Continued positive comments, including on his Twitter account, caused the authorities to stop him from leaving the country for a trip to South Africa in July 2011, possibly because they feared he would set himself up as a dissident preacher abroad. Odah and some others praised the trial of Hosni Mubarak while most were silent. Odah wrote: 'Sensible rulers will review calculations, speedily apply justice and prevent corruption, but despots will burn their people for fear of this moment.'

The Arab Spring fatwa issued by the Council of Senior Religious Scholars on 6 March 2011 stands out alongside the fatwa of 1990 authorising American military forces on Saudi soil as a classic example of Wahhabism rallying to defend Al Saud and bolster the Saudi-Wahhabi state project. It cited Quranic verses and Prophetic hadiths that call on believers not to fall into dispute and to uphold the principle of 'preserving the group'. 'God has blessed the people of this country in their unity with the leaders over the guidance of the book and the Sunna and he does not divide them with foreign (political) trends or parties with differing groundings', it said in the preamble. 'The kingdom has maintained this Islamic identity, and with its progress and development and consideration of permitted opinions, it has not and will not allow ideas from the West or East detract from this identity and divide the whole.' It went on to warn not only against demonstrations but against gathering signatures for statements asking for petitions.

> The council affirms that reform and advice has its legal channel which ensures the common interest and prevents corruption, that channel is not the issuing of alarming statements that provoke strife and collecting signatures for them ... Reform and advice in the kingdom is not through demonstrations and ways and means that provoke strife and divide the whole, and the religious scholars of this country have always declared this *haram* and warned about it.[41]

ANTI-SHI'ITE RHETORIC

The interests of the clerics and the authorities coalesced once again in their common horror at the rising power of Iran. They watched with alarm as Tehran-backed clerics, militias and parties dominated post-war Iraq, and saw Iran step in to back the Sunni Palestinian group Hamas after Saudi Arabia and other Arab backers gave up on the Gaza-based Islamists under Western pressure following Hamas's victory in the Palestinian elections in 2006. Saudi Arabia was concerned about Hizbullah's continuing strength as a player in the Lebanese political scene and as a paramilitary force, after Israel's withdrawal from south Lebanon in 2000. Those fears worsened when Hizbullah fought and survived a month-long war with Israel in 2006, and as a result the prestige of the Iranian-backed 'resistance' camp challenging the *Pax Americana* in the region rose sharply. Saud al-Faisal summoned ambassador James Oberwetter on 30 July to Jeddah to ask for a US call for a ceasefire in a war that confounded Riyadh's hopes and expectations and strengthened the leadership's view that the Shi'ites of the Eastern Province are a 'fifth column' for Iran that could be activated at any time. Saudi fury extended to Damascus, another ally of Iran and Hizbullah, which became the object of regular attacks in Saudi media and Saudi-owned pan-Arab media. 2006 was a pivotal year for Riyadh.[42]

In the early post-9/11 period Saudi media's tone was leaning towards the dovish with regard to Shi'ites. After becoming king, Abdullah told the Shura Assembly that 'enflaming sectarian conflicts and reviving regional hatreds and promoting one section of society over another contradicts the guarantees and tolerance of Islam and threatens national unity'. As sectarian violence worsened in Iraq in 2005 and 2006, and Hizbullah's showmanship vis-à-vis Israel captured popular attention, things changed. A proliferation of anti-Shi'ite statements were issued by Saudi clerics in 2006 – Abdulrahman al-Barrak said they were 'polytheist infidels' (*kuffar mushrikun*) – and the government used the 2007 Arab summit in Riyadh to showcase King Abdullah as the true 'leader of the Arabs' in the face of the popularity of Hizbullah leader Hassan Nasrallah. A fatwa by one of the most intransigent anti-Shi'ite figures of the Wahhabi *ulama*, Sheikh Abdullah bin Jabreen (who died in 2008), was recirculated during the Lebanon war. 'It is not permitted to support this Shi'ite party, to operate under its control or to pray for their victory. Our advice to Sunnis is to have nothing to do with them', the fatwa said.[43] Sahwa sheikhs – infused with the concerns of political Islam – were split. Nasser al-Omar's website published a notice telling followers that Hizbullah was a 'tool' in the hands of Iran's Revolutionary Guard; Salman al-Odah said the historic rift between Sunnis and Shi'ites was secondary in such times of conflict: 'Our bigger enemy is the criminal Jews and Zionists who don't even distinguish between children and combatants in their aggression.'[44]

Anger among the Shi'ite community deepened in the years following 2006. US diplomatic missives to Washington from 2006 to 2009 indicate increasing disillusion, notably among young people who questioned what Saudi identity and loyalty means to them in a country that continued to treat them as outsiders, second-class citizens and religious deviants. In February 2009 clashes broke out in Medina in the west of the country between Shia pilgrims – the figures cited are from 500 to 2,000 individuals – and religious police in which security forces intervened and used water cannon on the pilgrims.[45] The incident took place at the Baqia cemetery, located next to the Prophet's Mosque, a site visited by Shia pilgrims since it is the final resting place of many important figures from the early days of Islam. Young Shi'ites from al-Ahsa formed a large part of those involved in the clashes and arrested, and a Shi'ite preacher was stabbed.[46] The interior ministry prevented Saudi media from discussing the issue for several days, while Qatif preacher Sheikh Hassan al-Saffar was asked to help maintain calm and prevent protests. Several weeks later an unnamed popular cleric, described as the likely leader of Saudi Hizbullah – a group that opposes Saffar's conciliatory approach, follows Iranian Supreme Leader Khomeini as religious *marja'iyya* and subscribes to the theory of clerical rule – requested a meeting with US diplomats to discuss the tensions.[47] The preacher warned that there was a chance of an explosion of violence in the Eastern Province from loss of hope in Abdullah's 'reform process'. The preacher said that Shia would likely be 'slaughtered' in any government response.[48] Two weeks later Sheikh Nimr al-Nimr, an outspoken cleric known for his rejection of compromise with the regime, went into hiding for a time after he warned in a sermon that the Shia could seek secession from Riyadh one day if their situation does not improve in the Wahhabi state.

In this context, it is hard to understand the continued Saudi policy of repression without factoring in the presence of Wahhabi scholars and their influence on thinking at every level of the state. After the al-Qa'ida attack on the Abqaiq oil facility in 2006, Saudi officials expressed their view to the US government that an Iranian missile attack or sabotage activities by Shi'ites, perhaps via Saudi

Hizbullah and perhaps via Shi'ites who work at Aramco, were the biggest threat to oil security.[49] There is little evidence that the US government pressed Saudi Arabia on the illogic of its policy towards the Shia. It does not come up in the context of Secretary of State Hillary Clinton's visit to the kingdom in February 2010, where preparatory material put together by ambassador James Smith suffices itself with a line: 'The status of women, religious freedom, and human rights are ongoing concerns.'[50] However, the Riyadh chargé d'affaires outlines explains extensive security cooperation with the interior ministry: 'An in-depth analysis of Abqaiq's engineering plans and drawings, along with extended access to and discussion with key technical personnel, are being done to better understand the plant's specific vulnerabilities. The Saudis' willingness to share this level of technical detail with us on the world's most important petroleum facility is unprecedented in our relationship.' He puts this new openness down in part to two visits by President George W. Bush, during which he tried to do a Bedouin sword dance, which had clearly flattered the princes.[51]

Despite this, Abdullah launched his 'interfaith dialogue'. The project suited Saudi aims to place the country at the centre of global efforts to combat Islamist violence and fend off Western criticisms post-9/11, but was bound to rile the clerical establishment just as it was warming up to its job of presenting Shi'ism as a major threat to the Arabs and Islam itself. Some 500 religious scholars from around the world gathered at a three-day meeting in Mecca in June 2008 under the auspices of the World Muslim League. Days before, Barrak, bin Jabreen and 20 others tried to torpedo the meeting with a warning that Sunnis were being fooled by Hizbullah's posturing against Israel. The Mecca meeting was a superficial effort at best. Only a handful of the 500 invitees were in fact Shi'ite; they included only one Saudi Shi'ite, Hassan al-Saffar, and no Ismailis; there were also no Shia from Europe or North America. Al-Qa'ida taunted the Saudi *ulama* over going any distance at all with the king's pet project. 'If you don't resist this wanton tyrant (Abdullah) ... the day will come when church bells ring in the heart of the Arabian peninsula', Abu Yahya al-Libi said in a video posted on Islamist websites.[52]

The Iraqi invasion of Kuwait in 1990 unleashed conflicts of ideology, policy and practice that were constantly bubbling under the surface. It led to the most serious and prolonged rupture in the relationship between the ruling family and the clergy. But the dynamic after the 9/11 attacks in 2001 was different: the clerics realised that liberals saw this as their moment to press for reforms on their terms while Western pressure on Al Saud was intense. Ultimately they closed ranks with the royal family to keep the liberals out. From within the bosom of the state, superficial disputes with Abdullah and his clique notwithstanding, they pressed their advantage wherever and whenever possible. Still, Saudi liberals see over the last 20 years a break in the scholars' hold on society and their ability to enforce the ruler's will. Bin Baz was respected for his knowledge, but disappointed towards the end. The al-Qa'ida movement lost the interest of the people when its disregard for Saudi and Muslim victims became clear. The Sahwa movement succumbed to co-option. In addition, the information revolution has weakened the state clerics' monopoly of opinion. 'Society has changed fundamentally. Politically, we used to see fatwas forbidding elections and democracy. The official fatwa said that we have to obey the ruler and he cannot be removed or share in power. The political thinking that demanded absolute obeyance has collapsed; now we talk about participation. We could never go back now if we wanted to', says Abdulaziz al-Qasim, a former judge who became a leading liberal Islamist.

> Socially, fatwas used to say that women should completely cover their face, but now if you go to any market you see 90 percent of girls showing their face. There is a loss of confidence in the value of Saudi fatwas. They are seen as archaic, naive and in need of reform, and this a new. Young men and women do not obey fatwas like they used to – they go to Google, hear other opinions and discuss the issue.[53]

This atomisation of the *ulama* that Qasim describes is an important phenomenon, but it is not clear that it weakens the power of the clerical class at all. In fact the *ulama* seem to enjoy the plurality of media they are now afforded and have defied government efforts to unify them once more. Abdullah declared in 2010 that only clerics of the Council of Senior Religious Scholars could issue fatwas, an order that came after a string of clerical opinions that ran counter to his policies: council member Saad bin Nasir al-Shathri publicly challenged the mixing of the sexes at the King Abdullah University of Science and Technology (KAUST) and suggested that the *ulama* vet the curriculum; another council cleric, Saleh al-Luhaidan, suggested that owners of Arabic entertainment channels should face trial for un-Islamic programming; al-Barrak sought legal action against newspaper columnists he didn't like. Yet the king's ability to 'control' the *ulama* is limited: the mufti's standing among them is not strong and the council does not exercise formal control over the thousands of religious scholars. One of the central functions of a scholar of religion, whether he is imam of a mosque or judge or simply preacher, is to offer guidance to Muslims in response to their questions on any aspect of faith and practice. Clerics with their own websites simply began to avoid the use of the word 'fatwa', to keep government monitors away.

VELAYAT-E ALEM?

Post-9/11 the royal family faced renewed attempts by some of the *ulama* to suggest, expanding on Ibn Taimiyya's ideas of priestly primacy, that they can exercise political power in the regulation of public affairs. The Memorandum of Advice of 1991 implied, but did not say directly, that clerics should have an equal if not greater role in running the country.[54] The example of Iran since 1979, although Ayatollah Khomeini's *velayat-e fagih* was a Shi'ite innovation, demonstrated that the *ulama* did not have to remain beholden to a higher political authority in the land. Al-Qa'ida's call for revolutionary action against despotic apostate rulers and the wider movement of political Islam hinted at such possibilities. With Al Saud facing a crisis in its ties with the West after 9/11, Sahwa sheikh Nasser al-Omar and others suggested publicly that the *ulama* should be partners in political authority as opposed to the adjunct that they have been, providing advice to the Sharia state's ruler or legal guardian (*waliyy al-amr*; that is, the king), or even that they should have the right to take over rulership itself. His argument was that Surat al-Nisaa in the Quran allows for ultimate authority to lie with the *ulama*. Prince Talal bin Abdulaziz responded in an article in *Asharq al-Awsat*:

> I won't hide the fact that I was rather surprised by the idea that the *ulama* could be considered legal guardians since it has been axiomatic and customary throughout Islamic history that the oath of loyalty is given to rulers and sultans who become legal guardians on the basis of this oath. We have never heard of the oath being given to a religious scholar or judisprudent who becomes legal guardian. Moreover, we have never heard of a religious scholar claiming he could be legal guardian until now.[55]

King Abdullah's innovation of an 'allegiance council' of 34 princes established that it is only the Saudi royal family – the sons and grandsons of Abdulaziz Al Saud – who have the right to rule; indeed, it could be read as an attempt to shut the door to clerics tempted by Iran's example, al-Qa'ida's rebel yell or the game of parliamentary democracy to try to take matters into their own hands.

In 2006 the issue was still appearing in debates in Saudi papers. A columnist in *Al-Jazeera* who is from the Al al-Sheikh family attacked the idea of direct clerical rule as a deviation from Sunni norms. 'Islamic history has never ever known scholars such as Abu Hanifa, Malik, al-Shafi'i or Ahmed bin Hanbal (the founders of the four schools of Sunni Islamic law) to have asked that their followers should give their oath of loyalty to them, which means that the "partnership" of jurisprudents in political authority – which al-Omar calls for – has absolutely no historical justification', Mohammed bin Abdullatif Al al-Sheikh wrote.[56] Imputing the *ulama*'s temptation to claim ultimate jurisdiction over the state for themselves to the political Islam of the past generation, the writer – like Prince Nayef – blamed the Muslim Brotherhood (which has never suggested the Sheikh of Al-Azhar should be Supreme Leader).

The clerics have not stopped pressing for more. Popular preacher Ayedh al-Qarni outlines the role of the *ulama*. He attacks the modern state for marginalising the clerics – 'they were only there for giving fatwas, and even then only fatwas concerning issues of worship and conduct' – and suggests they should have as extensive a role as possible short of demanding a say in political decision-making. The *ulama* were 'sermon givers, prayer leaders, fatwa givers and judges'; they educated the people, preserved the identity of the nation and advised the ruler on what is right. 'Then the leaders of knowledge began to disappear in the age of the (modern) state that put Islam aside, so that the religious scholar's role became simply leading prayer, conducting marriages and supervising religious endowments', Qarni laments. He offers his thoughts on how to revive the role of the religious scholar and with it the Utopian society: the *ulama* should play their part by shunning personal gain and acting as points of emulation for the believer, but rulers must not sideline them. A new, more extensive body of clerical institutions should be established 'to manage the affairs of the nation', such as one for promoting knowledge of the hadiths, another for jurisprudence and providing fatwas, and another for safeguarding the correct precepts of Islamic faith such as *tawhid*.[57]

4
Segregated Nation

Sitting in the reception area of a Saudi newspaper office, we do nothing more damning than talk about the weather and the local press. The security guards eye us suspiciously – so much so that I avoid crossing my legs to escape the impression of being overly casual with my female interlocutor. In almost any other country it would be a routine exchange, but here a public meeting like this between a man and a woman could ruin her reputation and besmirch a family's honour. Najah, a young journalist, explains in almost a whisper that we are lucky we can even talk here. Hotel lobbies are a non-starter, she says, since women have been hauled off by the religious police for talking like this to strange men. I thought that was an exaggeration at the time, but after I left the country three years later I realised that the women I had talked to in hotel lobbies in Riyadh had either been Westerners or Saudis of another Arab origin, say Iraqi. Or perhaps we had met at press conferences or inside the diplomatic quarter where the religious police don't venture so often. The Commission arrested a Saudi woman and a Syrian work colleague she was having coffee with in a Riyadh mall in 2007. In Jeddah, the relatively liberal Red Sea port city, such encounters are less fraught with danger, at least between foreigners and Saudis, and its private beach areas and housing compounds are notorious for their raucous parties. But in Riyadh – a city essentially developed by Al Saud as a conservative Najdi counterpoint to Jeddah and its centuries-old cosmopolitan traditions – the office managers would pace around nervously if a woman visited any department on the premises in case the religious police found out and caused the company trouble.

Some half the population is off-limits to men for the kind of day-to-day contacts of most other places in the world. A modern city of 4 million, with a considerable number of people with a lot of money to spend, Riyadh tries hard to give off a cosmopolitan and sophisticated air. Its wide streets bulge with the latest sports cars and four-wheel-drives. Its vast shopping malls offer the latest fashions. Young men play the stock market in its endless street cafés.

But the familiarity stops there, because beneath the surface a system of gender segregation is in force which rigorously separates men from women unless they are close relatives. Women are removed from the glare of strangers, whether behind the tinted windows of cars, the high walls of villas or the monotone *abayas* and veils. In Riyadh I could not ask a woman in the street for directions, let alone approach her with questions about an issue of the day. At conferences we would sometimes witness the bizarre innovation of women speaking to the floor via loudspeaker from a concealed, segregated section – the norm in most universities. I wanted to meet the novelist Rajaa Alsanea after her bestseller *Girls of Riyadh* came out but she would converse with me only through email. Not everyone was like that. Film-maker Haifaa Mansour – who shot some of her films in the desert to avoid the eyes of the religious police – readily invited me over to her home in Khobar when I called her on a trip to the Eastern Province. But in Riyadh, when it comes to arranging meetings, always the same problem presented itself: where?

The power of the cleric is perhaps felt most strongly of all by Saudi women. Women are at the very centre of the Wahhabi concept of a moral society because they have the potential to create *fitna*, a term that signifies trouble or strife in society of various types. The civil wars over leadership of the early Islamic state are referred to as the *fitna* wars, but *fitna* can also be provoked by the allure of women; a woman who is *fatin* (a female name) can be alluring to the point of throwing the natural balance of men off-kilter. A woman loses her potential for provoking *fitna* once she is no longer reproductive; religious scholars such as Yousef al-Qaradawi say women may work as judges, for example, but only once they have reached menopause. At the same time women are regarded as inferior to men and best suited to home-making and child-bearing and child-rearing. When a girl enters puberty and teenage years she is expected to cover up completely in public, and in the Najd area those who show even their eyes tend to be those from affluent, liberal backgrounds, a minority. In public areas women should be accompanied by a male relative – father, husband or son – who acts as a legal guardian in all legal contracts or situations. Thus a woman can only obtain a passport with the approval of her guardian and is represented in court by the guardian. Thus women are also forbidden from driving cars. At the same time, homosexuality is generally tolerated and seen as youthful exuberance and rashness, as long as it does not become an overt sexual identity.[1] There is little rhetoric against Saudis who go abroad for periodic bouts of debauchery in Bahrain, Beirut or beyond, since the phenomenon helps maintain the purity of the Wahhabi home zone.[2]

Ideological obsession with the implementation of theory can produce deadly outcomes. In *The Origins of Totalitarianism*, Hannah Arendt argued that ideological rigour is a defining feature of totalitarian systems: if some races are superior, the inferior ones must be destroyed as human detritus; if society is to remain classless, periodic purges of certain social groups are necessary. Race policies easily overruled the profit motive in South Africa. Wahhabism in the nineteenth and early twentieth century was more extreme than it is today. Nineteenth-century travellers noted that Wahhabi strictures were a break on economic activity: objecting to sale and consumption of luxury items like tobacco, silk and coffee – even rice – not condoned in their view by the Prophet in hadith literature. This helped the Rashidi state, based in Hail in the northern Najd, become a major trading centre, outside the Saudi-Wahhabi zone, where Shi'ite and non-Muslim traders were welcome.[3] With regards to women specifically, Wahhabism today makes a strenuous effort to apply its theorising to the fullest extent possible, displaying an obsession with gender segregation that overrules economic utility and gives Saudi Arabia the semblance of one of Arendt's raging madhouses.[4]

The consequences for women of the ideological maelstrom in which they find themselves range from the trivial to the deadly. Doubts are habitually cast in media and forums over the authorship of novels published by Saudi women;[5] a plan to appoint a woman as Saudi ambassador in Washington to replace Turki al-Faisal in 2006 went nowhere because of the concern that embassy and foreign ministry staff would not cooperate with her.[6] Female university departments are locked during teaching hours and students cannot leave campus until a legal guardian or driver arrives, and even the entry of a male ambulance driver is difficult. Although the government department in charge of girls' education was moved to the formal control of the education ministry in 2002, many of these girls' schools remained without formal names because ministry cadres do not deem them worthy of them.[7] The design for the Noura Bint Abdulrahman University for Women, launched in Riyadh 2008, includes an underground tunnel where maintenance engineers can control water, electricity and air-conditioning without ever having to step inside the female-only precinct.[8]

American writer Naomi Wolf has written approvingly of a 'thriving Muslim sexuality' that lies 'behind the veil'. 'It is not that Islam suppresses sexuality, but that it embodies a strongly developed sense of its appropriate channelling – toward marriage, the bonds that sustain family life, and the attachment that secures a home', she writes, of experiences in Morocco, Egypt and Jordan.[9] But the corollary of sanctification of family life is commodification in public space. Capitalism has fully exploited women's segregation in Saudi Arabia, with ample royal help. The MBC Group owned by Walid al-Ibrahim, a brother-in-law of King Fahd, Prince Alwaleed bin Talal's Rotana and LBC, magazines owned by Alwaleed and the family of Prince Salman bin Abdulaziz, websites such as Elaph (run by a Saudi businessman) – these are the prime purveyors of a 'liberal' entertainment aesthetic that presents women as sexual objects in imitation of MTV and other Western outlets that the *ulama* deem inappropriate. Arab media often carry reports of fads among Gulf Arab women for plastic surgery to resemble the latest bubble-gum pop sensation from Lebanon, role models created by Saudi media who often lack charisma or talent. Western commentators tend to report positively about the vibrant, titillating music video culture in the Arab world, but in the Saudi context it clearly raises questions about cultural schizophrenia.[10]

On the one side there is Alwaleed's vulgar pop culture, masquerading as 'progress' and 'keeping up with the West', on the other there is the codified misogyny of Wahhabism in the form of the life's work of former mufti Abdulaziz Bin Baz. The clerics are no fans of the entertainment media – Alwaleed's own brother Khaled has denounced him as *al-amir al-majin*, 'the depraved prince' – but their view of women springs from the same well of misogyny. It was the death of Bin Baz in 1999 that helped pave the way for this entertainment media to come into existence. 'Bin Baz may have been one of the worst enemies of women in the 20th century. In what he wrote, announced, preached and offered official opinions on, he seemed to be disgusted with them', writes Lebanese political scientist As'ad AbuKhalil.[11] Bin Baz's influence was immense, and a vast body of material exists demonstrating his views on women and other issues; blind himself, he famously questioned whether the earth was really round. Many members of the ruling Al Saud family felt a personal bond with him and claimed to derive from him spiritual sustenance. Prince Sultan bin Salman talked in glowing terms of Bin Baz when I met him in 2007. The prince became the first Muslim to go into space as a payload specialist on board the

American space shuttle Discovery in 1985. He sought advice from
Bin Baz on how he could pray and fast, since it was Ramadan, while
in orbit, then headed to sheikh's home in Taif on his return to tell
him about his discoveries. The prince says he convinced Bin Baz
that the earth was not flat. 'He said people needed to travel more
and see evidence of the roundness of the earth. He loved it and he
said a few times he wished he wasn't blind so that he could see the
photographs', the prince said.[12] Professor of Law Khaled Abou El
Fadl concluded in his analysis of Wahhabi rulings in the Bin Baz era
that women were reduced to 'a mere physicality' through a highly
selective reading and choice of hadiths that contradicts the spirit
of the Quran.[13] Here are some Bin Baz fatwas:

- Bin Baz replies to a listener about women's clothes that attract
  the attention of men: 'There is no doubt that women must
  be pious in this and strive to cover their bodies with clothes,
  conceal all parts of the body from men, and on the head so
  that people are not seduced (la taftin al-nas) and so that young
  men and others do not associate with her, since this would
  cause an instance of immorality (al-fahisha) and forbidden
  things, and this is what girls should do wherever they are.
  They absolutely must strive to cover all their body, not to show
  head, face, chest or anything else. She must be well protected
  and covered, covering her attractive areas (mafatin) and body
  so that she does not damage herself or the young men who
  look at her.'[14]
- Foreign maids should not be hired because non-Muslim
  foreigners should not be permitted into the Arabian Peninsula
  at all. 'One should know that it is not permitted to bring infidels
  to the Arabian Peninsula', he wrote, citing a well-known
  saying said to come from the Prophet Mohammad. 'There
  must not be Jews, Christians, Buddhists, Communists,
  Idolaters and all those who Islam has deemed to be infidels
  unless there is an absolute necessity because of an unforeseen
  circumstance decided upon by the ruler, then they should
  return to their country.'[15]
- 'There should be no mixed teaching with girls in one place, or
  one school, since this is one of the biggest causes of fitna. The
  Muslim should also not shake the hand of a foreign woman
  if she extends her hand to him', he ruled, citing a saying of
  the Prophet where he stated he did not shake women's hands,
  a saying attributed to his wife Aisha apparently confirming

this of the Prophet, and a Quranic verse exhorting Muslims to take the Prophet's practice as the example to follow.[16]

- He praised the practice of taking four wives as assuring the chastity of women – by placing them safely inside marriage and outside the *fitna* zone – and the multiplication of the numbers of Muslims.[17]

'Guardianship' is the key mechanism for guaranteeing the segregated moral order. The *muhrim*, or male guardian, is a religious term which suggests someone whose presence protects the honour or virtue of the woman, who otherwise would be open to approaches from unrelated men, leading potentially to *fitna*. It is semantically linked to *ihram*, the state of ritual purity that a Muslim enters while performing pilgrimage in Mecca. A saying of the Prophet listed in the hadith collection of Tirmidhi and approved by Wahhabi clerics says that 'If a man is alone with a woman, there is a third person there who is Satan.'[18] Bin Baz's opinion was that 'A man should not be alone with a woman in an office, car or room, and he should be careful of this, since Satan could cause something with unforeseen consequences.'[19]

The New York-based rights group Human Rights Watch correctly homed in on these attitudes in a report published in 2008, *Perpetual Minors: Human Rights Abuses Stemming from Male Guardianship and Sex Segregation in Saudi Arabia*, in which it reached the conclusion that women are treated in Saudi Arabia as 'legal minors'.[20] 'While in the vast majority of countries governments only deny minors and those with certain mental disabilities the right to make decisions for themselves, in Saudi Arabia the government extends these limitations on legal capacity to fully competent adult women', the report said.[21] There was no better indication of how on target this description was than the government's rattled responses in domestic and international media via the government's official body established to discuss and address human rights issues, the Human Rights Commission. The responses evidenced an impatience with those who contrast the reality with the idealised picture wished for and presented by the liberal elements in government who must deal with the outside world. The Commission's spokesman Zuheir al-Harithy said the report had confused tradition with state policy. 'We know some customs and traditions prevent women having their complete rights, but you cannot say they are "legal minors". They are doctors, teach in universities, are elected to the chambers of commerce', he said.[22] Despite the Commission's angry reaction, its own report of 2007 outlined in considerable detail the problems of discrimination faced by women in the country. 'Adult women are not able to conduct their own affairs, which manifests itself from time to time in some situations', it said, citing the need for a guardian to acquire an identification card or passport.[23]

The Human Rights Watch report noted that women in general cannot open bank accounts for children, enrol them in school, obtain school files, or travel with their children without written permission from the child's father. Women are also prevented from accessing government agencies that have not established female sections unless they have a male representative, and the need to establish separate office space discourages firms from hiring women. Although there are no official rules requiring a guardian's consent for a woman to enter a hospital or undergo any medical procedure, many hospital administrations ask for it if those in charge are religious conservatives; sometimes drivers will provide the signature that the hospital requires. If a woman turns up at a hospital to give birth without a guardian she runs the risk of finding herself facing a criminal case for having an extramarital affair (which can also happen in the UAE). Women cannot get redress in situations of domestic violence or abuse because the guardian must approve their police statements or even their entry into a station, where all the police are men. Some women fear calling the police without a guardian around to approve it.[24] Women have trouble filing legal cases or being heard in court without a guardian. Since there are no specialised female sections in courts, so a woman must bring someone who can identify her, known as a *mu'arrif*. Yet, as Human Rights Watch noted, there is one area where women carry legal status equal to men: woman from the age of puberty bear full legal responsibility for any crimes committed.

In situations where guardians are no longer required, institutions will require a guardian's presence or approval for fear of consequences from religious authorities, even when buying a telephone card. When women take part in conferences such as the National Dialogue or other public events, they are sectioned off in another room and contribute via speaker system. The Ministry of the Interior said in 2008 that women over the age of 45 could travel without permission but airport officials will still ask for written proof that the male guardian approves their travel. Hospitals may only allow a woman to undergo some medical procedures if a guardian's permission is provided. The government is unwilling for the most part to challenge the cleric-sanctioned order. When women were not allowed to take part in municipal elections in 2005 it was argued that there were no separate voting booths for them to use; if women drive, special women traffic police will need to be employed to handle them on the streets and at registration. The clerics apply the most restrictive reading possible of a Quranic verse (Surat al-Nisaa, the Quran's fourth chapter, verse 34) referring to guardianship (*wilaya*), demonstrating a stubborn determination to disregard progressive interpretations appropriate to the needs of a modern society.

ECONOMIC COSTS

The modernisers in government have identified women in work as a national priority and women's education has improved since the 1960s but the clerics have given no ground in their belief that women's main role is as home-maker and child-rearer. The state has made some headway in persuading clerics that women should work but for the reason of advancing the economic position of the country, not as a principle in its own right. In 1970 only 16.4 per cent of women aged over 15 were literate; in 2005, 83.3 per cent were literate.[25] In the Bin Baz era, the Permanent Committee for Research and Fatwas disparaged university education as 'something we have no need for'. 'If a woman finishes elementary school and is able to read and write, and thus benefit from reading the book of God, commentaries and hadith of the Prophet, then that is enough for her, unless she excels in a field people need, like medicine, and that this does not involve anything not permitted such as mixing of the sexes', it said.[26] 'God commended women to stay at home. Their presence in public is the main factor contributing to the spread of *fitna*. Yes, Sharia permits women to leave their home if necessary, wearing a *hijab* and avoiding suspicious situations, but the general rule is that they should stay at home.'[27] The ruling family has challenged the clerics on these social issues only with extreme care. Article 153 of the Saudi Policy on Education says: 'A girl's education aims at giving her the correct Islamic education to enable her to be in life a successful housewife, an exemplary wife and a good mother.'

State universities generally do not run political science, engineering or architecture courses for women, who must study in separate all-women departments, and most languages are not offered to women. Universities seek permission from a woman's guardian over courses she wishes to study and the Ministry of Higher Education requires women who get scholarships abroad to be accompanied by a guardian (forcing many into temporary marriages referred to as *misfar*). Women's access to university libraries is restricted; they cannot enter many public libraries, instead having to send drivers to pick up books they have ordered by telephone in advance. The King Fahd University of Petroleum and Minerals in Dhahran does not accept women at all. King Abdulaziz University has its first women law graduates this year but the Ministry of Justice does not give them licences to practice. The King Abdullah University of Science and Technology (KAUST), opened to great fanfare near Jeddah in 2009, is the first institution offering unfettered academic freedom to women, but it is a bubble. The Labour Code of 2006 talks of equal labour opportunities without discrimination throughout the country but says women should work in fields 'suitable to their nature'.[28] In any case, employers tend to avoid women because they have to raise their wages to compensate for their transportation costs. The clerics insist that separate work spaces must be provided for women so that they do not mix with men. At a conference of government officials and religious scholars at the King Abdulaziz Centre for National Dialogue in 2008, clerics insisted on segregation in the workplace. 'Most agreed to open a wide arena for women to get jobs, since girls now graduate more than boys from universities. We cannot go on having 7 million foreigners and our graduate women in their houses', said the Centre's director, Faisal bin Muammar.[29] 'But how to establish it [is the issue], whether it is in separate or mixed places ... We need to make rules for it, which clerics, families and social leaders need.'

Hassan al-Husseini, a former teacher at the King Fahd University of Petroleum and Minerals and head of Employment, Human Resources, and Planning at Aramco from 1979 to 1998, believes that segregation is costing Saudi Arabia billions of dollars every year. Of the expatriates, about 1 million are female nannies working in private households, with another 1 million male drivers serving the same households. About 1 million expatriate women work in health services, education or are dependants of expatriate men (wives and children). The expatriates as a whole send about $50 billion in remittances annually to their home countries, and perhaps account for about $50 billion in annual spending in Saudi Arabia on housing, food, clothing, transportation, travel, and so on. 'If restrictions on Saudi women working and driving could be removed, then Saudi women could perhaps displace 2–3 million of the expatriates, and reduce the remittances by $20 billion, and increase domestic spending by about $20 billion ... Saudi female unemployment perhaps could be reduced from 70 per cent to about 50 per cent to 40 per cent', he says.[30] According to Husseini, limiting employment opportunities for women is costing Saudi Arabia about $40 billion a year; there is a vested interest in maintaining the situation, since the *kafala* (sponsorship) system for bringing in foreign workers allows Saudi citizens as individuals and institutions to charge a fee from foreigners they hire. This has become a major source of income for many Saudi princes, and one report says that princes alone caused an increase in the expat population from 4.2 million to 6.5 million between 1992 and 1995.[31]

In recent years, restrictions have been eased to allow some women into the economy, allowing women to open bank accounts or get business licences in their own name, though they will always require the approval of their male guardian. Women who travel without a guardian need his permission and carry a yellow paper that specifies how many days they are allowed outside and how many they've taken; they need his permission for a passport, and the foreign ministry issues a visa with permission allowing them to travel abroad over and above the passport. Women's participation in the labour market was at 5.4 per cent in 1992, 10.3 per cent in 2004, and was expected to reach 14.8 per cent in 2009.[32] Marriage is not necessarily an obstacle to work: 69 per cent of working Saudi women aged 15 or older were married (compared to 77 per cent for males). In 2005 there were 22,500 women-owned commercial enterprises, representing around 4.7 per cent of total registered businesses. As part of the government's eighth economic plan (2004–09), the cabinet passed a series of measures in May 2004 to 'enhance women's economic activity'. The labour ministry began opening offices for employing women in the private sector in 2004 after a cabinet decree of 1 January 2003. In 2006, women accounted for 2.2 per cent of the 5.6 million people who worked in the private sector, and only 13 per cent of that 5.6 million were Saudis.[33] Despite all this, 60 per cent of university graduates are women.[34] Rules allowing women to work as shop assistants in lingerie shops took eight years to go into effect in 2012 because of clerical and business resistance to replacing cheap foreign hires; the minister Gosaibi did not live to see the fruit of his long labour.

The ban on women driving has had a social and economic cost for Saudi Arabia. A high-profile attempt in 1990 to break the informal barrier to women driving provoked a decisive clerical opinion on the issue, leading to the interior ministry taking the decision to deny women licences and take action if a woman was caught at the wheel. In 1990, 45 women took advantage of the hopes and uncertainty unleashed by the Gulf crisis to drive their cars together through central Riyadh on 6 November of that year. Members of the educated elite, they were noticed by police and religious police and arrested. They were only released after male guardians signed guarantees they would not disturb the public peace in this way again; some were subjected to humiliating medical tests (for semen, drugs and alcohol), denounced as whores in mosques, received harassing phone calls and were monitored for months.[35] Those who had jobs lost them and the religious establishment agitated heavily over the incident, citing it as an example of the kind of moral pollution caused by the presence of American troops (and the influx of foreign media that followed them). Bin Baz cited six verses from the Quran to back up his logic that women must not drive. 'It is known that it [women driving] leads to corruption including being alone with men, unveiling, free mixing with men, committing that which is banned', he said. 'Pure Sharia has banned the means that could lead to that which is forbidden.'[36]

Since Abdullah assumed the throne in 2005, a number of senior princes including the king said publicly on various occasions that they had no personal problem with women driving, but the change could only be enacted once it was clear that society itself would welcome it. The argument is false on two grounds: Al Saud promote the very religious and social conservatism they cite as a block to the state taking action to grant women who wish to drive their rights because it suits their interests in other contexts, and Al Saud are smothering efforts by women from within society to claim the right for themselves. Therefore, when the senior princes talk of society welcoming women driving, it is clear which society they have in mind: only that of the religious conservatives. Fatwas from Bin Baz and Abdulaziz Al al-Sheikh were cited by religious forces in the Shura Assembly when some members tried to raise the issue in 2008: all members are appointed by the king. At that time Saudi newspapers reported with increased frequency incidents where women had taken to the wheel themselves. Usually they were stopped by police, and a guardian was required to sign a statement promising it would not happen again, though in one case a girl drove her relatives to hospital after they were burned in a fire. Advocates of reform long hoped the king would focus on the issue as an area to chalk up a clear reform success, since he did not follow through on hopes of setting up an elected parliament. The authorities, however, showed no sign of movement when a number of women took to the wheel in separate incidents – no organised group effort such as the one that failed in 1990 – in 2011, inspired by the Arab protest movements.

SOCIAL COSTS

Guardians also have the power to approve marriages and absolve marriages they deem unfit, though the mufti Sheikh Abdulaziz Al al-Sheikh spoke out against forced marriages in April 2005 and the media has tried to make an issue of underage marriages in particular in recent years, after some particularly egregious examples became public. The mufti upheld the principle of contracts to marry prepubescent girls, arguing that in Sharia law consummation of the marriage is a separate issue and they, or their guardians, can sue for divorce at a later date.[37] The case of Fatima Azzaz and her husband Mansour Timani was one notorious case. In 2006, police went to the couple's home in al-Jouf to tell them a court had divorced them at the behest of her eleven brothers and half-brothers who argued that they were in a position of guardianship over Azzaz and objected to her marriage to Timani, who they said had lied about his social status when he first proposed marriage. Although the case become known as a question of caste and class attitudes and the contrast between that naked tribalism and the Islamic Utopian claims of the Saudi state, it was in essence a question of guardianship. The trouble began with the death of her father, who Azzaz says was on good terms with Timani. In her view, her brothers felt her marriage should be an opportunity to advance the family's business interests and social connections. They belong to the Bani Tamim tribe and one of her sisters had married a wealthy merchant with good connections to some Saudi princes. Timani says he is a Shammari, hailing from the extensive Shammar tribe that stretches from Hail in north Saudi Arabia into Iraq and Syria. King Abdullah's mother was a Shammari tribeswoman. Although to many Muslims around the world Islam is strongly defined by its focus on equality between peoples and classes, and excess tribal zeal and partisanship is explicitly denounced in the Quran, for the Wahhabi judges in this case and others it was a relatively simple question of who the woman's legal guardian was and the guardian's right, in their view, to approve or disapprove of her marriage. They were not defending tribalism per se, though the case is an example of how tribalism and al-Wahhabiyya coalesce.[38] Senior clerics and the government only rarely speak out against tribal zealotry, and only when it threatens unity in the Saudi-Wahhabi state: buying tribal loyalty is an important element of Al Saud rule. 'I just want to be with my daughter and husband. I don't care if he's Shammar or whatever. What difference will your lineage make on the Day of Judgement? White, black, whoever you are – we're all the same then', Azzaz told me at the time.[39]

The story shocked many Saudis when it became public knowledge in 2006. The couple's fate after the first ruling had a tragic quality to it. They had first decided to flee to Jeddah, but when law enforcement agents caught up with them they decided each to retain custody of one of their two young children. Timani was free to go about his life with their daughter, while Azzaz chose to go to prison with their infant son rather than submit to her brothers' authority and return to the family home. She was later moved to a government home for orphans in Dammam. Incarceration was more protection than living in society at large. The interior ministry withdrew Timani's identification card and he was banned from leaving the country. In 2010 the newly-established Cassation Court overturned the ruling's keeping the couple apart – but implementation remained an issue. The head of the Human Rights Commission asked King Abdullah several times to intervene in the case. The idea of prison as the only refuge in a society that is itself something of a jail is striking. Novelist Abdo Khal touches on the theme in *Fusouq*, a satire on morality in which a police officer is charged with investigating the disappearance of a woman's corpse from her grave. The protagonist, who is convinced the woman staged her death to run off with her lover, muses that 'those who become familiar with prison no longer find life pleasant outside. They justify their continual return to prison saying that outside you need a spotless reputation to let you live your life.'[40] Later he notes that 'when you create a big prison, people have to find a way to escape'.[41]

Saudi women are also kept out of sports by the religious establishment and the state that turns to them for advice. In the wave of the re-evaluation and introspection that swept the country after the events of 9/11, the Ministry of Education debated whether to introduce physical education for girls in the primary and secondary school curriculums, but the idea was ultimately rejected in 2005. Religious figures, who dominate in the ministry, portrayed the victory against women's sports as a victory over a Western plot to secularise society through focusing on women's freedoms. In the Shura Assembly their supporters argued that exercise for boys had made little difference to the high levels of obesity; malls for women are enough. Sheikh Muhammed al-Habdan (moderator of website islamlight.net) published a series of widely-disseminated booklets railing against the idea of women in sports. 'The Muslim woman should realize that she is a target for corruption', he wrote in one concerning the evil of fitness clubs. 'There is no faster way to corrupt nations than the emancipation of women – that is getting her out on the street to entice men and ruin their morals.'[42] Leading lights of Wahhabism such as Abdulrahman al-Barrak suggested women could perhaps race their husbands in the desert for exercise because of a hadith that the Prophet did that with Aisha. Unofficial women-only sports clubs face the constant threat of closure. Two in Jeddah and one in Dammam were closed in 2009 by the Ministry of Municipal and Rural Affairs, which licenses male-only gyms.[43] Some hospitals house women-only gyms under the title 'health centres', supervised by the Ministry of Health. But costing at least 1,000 riyals ($266) a month, not so many Saudi women can afford membership. Women tried to challenge the situation with the sarcastic slogan 'Let her get fat!'

The result has been catastrophic for women's health, another factor in the creation of a model consumptive society. Typically, conservatives have tried to hedge, nuance and widen the argument in a bid to take the focus away from physical education as the solution to the failing health of Saudi women, an approach similar to that taken towards the question of segregation and women in the workplace. Health ministry statistics published in 2006 showed that obesity affects 51 per cent of Saudi women and 45 per cent of men, as well as 29 per cent of teenage girls and 36 per cent of boys.[44] Saudi women are also suffering from fragile bones. In one study of 483 Saudi women between the ages of 52 and 62, 34 per cent were found to have weak bones and 24 per cent were found to suffer from osteoporosis.[45] Saudi Arabia has one of the highest rates of diabetes in the world, affecting some 30 per cent of the population.[46] International shame is perhaps the only avenue that can produce any significant shift. Saudi Arabia was careful to send not a single woman to the Olympics in Beijing in August 2008, and that caught the attention of media and politicians. US Secretary of State at the time Condoleezza Rice spoke out publicly on the question while the Games were underway in Beijing. Saudi Arabia finally agreed two weeks before the start of the London Games in 2012 to send two women athletes after intense pressure from the International Olympic Committee (after Qatar and Brunei also agreed to ensure they had female representation). In the words of US-based dissident activist Ali Alyami, 'the Kingdom sets an unspeakable example for other Arabs and Muslims to emulate because other Muslims look to Saudi Arabia for religious guidance. These examples perpetuate discrimination against other Muslim women and non-Muslims who live in Arab and Muslim societies.'[47]

POLITICAL COSTS

Protecting the sanctity of the judiciary is a major concern of the state, both its religious pillars and its royal players. But foreign, specifically American, pressure over a particularly embarrassing example of judicial cruelty towards a woman forced the government's hand after a 19-year-old Shi'ite girl from Qatif in the Eastern Province was sentenced in November 2007 to 200 lashes of the whip and six months in prison for being alone with an unrelated man when she was attacked and gang-raped by seven other men. The seven men received sentences of between two and nine years in prison. The sentences came from the Supreme Judicial Council, a cassation court that raised the punishments against all parties – the woman was first sentenced to 90 lashes, and five years was the maximum sentence against any of her attackers. The young man she was with, who was also raped by the men, was not tried. According to Saudi women who spoke to the rape victim, she had asked to meet the man in order to retrieve photographs he had of her which she feared could be used to compromise her upcoming marriage – blackmail and smearing reputations through possession of photographs taken on mobile phones became common after the technology was introduced. The girl and her male companion were pardoned by the king a month later, but during that period the country's rulers faced intense scrutiny over the issue internationally while the justice ministry issued two separate statements defending at length the verdicts against the woman. The statements stopped just short of accusing the woman of adultery, saying that she was conducting an illicit relationship when alone with the man on the night of the rape, parked in a car in a dark area of Khobar. The judiciary said the woman was married, while her lawyer, whom the court took disciplinary measures against for defending the girl and talking to the media about the case, said she was merely engaged. Her husband called into a Saudi television programme to say she had not been married at the time.

At the same time, foreign minister Saud al-Faisal faced harsh questioning about the case while in Washington for a Middle East summit. 'Unfortunately, these things happen. Bad judgements occur in legal systems', he responded. 'It is a process that is still going on. This is being reviewed by a legal process and we hope it will be changed.'[48] For a brief period of two to three years, the US administration talked with uncharacteristic gusto about the need for democratic and other reforms in Arab countries, including Saudi Arabia, but went quiet once the Iraq project turned sour and Islamists did well in Egypt, the Palestinian territories and even the Saudi municipal election vote. The Qatif-girl case, however, received considerable attention on CNN and other American news outlets, and that provoked a response from the administration, however diplomatically the public statements were phrased. Asked by journalists, President George W. Bush had avoided direct criticism but said the king 'knows our position loud and clear' on the case.[49] That was a step up from a State Department spokesman's anodyne observation some days before that 'most would find this relatively astonishing that something like this happens'.[50]

The pardon when it came on 17 December was revealed through a statement by justice minister Abdullah bin Mohammad Al al-Sheikh on the front page of *Al-Jazeera* newspaper. In it, he said the king had the right to issue pardons 'in the public interest' while defending the legal system's 'integrity, justice and transparency'. In the evening of that day, the minister rang in to a call-in show on Al-Ikhbariya news channel to read out the royal order, which was addressed to the minister. 'The crime against this woman reached a disturbing level of brutality. Because the woman and the person who was with her suffered a level of torture and distress that was by itself enough to discipline them ... we would like you to close those parts of the case concerning them', it said.[51] The Bush administration stepped in again on the occasion of the pardon, placing the case in the context of US encouragement of judicial reform in Saudi Arabia. 'We would like not to see a repeat of this case', a State Department spokesman said. 'If the king's decision has an impact on that kind of thinking of those in the Saudi judicial system, I think that would be a good thing.'[52] The state had no interest in a public dispute with the religious authorities and has never acted with haste to appear to criticise them; the king only acted because of foreign pressure. Amnesties were issued before in cases where the jurisprudence of the *ulama* clashed with global realities and led to an international incident – notably the pardoning of British nurses found guilty of murder and of British and Canadian nationals found guilty of alcohol trading and murder. The pardon in no way implied that the persons involved were innocent nor impugned the integrity of the judiciary, or its obsession with guardianship.

What the Qatif-girl case ultimately demonstrated was the determination of the Islamic judiciary to maintain its ground and the supremacy of its moral worldview, and the commitment of Al Saud to preserving their position. In the view of Saudi Shi'ites, it also touched on the sectarianism at the heart of the system. 'These Wahhabi judges gave this sentence because the defendants are Shi'ites. Wahhabi ideology views non-Wahhabi women as loose, and Shi'ite women are whores. They see sexual promiscuity as nothing unusual for Shi'ites', said Ali Al Ahmad, the Shi'ite dissident based in Washington.[53] The idea that the woman was at least guilty of wrongdoing, even if the punishment was inappropriate or draconian, was prevalent among many educated men. During a visit to the information ministry not long afterwards, I raised the issue with one of the deputy ministers of information at the time, an alleged liberal light who published poetry. Yes it was a bad case, he said, but he wanted to relay his insight about what really happened. 'It seems that the girl was a prostitute', he said smugly. I asked him to elaborate. 'You can tell from the way the judges wrote their statement', he said.

The clerics made a controversial and abortive attempt in 2006 to restrict women's space for prayer inside the Grand Mosque in Mecca. The Grand Mosque is one of the few places where men and women can pray together in Islam, although technically there are separate spaces for each gender throughout the vast complex. The religious police patrol the mosque with sticks and often prod worshippers over attire they deem inappropriate, or stand around the Kaaba in a vain attempt to stop the throng of pilgrims adulating the black stone and the wall in which it is placed, and they might hassle women praying outside the prescribed areas. But within the central area around the Kaaba (called the *sahn*) they do not stop women, or men, praying, unless they choose to do it next to the Kaaba itself when the crowds are particularly heavy, such as during hajj. But in September 2006, plans were made public for the all-male committee overseeing the holy sites to place women in a distant section of the mosque while men would still be able to pray in the key central space, the *sahn*. 'The area is very small and so crowded. So we decided to get women out of the *sahn* to a better place where they can see the Kaaba and have more space', said Osama Al Bar, head of the Institute for Hajj Research. 'Some women thought it wasn't good, but from our point of view it will be better for them. We can explain to them what the decision is.'[54] The idea was bound to provoke a reaction from Muslims around the world, where Saudi obsessions with gender segregation are not generally shared, and in particular in North America where Muslim women have formed vocal lobbying groups. A US-based group called the Muslimah Writers Alliance began a web petition to lobby Saudi Arabia over the plans, called 'Project Grand Mosque Equal Access for Women'.

The trial balloon burst: several days later, Saudi papers quoted Grand Mosque administration saying an alternative plan to organise the crowds had been adopted. Pilgrimage generally presents Saudi clerics with the stark reality that most Muslims are not like them, or in their view that most of the world's Muslims are steeped in superstitions and traditions that have nothing to do with the true pure message of Islam, which they represent. It appeared discriminatory in a way that violated the basic right to be able to pray as close as possible to the Kaaba which Islam regards as the place where God's presence is most felt on earth. Of course, it is towards the Kaaba that Muslims around the world turn when praying. Some of the reactions included this from Suhaila Hammad, a woman member of the Islamic Jurisprudence Academy, based in Jeddah. 'Both men and women have the right to pray in the "House of God". Men have no right to take it away. Men and women mix when they circumambulate the Kaaba, so do they want to make us do that somewhere else too? This is discrimination against women.'[55]

WOMEN IN NEW SAUDI LITERATURE

Saudi literary output grew throughout the first decade of the twenty-first century, with a body of work that has offered representations of Saudi Arabia during a critical, transformative phase, and they depict an opaque and troubled society. Abdo Khal's *Tarmi bi-Sharar* (*Throwing Sparks*) won the International Prize for Arabic Fiction, or the Arabic Booker, in 2010, confirming a certain Saudi status in the Arab literary scene. Post-9/11 Saudi Arabia has thrown up many themes for discussion, from greater expectations for political and social rights, to economic boom and bust, to radical Islamist politics and insurgency. Women have featured prominently in this outpouring of expression, as writers and as subject matter.

Rajaa Alsanea's *Banat al-Riyadh* (*Riyadh Girls*) spurred interest among young women in writing. Around 50 novels were published in 2006 compared with 26 in 2005, the year Alsanea's book was published.[56] Written as a series of blog entries, *Banat al-Riyadh* concerns four friends and their experiences in love and marriage. It provoked a strong reaction from conservatives who said Alsanea was exposing private issues in a matter unbecoming for Saudi women and shaming the country and its values, while liberals were irritated by the book's success because they felt the book was being exploited to give the impression to the outside world that liberals were gaining ground against conservatives in Saudi society, as the government wants the West to think ('It's a piece of junk but it serves a purpose. She tries to present a positive image', said Wajeha Huweidar). The novel concerned women of the affluent class of society who have far more freedom to navigate the restrictions of Saudi society, indeed to escape it completely if they wish with trips abroad.

Other works have done more to bring out the alienation and restriction faced by women, and challenge the idea that the particular conservative religious cast of Saudi Arabia is an immutable cultural reality that has always been and always will be. In Badriya Al-Bisher's *Hind wal-'Askar* the protagonist Hind wrestles with the bitterness of her mother, who perpetuates the system of control. In the end, Hind's only escape is to leave the country itself, though she requires the approval of a sympathetic brother and her former husband, father to her one child, in order to fly out of the country. The novel records the myriad bureaucratic sleights that women bear suffer to establish their inequality in Saudi society, sleights noted in the Human Rights Watch report mentioned earlier in this chapter. Hind explains:

When I was young I loved school because it was the one place of enjoyment. Men understand that homes are created for women, the bars of their windows are the limits of their world. Women are used to bars, they are fond of them. They think it's the one safe place for them in this world and wild animals that could pounce on them lie beyond if they go out and men are mad wolves. In my country women grow old before their time, they become afflicted with depression, they fear illness, the illness of children and losing their husbands. Their premature ageing is a sign of damage and the end of their seductive years. Their roles are restricted and their value slips because they live in need all their lives, the need for their fathers before marriage, the need for their husbands, then their children when they grow old, so it's easy for their benefactors to lead them.[57]

Al-Bisher's book came out in 2006 talks of the period in 2004 when Islamist radicals fought the Saudi state. The novel brings up familiar debates in Saudi society at that time: are the al-Qa'ida insurgents good Muslims who must be brought back to the correct path, or are they people beyond hope to be rooted out and destroyed? The official religious establishment, whose ideology hardly differed from that of al-Qa'ida, was keen to promote the former view. Hind's brother becomes more zealous in his religion and Hind's column in a newspaper, published with her name, provokes him. He tells his sisters that women who do not hide their identity in public will be fuel for the fires of hell. But the system has mobilised women as much as men to do the work of perpetuating tradition:

> Men sit at the table of life and eat the cake in full, without feeling the slightest pang of conscience, while women observe them hungrily, only allowing themselves to smack their lips because of a tradition they are not responsible for. But they are its faithful guards. Over the years they have managed to mobilise women who became even more fierce than them in guarding it. My mother is one of those faithful guards. She always tells me when I ask how Fahd or Ibrahim are different from me: 'They are men and you are a woman. Don't you get it?' But I don't understand what 'woman' means. I ask her: 'Does this mean a woman is without a soul?' She says: 'Something like that. You'll accept it just as we accepted it before you, whether you like it or not.'[58]

In *Al-Akharun*, Siba al-Harz (a nom de plume) also employs the first person to tell the story of a teenage girl trapped in a vicious circle of exploitative, violent lesbian relationships. Light emerges at the end of a dark psychological trip through the internet, which has opened up new vistas for communication and interaction among trapped Saudi youth.

> I trembled and trembled and trembled. She covered me with her body and began stroking my hands with hers, but in vain. It was not the cold that made me shiver, it was something else, sunk in deep recesses and I knew not its nature. I couldn't stand or control any part of my body. I tried to focus on an idea to get me out of this worrying crisis of mine, but nothing helped. I really wanted to run away from Dee. So I turned around and drew away, putting my leg in front of my chest. She began licking the scratches on my back, that came from her nails, or the other scratches caused

by the rough carpet rubbing my skin. It led me to imagine that I was a morass of saliva and breath, that she was a cat and my wounds would not heal.[59]

Al-Akharun is interesting for the link it draws between escape from certain sexual confines to a latent political awareness. The protagonist is a Shi'ite from Qatif, where Shia rose in opposition to the social and political order in 1979–80 under the inspiration of the Islamic revolution in Iran and its call to fight oppression. For Harz's heroine, those events, and the controversial annexation of the Eastern Province to the Saudi realm many decades ago, are disjointed shards of memory that find focus in a moment of realisation. She discovers the repressed political history of Qatif through sifting through memories of events and comments made by relatives, then seeks recourse to the Internet to investigate further. She recalls what one of her girlfriends once said, now able to understand what she meant:

When I looked into it I found that the history of Qatif around 1400 AH had not been written down as if it was something we were only worthy of keeping silent over. Qatif was stamped with a different face and we all live it and will continue to live it. Our problem is that we are not aware of its details and folded-up truths, or our problem is that we are too ignorant to comprehend it. Sometimes I think I don't understand what happened because I am a woman. Women don't understand history because they did not record it, and history is just a corrupt policeman who is bought with money and force.[60]

The character, whose name we never know, establishes an online relationship with a young man, and while we do not learn where the friendship leads, a stage of hope, optimism and maturity has been reached. The male friend she finds on the internet is from Riyadh: Harz's protagonist has managed to cross sexual, geographical and political boundaries, thus she has found the potential to become a truly national figure in a country whose myths and ideologies prevent the projection of a convincing, inclusive national identity.[61]

Wahhabism's response to the post-9/11 challenge on women's status has not ignored the possibilities offered by literature. We have already noted the wide dissemination of Ayedh al-Qarni's *La Tahzan*, a second-generation adjunct to the core Wahhabi production since the 1980s of Quranic commentaries and pamphlets by key living and deceased preachers. *La Tahzan*, a tract to keep believers on the true path of religion, was not really aimed at women at all. It explicitly warned the reader: 'Do not crave all that you hear, do not trust every friend, do not reveal your secrets to a woman, do not run after your every wish.'[62] So in 2004 Qarni published *As'ad Imra'a fil-'Alam* (*The Happiest Woman in the World*), a lavishly produced volume which has been a bestseller, prominently placed in Saudi and other bookshops. Its premise is that the Muslim woman can find happiness by simply turning to religion, as elaborated from the Salafi perspective. The temptations of secularism, Western culture, literature or even thinking itself will not lead to contentment. He says:

> The way to happiness lies in purity of knowledge and culture, and this does not come from romantic imaginary stories that take the reader out of his reality and far from his world. You may find in that rose-tinted dreams, and the intoxicating drink of illusions, but its fruit is frustration, schizophrenia and deadly depression, or worse, such as with the novels of Agatha Christie which teach deception, crime and theft. I have checked the list of global masterpieces that won the Nobel prize and they are full of major mistakes and stupidities.[63]

Qarni goes on to shun alternate visions of womanhood and uphold the traditional family, conjuring up the kind of images of a magical world of wonders on prog-rock album covers from the 1970s. 'If winter closes the doors of your house and mountains of ice entrap you all around, then wait for spring to come and open your windows to the breath of pure air. Look afar and you will see the shimmer of birds who have returned to sing, and you will see the sun as its shines its golden rays above the tree fronds to create for you a new life, a new dream, a new heart', he writes.[64] Qarni builds up to his conclusion with an ecstatic crescendo:

> After reading this book, say goodbye to sadness, leave the world of pain, quit the home where there is depression, and move on like a nomad from the tents of despair and frustration. Come to the pulpit of faith, the *kaaba* of familiarity with God, the place of contentment in his judgement and fate, to begin a new life that is happy and new days that are beautiful; a life without hesitation, anxiety and confusion, and days without boredom, pessimism and irritation. When you do this, the call to faith will come, from atop

the mountain of hope, in the valley of contentment, to announce the good news: you are *the happiest woman in the world*.[65]

INDIGENOUS TRADITIONS

Wahhabi misogyny has left its mark on generations of Saudis, yet Saudi Arabia has the cultural and historical materials with which it can alter women's status if it wants to through its own traditions. Abdullah al-Ghaddami and Mai Yamani have documented at length the more liberal social customs of the Hejaz and which have been suppressed in stages during the region's journey as part of the Saudi realm.[66] Today women unveil in shopping malls and socialise in mixed-gender coffee shops and restaurants. A Jeddah businessman tried to establish a TV channel 'Uyoun Jeddah where unveiled Saudi actresses took the female roles (actresses in Saudi comedies and dramas are usually Bahraini or Kuwaiti). The status of women in south Yemen and the Dhofar region of south Oman demonstrates that Arabian conservatism is not an eternal reality or cultural specificity which subsequently acquired an Islamic stamp of approval, but a situation of its time, maintained and produced by political systems. Women played a role in political activity against the British in Aden, then formed their own trade union, joined the army and mobilised against forced wearing of the veil and in favour of women playing an active role in society outside the home. A law was enacted, modelled on Tunisia, to end polygamy and equalise divorce rights.[67] Serious measures were also taken in an attempt to end tribalism, unlike Saudi Arabia where the state periodically sheds crocodile tears over the strength of tribal identity, despite the central role given to certain tribes in the family-centred political system and the fetishisation of Bedouin traditions (namely the annual Janadiriyya festival). The six governorates set up in South Yemen broke up the old tribal lines that the British had maintained. Revenge among tribes was outlawed, *'urf*, or customary tribal law, was suppressed so that rural murder became a capital offence, and tribal associations were banned.[68]

In a study of coins and inscriptions on tombs and monuments of the Nabataean period, a tribal confederation that in its heyday from 100 BCE to 100 CE encompassed northwest Saudi Arabia, modern Jordan and southern Syria, Saudi scholar Hatoon al-Fassi argues that women had significantly more rights and a stronger social positions than they do in the modern state of Saudi Arabia. She argues that women were free to conduct legal contracts in their own name without the need for a male guardian. She notes that Nabataean queens had coins struck in their name and showing their face, with light hair-covering veils, while today Saudi clerics expound at length on television and in other forums on the complex rules over when women can and cannot reveal their faces, and surmises that women had acquired this independent status as a result of a change in trade patterns. Around 100 BCE the caravan trade from Yemen through Nabataean territory to Greece and Rome become more intensive, twice a year instead of once, and this resulted in the absence of men who were involved in this commerce. Women stepped into the breach. Fassi also argues – echoing a recent trend in recent Western scholarship of early Islamic history – that the rules and restrictions regarding women which appear in Islamic law have their origin in provincial versions of Greek and Roman law which were more restrictive than the customs of Nabataea.

In *Life As Politics*, sociologist Asef Bayat describes women in Iran taking back some of what the state has sought to deprive them of through a process he calls 'quiet encroachment of the ordinary' that has brought demonstrable improvements in the life of women in Iran. Women in Iran faced segregation, enforced dress codes and widespread surveillance after the revolution. But, Bayat writes, 'women resisted these policies, not much by deliberate organization campaigns, but largely through mundane daily practices in public domains, such as working, playing sports, studying, showing interest in art and music, or running for political offices'.[69] In the early 1990s, women and officialdom were engaged in a low-scale war over how to wear the veil, as many made their protest against the rules by deliberately leaving a small part of their hair at the front showing. Hundreds were arrested, but within a few years this fashion of wearing the veil had won acceptance among those who preferred it that way, even if conservatives viewed them as *bad-hijabi* ('wrong-veilers'). Women pushed their way into the workplace. By the mid 1990s, half of those employed in the government sector were women and more women than men were entering universities. I see little scope for success along these lines in the Saudi-Wahhabi state where gains are generally restricted to the affluent sectors of society. Iran's segregation and guardianship is not as draconian as Saudi Arabia's; it does not, critically, rise to the level of the law; women do not need men to represent them in matters of contracts: Iranian women succeeded in winning legislation that allowed single women over the age of 28 to study abroad without a guardian. Saudi women's gains are miniscule in comparison to Iran, where women are trying to reclaim ground that was once theirs. Jeddah, the natural candidate for producing an urban progressive movement, has been boxed in by various Saudi-Wahhabi stratagems and the Eastern Province Shi'ites are cut off from the comparatively liberal Shi'ite centre of Bahrain. The centre, the Riyadh region, is left to stew in its conservatism. The trope of substantive advance in women's status is part of the larger illusion of reform in the Saudi-Wahhabi state that the next chapter tries to address.

5
The Illusion of Reform

When politics professor Matruk al-Faleh was taken by Saudi state security forces in May 2008, his wife Jamila al-Ukla spent five days searching for him before finding out he was in prison. She checked hospitals and local police and called colleagues who worked in local human rights groups. When she tried to check his ransacked office on the campus of King Saud University a security guard removed her. Ukla eventually learned that state security forces had incarcerated her husband, a well-known political reform activist, in Riyadh's Uleisha prison. Within days of the eight-month ordeal, Faleh was moved to the high-security Haer prison, where most al-Qa'ida suspects and other political prisoners are thrown – his punishment for refusing to cooperate with interrogators. After some pleading, prison officials who felt pity agreed to take Ukla to see him there. 'I sat with him. We cried a lot. It was maybe 15 minutes', she said, speaking in their modest home on the campus of the university a week later. 'They had taken him there in blindfolds, handcuffed and chained, and they drove really fast to scare him. Why does he deserve to go to Haer? People have a mind to think and a dream to be better.'

Faleh is one of Saudi Arabia's more outspoken thinkers, one who remained in the country and resisted the temptation to campaign from the comfort of abroad. He was sentenced to seven years in jail in 2005 along with two others for organising a petition calling for Saudi leaders to set a timeframe for transforming the closed political system into a constitutional monarchy. King Abdullah pardoned them on accession to the throne later that year but the pattern of detention and harassment of democracy activists has continued unabated. Two days before his arrest Faleh had published a report detailing parlous conditions in the state security prison where Abdullah al-Hamed, an Islamist thinker convicted with Faleh in 2005, was being held at the time for encouraging the wives of al-Qa'ida suspects held without trial to stage public protests over their situation. Both Hamed and Faleh continued to campaign loudly over rights issues after the king let them out. Faleh tried to publicise the plight of hundreds of Saudis who are regularly banned by the interior ministry from travelling abroad because of political activities or opinions expressed in the media that the ministry does not like. In the Abdullah era, activists faced a revolving door of detention, release then re-detention, usually without any formal charges being laid (despite a six-month limit for detention without charge). Many liberals continued to believe that the king was unaware of who was being held or was incapable of challenging his half-brother Nayef for their release. 'When do you think Saudi Arabia will change?' Ukla asked. 'This is my country and I love it. How do you solve a problem if you are silent?'[1]

Saudi reform of the past decade is an illusion. The changes effected aim to keep the Saudi family and the Wahhabi clerics in power with essentially the same functions as they have had in the past. Opposition within the ruling family to Abdullah's reform process centres on the pace and extent of policy shifts which they see as unnecessary because, in their view, the degree of threat to the Saudi-Wahhabi system has been exaggerated, and the shifts could in themselves create new dangers. No one was talking about relieving them of their societal and ideological patrolling functions. The aim of the royal proponents of reform (*islah*) is to repackage Saudi Arabia and its Wahhabism as a beacon of moderation – promoting the term *al-wasatiyya*, or 'the middle way', as the key attribute of Saudi Islam – in order to neutralise threats to the Saudi state from the West. The Islamist violence against the state unleashed by al-Qa'ida in 2003 was a sharp wake-up call over the dangers of Wahhabi extremism. The clerics needs to be brought into line and knocked down a peg, but not to the degree that would provoke more Islamist dissent. (A diplomat put it this way: 'They [senior princes] were so frightened by what was in the justice system and education in 2003 and 2004 that they wanted to change it. They think if they don't succeed in justice reform they will not survive.') The government *ulama* and the Sahwa movement have learned the lesson of the Islamist challenge to Al Saud after the 1990–91 Gulf crisis – which ended up with many of them in jail. They made only minimal challenges to the state after 9/11 threw Al Saud into crisis, and focused their energies on the stronger threat that the liberal trend had come to represent. The champion of the reform camp took power in 2005 but his plans for a new social-economic order have been limited to what I call 'liberal enclaves', special zones such as the King Abdullah Economic City and the King Abdullah University of Science and Technology (KAUST), both essentially extensions of the liberal city of Jeddah. The *ulama* have largely acquiesced, consolidating the extensive areas of control they have over society rather than wasting their energies on attaining leverage in political decision-making, as some hoped to do in the 1990s. That losing game has been left to the some of the liberals who believed the royal rhetoric on a new era of change. These activists have suffered the continued wrath of the interior ministry with virtually no help from Abdullah, yet they still proclaim him their champion and view him as the country's saviour.

The battle between liberals and conservatives stretches back to the 1960s. King Faisal played off both camps. His Islamic foreign policy helped counter secular Arab nationalism and gave him leverage with conservatives and the *ulama* to introduce modernisations such as girls' education, and television and radio. He made no effort to stave off the progressive social trends of the 1950s and 1960s in Arab countries influenced by secular Arab nationalism. In the 1970s Saudi Arabia was a generally 'liberalising' society. Men and women began to mix in public spaces in some parts of Jeddah and some women began to shed their *abaya* in public. What is arresting about this development is that at the same time a regression in social freedoms began elsewhere in the Arab region because of the blow to secular Arab nationalism that the Arabs' defeat to Israel in 1967 represented. Egyptian preacher Sheikh Metwalli Sharawi famously knelt down in thanks to God for Nasser's defeat because he realised it signalled the end of a nationalist cultural paradigm that was regarded as atheistic by Islamists of various persuasions. Sharawi went on to become an immensely influential televangelist in the 1970s when Nasser's successor Anwar Sadat promoted religious groups as a bulwark to his Nasserist and socialist enemies. Saudi Arabia shared this sense of relief at the collapse of Nasserism. For Faisal, 1967 was a victory because a grave political threat to the Saudi realm for many years was in an instant removed; the agent of this removal, Israel, may have been distasteful to him, but the removal was all. The clerics shared Faisal's relief because their Islamic Utopia was safe, but they found that the cultural trend towards liberalisation was not halted. The modernisations continued and the sudden influx of oil wealth from 1974 onwards only accentuated the trend. It is striking that Saudi Arabia did not see a new social and political shift towards religion until after the events of 1979 – mosque siege, Iranian revolution and Soviet invasion of Afghanistan.

In *Hikayat al-Hadatha* (*The Issue of Modernity*), Abdullah al-Ghaddami describes the sudden changes he observed in society during his periodic returns from studying in London. Arriving in 1976, he recounts that he could not find a hotel to stay in Jeddah because prices were so high. He arrived in his hometown of Unaiza in the Najd to an airport full of businessmen in dark glasses and suitcases. 'No more did I heard people asking me about Britain and study, about thought and civilisation. Everyone talked about deals and deals, partnerships and speculation. People called each other "sheikh" and "businessman", and they had cars, cheques and bishts [cloaks worn by eminent personalities]. It was the *tafra* [great leap], mate!'[2]

Ghaddami identifies three stages of modernisation: one in the 1950s and 1960s when the administration in Riyadh was expanded and bureaucrats were hired from the Hejaz cities – strangers in a strange land, as he describes them; the second from 1975 to 1985 when the oil boom was at its height; and a third from 1985 onwards when intellectual trends in the West such as deconstruction and critical theory entered the kingdom, to huge controversy. The forces of conservatism were in the strongest position to resist in the 1980s after the decision taken by royal family after the events of 1979 to further empower the religious establishment. It gave the *ulama* the chance to have their way with a society far larger and more complex than that of the Najd when the Saudi-Wahhabi alliance was contracted over 200 years before. Decrees were issued in 1980 strengthening the powers of the religious and gender segregation was enforced throughout the country at all levels of political and social life. King Fahd decreed in 1983 that gender mixing was formally banned in public: 'Allowing women to mix with men is not possible, whether she is Saudi or not Saudi, since this is forbidden in Sharia law because of the evil, *fitna* and moral chaos it leads to.'[3] This pre-eminence of the conservative religious paradigm meant that as the country came into the era of law and legal codification from 1993 onwards, when the Basic Law came into effect, it was the conservative paradigm that was taken as the standard. When King Fahd took over in 1982, consolidating the power of the so-called 'Sudairy Seven' sons of Abdulaziz from the same mother, he promoted conservatives in the same way that Sadat had done in Egypt in 1970s, although he himself was far from religiously conservative or devout.

Even in Saudi Aramco's model town and headquarters in Dhahran, a relatively liberal enclave separated from the rest of society, the administration stopped hiring women for 15 years until 2000; women were stopped from teaching mathematics and English at Aramco training centres, and to this day women need permission to enter some buildings in Dhahran.[4] The Aramco trainee scheme where Saudi students are hired and trained abroad was restricted to men, and women only returned to the fold in 2007 (the benefits system discriminates against Western women too; all foreign women are hired with status as 'single' even if they are married, depriving them of paid flights home; foreign men are hired as 'married', giving them three flights home a year). The changes extended to schools. A supervisor (*muraqib*) was appointed by the Ministry of Education to each state school to check that pupils' behaviour accorded with the spirit of the times. They checked that prayer times were observed, how girls carried their bags or wore their *abayas*, and on whether the contents of bags would include magazines seen as spreading moral corruption. 'It was like a prison. Teachers behaved like imams in mosques, encouraging people to give money to Mujahideen in Afghanistan or praising those who fight there', says Wajiha Huweidar, a rights activist who lives in Dhahran. During the 1980s, some 45,000 Saudis received visas to go to Afghanistan to join the fight against the infidel Soviets, while the $20 billion cost of that war was split equally between Saudi Arabia and the United States.[5]

The conservatives were energised by the appearance of Ghaddami and 'modernisers' in the mid 1980s. Sahwa cleric Awadh al-Qarni accuses Ghaddami of 'begging at the tables of Western thinkers' and modernity which is 'materialistic, destructive, denying the afterlife, faith, the legacy of the prophets, religion as the reference point ..., springing from materialistic, Western philosophies'.[6] When Ghaddami published his book *Al-Khati'a wa-l-Takfir* (*Sin and Excommunication*), many conservative intellectuals, writers, journalists and clerics enjoined the battle against ideological threats from outside, and indeed the word *hadatha* ('modernity') was banned on state television (in the *ma'rakat al-hadatha*, 'the battle over modernity'). Islamists had found their new enemy and determined to battle them on university campuses, in literary clubs and in the media. Casette tapes were released condemning the modernisers and Qarni published his famous riposte *Al-Hadatha fi Mizan al-Islam* (*Islam's Judgement on Modernity*). In the wake of Ghaddami's work, writers such as Ghazi al-Gosaibi, Turki al-Hamad and Abdo Khal began publishing novels in the 1990s, bringing new names and faces to the battle in what was a developing genre for Saudi Arabia.

This battle between liberals and conservatives was interrupted by the 1990–91 Gulf crisis. It was a turning point not only for the government's decision to allow American troops into the country from where they would organise the effort to expel the Iraqis from Kuwait and restore the former British protectorate to its ruling family, but also for the backing that the religious establishment, fronted by Bin Baz, gave the authorities for this controversial move. The crisis dented the prestige not only of the ruling family but of their clerical allies too. Bin Baz gave a free pass to the Americans, in the face of major principles of al-Wahhabiyya that he championed. The foreigners in his fatwas were no longer 'infidels' (*kuffar*), but simply 'non-Muslims' (*ghayr muslimeen*). Bin Baz's fatwa, issued the same month as the invasion of 1990, first explained at length the criminal nature of the Iraqi invasion, exhorting the Iraqi leader Saddam Hussein to withdraw his forces and calling for a peaceful resolution. This was a preamble to the final section which justified Saudi Arabia's decision to rely upon foreign, American-led forces to repel the Iraqis. 'As for the Saudi government seeking the help of a group of armies of different nationalities, Muslim and non-Muslim, to repel the aggression and defend the country, this is permitted, in fact necessity makes it inevitable and demands it and the kingdom must undertake this duty', Bin Baz said. 'Defending Islam, Muslims and the sanctity of the country and its people [Saudi Arabia] is necessary and inevitable, so it [government] is excused over this and thanked for this mobilisation and desire to protect the country and its people from evil and defend it against an expected aggression the head of the state of Iraq may launch.'[7]

The invitation to American troops led to an era of protest in Saudi Arabia centred around demands for a range of reforms including popular representation, formulated for the first time in 30 years (though persecution of Arab nationalists and leftists continued throughout). This daring landed the leaders, a group of politicised clerics led by Safar al-Hawali and Salman al-Odah, in jail. From Afghanistan, the force of Islamist rebels who Saudi Arabia had built up throughout the 1980s made their opinion known too. Osama bin Laden exhorted the Saudi rulers to oust the American forces, offered to lead a force fighting the Iraqis himself, and backed the subsequent demands for reform. After moving to Sudan in 1994 he organised his own attacks against the American troops, who had never left Saudi Arabia, in Riyadh and Khobar in 1995 and 1996. With the 9/11 attacks in 2001, however, Saudi Arabia's rulers were under pressure to do something about al-Wahhabiyya itself.

Surat al-Baqara (the Quran's second chapter) contains a verse with the phrase *umma wasat*, usually taken to mean a community is that balanced, or follows the middle way or path; that is, does not go to extremes. The derived abstract noun *al-wasatiyya* suggests 'centrism' or 'the middle way'. In the 1960s, Egypt's Ministry of Religious Endowments published *Wasatiyyat al-Islam* (*Islam's Middle Way*), a response to the Muslim Brotherhood's challenge to Nasser. Yousef al-Qaradawi, a cleric associated with the Brotherhood, picked up on the concept in his 1971 book *Hatmiyyat al-Hall al-Islami* (*The Inevitability of the Islamic Solution*) and he has often discussed it in his weekly show on Al-Jazeera television, *Al-Sharia wa-l-Hayat* (*Sharia and Life*). In 1998 another secular regime in opposition to Islamists employed the term. King Hussein of Jordan used the word to counter domestic opponents and literalist interpretations of the Quran and Sunna. After the 9/11 attacks, the phrase took off in Saudi media. It was one of the main topics of a summit meeting of the Organisation of the Islamic Conference in Mecca in 2005 that discussed challenges confronting the Muslim world, and the word appears four times in the summit's final communiqué.[8] Under Abdullah, Wahhabism presented itself as the 'middle way' between the zealotry of al-Qa'ida and others who turn to violence to realise God's design, on the one hand, and liberals who seek to water down the role of the cleric, on the other.

DOMESTIC REPRESSION IN THE ERA OF *WASATIYYA*

It has often been said that the Saudi government crushed Juhaiman's revolt in 1979 only to proceed to implement Juhaiman's agenda in the subsequent years, and that was the promise the *ulama* extracted from the Saudis to sanction their military action against him. After 9/11, the tide turned and liberals in government gained the upper hand. Their hope, Abdullah, became king. But what does the reform agenda mean, how meaningful are the reforms touted in Saudi and Western media and government circles?

After 9/11, Abdullah as crown prince and his allies in government and the royal court began efforts to place some limits on Wahhabi influence in some areas of state policy, a turf war of sorts, while Saudi liberals began to speak up more forcefully in their demands for political and social reforms. If, after 2001 the reform drive was based on improving the family's standing with its Western friends for fear of ideas of replacing Al Saud, after 2003, the year al-Qa'ida launched its operations against the Saudi regime, it was driven by fear that Wahhabism – a threat far closer to home – could succeed in supplanting Al Saud. 'The state is proceeding, with the help of God, in its gradual and studied course of reform and will not allow anyone to stand in the face of reform', Abdullah said in a televised speech to Saudis in 2004. 'We will not allow anyone to stand in the way of reform whether through calls for immobility and stagnation or calls to leap into darkness and reckless adventure.' In that speech he went on to warn against the 'provocative' and 'extremist' positions on either side, backing *'wasatiyya* that does not go too far and moderation that does not waver' – a warning to Islamists and the Saudi liberals that both should limit their demands.[9] The government responded to demands to alter school textbooks, girls' education was moved to the education ministry then placed in the hands of a female deputy minister, and the press acquired a new boldness in debating these social issues. Between 2003 and 2006, 1,300 of 70,000 Friday prayer leaders were sacked, though some later returned to work.[10] Reflecting the wider conflict in society, Abdullah set up the Abdulaziz Centre for National Dialogue in 2003 in an effort to promote a new era of openness and reform, but interior minister Prince Nayef was just as keen to cooperate with the clerics to challenge liberal excess in the media. In 2004, the government announced it would hold elections for half of the members of municipal councils, a step in the direction of the democratic path the country was on in 1960 but which King Faisal snuffed out. These elections, packaged as *al-musharaka fil-hukm*, or 'participation in governance', took place in 2005 under American pressure to match democratic developments in Iraq but they were as far as the ruling family was prepared to go in democratic reform: elections scheduled for 2009 were shelved indefinitely but revived in 2011 after the authorities succeeded in preventing the regional pro-democracy protest movements spreading to Saudi Arabia.

Some 40 per cent of the material in state education concerned religion through courses on *tawhid* ('unitarianism', the central tenet of Wahhabism) and Islamic jurisprudence, as well as history, geography and Arabic language. The theme running through the religious material is that Saudi Arabia is the only land where God's moral order is established on earth; all others, Muslim or otherwise, are deviants to one degree or another. Theology texts used by 13- and 14-year-olds enjoin Muslims not to befriend Christians and Jews because 'emulation of the infidels' could leads to liking them. 'It is the duty of a Muslim to be loyal to the believers (Muslims) and be the enemy of the infidels. One of the duties of affirming the oneness of God is to have nothing to do with his idolatrous and polytheist enemies', textbooks stated.[11] 'Muslims should not imitate the infidels in music and art or frequenting theatres and cinemas. All these are frequented by the wayward and those who have strayed from earnest life.' This language was still in use in 2006, and the government said it would take years to overhaul the education system in the face of opposition from clerics who remain entrenched in the education ministries.[12] Educationalist Hassan al-Maliki was sacked from the ministry in 2002 over a study he prepared on Wahhabi zealotry in the school curriculum. 'Throughout school you hear Mohammed ibn Abdulwahhab's name more than the Prophet's', he says. 'I was prevented from travelling and writing the papers. They took some ideas and ignored rest: they took the part that says you have to look for mitigating circumstances before deciding someone is a *kafir*. But now they use coded phrases for *takfir*, like "innovator" [*muhdith*].' Reforms of Friday sermons, monitored by the Islamic affairs ministry and the interior ministry, have been no more effective, he says: 'Friday sermons attack media, secularists, curriculum reformers, other Muslims. There is no seriousness in the Islamic Affairs Ministry in moderating imams, as long as they don't attack the king.'[13]

In many ways, it was not that Saudis were taught to hate, it was that in state schools they were not seriously educated at all. While education produces Saudis lacking in basic English skills and steeped in religion, images of cosmopolitanism are sold to the uneducated masses through the liberalised economy of recent years. Mobile phone operator Mobily began running ads in October 2008 in which the CEO announces to a press conference that all international calls would be free to certain Arab countries. A Frenchman in the audience asks in French if this can be extended to the whole world, to which the CEO responds in French that yes, it would be apply to France, Switzerland and other European countries, and the crowd erupts in applause. Saudis are being sold Mobily as the choice of the 'average sophisticate' who understands the world, while in reality the outdated education system is producing nothing of the sort among the great majority of Saudis. Saudis are neither expected nor encouraged to play a productive part in the national economy because of the import of millions of blue-collar foreign workers in a no-tax-for-no-representation state. In Saudi Arabia this ignorance and indolence – which must be seen as a product of state policy – backfired when young Saudis found themselves vulnerable to the activist politicisation of radical Islam. Saudis also enjoyed free health care, cheap petrol and electricity, housing and social insurance benefits, though many in impoverished areas remain at the level of the blue-collar workers. Estimates in 2008 put the number of Saudis who earn less than 7,000 riyals a month at 80 per cent of population. The average government employee – where the brunt of the Saudi labour force is and wants to be – earned 5,000–6,000 riyals a month, with an entry level of 2,500–3,000 riyals a month. Numbering around 1 million, government employees enjoy generous amounts of holiday leave, flexible working hours that allow work on the side, and access to housing and other bank loans. Partly-privatised industrial giants Aramco and SABIC offer higher wages to the cream of Saudi high-school achievers.

The interior ministry came down hard on supporters of democratic reform. In 2003 some of the Islamist reformers associated with the Sahwa movement joined with liberal reformers to present petitions to Abdullah as crown prince for constitutional reforms, political participation, fair distribution of wealth and judicial independence. Groups of reformers, including Shi'ite activists and campaigners for women's rights, submitted further petitions that year. Three reformers involved in the petitions – from leftist (Ali al-Dumaini), nationalist (Matruk al-Faleh) and Islamist (Abdullah al-Hamed) backgrounds – were among a group of 13 arrested in March 2004, but then tried and convicted in May 2005 for promoting democratic reforms and talking to the foreign media about it. Their petition for a 'constitutional monarchy' also contained a demand for a timetable for democratic changes. 'The new thing on the previous petition was the timetable. We said the people are expecting a timetable instead of vague talk and the petition included important ideas like separation of powers, protecting public revenue, protecting public land and equal opportunity', says Mohamed Said Tayeb, one of the original group of 13 detainees who was later released.[14] Tayeb had a terse exchange with Nayef in March 2004 in which the minister complained about meetings reformers had with foreign diplomats. He was also upset that Tayeb had named a son of his after Egyptian leader Nasser. Nayef accused the reformers of seeking to turn the Saudi king into a meaningless figurehead like Britain's Queen Elizabeth (similar complaints were made by Bahrain when it charged 23 democracy campaigners of planning a 'coup' in 2010). 'Reform Wahhabism' is wishful thinking, says Tayeb – a man who was among those jailed by Faisal in 1969 when he was seeking to consolidate his survival of Nasserism and defeat of Saudi opposition movements. 'I was in a room alone from the first to the last day. It was long and very hard', he says.

With King Abdullah's formal assumption of power, the interior ministry adopted a different strategy towards cracking down on reformers. It began to tar activists as sympathisers of Islamist militants, threats to public order, or simply to say nothing at all to justify their arrest, avoiding direct mention of reform activities, which would only attract the attention of international media and Western governments. In February 2007, ten men were arrested in Jeddah for allegedly collecting donations to 'finance' terrorism because they were involved in raising money for Iraqi Sunnis. One of them, Saud Mukhtar al-Hashemi, had planned to set up a political movement called the Rally for Reform (*tajammu' min ajl al-islah*) and publicised another petition to the king for parliamentary democracy, termed the Islamic Constitution petition, which played more plainly to the themes of political Islam.[15] Hashemi was a public figure who held a popular weekly salon at his Jeddah home. Under the auspices of the Saudi Red Crescent he raised money for Hamas and Iraqi Sunnis and hosted Hamas figures on an official visit to the kingdom in 2006 at salons attended by interior ministry officials. In 2010 the authorities quietly issued an indictment against the men, plus six others, for supporting terrorism and attempting to overthrow the government, and began trying them in an interior ministry villa in north Jeddah in 2011, an improvised special court under the ministry's jurisdiction. The case was kept entirely out of Saudi media until July 2011 when *Asharq al-Awsat* ran a story declaring to the public the 'trial of a "secret organisation" that tried to take power in coordination with al-Qa'ida' – rather more than the initial publicity tar which implied they had funded al-Qa'ida types in Iraq (many potentially did, the American attack on Falluja in 2004 fired public imagination, and clerics including Salman al-Odah issued public statements of support for the Sunnis).[16] An internet blogger, Fouad Farhan, was detained for three months in 2007 after he ran an online campaign over the detentions, saying the charges could not be taken seriously.

The case is interesting because it also appears to have its origin in Prince Nayef taking offence at independent-minded Saudis in favour of parliamentary democracy (with or without parties who can form governments). Some months before the arrests, they were summoned to a meeting with Nayef in which he warned them to stop their campaigning for political reforms. The meeting ended on a sour note because they argued back, according to an associate of the group who was there. 'Some of them were opinionated and spoke back to him as if he was normal person and not a prince, they did not give him what he thought should be given in terms of due respect and follow the normal protocol on how to speak to royalty. They said "you do what you want, we are fed up going to jail but one more time in jail won't make a difference to us"', he said of the conversation.[17]

In November 2007 Abdullah al-Hamed was jailed again for six months for encouraging women to stage protests in Buraida over the indefinite detention of their husbands on suspicion of being linked to al-Qa'ida. Around 3,000 were arrested from 2003 to 2007, but nearly 1,500 were released through a 're-education' or 'correction' (*munasaha*) programme that received considerable media attention. The women claimed their men were tortured by prison authorities because they refused to be inducted in the correction programme, which won the kingdom praise from Western governments and much positive coverage in Western media.[18] The programme stirred up much debate after it transpired that some who had been inducted in the programme, as well as some Saudis whom the United States returned to Saudi Arabia from Guantanamo Bay, had moved to Yemen where they helped al-Qa'ida regroup as al-Qa'ida in the Arabian Peninsula. However, the soft treatment for those who had been 'corrected' on the programme and returned from Guantanamo – financial help with housing, education and marriage – simply reflected the elevated status of Wahhabism in the kingdom and the fact that the jihadist strands within Wahhabism had fallen out of favour with the state. 'Correcting' individuals also maintained the fiction that there is no 'correcting' required of the Saudi political system itself and of Al Saud's position in it.

US pressure withered after some public criticisms in 2004 and 2005, when the administration of President George W. Bush was stridently promoting a democracy agenda in the Arab countries. By contrast, just before he left office in 2009, Bush performed a Bedouin sword dance with Saudi princes in front of TV cameras. He said nothing about the fate of political reform. Saudi princes blithely lectured American diplomats on the ill-effects of democracy. Elections had only encouraged tribalism despite a large Saudi aid programme to Yemen, Saud al-Faisal shamelessly told US ambassador James Smith in October 2009, despite the fact that Riyadh funds the tribes through direct payments; Faisal also cited the arrest of the Jeddah reformers as a sign of progress in Saudi efforts to combat terrorism in February 2007.[19] Some activists refused to lie down. Hamed organised the 2007 reform petition and issued a separate statement calling for Prince Nayef to face trial for the police state with increasingly bloated and intrusive security apparatus he had created – Hamed's stance on this is a noteworthy milestone in the evolution of Saudi Arabia from retro-Islamic state to modern police state. I met him once during a visit to a hospital in Riyadh in 2007 where rights activist Ibrahim al-Mugaiteeb was convalescing. 'There is no country in the world that knows the repression that Saudi Arabia now knows', he said. 'There are two elements to Islam, there is the ritual element that requires doing prayer and the civil element that requires justice and freedom. There is neither justice nor freedom so it's not an Islamic state.' This is the kind of argument the Sahwa movement made in the 1990s: Hamed was one of the founders of the group that set up the Committee for the Defence of Legitimate Rights (CDLR) in 1994 with Fagih and Mas'ari. He said the only democracy activists left standing were those prepared to go to prison and that the call for democracy within an Islamic context was frightening the authorities. 'Right now in the Al Saud salons they are saying this is a call for a Khomeini state', he said; that is, a project to further empower the clerics.

Another attempt to create a political party was made in February 2011 by another figure who was involved in the CDLR and Sahwa activity of the early 1990s, Abdulaziz al-Wohaiby. Eight members were arrested for calling for protests in February when they announced the formation of their Umma party. All but Wohaiby were released within days, with most of them denying any involvement or promising to quit. Generally speaking, the Umma party people got off lightly compared to the treatment of the Jeddah reformers. Hashemi, Suleiman al-Rushoudi and the others in the Jeddah group have more prestige in the small circle of the opposition intelligentsia than Wohaiby and his followers. They are familiar figures in Jeddah society, indeed in Saudi Arabia generally through Hashemi's work with the Saudi Red Crescent. Hashemi had the credentials to make of himself a credible civilian politician, something Saudi Arabia has not had since the era of King Saud. They were alarming enough to warrant a meeting with Prince Nayef in 2006 in which he lost his temper. Wohaiby is less of a threat. Saudi rights activist Mohammed al-Qahtani was of the view that the government might even have let Wohaiby get away with his announcement of setting up a party if he had not also called for street mobilisations. 'They made tactical mistakes and could have avoided detention altogether. If you understand the psyche of this regime, you can do things', he said. 'The guys in Jeddah are far more important in terms of their status in society.'[20]

These are just some of the more well-known cases, but there are thousands of others who have disappeared into detention without charge and beyond the remit of what laws there are governing security offences, political crimes and detention: the independent Saudi Civil and Political Rights Association, set up in 2009 by a group of rights and opposition activists from different political trends including Abdullah al-Hamed, estimated that a staggering 30,000 people were being held over security issues in 2011 (a figure the government rejected). The arrests and imprisonment are handled largely by the state security investigations department, the equivalent of the hated state security investigations body in Egypt whose premises around the country were ransacked after Mubarak left office in February 2011. Saudi apologists like to depict a state of repression-lite – the Saudi way is allegedly softer and involves subtle persuasion through short spells in prison where there is usually little mistreatment. Mamoun Fandy goes further, writing in *The Politics of Dissent* that the Saudi authorities never committed an act of mass violence like the regime of Hafez al-Assad did to crush Muslim Brotherhood opponents in Hama in 1982. The statement suggests that Syrian – and why not Israeli or Iraqi, for that matter? – mass violence is the red line in repressive behaviour. Egypt and Tunisia were brutal police states without resorting to the more eye-catching actions of their regional peers. Saudi authorities have not flinched from resorting to draconian measures when they saw fit, however. Britain was allowed to bomb recalcitrant Bedouin from the air in 1930. Indiscriminate violence and murder was committed by Abdulaziz's Ikhwan army in its conquest of the Hejaz. Violence was used to break up the labour movement in the Eastern Province oil zones in the 1950s. In 1987, Saudi police opened fire on Iranian pilgrims in Mecca for the hajj who tried anti-American protests; in the ensuing melee 402 people died. Saudi Arabia worked with Bahrain to apply mass violence against the protest movement during some two months of martial law in 2011.

The state through an extensive interconnected network of security apparatus, media monitoring and Wahhabi thought control in fact practices rigorous repression. Zaki Badr, the Egyptian interior minister, under whose watch the use of torture rose markedly in Egypt during the 1980s, became an advisor to Saudi security forces in the 1990s. Before the uprisings, Arab interior ministers met yearly to coordinate on policy: Nayef was the doyen of Arab security chiefs. Many of those arrested during the period of ferment after the 1991 Gulf war reported torture. Mohammed al-Mas'ari, who fled to Yemen then London after six months of detention over the CDLR in 1993, recounted his ordeal in Western media and in an Arabic book he published once abroad (he was whipped on the back and the soles of his feet, punched, spat upon and deprived of sleep in a fully-lit cell monitored by cameras 24 hours a day). Rights activist Ibrahim al-Mugaiteeb was of the view in 2009 that deputy interior minister Mohammed bin Nayef should be credited for banning the systematic use of torture since around 2003/04. Nayef's son repeated the same to US diplomats in 2008.[21] Certainly there have been no reports of the more well-known political prisoners of the years since 2001 suffering the kind of violence in detention that Bahraini doctors, opposition leaders and rights activists suffered in Bahrain after martial law was introduced to stop the protest movement of February and March 2011. Many people hauled in on minor offences are held for a few days or a week and then released if they sign a pledge not to reoffend: the blogger Fouad Farhan or Mohsen al-Awajy, for instance. The rights of the Jeddah activists, however, were still abused: they were held in solitary confinement without medical attention without charge for four years. The families of men arrested on suspicion of links to al-Qa'ida and who refused to join the 'correction' programmes say they were beaten, and one attempt to stage a protest at the interior ministry headquarters in Riyadh in March 2011 was in fact a call for the release of relatives held for years without charge. In 2007, prison guards in the Haer prison where political and security detainees are often held were caught on mobile -phone video whipping two teenagers with what looked like plastic tubes.

Anyone who does not conform to Wahhabi orthodoxy on correct behaviour is liable to face abuse, be they Shi'ites in the Eastern Province, Ismaili Shi'ites in Najran in the far south, or non-Muslim foreigners. Nine foreigners were arrested in 2000 on suspicion of the murder of one Briton and the attempted murder of three others in bomb attacks linked to turf wars over alcohol sales and smuggling. Some were forced to confess to the murders on television as well as to working as intelligence agents, for which they were sentenced to death; they were granted royal pardons in 2003 and some have published accounts of how they were tortured over two years to force confessions and just for fun (such as mock beheadings). An American among them was released early on through the efforts of the US embassy. Briton Sandy Mitchell has said he still suffers trauma from the experience.[22] Had they been Asian it is not likely they would survived, whether they were guilty or not. Sheikh Ahmed Turki al-Saab, a tribal leader among the Ismaili Shi'ite community in Najran on the Yemeni border, was tortured for months after clashes between Ismailis and police in 2000. 'The fatwas make the state security police officers hate you', he told me in 2006. He said he was beaten and electrocuted by officers he regularly saw around town: 'They said "Don't you hate the Saudi state?"' Shaheed, the son of a Shi'ite cleric, told me about the deep sense of being a second-class citizen when I visited Qatif in the Eastern Province in April 2003. 'You wouldn't believe the things they say about us. It's in the school textbooks that we are infidels and heretics, and we have to sit there and listen to this at school', he said. 'The police treat us like we're subhuman. They're not that bad with other Saudis, but with us they think we're like animals.' Yet Mansour Nogaidan, the former Najdi Wahhabi zealot who embraced secularism, said he had never faced maltreatment during his former life. 'If I forget my identity card I don't fear being stopped at a road checkpoint, for example. I've been arrested five times by state security but I was never dealt with badly or humiliated. There are some who are tortured, but it's a minority', he told me in 2003, shortly before quitting the country to settle in the UAE.

A 2011 complaint to the interior ministry by the Civil and Political Rights Association listed numerous cases of arbitrary torture and cruelty carried out with impunity by state security officers, and said that repression without impunity from security officers had got worse. In the Association's view:

> The practices of the Directorate of General Investigation [DGI] under your administration match that of the vicious Savak system that operated under the late Shah of Iran's government. It is too similar to the 'state security' department under the toppled dictator Mohammad Hosni Mubarak of Egypt. DGI's conduct is no difference than that of the 'investigation department' of the eloped Tunisian tyrant Zine al-Abidine Ben Ali, and to the various 'security apparatus' which oppress people in different Arab countries.[23]

The report focused specifically on the state security apparatus, which became an increasingly obtrusive force over the past decade. It mentioned cases of individuals arrested for promoting political and human rights issues in the era of the uprisings, though since there were hundreds of Saudis talking freely about such issues on blogs and to the foreign media it was not clear why particular individuals were singled out for harassment. It mentions one Association member whose son was taken at gunpoint from his car, beaten and held in solitary confinement: he lost the hearing in one ear from the beatings. Some people languish in prison without charge as if the state had just forgotten about them. The report cites many cases of denial of medical care. Regarding torture, it says:

> DGI agents torture detainees mentally and physically to extract confessions by force. Among the methods used, according to the testimonies of the prisoners and their families, are the deprivation of sleep for days, hanging the defendant in an upright standing positions for days, long solitary confinement until the prisoner breaks down and hallucinate, threats of sexual assaults, and luring the young prisoners by false promises to confess to crimes they didn't commit. Such cruel practices are examples of the systematic crimes committed by DGI against citizens and legal residents, too many to list in this letter.[24]

The suffering of foreigners on low incomes – mainly Asians and Africans – and visa overstayers looking for work goes almost entirely undocumented. In *Fusouq*, Abdo Khal depicts a society where there is no rule of law in the modern sense and where officers of law enforcement act with impunity. His hapless police officer, vexed by the disappearance of a girl from her grave, muses on what his job has taught him about society: 'The country is naked in the police station; the ideal society disappears under the filth that pours from every corner. Filth that horrifies you from the many appalling crimes: adultery, sodomy, molestation, rape, theft, drugs, disputes, murder, absconding fathers, fleeing girls, treachery, financial cases, fraud, deception, great and small complaints, streams of filth risen to the surface of the earth with too few channels to run it off.'[25]

For the government, political reform has been a game of deflecting attention and diverting minds. When world oil prices began to rise in 2002, the state launched a project to encourage mass participation in the stock market, a means of distributing wealth that gave people a sense of having a piece of the pie but a poor excuse for real wealth redistribution. The authorities had the sanction of the *ulama* for the project, though the hysteria surrounding stock investment soon became discomfiting since it smacked blatantly of gambling. By early 2006, 9 million people, or half of the Saudi population, were shareowners after a string of initial public offerings in companies that remained government-controlled. When the inevitable bourse crash hit that year after sophisticated speculators drove up prices, millions of Saudis were affected. The idea, attributed to Abdullah, had been to make sure that much of the oil wealth was kept in Saudi Arabia, unlike the 1970s when much was placed in foreign banks and spent abroad. Saudis were so desperate to get a piece of the action that teachers were absconding from classes to play the bourse and Saudis fought in bank queues to enlist in some IPOs (initial public offerings). The contrast between the wealth of the ruling elite and unprecedentedly huge budgets afforded by oil receipts, on the one hand, and the suffering of ordinary Saudis, on the other, was striking. Abdullah was valued by *Forbes* magazine that year at $21 billion. Shortly after publication of the *Forbes* story, the king announced plans for cheap housing, a fund for poor low-wage-earners and lower fuel prices. Abdullah had made a conscious effort to style himself the caring king and a man of the poor. As crown prince he brought the issue of poverty into public debate with a visit to a poor district of Riyadh in 2002.

I visited the area myself in March 2003. Though it was mainly mudbrick and stone buildings, they were often prettily decorated and obviously were part of a previous urban tradition, before air-conditioning and breeze-block apartments. Modern Riyadh has essentially expanded around this ancient village. The dusty streets with garbage, the graffiti and plethora of expensive cars, all reminded me of poor districts you seen in Cairo. Here the difference was relative: others were living in the lap of luxury. The point my information ministry minder Mohammed made was that these people were the unlucky ones, the rural migrants who hit the city after the 1970s oil bonanza. Most of them came from Jizan and Asir, the poor mountainous regions south of the Hejaz and bordering Yemen which the authorities had largely forgotten about (and where a number of the 9/11 hijackers came from). Part of the government's sudden interest in the poor was that they could provide more foot soldiers for militant Islam in the kingdom – sociologist Asef Bayat has argued that Islamist movements have traditionally been more interested in the educated middle classes and shown a certain indifference to the poor.[26] 'Eighty years ago my grandfather came from Taif in the west to live in this Riyadh neighbourhood', Mohammed said. 'During the *tafra* in the 1970s the state gave him a house in a new neighbourhood. These people came afterwards.' We stopped a few people to talk to them. They said local charities provide food and clothes and sometimes pay rent for the residents. A shop assistant called Ibrahim said he had had to leave school to support his family of 14 so he was unlikely to find a government job. 'We see all the money they have while we have nothing here', he said. It was down this road we were standing on that Abdullah had walked almost a year before. 'It was strange. He came down this street and asked about us. For 15 years I saw no development here. To be honest I haven't noticed any difference since he came', Ibrahim said.

LIBERAL ENCLAVES

The unresolved debate between conservatives and liberals continues under Abdullah and continues to produce unusual outcomes. Within the first months of Abdullah's term as king, the Saudi government pursued a number of policies to improve the kingdom's economic profile. Saudi Arabia became a member of the WTO and the limits were raised on foreign stakes in sectors such as banking, telecommunications services, wholesale, retail, and franchising. These reforms were intended to answer the economic priorities of diversifying from dependence on oil revenues, finding jobs for young Saudis and opening up foreign investment. But they had another function too, one that was more transparent in a centrepiece of the early period of Abdullah's reign: the establishment of 'economic cities' where, freed from the influence of the Wahhabi clerics, Saudis would live, work and study as productive members of a modern economy.

The lead project was the King Abdullah Economic City, which was announced in December 2005. Three more are planned for Jizan, Hail and Medina. The King Abdullah Economic City has been sold in publicity material as a hypermodern, eco-friendly melange of port and industrial zone, financial centre, residential quarters, luxury resort, and schools and colleges – a Dubai on the Red Sea coast. Officials let it be known in foreign media that women would be allowed to drive cars, schools and universities would be co-educational, the gender restrictions in public places would be relaxed, and Prince Alwaleed bin Talal's entertainment firm Rotana would operate cinema houses. Housing 2 million people by its completion around 2020, the city is to be a model of urban renewal and modern education, as well as a zone where the strict rules of the Utopia were put in abeyance. Though no one said so publicly, the city was intended to be a liberal enclave in Saudi Arabia's sea of religious conservatism. As such, the project encapsulated the hopes of socio-economic reform that the Saudi liberal class invested in King Abdullah when the long, dark night of King Fahd's reign finally came to an end. 'Saudi Arabia today doesn't offer the kind of services that are required. There is a lack of infrastructure and basic urban aesthetic beauty is also missing', says Fahd Al-Rasheed, chief executive of Emaar Economic City, a subsidiary of Dubai's Emaar and the City's developer. 'We have 60 per cent of our population [aged] under 30 and these people need places to live. So we are going to create the educational opportunities of them to come, study and work ... We looked at so many cities. There was Brasilia and Canberra but these were planned by governments and there was no economic plan. Ours was developed based on economics – what are the industries and services we can bring – and then do a masterplan based on that.'[27] In 2005, Emaar Economic City proclaimed 'the dawn of a kingdom in a new colour'.[28] Before it really got off the ground, the project ran into bureaucratic and financial troubles.

The Saudi-Wahhabi state contains other liberal zones where Wahhabi social control is relaxed. They include parts of Jeddah where some restaurants play music and allow unrelated men and women to sit together, on the assumption that the religious police will not drop by. Jeddah's summer festival included a cinema section in 2006, 2007 and 2008, and concerts have featured rappers, reflecting the more liberal social attitudes of the Hejaz region compared to the Najd. The religious police generally avoid the diplomatic district in Riyadh and the town of Dhahran on the Gulf coast that houses state oil firm Aramco. They maintain a light presence in neighbouring Khobar, but a strong presence in the more conservative Dammam in the same Eastern Province vicinity.

In 2009 the King Abdullah University of Science and Technology (KAUST) was inaugurated at a lavish ceremony north of Jeddah next to the economic city, the latest addition to the small set of liberal enclaves. KAUST has been fêted in Western media as one of the final gambles of an octogenarian monarch in his twilight years to outflank the repressive clerics: in fact it confirms that the king and the liberals are incapable of reforming public space, hence the resort to extraterritorial zones ('this might just be the last chance the king gets to institutionalize his progressive legacy and improve the future of his troubled land', *Newsweek* wrote[29]). KAUST breaks with tradition on many fronts. It is run by Saudi Aramco, widely seen as the country's most efficient and modern corporate institution, whereas the King Abdullah Economic City, which the king placed in the care of the then investment authority chairman Amr al-Dabbagh, has been hampered by obstruction from businessmen and other government departments.[30] It has a foreigner, from Singapore, as its president, as well as faculty hired from around the world at immense expense. It has a huge $10 billion endowment said to be from the king's own pocket. Its curricula are designed by Western consultants rather than the education ministry where, despite the hype, Wahhabism reigns.

Domestic media has never presented the economic city concept in the way it was described to foreigners. When I used the phrase 'liberal enclave' in a story in 2008, there was a visceral reaction from conservatives who, it seemed to me, were provoked by the presentation of KAUST's place in the struggle between reformers and *ulama* in such stark terms. Sabq.net, a news website close the interior ministry, ran several stories attacking me personally over my story.[31] The launch of KAUST was met with a vocal challenge by some clerics to the idea of a desegregated zone, a double threat in that involved the area of education, a traditional preserve of the clerics. One member of the Council of Senior Religious Scholars was sacked by Abdullah over his criticisms. His removal mirrored an incident in 1985 when Sheikh Abdullah al-Qa'ud was removed by King Fahd after he publicly criticised state television for broadcasting music and singing, but it was a bit late in the game for Abdullah to begin stamping his authority in such a manner when for several years most of his reform ideas, as one ambassador put it, 'disappear into a black hole'. The power of Prince Nayef's interior ministry was such that it operates almost as an entire state within the state. It has over 700,000 employees in its various arms, almost as much as the rest of the government bureaucracy, and most governors around the country are answering to the ministry rather than to the king. Deputy minister Mohammed bin Nayef, as head of domestic security, is one of the lowest-level government officials from any country in the world to be granted an audience with President Barack Obama on trips to Washington. When US officials come to Riyadh it is him they want to see. Abdullah is nominal leader of the liberal trend but with little ability to control events. When pressured on the issue of the king's reform proclivities, a Sahwa figure said to me dismissively: 'The king is out of the arena, simply he is out of the arena.'[32]

The religious establishment has not stopped challenging the social liberalisations of the king. For every step forward, there is a step back that makes the elucidation of a 'trend' hard to prove. Mecca governor Khaled al-Faisal ensured that a full-length comedy film made by Prince Alwaleed bin Talal's Rotana company was shown to the public at culture centres in Taif and Jeddah in December 2008. The religious police were obliged to back down and remove their initial objections, and the head of the body, Ibrahim al-Ghaith, was removed by the king a few months later. But the Jeddah film festival, which had run for three consecutive years, was stopped by the interior ministry in the summer of 2009. 'The king goes to parliament to talk about the need for women to participate but when it goes down to lower levels there is resistance', said Abdullah al-Alami, an educationalist from Khobar.[33] He cited continued insistence on gender segregation in the workplace, schools and universities, consolidating their control in return for the concession of the liberal zones. 'I am really concerned that these people have become stronger than we think they are and it will be virtually impossible to change the situation', he said.

JUDICIAL REFORM

The fate of two policy initiatives in the era of King Abdullah illustrate well the reticence of the clerics over the king's reforms and their ability to stymie policy: justice system reform and his initiative for 'interfaith dialogue'. Control of the justice system lies at the very heart of the idea of definition of Saudi Arabia as an Islamic state. There have been some attempts to meddle with the extent of clerical prerogatives there before; Abdullah began a new chapter in the tussle in 2007. He issued a royal decree in October of that year announcing plans to reorganise the court system, establishing an appeals court and bringing a series of commercial tribunals working inside the ministries under the name *lijan* (committees) into the Sharia court system. Some ministries established a series of tribunals for issuing trade licences and judgments in various types of commercial and other disputes with the power of normal courts. The commercial tribunal judges are officials of different ministries. The system, set up by King Faisal, irked the cleric-judges and then Mufti Mohammed bin Ibrahim fought Faisal over these courts before his death in 1969. There are also grievance courts (*mazalim*) which answer directly to the king but are Sharia-based. Previously, the Ministry of Justice did not represent the entire justice system, because of the grievance court and industrial tribunals. The issue came up in the Memorandum of Advice, the central document of opposition politics in the 1990s: it sought more *ulama* appointed as 'advisors' to ministries with tribunals outside their control.

The reforms envisage a number of specialised courts. The labour committee, or chamber, becomes the labour court (*mahkama 'ummaliyya*); a commercial court (*mahkama tujariyya*) will be formed from the rest of the non-Sharia committees (around 50 of them), plus the commercial chambers of the Sharia court and grievance court; a personal status court (*ahwal shakhsiyya*) will be formed from the Sharia court; a general court (*mahkama 'amma*) will emerge from the Sharia court; and a formal appeal court (*mahkamat isti'naf*) will be established, replacing the appeals system. At present, an appeal consists of a memorandum reviewing the case as already presented prepared by Sharia judges and given the grandiose title *tamyeez*; the reform envisages a formal court of appeal as a second stage of litigation. A third stage will be represented in the new arrangement through the Supreme Court (*al-mahkama al-'ulya*) to act as a court of cassation, which began operations in 2010 and will save the king and the *ulama* the embarrassment of royal pardons for troubling cases that hit the international media. The grievance court will be transformed into an administrative court circuit with the three stages of first instance, appeal and cassation. The Supreme Justice Council, headed for many years by Sharia court chief Sheikh Saleh al-Luhaidan until February 2009, is to remain but reduced to a body that merely administers the affairs of the judges manning the courts. The Sharia court judges will now cover the entire system and the judges who sat in the tribunals will become their assistants.

It is clear that the revamp aims at streamlining the system, but the controversy lies in whether the reforms will train judges in some specialisations outside the Hanbali school of Sharia as interpreted in the Saudi context – Wahhabism – and in some specialisations outside the realm of Sharia altogether. The implication is there, but it has not been stated openly. Many clerics of the Wahhabi religious establishment thus view the reforms with suspicion. The justice ministry has been charged with implementing the reforms. Although they are Sharia judges with training first and foremost in Sharia law, the judges will receive training in different fields. Training is taking place at the Judiciary Institute, which is a part of the notorious Imam University in Riyadh, a bastion of Wahhabism, but the justice ministry has sent judges to the United States, Holland, Britain, Austria, Singapore and Malaysia for training on modern methods of 'judicial administration'.[34] The Minister of Justice said in 2008 that the concept of precedent and codification of laws for that purpose would be introduced throughout the system; the Ministry of Justice is said to be preparing a penal code. This could help reduce the inconsistencies in rulings which became quite stark in recent years. Judges have complete discretion to impose sentences except in cases where Sharia outlines a punishment. Rape is not one of those, and a judge could impose anything from no sentence at all to death. In 2006 a judge sentenced four men to between six and twelve years' imprisonment each for sexually harassing women in Riyadh, while the same year three men convicted of raping a twelve-year-old boy received sentences of between one and two years in prison each and 300 lashes.

'We didn't have general criminal law so things were left to each judge's view. The idea of the penal code is it will control these acts, and in addition that codification of verdicts will help judges look back for consultation and we'll have a history to build on', says Majed Garoub, head of the Jeddah Bar Association.[35] In 2007 the Ministry of Justice began issuing a register of rulings, though it is not comprehensive. In 2010 media reports said the Council of Senior Religious Scholars had spent a week debating the issue, and while the reports said there was broad agreement, it was possible that the headlines reflected the desire of newspapers and their owners for that to be the case. A report in *Al-Hayat* for example, from March 2010 said in its headline that the clerics had 'approved' codification but the body of the story adumbrated at length the objections some members of the council had (it named five of them). These included Quranic verses, such as verse 105 in Surat al-Nisaa which says the Quran was revealed 'so that you may judge among the people according to that which God has shown you' as well as an objection to the idea of one judicial opinion from one place and time being obligatory for all judges from then on. 'It disrupts the link to the books of jurisprudence, limits the judges and halts the process of *ijtihad* and intellectual activity required to meet the needs of changing life and confronting new systems, customs and practices', the report said.[36] The tribunals and grievance courts already codify and use laws as the basis for future rulings. These courts do not suffer from the shortage of judges which is chronic in the main Sharia court system. There are only a handful of judges in Shi'ite courts in the Eastern Province, forcing many Shia to use the Sunni courts (common practice in the Ottoman empire, where individuals were free to make use of various legal schools, but not in Saudi Arabia).

The reforms go back to 2001 and partly had membership of the WTO in sight, which Saudi Arabia achieved in 2005. A litigation law, or code of legal practice (*nizam al-murafa'at*), was promulgated in 2001, giving plaintiffs the right to legal representation. However, no regulations on implementation have been published regarding this litigation law, which the then Sharia court head Saleh al-Luhaidan and the interior ministry are widely presumed to have opposed. The law is not only widely ignored by judges as well as the interior ministry, it does not affirm the right to be informed of protections guaranteed under law, it does not insist on a lawyer's presence before interrogation begins, it does not prevent comments made to a lawyer being used against the suspect, and it does not provide legal counsel for those who cannot afford it.[37] To take one example, four Sri Lankans were arrested in March 2004 for armed robbery, but had no chance to inform their embassy of their situation, obtained no legal counsel and, on the morning of 20 February 2007, they were taken without warning to a public square in Riyadh for execution by beheading, after which their bodies were left on display for an hour as a warning over crime.[38] In another case, a biochemist at a hospital in al-Baha was the subject of legal action raised by the husband of a woman whose research work he had supervised. The husband claimed the biochemist was guilty of *takhbeeb*, or sowing discord in his marriage with the purpose of separating the couple, who in fact divorced. The husband claimed the biochemist had indulged in this through telephone conversations with his wife ostensibly concerning her research work. At the beginning of the case in 2007, the judge dismissed the request of the biochemist, Khaled al-Zahrani, to have a lawyer. When the verdict came a year later, he was sentenced to eight months in prison and 800 lashes of the whip, while the woman in question – who never appeared in court at all – was sentenced to three months in prison and 200 lashes.[39] Lashes, apologists often argue, are often no more than a token brush on the body, but there's no guarantee of that.

Another case I came across in 2006 highlights the arbitrary justice of Saudi Arabia in the question of land ownership. In 1995 Suleiman al-Sharif, an incense trader, put together 5 million riyals to buy a plot of land in Jeddah. 'One day in 2002 I heard that bulldozers were churning up the land and knocking the wall down. I went there and asked them to stop', he said, speaking in his modest apartment where I met him in July 2006. Police held him for eight days after he went to register a complaint because as far as they were aware most of Sharif's plot was Ministry of Defence land that had been granted to a daughter of defence minister Prince Sultan. Sharif spent months lobbying governors, appealing to human rights groups and trying to raise legal action, but in 2006 the princess sold the plot for 58 million riyals ($15.5 million) – a profit from nothing. Sharif said he had been offered 11.6 million riyals to go away quietly and end the legal dispute, in a deal that would give the judge involved his own share, but he was loath to give in to the theft and thuggery of the ruling family. 'They think "okay just give the guy a few millions", but this is about rights', he said over coffee and dates. The judge, he says, told him: 'You're a poor guy but you're sensible so why go to jail or have problems?'[40] Sharif said he voluntarily ceded 40 per cent ownership of his remaining plot to another Saudi princess: 'It's protection so that this doesn't happen again.' Sharif's story is typical of the legal chaos that plagues the Saudi property market, and helped to hold up mortgage law for years, but it highlights the rapacious behaviour of the royal family towards land for more palaces or that can be rent or sold for huge profits, behaviour which Abdullah tried to curtail after he became king because he knew how unpopular it was making the family.[41] With land values rising and new laws on the horizon, a race has been on to establish ownership of land. 'There is a link between the real estate boom and the royals' hunger for land. Land has been seized over the past 30 years across the country. I estimate a minimum of 20 percent of the country's land has been seized illegally', says Ali Al Ahmad, the opposition activist based in Washington.[42] The best hopes of reformers are summed up by Abdulaziz al-Gasim, a former judge now associated with the liberal trend: 'The court reforms are not fundamental but they could be radical, depending on how they are applied. They have opened the door to cleansing the judiciary of the conservatism that has dominated up to now. The judges will remain clerics, but clerics of a different style.'[43]

An incident involving Sheikh Saleh al-Luhaidan in September 2008 illustrates the determination of the Wahhabi clerics not to cede ground over their central judicial prerogative. Luhaidan stoked controversy with comments to a well-known radio show *Noor 'ala al-Darb* (*Light on the Path*) on the state-run Quran Station, a weekly programme where senior clerics take listeners' calls and offer opinions. One caller asked him what advice he had for the owners of Arab television stations airing entertainment shows during Ramadan. In his response, Luhaidan, also a member of the senior clerical body, seemed to be deliberately provoking controversy by saying raising the prospect of trial with a possible death penalty as its end result: 'I want to advise the owners of these channels that broadcast programmes containing indecency and vulgarity and warn them of the consequences ... They can be put to death through the judicial process (*qadaa'an*).'[44] Saudi liberal media seized on the comments to depict the clerics as dangerously out of touch, suggesting that Luhaidan was encouraging vigilantes to implement his orders to assassinate television chiefs. That media included those owned by Saudi princes and their supporters who, Luhaidan's implication was, could themselves find themselves in court.

The incident was on the surface ridiculous in that it was hardly as if Alwaleed, King Fahd's sister or her family, or the manager of Al-Arabiya in Dubai were seriously worried about attacks to their person. But Luhaidan's words seem calculated to speak to a deeper and more pressing issue – the long-running, unresolved struggle over judicial power within the Saudi government. Luhaidan was seeking to re-stake the Wahhabi *ulama*'s claim on their judicial prerogatives. The key phrase was *qadaa'an*. For Luhaidan there was no need to clarify this point further in his initial comments, since for the Saudi clerics the process is all; they could not conceive of a moral-criminal issue in any other fashion. In classic Sunni legal thinking, as we have seen, God's justice is dispensed by His cleric-lieutenants on earth who are to be found in Sharia courts ready to pass judgment based on the divine law.

In this context, the most interesting element of the incident was Luhaidan's defence of his original comments in an unusual appearance on Saudi Arabia's government-run Channel One where he came out fighting in defence of the Sharia courts and clerical justice.[45] The state had its own interest to make clear that Luhaidan had been talking about a judicial process and not issuing a call to arms. His interviewer set the tone by mentioning in his preamble that Luhaidan's fatwa had been 'falsified' by 'biased media' before repeating the original question seeking Luhaidan's advice to owners of entertainment channels. Luhaidan's lengthy response began with an outline of his personal history as a religious scholar who graduated in 1960 from the Sharia College of al-Imam ibn Saud University in Riyadh then immediately found work in the office of the then mufti Sheikh Mohammed bin Ibrahim, a man who clashed with King Faisal over attempts to modernise the judicial system. For 50 years, Luhaidan stressed, he has given service to the spread of God's moral ordinances through issuing fatwas, adjudicating in Sharia courts and preaching in mosques. He discussed his relationship with successive kings and senior officials of state and pointed out that he was the only one of the original 14 members of the Supreme Council of Religious Scholars established by former mufti Mohammed bin Ibrahim who was still alive. Turning finally to his fatwa, he said it was a matter of proper judicial procedure rather than a call to vigilantism. 'Of course, the judge does not pull out his sword and kill whoever he wants, a case is filed by the concerned parties to the general prosecutor and the judge hears the case and issues his verdict and if he thinks they deserve severe punishment it is passed on to the further authorities to review the judgment and then to the highest authority', he said.

> I don't think that someone who had lived and worked all this time among the senior *ulama* would rush to make a statement in the way that biased parties have rushed to falsify and say I issued a death verdict against satellite TV channel owners. I ask God to guide these people and strengthen their understandings, and I ask God to increase this kingdom in its resolve for right guidance in the face of the biased parties, since this country has lived through a period of changes in neighbouring countries in terms of revolutions, disturbances and hesitancies. Yet it has remained firm because it is on the right path, did not follow a vain cause and it attained the approval of God.[46]

With these comments Luhaidan was appealing to Al Saud on the key issue on which they both agree: that the polity of Saudi Arabia has survived, despite numerous predictions of its imminent demise, because they have stood together and shared in power. Of course, Luhaidan would never phrase it like that. But the clerics' free hand to administer Sharia law in the courts is a central function they perform as their part of the bargain, and hand-in-hand al-Wahhabiyya and Al Saud have fended off Baathism, Nasserism, communism, Shi'ite revolution and formed a working relationship with Western neo-imperialism in the post-colonial age – quite a collection of 'disturbances'. Further, Saudi Arabia is surrounded by polities that have jettisoned elements of the conservative Sharia system the kingdom adheres to: women can drive and alcohol is publicly accessible. For Luhaidan, right guidance has prevailed in Saudi Arabia, and if the Al Saud are thinking seriously of diluting clerical control of the judiciary, he wanted to say, the risks to both partners will be considerable.

Luhaidan overplayed his hand. After the fasting month of Ramadan was over, he was one of many senior clerics who met with King Abdullah in Mecca in the traditional manner during Eid al-Fitr. State television carried images of Luhaidan greeting the king. They embraced, but the king quickly moved on to someone else and Luhaidan appeared to be left standing, jilted, when expecting more.[47] Text messages circulated among politically-attuned Saudis asking whether this was a royal snub for the TV fatwa. Five months later he was removed by the king. Luhaidan will fear that his absence in itself will open a threat to the Wahhabi judiciary, but he had already sent his warning loudly and clearly.

'THE DIALOGUE OF RELIGIONS'

In 2008 King Abdullah launched his project to create a forum for dialogue among Muslims, Christians and Jews, an 'interfaith dialogue' that aimed to promote 'the middle way' and 'moderation' that he had been touting inside Saudi Arabia since 9/11 as a panacea for various international conflicts and woes. A three-day meeting was convened in Mecca in June 2008, bringing together Sunni clerics from around the world and a few Shi'ites in preparation for a larger forum with non-Muslims that would win international attention. The most prominent figure to turn up in Mecca was former Iranian President Akbar Hashemi Rafsanjani, providing a Sunni-Shi'ite reconciliatory photo-op of the king, his Wahhabi mufti and the Iranian cleric. The king's opening speech was carried on state television in which he talked of Muslims as one, holding a hand outstretched to the rest of the world. 'You are meeting here today to say to the world with pride that we are a fair, honest, humanitarian and moral voice, a voice for living together and dialogue', he said. 'How difficult the Islamic nation's challenges are at a time when the threat from extremism among its own people, and others, is all around ... This call is intended to confront the challenges of isolationism, ignorance and short-sightedness.'[48] The king appeared to have won the backing he wanted at the Mecca meeting for a gathering of different religions that appeared to signal a new tone in the Wahhabi establishment: open to Shia, open to other faiths, open to the world.

Due to continued Wahhabi opposition to the very idea of talking to the infidels on an equal footing, the conference was held outside Saudi Arabia in Spain in July 2008. The word 'religious' was removed from the conference's official title (it became the International Conference for Dialogue) and not even the state mufti turned up in Madrid to parley with the Buddhists, Hindus and

Sikhs who were shown on Saudi state television shaking hands with the king. In fact, the Saudi information ministry was having such difficulty persuading Saudi clerics and Islamist thinkers to attend that some secular intellectuals from Saudi universities were pressured into joining the Saudi delegation to fill out numbers. The list of invitees was governed by the desire to find Saudis who knew the West and spoke English rather than enjoyed a reputation for knowledge of Islamic theology.[49] The forum was dominated by disputes shown live on television between American Jewish figures and Arab Muslims and Christians over Zionism and Israel, and Saudi Arabia resisted calls from Jewish figures for a follow-up meeting on Saudi soil. The dialogue came up against the reality of entrenched clerical conservatism, and in so doing it was reduced to a public relations exercise. Not a single member of the council of clerics, including the mufti, attended Madrid, and Abdulrahman al-Barrak and other Wahhabi clerics indicated their opposition to the idea from the outset with a statement attacking Shi'ism for its 'infidel precepts' several days before the meeting in Mecca. 'It was the rejectionist Shi'ites who began the practice of visiting graves and building shrines', it said.[50] The mufti was of course not a signatory to such the statement, but he set the tone during sectarian fighting in Lebanon in May 2008 when he said that groups who 'raise the banner of Islam but have nothing to do with Islam' were exposing Lebanon to the danger of Israeli reprisals.[51]

The interfaith project was part of a wider project to reform Wahhabism so that it never again produces rebels against the Saudi state and to convince the outside world that in so taming the movement it will never again threaten Al Saud's friends in the West. While all within the family and government agree that this is necessary in as far as it means warring al-Qa'ida ideology, there is wide disagreement over whether this should extend to include the social powers of the clerics, their grip on the judiciary and the system of morality they maintain in society. Indeed, it is not clear if the king himself – the nominal leader of the reform trend – really supports rolling back the Wahhabi morality system. Those who believe in political reforms to stymie Wahhabi power are even fewer in number. 'The king isn't democratic, he doesn't believe in modernisation to the end', says former judge Abdulaziz al-Qasim. 'King Abdullah believes there is a problem with the traditional religious establishment and Salafism that violates the bases of the state. He wants a new social contract based on the rights of the citizen and the right of the state. It's about the state in the modern sense of the word, without words like *takfir* and jihad.'[52] What would al-Wahhabiyya be without these concepts? It was not long ago that the regime indulged *takfir* and jihad when it sent thousands of Saudis to Afghanistan or encouraged them to fight in Bosnia or Chechnya, or even Iraq after 2003, and it is unlikely to hesitate before trading in the language of *takfir* or promote jihadists in distant lands again when it suits its interests.

THE REFORMER KING IN WESTERN MEDIA

The narrative of the reformer king bravely challenging the radicals who want to stymie his plans for comprehensive social, political and religious reform has been heavily promoted by some Western media, politicians, diplomats, analysts and academics who like to contrast him to his hawkish half-brothers.[53] To believe the rhetoric, Abdullah wants women to drive, parliament elected, the courts to ditch Sharia judges and al-Wahhabiyya reduced to Sufism. He not only wants it – it's easy to want – but he will make it happen. *Newsweek* wrote in May 2008 that the king hopes to 'outflank the repressive clergy' with his Aramco-run KAUST. The article fails to mention how the regime has crushed proponents of political reform who oppose publicly the arbitrary powers of the state's coercive bodies in the form of the security forces and religious police. Reform simply means the clerics moderating their positions to allow for economic development to provide jobs for the burgeoning youth population and rejecting the ideology of *takfir* in as much as it threatens the Saudi rulers, leaving the autocratic family untouched in their powers and their Western-friendly foreign policy. 'Ever since King Abdullah came to the throne three years ago, his government has been slowly implementing progressive reforms to counteract the extreme Wahhabi doctrine that many blame for fostering terrorism at home and abroad and for squelching innovation', it said.[54] The theme of such articles, which have been many in number since Abdullah took the throne, is that he has so little time to do his work since he is already in his eighties and conservative forces will turn back the tide of reform.

Instances of reform in action cited by Western media often miss the bigger picture. Sheikh Kalbani received a positive profile in the *New York Times* when he was appointed the first 'black' imam of the Grand Mosque in Mecca but brought bad publicity to the country a month later when he said Shi'ites are heretics who must not be given a place on the Council of Senior Religious Scholars.[55]

The *New York Times* reported on an all-girl rock band in Jeddah; but they did not tell readers, and probably were not aware, that the band broke up after the article was published because of threats it provoked from Salafis.[56] The New America Foundation placed numerous articles in the US media lauding Abdullah as the reformer for the times: one claimed that 'a new day seems to be dawning for Saudi Arabia', and that 'as the kingdom gets its own house in order, it's time it moved to assertively shape a more moderate, prosperous Muslim world. King Abdullah clearly sees himself in this role.'[57] An academic paper wondered in 2005 if there was a new 'spring in Riyadh'.[58] And Robert Lacey paints a positive portrayal of Abdullah the Reformer in his *Inside the Kingdom*, where princes have free rein to peddle their version of Saudi relations with bin Laden and al-Qa'ida throughout the 1990s and present the family as battling the clerics for reform after 2001.[59]

This merry folderol continued after the protest movements spread throughout the Middle East. A Carnegie Endowment for International Peace analyst claimed in the aftermath of Mubarak and Ben Ali's fall from power that 'the Arab autocracies were, or are not, held in place by any external power framework'.[60] He went on to cite the 'independent-minded King Abdullah' as an example of this. This theme often came up in discussion of US-Saudi relations: token displays of cranky strong-headedness such as Abdullah's reference to 'illegal occupation' in Iraq in his Arab League speech in 2007 or stubborn refusal to meet Iraqi prime minister Nouri al-Maliki because of Shi'ite sectarianism and close ties to Iran are cited as indications of a putative independence, as if anything less than 100 per cent rubber stamping of Washington's every desire means the game's up, no more best friends forever. In the same fashion, a rift of alleged import was posited in US media and policy circles in the wake of the uprisings as Riyadh seethed in anger over Barack Obama's abandonment of old friend Hosni Mubarak, as if the US and Saudi leaderships were not on the same page in limiting the damage from the protest movements. For example, they coordinated positions throughout the political crisis in Yemen – Ali Abdullah Saleh only left once Riyadh had ensured his system could survive with him – and Riyadh's sudden *prise de position* against Damascus in August 2011 came in the days after the US Secretary of State called publicly on Arab states to do their bit to pressure the Syrian leadership. Britain's ambassador declared Abdullah as 'the architect of domestic reform' on his return after illness in February

2011.[61] Neither was interested in the trial or conviction of Mubarak, who had been a close friend of three decades to both governments.

In 2008 the Saudi-US Relations Information Service ran an interview with Mark Weston, the author of a glowing history of Saudi Arabia, *Prophets and Prince: Saudi Arabia from Muhammad to the Present*. The research was supported by the King Faisal Centre for Research and Islamic Studies and offers the standard defence of Al Saud in its Abdullah-led format. Most Saudis prefer the royals as a middle way between conservatism and liberalism and would vote for them in free elections, while Islamists would come second and the Western-style liberals would come third. He says that Abdullah's main achievement has been to take Saudi Arabia into the WTO as well as establishing the allegiance council to decide royal succession. The term 'absolute monarch' is not correct, he explains.

> Saudi Arabia is a consensus society and the King consults so many people before any decisions are made. He has to consult his brothers. He consults the senior clerics. He consults businessmen. He consults professors. So nothing gets done in Saudi Arabia by the will of just one person. Abdullah is not a dictator. He is not an absolute monarch. He is a little bit more than first among equals but every decision is made by the group – the group being the senior princes of the Royal Family but they consult many people.[62]

The interfaith dialogue, Weston says, is an excellent example of the attempt by Abdullah and his clique to effect a gradual change in clerical thinking by exposing them to the outside world and other Muslim trends, so that one day even a church could be opened. He repeats the king's line that the entirety of Saudi Arabia is equivalent to the Vatican – the comparison, though strained, only works when applied to the holy precincts in Mecca and Medina – and so churches cannot be built in such a holy land. He cites a discussion in the Shura Assembly on women driving as a sign of social reforms moving apace, though the proposal was shot down. On political reform there is less room for sophistry: 'It's been more disappointing mainly because the municipal councils that were elected in 2005 haven't yet done anything.'[63] The king's announcement in 2011 that he was granting women their right to take part in the 2015 elections to half the seats of a toothless municipal body and their right to sit in the only marginally less toothless quasi-parliament was also held by defenders of the regime as a great stride towards reform.

What these arguments don't explain is that the reforms are driven entirely by the desire to protect the extraordinary power and privileges of the Saudi royal family. Like Faisal before him, Abdullah realised that the United States required clear measures to moderate the regime's ultra-conservatism. It also seeks to remove from the historical record the repression of political critics languishing in jail with no regard for due process, as well as the hundreds of unnamed detainees held in Saudi prisons, and the control of the Saudi media, which attacks the religious police and clerical excess within boundaries moved at will by the ruling family. They also fail to explain why the ruling family is not interested in breaking the historical divvying up of power between themselves and the Wahhabi clerics, despite the desire to dilute their influence, or explain that in the absence of popular representation it these very same clerics who provide legitimacy to Saudi family rule. It does not explain why forces outside the Saudi family or its clients are forbidden from developing social and political constituencies, so that the 'liberal' Saudi media (MBC, Rotana, LBC, Orbit, ART, Al-Watan) is in the hands of the royal family and its allies, and there are no political parties, or attempts to prepare the ground for an opening up of the political process, so that a populace described as 'not ready' by Mohammed bin Nayef acquires the maturity he thinks it lacks.[64] As for absolutism, rulers with no constitutional or legal impediments to their ability to act were in hardly less of a need to consult others in taking decisions in any other era of history. Abdullah does not have to be Saddam Hussein or Genghis Khan to deserve the epithet 'absolute ruler'.[65] If the Saudi ruling family has been a 'headless tribe' in recent years, to use Madawi Al-Rasheed's phrase, it speaks more to the circumstances of Abdullah's weak rule than the institution of monarchy. And, one may ask, since when has a group of brothers ruling in concert been a stunning improvement on just one of them doing it alone?

As one ambassador – who was more frank on these issues than US diplomats in the Wikileaks documents – put it once in a conversation with me, the king heads the group within the ruling family that understands that modernisation and increased links with the outside world are good publicity for a regime that realised in the aftermath of 9/11 that one day an American government might well decide it's time to get rid of Al Saud. The king is 'not a real reformer, but he's more conscious of PR than the others are', the ambassador said.

They haven't prepared a move to democracy in parties and free speech; they don't want to give up power and they fear the Islamists will be elected in any free elections. If you look at the Qatif-girl case, it was not so much because of injustice that she was pardoned, it was because it made the country look appalling and medieval. Abdullah can see this is a problem, especially post-9/11. So he looks reasonable, he talks to the Pope, he holds conferences, he has interfaith dialogues. He's saying 'we're a *nice* despotic medieval system'.

In the view of this reform wing of the family, 'there should be only gradual change while maintaining the position of Al Saud *and the clerics*', he said (my italics). The regime offers the same argument as Abdullah's old chums Mubarak and Ben Ali that democracy cannot be trusted because Islamists will win. The king must also surely be mindful of the fate of King Saud. He was deposed in 1964 after Faisal and his allies in the clerical establishment took fright at the democratic concessions he was prepared to make to the leftist and Arab nationalist trend. If the king precipitously acted to dilute Al Saud power, he could well face the same fate. And while it appears there were differences in policy and approach between the king and Nayef, they do not rise to the level of conflict between Saud and Faisal.

What the king was interested in until the 2011 uprisings was a rolling back some of the powers given to the religious establishment after 1979. This has been quite clear from the attempts to reduce the emphasis on Islam in the country's sense of identity in favour of Saudi nationalism. Plans to celebrate the third Saudi state were stymied by the *ulama* in 1950. The state concluded in the 1960s that nationalist identity implied a submissive role within Egyptian-led Arab nationalism and threatened the rule of Al Saud themselves. King Faisal deliberately developed an Islamic identity for the country from 1964 to his death in 1975, placing Saudis as a people of special favour and bounty in the global Islamic community. The permanent fatwa council of the Council of Senior Religious Scholars headed by Bin Baz duly condemned nationalism: 'God brings Muslims together through Islam and the sense of brotherliness in Islam, and the nationalist obsession is a point of destruction and division for Muslims as a whole if it means pride over Muslims from other countries.'[66]

In 1999, however, the government celebrated 100 years of Saudi Arabia. The celebration was linked to the Christian calendar and it challenged the Wahhabi notion that there could be only two national celebrations, Eid al-Fitr marking the end of Ramadan and Eid al-Adha during the hajj pilgrimage: anything else is an innovation and imitation of the ways of non-Muslims. The 1999 celebration furthered the cult of Abdulaziz as the founder of the nation. Numerous artefacts connected with points in his life are collected in the National Museum, venerating his person in a way that in fact runs counter to Wahhabi teachings, and he is presented by the state as a kind of Arabian superman – warrior, scholar, moderniser, father, tribal chieftan and pious Muslim. Once installed as king in August 2005, Abdullah took things further with the announcement that 23 September would be Saudi Arabia's National Day (al-yawm al-watani) to be celebrated every year. The event has evolved with an open linkage to the king's promotion of wasatiyya and tolerance. In deference to the clerics, the national day is not an Eid in official terminology, in the same way that the commercial tribunals were lijan and not mahakim, and laws are nuzum not qawaneen. This shift towards nationalism has created some conflict with the dominant notion of Saudi Arabia as Utopia for all Muslims. It has had consequences for migrant labour communities. Faced with rising crime in Saudi cities, the Saudi media ran a campaign in 2007 singling out Bangladeshis as a destructive and unwanted presence. Bangladeshi diplomats linked this to a more nationalist approach towards Asian workers, who had been welcomed since the 1970s as primarily Muslims in the land of Islam but now faced labour ministry attempts at 'Saudisation' in many spheres, forcing companies to replace some foreigners with Saudis. The Islamic Utopia is bending to accommodate more intrusive security forces, modernisations in the judicial and legal systems and attempts to 'nationalise' the labour force.

Military and security forces have played their role in this attempt to produce a national identity around the Saudi family name, a result of its tussle with the al-Qa'ida insurgency. Yet there are limits: it is the security forces, rather than the military, who are lauded as protectors and paragons of the state. In Colonial Effects, Joseph Massad notes the role the military played in Jordan. 'The military was the central vehicle for the advancement of a new culture that is nationally defined and governed by the laws of the nation-state. From music to clothes to food to the very "tribalist" culture that Jordanian national culture came to represent, the Jordanian army was a central instrument in its formation', he writes.[67] Saudi Arabia's National Guard, an elite Bedouin force in charge of domestic military security established by Abdullah in the 1960s, holds the Janadiriyya festival each year outside Riyadh – a celebration of Bedouin folklore and tradition with camel racing, traders selling trinkets and Arab intellectuals invited to speak at seminars and accept Saudi gifts in return for being a fan of Al Saud in Arab media. But Saudi Arabia never quite accorded military institutions, even Abdullah's pet project, such a role, as a consequence of the ruling family's constant fear that a strong indigenous military could become a tool for removing them. So when the desire emerged to look beyond Islamic institutions to boost national unity, the security forces were a safer bet. Thus the interior ministry has played a notably more prominent role than the military in the National Day celebrations and the government-orchestrated media fanfare around the event.

6
Foreign Policy Adventurism: Iran and Palestine

In April 2008 then commander of the multinational forces in Iraq, General David Petraeus, and US ambassador to Baghdad Ryan Crocker had a series of meetings with some of the senior Saudi princes, including the king and the ambassador to Washington, Adel al-Jubair, over two days in Riyadh. Iraq was on the agenda and what Saudi Arabia could do to help stabilise the situation there for the Americans. Al Saud had one concern, the US diplomatic cable that details the discussions shows: Iran. The Saudi princes explained that they would not send an ambassador to Baghdad or open an embassy until they were satisfied the security situation had improved and the Iraqi government had implemented policies that benefit all Iraqis, reinforce Iraq's Arab identity, and resist Iranian influence. But it is the king himself – contrary to the carefully constructed image of him as a dove – who repeatedly implores the Americans to take military action against Iran's nuclear energy programme. 'Al-Jubair recalled the King's frequent exhortations to the US to attack Iran and so put an end to its nuclear weapons program. "He told you to cut off the head of the snake," he [Jubair] recalled to the Charge, adding that working with the US to roll back Iranian influence in Iraq is a strategic priority for the King and his government', the cable written by chargé d'affaires Michael Gfoeller says.[1] It's not clear from the text whether the 'head of the snake' is Jubair's description of Iran or the king's words, or whether he is recalling a conversation during the two days of meetings or a previous occasion; Jubair has a habit of embellishing translations. But his words reflect the kind of colourful allegory Abdullah is wont to use (he once told Muammar al-Gaddafi at an Arab League summit that 'the grave is before you'), and whether he used those words or not, his hawkish position is evident, as it is in numerous other encounters with American diplomacy documented in the Wikileaks cables.[2]

Saudi Arabia and Iran have been locked in a battle of wills over regional influence since 1979. Before that the fact that both regimes were friends of the United States mitigated the scope for destructive rivalry. Since the revolution, Tehran has viewed Al Saud as Western lackeys with no regional clout or allure for the masses other than their money and ability to spread it around, publicly, privately, mischievously. Riyadh sees Iran as a force for agitation against the American-dominated regional order in which Saudi Arabia has happily made itself a central element. Both claim leadership of the Islamic world. Saudi Arabia bases this on its control of Mecca and Medina and promotes a Sunni fundamentalist cult of the Prophet as the true Islam and Shi'ism as an aberration. Iran likes to think of itself as a polity for all Muslims, not least because its foreign policy champions causes that challenge Western hegemony in general, be they Arab, Muslim or Third World (backing the Sunni Palestinian group Hamas, for example), but on the ground its first and most natural allies have been Arab Shi'ites and thus it has been hard for Tehran to shake off the sectarian nature of its policy reach: from its attempts to stir the Saudi Shia to action in 1979/80 to the creation of Hizbullah in Lebanon, to the Shia militias in Iraq that engaged in bloody communal warfare with Sunnis after the fall of Saddam Hussein. Tense relations between the two countries eased for a period during the presidency of Mohammed Khatami but sharpened once more with the populist nationalism of Mahmoud Ahmadinejad, with both its religious and irredentist themes. Even squabbling about the name of the Gulf – is it 'Persian' or is it 'Arab'? – has intensified in the Abdullah/Ahmadinejad era. The 'fall' of Iraq to Shi'ism and Iran's push for nuclear energy have pushed relations between these two countries to their lowest ever in the modern era: Riyadh views the prospect of a nuclear -weaponised Iran as a game-changer that could threaten Al Saud rule, always fundamentally fragile, while Iran has to bear in mind that a second Saudi-Pakistani collaboration that affords Riyadh the same tools would be a threat too, though less so.

As a major theme of Saudi foreign policy over the past decade, Iran has exercised Saudi minds more and more with each passing year to the point of obsession. Saudi leaders feared that Hizbullah operative Emad Mughniya was killed by Syria or with its blessing in a deal with Israel and the United States that could lead to a rapprochement between Washington and Tehran.[3] Riyadh was so convinced that Iran was backing the Zaydi Shi'ite Houthi movement rebelling against the rule of Ali Abdullah Saleh in 2009 that it ensured a flow of armaments to Saleh's army, including weapons it bought especially for the purpose from Czechoslovakia and Bulgaria,[4] helping make homeless some 150,000 people.[5] The foreign ministry told American diplomats in Riyadh that Saudi Arabia should be 'consulted in advance' on US policy movements with Iran.[6] Saudi Arabia was so panicked by the rising prestige of Hizbullah after the Israelis failed to destroy the movement after two weeks of the Lebanon war in 2006 that ambassador James Oberwetter was summoned to a meeting with Saud al-Faisal in Jeddah to beg Washington to call for a ceasefire.[7] It was the Lebanon war more than anything which propelled Riyadh to engage in a period of public diplomacy that Al Saud had more or less ditched after the death of King Faisal. The kingdom began to project itself forcefully as the leading voice of the Arab world and Sunni Islam in the face of challenges from Iran and its allies. Abdullah was promoted as not only the 'king of the Arabs' but the leader of mainstream Islam itself. It is also clear from the body of US diplomatic cables released by Wikileaks that Saudi princes followed a clumsy and counterproductive policy of security repression in Shi'ite areas of the Eastern Province to prevent the development of Iranian-backed Shi'ite paramilitary cells who could target oil installations. Shi'ites in Arab countries perceived there to be a Shi'ite revival; US diplomats recounted in reports for the State Department in Washington the deep disillusion among Shi'ites of the Eastern Province that they could not be part of it.[8] In 2011 it was rare to find a Saudi official or intellectual inside the country who did not subscribe to the theory that Saudi Arabia's intervention in Bahrain was necessary to pre-empt an Iranian invasion of the island, or that Bahrain's Sunni Muslims were a demographic majority.

Fortunately for Riyadh, its Iranian obsession has dovetailed with American priorities as both countries grappled with Iran's interventions in the Arab countries – Iran's financial and logistical aid for popular political-paramilitary groups Hamas and Hizbullah and its cultivating of Shi'ite clerics and politicians in Iraq, all of whom were viewed as tools of Iranian foreign policy. The underlying theme of Saudi diplomacy in the immediate years following the 9/11 attacks in 2001 was appeasement of the United States. This manifested itself in Saudi Arabia's policy of 'moderation' on the Israeli-Palestinian question and close coordination with the White House over the invasion of Iraq, as Riyadh tried to deflect America's fury and desire for revenge towards other targets. The outbreak of al-Qa'ida violence in Saudi Arabia a month after the fall of Baghdad finally put Saudi Arabia and the United States on the same page in President George W. Bush's 'war on terror', after a period of protestation from hawks within the ranks of the senior Saudi princes – Prince Nayef – over cooperating with American officials in their war. Shaken by the jolt to the historic relationship with the United States government, the Saudi regime exploited the windfall from the second oil boom to diversify its portfolio of powerful friends, building political, military and economic ties with China, Russia and other countries. Saudi Arabia became less important as an oil supplier to the United States during the first decade of the twenty-first century as America sought to lessen its reliance upon Saudi Arabia.

A nuclear Iran would be unbearable for Al Saud. Nuclear weapons would raise Iran to the status of most powerful and prestigious country in the Gulf, and that would engender regional pressure on Saudi Arabia to take positions on foreign policy issues that would not please the United States: Egyptian street mobilisation against Israel following the fall of Mubarak was troubling for similar reasons. At the same time, the Wahhabi clerics are likely to view Al Saud's failure to stop their Shi'ite nemesis eclipse Saudi Arabia in this manner as a breach of the contract between the royal family and the *ulama*. Neither would al-Wahhabiyya take kindly to a rapprochement between Iran and Washington and the boost to Shi'ism it would give. Saudi Arabia has already stated it will begin its own civilian nuclear energy programme, under international supervision, in order to stave off such an eventuality, while at the same time keeping on good terms with the Americans. Meanwhile, Saudi propaganda has worked assiduously to create anti-Iranian sentiment among the Arab Sunni public, playing on Sunni/Shi'ite and Arab/Persian themes, battling against the reality that Israel, which already has nuclear weapons, is viewed by Arab publics in general as a greater threat than Iran.

Shared interests in regional foreign policy helped to win American favour in another way: purchases of American arms. In this Abdullah's policies mirrored those of Faisal, who oversaw a huge hike in defence spending from 243 million riyals in 1961 to 414 million in 1963 and 925 million in 1970, allowing for Saudi intervention in neighbouring states and consolidating US protection of the regime. 'The list of major and minor contracts represented a huge, successful manoeuvre by Western capital as a whole: it funnelled back to Europe and North America up to 1,000 million pounds in the period of 1965–71 thus diverting up to one third of all the revenues paid to Saudi Arabia in that period', Fred Halliday wrote of that time.[9] Like Faisal, Abdullah also realised that Western powers required some steps to moderate the regime's ultra-conservatism. The oil price hike was mitigated for Western countries by a large capital flow from Saudi Arabia to their economies: Britain won a £3 billion deal on technical and economic cooperation in June 1974 and US contractors took the lion's share of deals for rapid modernisation of cities, industry and infrastructure. Saudi revenue jumped from $2.8 billion in 1972, to $4.9 billion in 1973 and $19.4 billion in 1974.[10] During the 1980s Saudi Arabia ran up an arms bill of $30 billion with US firms which it had trouble paying back in the 1990s.[11]

In 2006 Saudi Arabia began expanding its military arsenal with major defence contracts. In 2006 Saudi Arabia bought 24 UH-60L Black Hawk helicopters, radios, armoured vehicles and other military equipment from the United States worth more than $6 billion, and France and Saudi Arabia signed a defence cooperation agreement involving the sale of helicopters and tanker aircraft. Britain won a £4.43 billion contract in September 2007 to deliver 72 Eurofighter aircraft, the latest in a series of arms contracts since the 1980s referred to as al-Yamamah and costing Saudi Arabia a total of around £43 billion. This is the contract that forced the British government to close a serious fraud investigation into whether Britain's BAe Systems had paid bribes to Saudi officials including Prince Bandar bin Sultan, son of the late Prince Sultan bin Abdulaziz. Reports in 2008 said Saudi Arabia was interested in buying 150 T-90 tanks, 160 helicopters and air-defence systems from Russia for more than $2.2 billion, perhaps in return for Moscow curtailing its cooperation with Iran in its nuclear energy programme.[12] The US government also lobbied intensely for Saudi Arabia to buy commercial airliners from Boeing, a deal worth $3.3 billion for twelve 777-300ER airliners that went through in 2010,[13] and in 2010 the Obama administration notified the US Congress of plans to sell as many as 84 F-15 fighter jets, helicopters and other gear to Saudi Arabia worth an estimated $60 billion, one of the biggest single US arms sales ever. In 2011 it became public that this figure could rise to $90 billion.

FOREIGN POLICY THROUGH US EYES

The Wikileaks material strengthens two conclusions about Saudi diplomacy: massive overt and covert interference in the affairs of other countries and the chaos and contradiction of what is benignly referred to as 'Saudi foreign policy'. The US State Department is aware of the ineptitude but bears with the Saudis for the sake of what is judged to be American national interest. The major arenas for intervention are Lebanon, Yemen and Pakistan. Lebanese politicians of the pro-West 'March 14' movement take orders from Riyadh, Yemenis and Pakistanis accept Saudi dictates; Riyadh finances its allies in Lebanon and Yemen in a haphazard and counterproductive manner, which runs contrary to the facts and counter to public sentiment. The cables reveal lies (democracy activists are al-Qa'ida financers), contradiction (low-level foreign ministry bureaucrats are dovish on Iran,[14] facilitating a 'tidal wave' of arms into already chaotic Yemen, foot-dragging on funds flowing to Afghanistan/Pakistan-based groups like al-Qa'ida, the Taliban and Lashkar-e Taiba[15]), panic (Lebanon, during the war of 2006 and street fighting in 2008 between March 14 militias and Hizbullah), bloodlust (Yemen's fight with the Houthis) and paranoia (Iran, *passim*). Saudi Arabia provides funds to the Lebanese army to destroy the Fatah al-Islam militant group in the Nahr al-Barid refugee camp in 2007 after the presence of Saudi nationals embarrassed the government. Saudi Arabia tries in vain to keep Pervez Musharraf in power as president in Pakistan, and senior princes appoint and approve ministers in Lebanon and direct its allies of the March 14 coalition on what to do. Walid Jumblatt, the Druze sectarian leader, seeks Saudi permission to attend talks in Qatar to resolve the crisis in May 2008 after the March 14 government's decision to ban Hizbullah's telecommunications network provoked street fighting: he gets it twice, from Saud al-Faisal and Bandar bin Sultan, the former ambassador to the United States. Chargé d'affaires Michele J. Sison writes: 'Walid had asked to see King Abdullah of Saudi Arabia, but Prince Bandar told him there was no need, he had the Saudis' blessing to go to Doha; "we want you to go to Doha." Prince Faisal told him in a separate conversation that, "We are with you. Go ahead, go to Qatar."'[16]

The Saudi meddling in Yemen revealed in the US diplomatic reports is particularly striking. They paint a picture of Yemen as a country Saleh reduced to vassal status. Saudi Arabia funds the government as well as tribal leaders to secure support for Saudi policies and prevent the emergence of a non-tribal, non-sectarian democratic culture, and Saleh has facilitated the inroads of Wahhabism into Yemeni society. One might wonder why Saleh, a Zaydi Shi'ite, would promote Wahhabi puritanism: the reason is because of Wahhabism's traditional quietist obedience to the ruler. Saleh's encouragement of Salafism was just another ruse to buy support and outfox his opponents. The Zaydi Houthis are the exact opposite: they are inspired by the idea of revolt against an unjust ruler. One report from the US embassy in Sanaa cites the opinion of Mohamed al-Mutawakel, head of the opposition Union of Popular Forces party. 'Mutawakel explained that Salafis believe that as long as a government is in any way Islamic, Muslims should not try to overthrow it. Zaydi teaching, by contrast, admonishes adherents to work to change any government that fails to "achieve justice." Mutawakel believes, as do other embassy contacts, that the ROYG [republic of Yemen government] considers a Salafi presence as a pacifying force in a country facing unrest in both the north and south.' Although Saleh worked hard at building a close relationship with Riyadh, he and other Yemenis were still treated with disdain by the Saudi princes, meeting only Crown Prince Sultan and not the king on his official visits to Saudi Arabia. One of Saudi Arabia's long-term strategic goals in its Yemen policy is to secure a passage to the Arabian Sea, thus bypassing the Straits of Hormuz.[17] Saleh was aware of this goal, but Saudi Arabia was paying supporters in the army, tribes and government to ensure that Saleh's successor gave in (Najrani Ismailis believe the largesse shown to Yemeni tribes is an extension of the same policy).[18]

In other cables from November 2009, diplomats express concern with Saudi policy towards the Houthi rebellion, which at that time was five years old and had escalated to a new level of violence with Saleh's 'Operation Scorched Earth' to crush the Zaydi Shi'ite movement. American diplomats describe Saudi thinking on eradicating the Houthis as 'delusional' and express the fear that Saudi Arabia, which became publicly embroiled in the conflict after Houthis seized some Saudi territory, will act 'irrationally' and kill lots of people with American-supplied state-of-the-art weaponry. Some of the weaponry provided to the Yemeni army is likely to make its way onto the black market and into the hands of al-Qa'ida fighters. One report refers to Saleh's claim that an Iranian ship bearing weapons for the Houthis had been seized off the coast. 'In fact, sensitive reporting suggests that the ship was carrying no weapons at all. It is, in fact, the amount of weapons the SAG [Saudi Arabian government] and at least one other neighbouring state, the UAE, seem intent on throwing at the Yemeni government that strikes us as a cause for serious concern', it says.[19] 'We urge the Department to engage in Washington and in relevant capitals to convey to these "friends of Yemen" that they are undermining their goal of a stable and secure Yemen by providing large amounts of money and military assistance to President Saleh.'

The grand aims of foreign policy under Abdullah were hampered by the lack of an institutional ability to support such a role. Saudi foreign policy tends to grind to a halt in the summer months when the foreign minister and key officials are on holiday. Defence spending is similarly chaotic. Different wings of the Saudi defence and security apparatus are in the hands of different princes and they do not necessarily coordinate arms purchases.[20] Much of the equipment bought by the National Guard and the interior ministry was the kind of material that would be of use domestically rather than in the large-scale defence operations that fighting with Iran would incur, a European diplomat noted to me in 2008. He surmised that equipment such as tanks, gunships and armoured vehicles could be aimed at domestic suppression in the event of any localised conflagration, as well as strengthening the position of key princes should any confrontations deteriorate in the future over the vexed question of the succession after Abdullah.

The king comes across as a comic figure in the American diplomatic cables, offering whacky nuggets of wisdom on world problems and revealing obsessive sentiments against Iran that border on the racist, and all delivered with the self-confidence of someone who receives his American pilgrims as if he was the Oracle of Delphi. Conforming to Wahhabi orthodoxy, he derides Iranian Shia for worshipping 'domes, statues, and individuals'.[21] He meets the ambassador and White House counterterrorism advisor in March 2009 to discuss relations after Barack Obama became president. Brennan hands the king a letter from Obama and the king reveals that he has just completed a meeting with the Iranian foreign minister Manouchehr Mottaki in the same room, during which he issued a warning for Iran that it has one year to improve its relations with Saudi Arabia. 'When challenged by the King on Iranian meddling in Hamas affairs, Mottaki apparently protested that "these are Muslims." "No, Arabs," countered the King, "You as Persians have no business meddling in Arab matters"', the cable reports.[22] '"Iran's goal is to cause problems," he continued, "There is no doubt something unstable about them" He described Iran as "adventurous in the negative sense" and declared "May God prevent us from falling victim to their evil."' The king reveals that he is worried for Obama's personal safety and offers the advice that America must restore its credibility in the world – for Saudi Arabia's sake first of all, one imagines, though he doesn't say that. The king receives an assurance that although he is a light unto nations, 'President Obama would remain strong on counterterrorism', the cable says.[23] The king gets an idea in his head – finally a wholesome use for Bluetooth technology, which Saudis had been making heavy use of as a means of flirting in quiet anonymity in public places, driving the clerics potty:

> 'I've just thought of something,' the King added, and proposed implanting detainees with an electronic chip containing information about them and allowing their movements to be tracked with Bluetooth. This was done with horses and falcons, the King said. Brennan replied, 'horses don't have good lawyers,' and that such a proposal would face legal hurdles in the U.S., but agreed that keeping track of detainees was an extremely important issue that he would review with appropriate officials when he returned to the United States.

Talking of horses, the American officials lead Abdullah into some soft banter on the topic of one of his favourite animals. 'The King appeared alert and at times animated, entertaining his guests with anecdotes about his encounters with Iranian leaders, and throwing up his hands in complaint when asked if he spent time with his horses: "I see them on television when they race," he said. "I love horses," he exclaimed, "every couple of weeks I get to see them, and then I have a very calm and restful sleep."' The conversation wouldn't have been complete without the old in-joke about what a dangerous neighbourhood Saudi Arabia lives in – a favourite trope among the Arab leaders who need to please Washington and one that Mubarak often trotted out in interviews with American media. When the diplomatic reports first became public in 2010, Prince Turki al-Faisal led the way in Saudi efforts at damage control, dismissing them as inaccurate prattle, 'a hodgepodge of selectivity, inaccuracy, agenda pursuit, and downright disinformation'.[24] What the reports represent, however, is a record of what senior princes involved in key policies and decisions over the years said in unguarded moments of considerably more candour and alacrity than we get in the air-brushed PR that princes spout in many published works of the decade following 9/11.

The fact is that Saudi foreign policy post-9/11 offered Iran the opportunity to fill a void in Arab backing for the Palestinian cause. Saudi Arabia, once a major funder of the Palestinian Liberation Organisation, Hamas and the Palestinian Authority in Ramallah, aligned itself with the Western policy of ostracising Hamas and demonising the concept of armed resistance to Israel as an occupying power. 'Resistance groups' turned to Iran because Saudi Arabia, Egypt and other Arab governments reneged on traditional functions in support of the Arab responses to Israel post-1967.[25] Saudi Arabia was joined by not only Egypt in the venture to please Washington, but Jordan, Bahrain and the UAE. Collectively they blamed Hizbullah for Israel's month-long assault on Lebanon in 2006 and blamed Hamas for Israel's month-long assault on Gaza in December 2008–January 2009. These policies culminated in the stark statement by Egypt's foreign minister Ahmed Abu al-Gheit during the Gaza war that Palestinians had no need for armed resistance, and provision of weapons (via sea or tunnels from Egypt) was not the way to help them. No Arab government had dared suggest such a thing; to publicly question the principle of resistance to Israel occupation – even if the Israelis argued Gaza was no longer 'occupied' – was something of a Rubicon in Arab politics. The Egyptian minister's words signified the final shift of key Arab states into the discursive territory the United States and Israel had prepared for them since the Oslo Accords of 1993. Later in 2009 Egypt began construction of a security wall along its border with Gaza in coordination with Israel, which had already fenced off the rest of the territory.

These shifts, I would argue, were one element in the series of circumstances that brought about the Egyptian uprising in January 2011: the perception that Egypt was pursuing foreign policy goals that served an American and Israeli agenda and utterly denuded of any concessions to the Arab nationalist and populist impulses of the region. While Saudi Arabia – the ante-state whose ante-foreign policy had always worked to undermine every possible revolutionary impulse in the region – was able to get away with this, Egypt could not. Even during the Gaza war, Saudi Arabia's mufti was dissing the notion of resistance. 'No good comes from protests', he told a gathering in widely reported comments. 'They are just useless rowdiness and noise.'[26] Indeed, Arab regimes have always been ambivalent about the Palestinian uprisings. The model of Palestinian resistance is a threat because it demonstrates what popular action can do and provides a template of mobilisation for rights elsewhere. Mubarak's regime made the mistake of elevating Saudi counter-revolution in the dark to the level of public policy.

9/11

The 9/11 attacks in 2001 were a nasty jolt for the Saudi regime. Different members of the royal family put out different theories on who was behind the attacks before the nationality of 15 as Saudis was acknowledged in February 2002. The dominant theme was that it was an Israeli plot to ruin Saudi-US relations, and Riyadh subsequently drew closer to Israel, through back channel contacts and policy alignment. Prince Nayef publicly blamed what he termed Zionism on numerous occasions including as late as December 2002. He was possibly referring to the anti-Semitic conspiracy theory that most Jews who worked in the Twin Towers had not turned up to work that day in the knowledge that the attack was coming. Adel al-Jubair, then spokesman at the Washington embassy, played damage control denying the essence of the comments by Nayef and affirming that in his view no one but bin Laden was behind the attacks. Nayef said the media and Zionism – by which he meant Israel and its lobbies, rather than the ideology as such – had tried to ruin 'a relationship of mutual understanding' between the United States and Saudi Arabia that he posited as having begun in earnest with the meeting between Roosevelt and Abdulaziz. 'We know that the Jews exploited the events of Sept. 11 and turned American public opinion against the Arabs and Islam and this is the aim they have had for a long time. We place big question marks and ask, who carried out the Sept. 11 events and who benefits from them. Who benefited from the Sept. 11 events? I believe they are the perpetrators of these incidents.'[27] He also denied the existence of militant sleeper cells in Saudi Arabia – seven months later al-Qa'ida operatives launched a campaign inside Saudi Arabia with the suicide-bomb attacks in Riyadh in May 2003.

Though there have been efforts to exonerate Abdullah of sharing in this thinking – see Robert Lacey's *Inside The Kingdom*, where Abdullah is reported to have had tears in his eyes as he contemplated photographs of the young Saudis who carried out the 9/11 attacks[28] – he also blamed the al-Qa'ida violence that erupted in 2003 on 'Zionism', meaning Israel. He spoke after militants stormed energy industry facilities in Yanbu in 2004, killing six people including two Americans, one of whose corpse was dragged through the streets from the back of a car. 'Your country is being targetted and you know who is behind all this – behind it is Zionism, that's clear now. It's become clear to us and I say not 100 percent but 95 percent that what happened now has Zionist hands behind it. Unfortunately, they duped some of our people, they duped them and got them in trouble and the latest of it is what happened in Yanbu', the king told a gathering of princes, ministers and commoners in Jeddah in comments shown on Saudi state television and carried in Arabic newspapers.[29] The United States government complained about the comments.[30] When Saud al-Faisal spoke publicly a few days later he said the attacks were part of a wider Zionist campaign to destabilise the country since Israeli funding had made its way to the Saudi dissidents in London, Saad Fagih and Mohammed al-Mas'ari, whom the interior ministry had accused of links to the attack in a statement. The Saudi leadership was convinced after 9/11 that Israel's lobbies were actively trying to widen the rift between Washington and Riyadh to breaking point ('They're after us', an advisor to Abdullah told me in March 2003, waiving a copy of Dore Gold's *Hatred's Kingdom*).

Nayef also blamed Egypt's Muslim Brotherhood for the political radicalisation of Wahhabism that bin Laden and al-Qa'ida represented, though it was the Saudi government in the first place who had welcomed Brotherhood cadres to Saudi Arabia in the 1970s. Nayef said the kingdom had evicted some of those Brotherhood members. 'The Muslim Brotherhood is the source of all of our problems in the Arab world', he said.[31] The Brotherhood's leader, Ma'moun al-Hodeiby, puzzled at the accusation. 'If any of them had done anything against Saudi Arabia the kingdom would naturally have acted to end their presence there and had they acted as a group against the country they would have been expelled en masse in a clear manner to all', Hodeiby said. 'They never tried to form a formal Brotherhood group there, that was a red line that the Brotherhood observed in the kingdom.' But he also noted that the Brotherhood publicly opposed the entry of 'colonial forces' into Kuwait to evict the Iraqis in 1991, and here lies the problem.[32] Saudi Arabia's problem was with any force, Islamist or otherwise, seeking an active role in politics and decision-making, not least foreign policy, the arena where Riyadh understands American expectations are highest in return for its protection.[33]

The US government began to suspect that the controversial family it had propped up for decades, at considerable cost to international human rights standards, had been playing a double game through funding and promoting Islamist guerrilla activities against it. Reports emerged that charity money from many ordinary Saudis had reached al-Qa'ida, an organisation that emerged from among the Arab Mujahideen who Saudi Arabia and the United States did so much to create in the 1980s. In October 2001, North Atlantic Treaty Organisation (NATO) forces stormed the offices of the Supreme Saudi Authority for Aid in Bosnia set up by Prince Sultan where they found pictures of the US embassies in Kenya and

Tanzania before and after the al-Qa'ida attacks of 1998, pictures of the Twin Towers in New York, and of the US destroyer *Cole*, attacked in Yemen. Swiss banks stopped the movement of funds in accounts held by Saudi princes, money which totalled $800 billion, after American pressure. Some Saudi diplomats were removed from the Saudi embassy in Washington by the federal government and even Aramco officials found difficulty getting visas to enter the United States.[34]

A briefing to Pentagon officials in August 2002 by Laurent Murawiec, a French analyst from the RAND Corporation, described Saudi Arabia bluntly as the enemy, and it not only leaked out to the public but apparently made quite an impression with US officials. The presentation, which came in the context of US preparations for an invasion of Iraq to bring down the regime of Saddam Hussein, stated 'Iraq is the tactical pivot; Saudi Arabia the strategic pivot, Egypt the prize', and suggested 'taking "Saudi" out of Arabia' by splitting the country up with the Hejaz returning to its Hashemite rulers of old (and surviving only in Jordan), with control of Mecca and Medina handed to an international body of non-Wahhabi clerics, and US troops taking control of the oil zone in the Eastern Province. 'Saudi Arabia supports our enemies and attacks our allies', the analyst said. 'The Saudis are active at every level of the terror chain, from planners to financiers, from cadre to foot-soldier, from ideologist to cheerleader.'[35] The analyst was a disciple of Richard Perle, a neo-conservative ideologue who headed the Defense Policy Board where the presentation was given. RAND had captured the zeitgeist. US Central Command chief General John Abizaid said in 2004 that Saudi Arabia had become a 'strategic problem', and Paul Pillar, a CIA analyst, presented a study to a National Intelligence Council conference in 2003 titled 'The Middle East to 2020' that suggested the possibility of Islamists toppling Al Saud.[36]

The idea of war against Iraq disturbed the Saudi leadership but their response was to work with the Americans, the better to steer the desire for revenge to other shores and discourage ideas of focussing US attention on Saudi Arabia. Saudi Arabia encouraged the US invasion, while publicly opposing it, in the hope that it would bring a more palatable Sunni strongman to power. They did not imagine it would empower the Shia and realign Iraq towards Iran. The idea that 'Saudi was next' was popular in the Arab media at the onset of the Iraq invasion in 2003. On Saudi television, preachers pronounced that Saudi was the real target of the war on Iraq and columnists in papers close to the state argued back nervously that the fears were exaggerated, while being careful to avoid mentioning the kingdom by name. 'There have been fears that this war will not end at Iraq and will include other countries in the region, according to an American strategy these people see to redraw the regional map', one Saudi daily said.[37] US political scientist Samuel Huntington argued there was a coming 'clash of civilisations' in a book he published in 1996 that borrowed a phrase first used by historian Bernard Lewis in 1990, but his thesis found new impetus after 9/11. Islamic civilisation would emerge as a major challenge to the West, he wrote: Saudi Arabia seemed to fit the bill. Saudi pan-Arab media warned that both al-Qa'ida and the neo-conservatives had Saudi Arabia in their sights. 'Al-Qa'ida wishes to reign supreme in Saudi Arabia once it brings about its collapse, even if such a collapse means a total break-up of the kingdom and the installation of a radical Islamic government on only a portion of its land', *Al-Hayat*'s New York bureau chief Raghida Dirgham wrote. 'But a clique of American and Israeli extremists is also working to bring about the collapse and break-up of Saudi Arabia.'[38]

The fact that in 2008 public discussion in the United States still brought up the question of whether to get rid of Al Saud demonstrates the strength of the bad feeling towards Saudi Arabia and the amount of space it has taken up in policy discussion in the United States since the tragic events of 2001. The Council on Foreign Relations published the dialogue of a panel on 'Democracy and America's Role in the World' that was held on the sidelines of the Republican Convention in September 2008. The moderator, Brian Atwood of the Hubert H. Humphrey Institute of Public Affairs at the University of Minnesota, commented that 'We've had little success in promoting democracy in Egypt, although some, and we don't even try in places like Saudi Arabia.' Michael Gerson, a Council on Foreign Relations member, stated the policy line that has traditionally dominated Western thinking on Saudi Arabia and which was boosted when Islamists did well in the municipal council elections of 2005. 'I don't believe anyone in the Bush administration would ask for national elections tomorrow in Saudi Arabia. The outcome of that election would be far worse than the current situation, which is really bad.' Asked the question 'what to do about Saudi Arabia', the veteran American diplomat Henry Kissinger replied: 'It's an issue that has defeated every administration that I've ever observed. I think everybody, if they were given truth serum, would recognize that this is an unviable system, and nobody has been willing to face the consequences of overthrowing that system.' Kissinger also noted that 'enlightenment' wins the Saudi regime friends and time, and King Abdullah has had success convincing the world that enlightenment now guides government policy. Kissinger's comments provoked a public Saudi response. Prince Turki al-Faisal criticised Kissinger in a speech at the National Council on US-Arab Relations. 'From one who is considered the elder statesman of America ... (this is) not very statesmanlike. Is Dr. Kissinger calling for the overthrow of the Kingdom? And for what?' the prince asked. 'The United States should also stop deluding itself, if that is the case as Mr. Kissinger has described, that Saudi Arabia can be overthrown.'[39]

In surveying how they could repair their broken relations with Washington and save themselves, Saudi leaders realised the United States was now focused on the links between Al Saud and the Wahhabi clerics, whom American analysts had homed in on as responsible for producing a generation of Muslims full of hate for America. Crown Prince Abdullah had the upper hand over his reluctant half-brothers Prince Nayef and Prince Sultan to push forward with some modernisations that would gradually roll back the influence of the clerical establishment while not tampering with the fundamentals of the relationship between Al Saud and al-Wahhabiyya. Now was the time to execute a new plan to reformulate Wahhabism as a sufficiently politically and economically liberal force to accept Saudi Arabia joining the WTO and 'normalisation' with Israel: Wahhabism without jihad and *takfir*. American English-speaking Sheikh Hamza appeared each Friday, on the MBC1 channel of King Fahd's brother-in-law, with a group of Western-dressed Muslims with near short-haircuts discussing such ideas as 'tolerance' and 'liberalism' in what was an early test balloon by the Saudi regime on how the public would react to the plan to repackage al-Wahhabiyya.[40]

Under Abdullah's guidance, the government seized the initiative after reports that the morality police prevented firefighters entering a girls' school in Mecca. The separate cleric-run General Directorate for Girls' Education was summarily dissolved and merged with the Ministry of Education, something the clerics had resisted for years. The press was given a green light to engage the liberal-con-servative debate more forcefully and risk attacks on the religious police. The ministry was also renamed from Wizarat al-ma'aarif (Ministry of Knowledge) to Wizarat al-tarbiyya wal-ta'lim (Ministry of Upbringing and Education, the phrase used throughout the Arab region) as a sign of the new phase of modernisation in education, which included a new English-language textbook (written by women) with a generally liberal tone in the Saudi context featuring Christian/Common Era dates and American greetings.[41] Identity cards were issued to women and a drive was established to employ women in large companies and banks (in the counterpunch, religious police insisted on separating men from women inside banks in 2007 and the banks caved.) The Saudi embassy in Washington opened a lucrative contract with PR agency Qorvis.

PALESTINE

After the crisis of 9/11, Saudi Arabia instituted a major policy shift on the Israeli-Palestinian question. In an interview with *New York Times* columnist Thomas Friedman, Abdullah made an offer of complete normalisation of relations between all Arab countries including Saudi Arabia and Israel in return for an Israeli withdrawal to the pre-1967 borders. Saudi media, caught unawares, tried to present it as a slip of the tongue, but it was a carefully prepared move to get maximum media attention and win the affection of the American public. During a dinner with Abdullah, Friedman said he explained to the king his idea of a land-for-peace deal between Israel and the Arab countries. To this Abdullah responded:

> This is exactly the idea I had in mind – full withdrawal from all the occupied territories, in accord with U.N. resolutions, including in Jerusalem, for full normalization of relations. I have drafted a speech along those lines. My thinking was to deliver it before the Arab summit and try to mobilize the entire Arab world behind it. The speech is written, and it is in my desk. But I changed my mind about delivering it when Sharon took the violence, and the oppression, to an unprecedented level.[42]

The link to the tensions between the United States and Saudi Arabia because of the 9/11 attacks was clear. Friedman asked Abdullah why Saudi Arabia had never apologised for the fact that 15 Saudis were involved in 9/11. He quoted Abdullah:

> We have been close friends for so long, and we never expected Americans to doubt us … We saw this attack by bin Laden and his men as an attack on us, too, and an attempt to damage the U.S.-Saudi relationship … We were deeply saddened by it and we never expected it to lead to tensions between us. But we've

now learned that we respond to events differently ... It is never too late to express our regrets.

Abdullah expressed his regret well, with a new policy on Palestine; to help sell this shift back home, the king talked not only of his pain over Palestinian suffering but President George W. Bush's too. He showed Bush pictures of destruction at a meeting on Bush's ranch at Crawford in Texas in May 2002: 'He listens and debates politely but was not fully informed about the real conditions in the region, especially the conditions suffered by the Palestinian people.' Bush's qualities as a compassionate listener were 'good news' for Palestinians, the king said.[43] This meeting, which reports have said was in fact highly strained, has been depicted by some writers as an indication of a crisis in relations brought on by Abdullah's fury over Palestinian suffering. David Ottaway describes Palestine as Abdullah's 'obsession' in his biography of the Saudi ambassador of the time, Prince Bandar.[44] Robert Lacey even tells us that Abdullah had tears in his eyes.[45] Both Ottaway and Lacey fall into the trap of construing Saudi Arabia's unpopular, overly pro-American policies as the product of the machinations of Bandar bin Sultan, whom they and others argue fell definitively out of favour with Abdullah in late 2007.[46] It was very clear from within the Arab world that Saudi Arabia and other Arab governments' concern over Palestine once the intifada erupted in 2000 was driven by fear for domestic stability because of popular anger not just at Israel and the United States, but at their own governments whose political bankruptcy was so exposed by the situation in Palestine. For similar reasons, he refused to budge over American prodding to make moves towards normalising ties with Israel as an 'incentive' to Israel on peace talks with Palestinians, in 2003 in a post-Iraq war meeting in Sharm al-Sheikh and in 2009 after Barack Obama assumed the American presidency.

The Thomas Friedman peace plan quickly mushroomed as a means for all the Arab leaders allied to America, not least Egypt's President Mubarak, who was under popular pressure to take a stronger stance against Israel but could not because Washington backed Israeli Prime Minister Ariel Sharon in his effort to crush the Palestinian uprising, to improve their position with the United States. The plan became an official Arab League initiative at a summit in Beirut in March 2002 that Palestinian leader Yasser Arafat was unable to attend because Israeli forces had besieged his offices in Ramallah. In fact Israeli forces stormed the city of Jenin in one of the most violent and controversial chapters of the intifada that begun in September 2000, ignoring the fact that Saudi Arabia had offered this major concession. The Saudi plan was effectively a rehash of a vaguer one presented by King Fahd in the early 1980s and rejected by an Arab summit in Fez, Morocco, in 1981. Intended to counter Egypt's go-it-alone policy of peace with Israel begun in 1977 with Sadat's visit to Jerusalem, the Fahd plan talked of an Israeli withdrawal from all occupied territories and an independent Palestinian state and a promise, implicit, to recognise Israel. Had Abdullah's plan been introduced through the normal diplomatic channels it would probably have gone nowhere because it was short on details, simply talking about comprehensive peace in return for land, which played well in the court of international public opinion.

At Saudi instigation, the Gulf Cooperation Council (GCC) countries shifted their position on Israel and the Palestinians in the decade following 2000 to conform with Washington policy and the requirements of 'moderation'. The GCC gave its full support to the Arab peace initiative, 'a major transformation of the GCC position on relations with Israel', according to a study by the Middle East Studies Centre in Amman.[47] This was despite Israeli's escalations of its operations against the Palestinian uprising that began in 2000, destroying Palestinian Authority institutions, and the Israeli government's cool response to the initiative. The summit, held in Bahrain in 2004, for the first time talked of a 'viable Palestinian state living side-by-side with Israel', mirroring the new language of the administration of George W. Bush that held it was not reasonable for Israel to give up all settlements in the occupied territories. It also conceded the Israeli and American position that the death of Palestinian leader Yasser Arafat removed an obstacle to a resolution of the conflict, declaring 'the importance of seizing the appropriate circumstances and opportunity presented' for obtaining Palestinian rights. The 2005 summit in the UAE welcomed Israel's dismantling of settlements and withdrawal of troops from inside Gaza, though it had condemned the plan for unilateral withdrawal in 2003, and declared that the 'road map' peace track led by Bush was in complete conformity with the Arab peace initiative which Israel had rejected primarily because of its call for a just solution to the Palestinian refugee issue. The 2006 summit in Riyadh repeated the reference to a 'viable state' and added to it a call for an end to 'violence and counter-violence' – the first time Gulf leaders had qualified the right of Palestinians to resist occupation. In 2001, for example, the summit distinguished between resistance activities and acts of terrorism; now, resistance was only justified as a response to specific Israeli military actions, not a natural right vis-à-vis military occupation. The 2007 summit in Doha used the phrase 'Palestinian-Israel conflict' for the first time, distancing the Arab countries from it, and expressed support for a Palestinian state according to the vision of Bush, who had set a timetable for ending negotiations by the end of 2008. 'The GCC position on a resolution was almost linked to the American position and the GCC was keen to continually praise American efforts despite the consensus in the Arab world over its bias towards Israel in the peace process. But the overlap in economic, political, security and military links between the GCC and the United States does not allow them enough room for maneuver', the study says.[48]

Abdullah was careful enough to play to the gallery while developing the new Saudi policy on Palestine. He issued public warnings against an invasion of Iraq, which by early 2002 had emerged as a possibility the Bush administration was seriously considering. 'Any attack on Iraq or Iran should not be contemplated at all because it would not serve the interests of America, the region or the world, as there is no clear evidence of a present danger. Iraq is contemplating the return of the inspectors, and the U.S. should pursue this because inspectors can determine if Iraq is complying with the U.N. resolutions', he said.[49] Yet Saudi Arabia's exact position on the Iraq invasion was not clear. While on the one hand the king and his foreign minister acted in consort with other Arab leaders to avert the war, testimony subsequently published suggests that the ambassador in Washington, Prince Bandar, was actively encouraging a war with the king's blessing.[50] Embarrassed by these revelations, Saudi officials have tried to present the support for the Iraq war as the work of freelancing ambassador in Washington Prince Bandar, who, the argument goes, did not represent the position of the king or the elders of the family generally.[51] As early as August 2002, media reports said Saudi Arabia secretly supported a US move to bring down Saddam Hussein and end what had been a secular, Arab nationalist nuisance for three decades.[52] It became public knowledge later that, despite fervent Saudi denials at the time, the American air operation during the Iraq war was conducted from the Prince Sultan Airbase at al-Kharj south of Riyadh, which had coordinated the policing of Iraqi no-fly zones established after the 1991 Gulf war as well as the Afghanistan war in October 2001.[53] Abdullah approved their use on condition that the US would leave Saudi Arabia once the war was over.[54] During the Iraq invasion, the US air force also made use of the northern Saudi airstrips in Arar and Tabuk.

The Arab peace initiative came round again in 2007 during Saudi Arabia's hosting of an Arab summit it had declined the previous year. Saudi Arabia was still locked into its traditional preference for quiet behind-the-scenes diplomacy, despite Abdullah's accession to the throne. Riyadh's concerns about Iran, its nuclear energy programme and its Shi'ite allies in Iraq and Lebanon had reached fever pitch. Saud al-Faisal engaged in public attacks on Iran in 2005, but it was in 2006 that events provoked Saudi Arabia into changing its diplomatic strategy to present itself as the leading Arab state, the leading Sunni Muslim state and the state best-placed to defend Sunni Arab interests against Iranian expansion. While Iran stepped into the breach left by the Egypt and Saudi governments' disconnect from the mainstream Arab nationalist street (their disinterest in Palestine), the Saudi regime saw its needs served by stepping up to fill the gap created by Egypt's distraction with increasing domestic discontent and the effort to establish Gamal Mubarak as Mubarak's heir. The huge revenues flowing into Saudi state coffers during this time also fed the diplomatic drive, allowing the country to emerge as a regional leader – but this position of leadership relied heavily on rentier wealth and lacked an institutional capacity for managing foreign policy, and that was another drag on Saudi Arabia's bid for the title 'leader of the Arabs'. The shift in Saudi policy on the Israeli-Palestinian conflict was such that the US State Department was surprised to find the kingdom for the first time offering a detailed breakdown of its financing of the Palestinian Authority, from a presumed desired to demonstrate it was being 'helpful', diplomats noted, in realising their common interests.[55]

LEBANON 2006: 'IRRESPONSIBLE ADVENTURISM'

In 2006 sectarian fighting threatened to drag Iraq into a civil war and Saudi clerics and media focused on minority Sunnis suffering at the hands of the Shi'ites. In the summer of 2006 Iran's Lebanese ally Hizbullah found itself embroiled in a major military conflagration with Israel that Saudi Arabia, following the line of Western capitals and media, uncharacteristically blamed publicly on Hizbullah because it had kidnapped two Israeli soldiers from across the border into Israel in the hope of swapping them for Lebanese held by Israel. 'A distinction must be made between legitimate resistance and uncalculated adventures undertaken by elements inside (Lebanon) and those behind them, without recourse to the legal authorities and consulting and coordinating with Arab nations', said an official Saudi statement released on 14 July, a few days into the fighting.[56] 'These elements should bear the responsibility for their irresponsible actions and they alone should end the crisis they have created.' Again, government officials have tried to disseminate the idea that Bandar was behind a diplomatic posture that did not put the kingdom in a good light before Arab public opinion: Ottaway cites a government source for the claim that Bandar planted the statement on SPA (the Saudi Press Agency), yet the key phrase 'adventurism' was repeated in Arabic on numerous occasions by Saud al-Faisal.[57]

American diplomatic cables from during the war reveal US and Saudi concern about the unpopularity of the Saudi position during the war, during which Israel imposed an air and sea blockade, bombed Beirut's international airport and invaded south Lebanon (killing over 1,100 Lebanese civilians). 'Grassroots anger toward the government has been fueled by what many are calling a surprisingly weak government position vis-a-vis Israel and Lebanon', a report from the consulate in Jeddah says.[58] A politics professor at King Abdulaziz University in Jeddah tells diplomats that the Saudi government statement had been an object of ridicule among his students: 'Noting that "they all laughed" about the July 14 statement [he] explained that the broader feeling is that Israel over-reacted in their attacks and that the Kingdom should not just pretend to be neutral when innocent Arabs are being killed.'[59] Over two weeks later, after it became clear that Hizbullah was surviving and capable of hurting Israel with rocket fire, a panicked-sounding Saud al-Faisal[60] summoned the US ambassador to explain that the war was moving towards a 'full victory' for Hizbullah: 'What is occurring is strengthening Hizbullah, not weakening it. These are the damage assessments we are getting from a wide variety of intelligence and other sources.'[61] Mubarak could not bring himself to utter the group's name when swarmed upon by press cameras, preferring the colourful colloquial Egyptian designation *il-bita' da* ('thingy') instead.

Saudi Arabia, Egypt and Jordan appeared to have colluded with Western powers to see the war prolonged for the sake of allowing Israel more time to finish off Hizbullah. Syrian President Bashar al-Assad, backer of Hizbullah, taunted Arab leaders as 'half-men', and Hizbullah employed street protests and a sit-in outside the cabinet offices in central Beirut to bring pressure on the Saudi and US-backed Siniora government to increase the number of seats Hizbullah and its allies had in cabinet, a victory that remained despite the fact that the Saudi and US-backed coalition of Saad al-Hariri won parliamentary elections in 2009. Western governments isolated Hamas by cutting off funding after its victory in Palestinian parliamentary elections in January 2006, and Saudi Arabia, although it had publicly backed Hamas as legitimate victor in a vote called for and supported by Washington, fell in line with the international effort to stop funds flowing to the Palestinian Authority under Hamas control. Hamas therefore turned to Iran for financial backing. Saudi Arabia watched as Iran was able to play hero by backing the Palestinians in the occupied territories and the Lebanese who backed Palestinian resistance; King Abdullah talked on a number of occasions of the danger of allowing Iran the chance to pose as champion of Arab-Islamic causes, but Saudi policies continued to produce that outcome.[62]

With the infrastructure damage to Lebanon in 2006, Saudi Arabia saw some of its own money go up in smoke, having consistently acted to support the Lebanese pound since the civil war ended in 1990. Competition emerged post-war to help the country stand on its feet. Saudi Arabia transferred $1 billion to Lebanon's central bank in late July when Israel's offensive was still in full swing to prop up the Western-backed government of Fouad Siniora. Through Iran, Hizbullah led its own reconstruction effort. Saudi Arabia played the lead role in the following months in whipping up anti-Shi'ite sentiment while Nasrallah became a hero not only to Shi'ites, who displayed his and Iranian revolution leader Ayatollah Khomeini's picture prominently in the Saudi Eastern Province, but to many other Arabs, who interpreted Nasrallah's actions in nationalist terms. Thus, Egypt's state-owned press began attacking Shi'ism in its editorials, though there was no particular dislike for Shi'ism per se among ordinary Egyptians.

In early 2007, fleshing out its new diplomatic aggressiveness, Saudi Arabia played host to Palestinian unity talks in February 2007 with the hope of ending street-fighting between Hamas and Mahmoud Abbas and Fatah. The two sides agreed to establish a unity government of both parties, but the United States, the European Union, Russia and Israel ultimately rebuffed it – or failed to lift their embargo on the Hamas-led government – because there was no explicit commitment to recognise Israel, a state without defined borders, and commit to past peace deals. The reconciliation effort had irritated the Bush administration in the first place as an example of Saudi diplomatic freelancing and straying from the line of no talks with a group, Hamas, it deemed terrorist. The summit could perhaps be viewed as Saudi Arabia's one misguided attempt to play the populist card and challenge Iranian policy on those terms, though it was based on propping up a regime in Ramallah that only survived via Israeli and Western will and tried to smother Palestinian attempts at even peaceful resistance and civil disobedience. Within months fighting returned and the deal finally unravelled with Hamas's defeat of Fatah forces in Gaza, leaving only the West Bank in Fatah hands. The Saudi effort was widely seen as a failure.

The Arab summit of 2007 played a central role in Saudi diplomacy during this time. Perhaps the high-point of Abdullah's foreign policy, the summit was Saudi Arabia's chance to pose as the voice of moderation through reinvigorating the Arab peace initiative of 2002 and dousing the flames of apparent radicalism sweeping the region. The slogans used by the Saudis during the summit reflected the idea that Saudi Arabia's non-confrontational approach to the Israeli-Palestinian conflict was the best way to solve it: 'Unity behind a just cause provides strength', 'Welcome to the country of peace and humanity'. The king remained true to his carefully constructed 'Arab nationalist' image by terming the American military presence in Iraq an 'illegitimate occupation', though a full four years after it began that rang hollow in many ways (both Lacey and Ottaway read it as a sign of a major rupture in relations with Washington). It was clearly grandstanding for the occasion, an attempt to wrest the title 'leader of the Arabs' from people like Nasrallah when the lights were turned his way. Indeed, his crown prince Sultan sounded a different note entirely in an interview several months later – 'Whether the American and other international coalition forces in Iraq should remain or withdraw is an issue that concerns the Iraqi people and its government.'[63] The concerns of Western foreign office mandarins in the 1990s over Abdullah's alleged 'Arabism' and anti-American tendencies came to nothing, with his peace initiative in 2002 and agitating against Hizbullah and Iran since 2003 (though paranoia and doubt are never far away: one amusing US diplomatic cable from 2006 surmises the king could be a closet Hizbullah lover[64]). Those concerns were always out of place: a US diplomatic cable from 1996 states that Abdullah was an ardent friend of the United States who 'repeatedly and emphatically stressed his personal commitment to a strong U.S.-Saudi bilateral relationship', and describes him as an architect of the bloc of Arab 'moderates'.[65] In fact, once Abdullah became king, the epithet *saqr al-'uruba* ('falcon of Arabism') gave way in Saudi media to *malik al-insaniyya* ('king of humanity').

Lebanon remained hamstrung by the political crisis with Hizbullah. Hizbullah and its allies overran areas controlled by the governing bloc's parties and militias in May 2008 – 'Hizbullah's coup' in apoplectic Saudi media – after a move by the cabinet to ban Hizbullah's independent telecommunications network, which had been crucial to its survival during the 2006 war. The result was a Qatar-brokered deal that finally gave the Hizbullah opposition the third-plus-one seats in cabinet that would allow it to block decisions; it was a defeat for Saudi Arabia, though it made up ground the following year via massive funding that allowed its March 14 allies to win general elections. Syria was finding success in rebuilding ties with Western powers, taking a leaf from the Saudi book by activating the Israel card – Turkey set up an informal negotiation process. Saudi Arabia was not happy at these developments. 'More and more Saudis begin to see Syria as having allowed a strategic threat into our part of the world, allowing the Iranians to penetrate the area. Saudi Arabia is really bothered by Iran's ideological moves surrounding us. The problem with the Iranians is they just deal along sectarian lines', said Jamal Khashoggi, then editor of *Al-Watan*. 'The king is personally unhappy with the regime there. We can wait until a serious change happens in Syria.'[66] Saudi Arabia's chance was to come in 2011, a chance to make common cause with parties willing to take down an enemy but to deflect attention from the rumblings of discontent at home.

SHI'ITE CRESCENT

Saudi Arabia identified a new Shi'ite threat after the invasion of Iraq in 2003 removed Saddam Hussein and his Baath regime, which Riyadh and its Western allies had seen as a buffer against Iranian revolutionary expansionism. Post-invasion Iraq, with Shi'ites in the ascendant, was a markedly different country from before. A secular Arab nationalist state that had belatedly veered into Sunni political Islam during the 1990s had become a Shi'ite Islamic state overnight. Shi'ite iconography and slogans sprang up everywhere, the call to prayer on state television came in a Shi'ite format, Shi'ite clerics in clerical attire were powerful figures in government, secular Shi'ite politicians as well as the clerics would seek audiences with the reclusive guru of Iraqi Shi'ism, Grand Ayatollah Ali al-Sistani, whom Sunnis cursed for his Iranian upbringing. One word form

Sistani could change the political course of an entire nation. It was the Najaf-based Sistani who laid down the principle for Shi'ites that they should work with the new US-formed order through democratic elections rather than fight the Americans as occupiers. It was Sistani who called on Shi'ites to resist the temptation to engage in all-out revenge against the suicide-bomb attacks of Sunni insurgents like al-Qa'ida in Iraq, who would kill dozens of civilians at a time in mosques, markets and bus stations with the stated aim of provoking civil war with the Shi'ite community. And it was Sistani who in August 2003 scuppered the plans of America's occupation administrator Paul Bremer to appoint members of a council to draft a new constitution, which would have delayed the process of elections and handing power to Iraqis. Sistani's prime concern was unequivocally Shi'ite interests, though as a leading Shi'ite figure who did not subscribe to the theory of *velayat-e fagih*, he was not Iran's favoured scholar. Ahead of the parliamentary elections in December 2005, he instructed believers to do three things: turn out to vote, avoid voting for candidates who were not 'religious', and not to vote for weak candidate lists so as not to split the Shi'ite vote.[67]

Radical Sunni Islamists from around the Arab world made common cause with Sunnis in Iraq, most notably under the al-Qa'ida aegis in a group led by the Jordanian Abu Musab al-Zarqawi. In their view, the Shi'ites were not only 'rejectionists' (*al-Rafida*) who follow a deviant version of Islam's true monotheistic message, they were also opportunists who were prepared to accept the occupation of their country for the sake of gaining power; they were also prepared to allow another foreign actor, Iran, unprecedented influence for reasons of politics and ideology. The broad anti-imperial aims of al-Qa'ida's ideology were shared by the Arab mainstream, both government and opposition. On the eve of Iraq's elections in 2005 that brought Shi'ite parties to power, Jordan's King Abdullah spoke of a 'Shi'ite crescent' running from Iran into south Lebanon. Fissures later appeared between Arab governments and opposition groups over an American exit from Iraq – the governments fearing that Iraq would be vulnerable to even more Iranian influence if US forces left before fixing the political system to ensure the Sunnis more clout. By late 2005, when Arab governments showed their opposition to a quick US withdrawal at a Cairo conference for reconciliation between the Iraqi factions, a civil war between Sunnis and Shi'ites had become a real possibility. Nationalist and Islamist opposition groups around the region simply wanted the Americans out.

Sunnis suspected that the Shi'ite paramilitary group known as the Badr Brigades was behind sectarian murders of Sunnis which appeared to be in response to the wanton violence of al-Qa'ida and other groups, often targeting the families of men who had worked for the Baathist police or intelligence services. The Badr Brigades were the military wing of the Supreme Council for the Islamic Revolution (renamed Islamic Supreme Council of Iraq in 2007), formerly an Islamist dissident group led by Abdulaziz al-Hakim (d. 2009) which was based in Tehran before the invasion of 2003. Sunnis accused the Badr group of working from within the Shi'ite-dominated interior ministry to carry out sectarian violence. The minister Bayan Jabr Solagh became an object of suspicion in the wider Arab media. He was asked directly in an interview on Al-Jazeera about accusations that he was not Arab at all but Iranian. 'I'm proud of being an Arab', he responded, linking himself to the Zubeid tribe of Emara in south Iraq.[68] Sunnis complained they were being shut out of government jobs, especially if they had Baath party connections. Following on the Jordanian monarch's comments about Shi'ism, the Saudi foreign minister said publicly in September 2005 that Iraq was being 'handed to Iran' and Sunnis were no longer equal citizens. 'We fought a war together to keep Iran out of Iraq after Iraq was driven out of Kuwait', he told the Council of Foreign Relations in New York, referring to the first Gulf war in 1991 when Saudi Arabia fought with the United States to liberate Kuwait after the Iraqi invasion. 'Now we are handing the whole country over to Iran without reason.'[69] Jabr described Saud al-Faisal as a 'Bedouin riding a camel'. 'This Iraq is the cradle of civilisation that taught humanity reading and writing, and some Bedouin riding a camel wants to teach us. This talk is totally rejected', he said.

> There are regimes that are dictatorships; they have one god, he is the king, he is God of heaven and earth, and he rules as he likes. A whole country is named after a family. If we open these topics without inhibitions, it is neither to our benefit nor to theirs … I wish they would give women their rights and let them drive, let alone vote. In Iraq, a woman can be head of state and can become a minister.[70]

Hosni Mubarak said on Al-Arabiya television that most Shi'ites were 'loyal to Iran and not to the countries they live in'.[71]

The death of Saddam Hussein, though he was despised for his secularism, played into Saudi-Wahhabi sectarianism. Hussein was put to death on the Eid al-Adha during the hajj pilgrimage in January 2007. Film of the hanging showed Shi'ite officials and prison guards in the Iraqi government jeering at the once-feared dictator and chanting the name of Shi'ite cleric Muqtada al-Sadr. The images went down badly in Saudi Arabia, for not only religious but tribal and Arabist reasons. Saudis passed around pro-Saddam poetry in mobile phone text messages and a Gulf newspaper carried an anonymous poem, widely assumed to be the work of poet-minister Ghazi al-Gosaibi, that threatened revenge: 'Prepare the gun that will avenge Saddam. The criminal who signed the execution order without valid reason cheated us on our celebration day. How beautiful it will be when the bullet goes through the heart of him who betrayed Arabism.'[72] 'The timing shows how much Shi'ites hate Sunnis in Iraq and all the Islamic world', the Sahwa cleric Nasser al-Omar wrote on his website. 'They want to link Saddam to Sunni Islam, blame Sunnis for his mistakes and show his execution as a victory for Shi'ites.' He employed the sectarian language shared by al-Wahhabiyya and al-Qa'ida, describing Shi'ites as 'Safavids', the name of the fifteenth-century dynasty that established Shi'ism as the state religion in Iran, and 'sons of Ibn 'Alqami', a reference to a Shi'ite minister whom Sunnis say connived with the Mongols in the 1258 fall of Baghdad. 'We have to protect Sunni societies from the Shi'ite invasion', the Egyptian Brotherhood-linked cleric Yousef al-Qaradawi said in 2008, though reflecting the outlook of modern political Islam he drew a line at condemnation of Hizbullah's actions against Israel.[73]

In the Wahhabi view, Shi'ism itself had gained prestige through Hizbullah's actions. Taking the Saudi regime's position of non-action in the regional arena as his base, the Saudi mufti said that challenging the Israelis would only provoke them into more bellicose measures against Muslim interests. Hizbullah exposed Lebanon to Israeli reprisals, he said. 'The prearranged, organised revolutions happening in Lebanon, that have been so well-prepared, by those who are considered to be part of Islam and who raise the slogans of Islam, while Islam is in fact innocent of them, these people have come in order to prepare the way for the Jews and the great powers, to prepare the arena for them and ease their entry and help them control countries of Islam in every sense', he said. 'These steps were not random, they were to prepare for evils that I pray to God to stop.'[74] The comments amounted to a circular justification from the Saudi regime's high priests for its pro-Western foreign policy and facilitation of US-Israeli interests.

ISRAELI OVERTURES

Saudi Arabia has no official relations with Israel. Saudi policy was to remain aloof from the conflict in Palestine before the events of 1947–49 that saw Palestinians lose their homeland and the state of Israel established. This was the period of Mandate Palestine when the territory was under the control of Britain, Abdulaziz's close ally. A unit of some 3,000 troops was sent to fight with Egyptian forces in 1947. Palestinian refugees were hired at Aramco at the behest of the government, but their numbers were kept low since neither the Saudis nor the Americans had an interest in creating a centre of dissent. Saudi Arabia's main concern was to hold the Hashemite monarchies of Jordan and Iraq in check. King Abdullah of Jordan had the hope of expanding his realm westwards to include Palestine, and indeed the war of 1948 left Jordan in control of East Jerusalem and the territory that came to be known, from a Jordanian perspective, as the West Bank. In the 1960s King Faisal made Saudi Arabia a key funder of the PLO, which was presented as part of his pan-Islamic policy, and in 1973 he infamously instituted the oil embargo. Saudi Arabia was not interested in a Palestinian-leftist victory in the Lebanese civil war when it broke out in 1975, a time which fortuitously for Al Saud coincided with the era of massive oil wealth following the embargo. Saudi money was used to prop up Syrian control in Lebanon and back Christian and Sunni Muslims of its choosing, as well as its own men within the PLO.[75] Bashir Gemayel was invited to visit the Saudi leadership in Saudi Arabia shortly before Israel installed him as president-elect after its invasion in 1982. Following the Oslo Accords of 1993, which established Palestinian self-rule zones inside the occupied territories administered by the Palestinian National Authority under PLO Chairman Yasser Arafat, the mufti Bin Baz issued a fatwa legitimising the principle of 'peace with the Jews'. The Saudi government thus hoped to provide the clerical cover for any normalisation with Israel that the Israeli-Palestinian dialogue might require for states of the Arab League, which gave its blessing to this peace process.[76]

Following his Arab peace initiative, Abdullah made subtle overtures to Israel despite rebuffing US requests for more substantial public-grandstanding gestures on normalisation in 2003 and 2009. Saudi Arabia allowed several Israeli journalists to enter the kingdom to cover events such as the Arab summit of March 2007, and commentators in Saudi media promoted a soft approach. Prince

Faisal bin Salman prevented a piece running in *Asharq al-Awsat* ni which an American official, Philip Zelikow, executive director of the 9/11 commission, said the Iraq war had been fought because of Iraq's threat to Israel, not to the United States.[77] When Turkish prime minister Recep Tayyip Erdogan argued with Israeli counterpart Shimon Peres at the Davos World Forum in 2009, *Al-Hayat* columnist Raghida Dirgham criticised his behaviour on Al-Arabiya television as 'beyond what's reasonable'. Foreign media reported several informal meetings between Israeli officials and Prince Bandar bin Sultan in 2006, in the context of his shuttle diplomacy concerned with limiting Shi'ite-Iranian influence in Iraq and Lebanon. Saudi Arabia only stepped up to deny these reports when they concerned the king. Israeli paper *Yedioth Aharonot* reported in September 2006 that he had met with then prime minister Ehud Olmert, a report picked up by Al-Jazeera television before its rapprochement with Riyadh. 'The news is completely fabricated and that the kingdom is carrying out its nationalist role transparently and does not have declared and undeclared policies', the Saudi Press Agency cited a foreign ministry source as saying.[78] The idea that the maverick Prince Bandar was acting solo – as Saudi defenders claim regarding his support for the American invasion of Iraq – was again useful in deflecting these reports and the criticism they could bring (though he still had the confidence of the king to be despatched to various capitals, including Moscow in 2008 where he concluded a deal on military cooperation).[79]

The revival of the peace initiative in 2007 helped pave the way for the Annapolis conference later that year in the United States, which hoped to revive talks between the Israeli government and the Palestinian Authority under Abbas. The idea behind the conference in the final stretch of George W. Bush's presidency was to marginalise Hamas by showing progress in peace talks leading to an independent Palestinian state. Saudi Arabia insisted there must be an Israeli agreement on suspending work-in-progress building Jewish settlements in the West Bank and other steps for the conference to be worthwhile attending. In the end, Saud al-Faisal went. Abdullah's interfaith initiative of 2008 formed the backdrop for the next stage in the long dance between Tel Aviv and Riyadh. The initiative led to a two-day United Nations general assembly meeting in New York on promoting the 'culture of peace', at which the king and a number of world leaders spoke, including Israeli president Shimon Peres. Peres, Abdullah and others, including the head of Al-Azhar, attended a dinner together (a photograph of Mohammed al-Tantawi shaking

Peres's hand circulated afterwards, causing the Sheikh of Al-Azhar to say he did not know whose hand he was shaking). Peres took the chance to praise the Arab peace initiative. 'Your majesty, the king of Saudi Arabia, I was listening to your message. I wish that your voice will become the prevailing voice of the whole region, of all people. It's right, it's needed, it's promising', Peres said, addressing the assembly and the king directly. 'The initiative's portrayal of our region's future provides hope to the people and inspires confidence in the nations.'[80] Israeli politicians began to speak positively of Saudi regional policy during the reign of Abdullah.

The UN conference on world peace, sponsored by Abdullah and UN Secretary-General Ban Ki-Moon was in itself probably the only success of Saudi foreign policy in the period since 2001, since it confirmed, if confirmation were needed, that the crisis brought about in the kingdom's relations with the United States and other countries was indeed over. In the words of one commentator, 'Who would have thought that just seven autumns after 9/11 the king of Saudi Arabia would be welcomed to Manhattan and feted as the inspirer of a dialogue for religious tolerance and peace?'[81] Who, indeed? Addressing the leaders of the Western countries it had wrestled with and sought to mollify since 2001, including Bush, the British prime minister and the Israeli president, the king had overseen a stunning turnaround for Saudi Arabia in terms of its global standing after the debacle of 9/11. Abdullah could banter with German foreign minister Frank-Walter Steinmeier in 2008 about troublesome states which responsible countries like Germany and Saudi Arabia, the weight of the world on their shoulders, must deal with. 'Why can't we exchange neighbours? We would even take Kosovo!' the king joked.[82]

7
The Saudi *Cordon Sanitaire* in Arab Media

Following the 9/11 attacks, the Saudi government made a strategic decision to open up the country to unprecedented domestic debate in the daily press as well as to the presence of foreign media. The changes of the decade following 9/11 are significant and have certainly impressed friendly foreign states, who are looking for policy changes that they believe will weaken the reach of radical anti-American ideology in the country. A US diplomatic cable from May 2009 concerning Saudi media concludes:

> In keeping with other initiatives such as the Interfaith Dialogue and plans for educational reform, the SAG [Saudi Arabian government] has clearly made a strategic decision to open the country to outside opinion, perspectives and culture to root out the vestiges of the extremist ideology and vision that threatened their rule. At the same time, they have refined their methods of control over editors and journalists in an effort to control the spread of these and other dissident ideas.[1]

These control mechanisms within Saudi Arabia fit into a wider pattern of control concerning the entire Arab region that has its origins in the crisis Al Saud faced during the Gulf crisis of 1990–91.

My own experience with the control mechanisms of Saudi media began in 2006, when I was called into the Ministry of Information over a story concerning Ismaili Shi'ites in the Najran region and a protest they attempted to stage about perceived marginalisation. A majority of the population in Najran, they had revolted against the local governor – a son of King Saud – in April 2000, besieging him in a local hotel after the arrest of an Ismaili cleric. Following that, 90 men faced trial in Riyadh and hundreds of Ismailis in the government bureaucracy were transferred to elsewhere in the country, while the authorities devised a scheme to settle Sunni tribes from Yemen who had long been resident in the area in an effort to dilute the Ismaili majority. When I visited in 2006, I found the information ministry in Riyadh ringing to enquire about my wherebouts within an hour of arrival. The following evening a security officer and a religious policeman knocked on my hotel-room door and waited until the next morning to escort me to the airport, but fortunately I had already managed to squeeze in nearly two days of investigation. I saw large tracts of confiscated land where housing projects were underway for Sunni tribes of Yemeni origin – prim towns with grid street designs, one-storey villas, street lighting and electricity. At that stage 10,000 had been settled, but Ismailis said the plans could extend to some 50,000 people among the tribes. Large billboards signed in the name of Yemeni tribal leaders had been erected to thank the local governor and Crown Prince Sultan for funding the housing projects. In a deserted office whose door had not been locked, we perused maps on the walls outlining elaborate plans for entire new districts. But none of it was for the Ismailis who have lived in the main town for centuries. 'There are families here who cannot get a new house or a legal deed to the land they live on. Even the children of the newcomers are given plots of land. It's a form of racial discrimination', said Nasser, a teacher who drove me around these sites. 'It is our ancestors who are buried here. But psychologically they make you feel like you are a stranger in your own land.'

The story that provoked a call from the office of one of the deputy ministers responsible for foreign media, preceded that visit by one month. Dozens of Ismailis had taken up a spot by the roadside near the airport, raising banners to protest against their situation. The deputy minister explained that he had made his own checks into the report and had been informed by police that no protest had taken place. Therefore, no protest had taken place and I should be more careful about who I speak to. I explained that I had avoided writing that there were large numbers involved since I was aware from demonstrations in Egyptian university campuses of the exaggerations protesters often indulge in; I had also tried to get an interior ministry comment but the spokesman failed to respond. What stuck out from this exchange, however, was when the minister – who cultivated the image of a liberal intellectual with his poetry and press columns – tried to press his point about who to trust. He turned to my colleague and asked him where he was from. 'I'm Jordanian', my colleague said, hoping that would command more respect than admitting he was Palestinian. 'Ah, well as you know, the Arabs are liars.' I should not have been shocked at this internalisation of a nasty Orientalist cliché, but I was. The idea seemed to be: amid a sea of liars, the only voice of authority and truth is that of the state. We all chortled at the comment, which at least afforded us the opportunity to part on a contrived upbeat note.

The second time I was summoned was in early 2008. Sheikh Abdulrahman al-Barrak had issued one of his famous fatwa bromides, this time suggesting that two liberal writers in the press deserved to face trial for suggesting that followers of all three monotheistic religions, Islam, Christianity and Judaism, were on a par in God's eyes. If they failed to repent in the face of a guilty verdict then they deserved the death penalty, he said. Again I found the deputy minister's office on the phone. What seemed to have irked the authorities was that the story had been picked up by CNN. That meant Barrak's fatwa had the potential to become a political issue between Washington and Riyadh, as happened with the Qatif-girl case, referred to in Chapter 4, a few months before. It should have been made clearer, he said, that Barrak does not speak for the Saudi government: that is the mufti's job. The story I wrote had explained that Barrak was regarded as the highest independent authority among Wahhabi *ulama*, but I said I would make sure in future to point out that there is also a mufti who represents the view of the Saudi state on religious matters and who advises the authorities when required.

By the time the third summons came in November, I had been verbally attacked over the summer on some websites for stories concerning the relatively open atmosphere in Jeddah and the 'liberal enclaves' the king hoped to establish with the King Abdullah Economic City and KAUST, where al-Wahhabiyya's strict rules on gender segregation and other social issues were expected to be put in abeyance. The story that finally tipped the scales against me was one that I did not imagine, naively, would cause any trouble at all. The state news agency announced that Prince Sultan would leave the country for medical treatment, but did not give details. It was well-known he had been treated for cancer of the colon but the problem had persisted. The published story in question had included that background, sourced to diplomats and people close to Sultan. Within half an hour of the article going out, the ministry rang. The meeting the next day was not pleasant. The deputy minister maintained a menacing cordiality. 'You're the person we should talk to. It seems you know better than we do what's going on in the country!' the minister began. I laughed nervously as we shook hands, and then after we settled down in our seats he made his lunge for the jugular: 'I need you to tell me who your sources are', he said with icy calm and a false smile. He had his pen poised over a piece of paper as if he really expected me to tell him. I said journalists had gone to jail in other countries to protect sources and that, even if I wanted to comply, I work for an institution that doesn't allow it. The best I could do was to pass on his request and his concerns to my bosses. At this, the minister erupted. I thought I was so smart, I was just like Gordon Brown (who had come seeking Saudi emergency funding for the IMF a few days before), I reminded him of the behaviour of British colonial officials a century ago. 'You have to pack your bags!' he rasped, by this point on his feet in anger. 'And I don't want to see your name on any story until you've gone.'

It seemed to me that such endings were the inevitable conclusion of the Saudi experiment in opening up to foreign media, and it was the first of a series of skirmishes with Western correspondents in the country or hoping to work there. Major changes in the development of Saudi media policy first took place in the wake of the Iraqi invasion of Kuwait in 1990. The crisis had two serious consequences for Arab media generally: weakened by war and international sanctions, Iraq drew back its funding of Arab media outlets, and alarmed at the dissent the crisis had unleashed, Saudi Arabia decided to upgrade its presence. The war and Saudi Arabia's backing for it posed questions of image and legitimacy for Saudi Arabia both domestically and in other Arab and Muslim countries. Using their financial resources, the royal family and its allies acted to drown out secular-nationalist and Islamist opposition critiques of the kingdom. Like other regimes in the region, the leadership perceived satellite television as a threat, and while the religious establishment would make its own war on the phenomenon of domestic viewership – with the religious police confiscating satellite dishes throughout the 1990s – the government realised it could not hope to hold back the tide in the long run. Dishes were banned, but those with affluence and influence did what they wanted behind the walls of their villas. The solution was to dominate the expanding airwaves with Saudi propaganda and innocuous entertainment that would keep out criticism and other subversive material.

In 1991 Walid al-Ibrahim, a Saudi businessman married to a sister of King Fahd, launched the Middle East Broadcasting Corporation (MBC), a news channel billed at the time as the Arab CNN in an attempt to frame political events in the Arabic language from a Saudi leadership perspective and create a Saudi discourse for the Arab world. This coincided with the relaunch of Lebanese daily newspaper *Al-Hayat* in 1988 with Saudi funding from Prince Khaled bin Sultan, deputy defence minister and leader of Saudi forces during the 1991 Gulf war, and Lebanese owner Kamal Moroue was subsequently forced out in the early 1990s as Prince Khaled took over ownership. Throughout the 1990s, sons of Prince Salman assumed and consolidated control of the pan-Arab daily *Asharq al-Awsat*, set up in London in 1979. The Saudi Media and Research Group (SMRG) publishes it; SMRG is partly traded publicly but part-owned by Prince Alwaleed bin Talal and businessman Mohammed Hussein Ali al-Amoudi, but it remains controlled by Prince Salman who maintains close supervision of its editorial line. Then followed the satellite entertainment network Orbit set up by Prince Khaled bin Abdullah bin Abdel-Rahman (via Mawarid Holdings) in 1994 (which joined with Showtime to form OSN in 2009, with a 50 per cent stake held by Kuwait investment firm KIPCO, which is linked to the ruling Al Sabah) and the entertainment network ART (Arab Radio and Television), set up in 1994 by businessman Saleh Kamel with funding from Prince Alwaleed bin Talal. In 2003 Alwaleed bought Kamel's 49 per cent stake in Lebanon's LBC International satellite television station, and in 2008 he raised his stake to around 85 per cent. Buying influence in the Arab media was an old game among oil powers in the region, but with the end of the Gulf war it was Saudi Arabia that seized the initiative in televisual media (Iraq was still able to buy support in Egyptian opposition newspapers in the 1990s).

The Saudi plan met with opposition and challenges. Qatar's Al-Jazeera entered the fray in 1996 with a ground-breaking approach that filled the glaring gaps in political and social coverage of the Saudi media, with frank discussions of the internal situation in Arab countries where opposition and government figures were equally welcome to offer their viewpoint. Saudi Arabia's delayed response to Al-Jazeera came in 2003 with 24-hour news broadcaster Al-Arabiya. Part of the MBC network, Al-Arabiya came on air after 9/11 and just in time for the Iraq invasion when Saudi leaders were correct in assuming they were due for a round of anti-Saudi sentiment in the Arab region similar to that which followed the 1991 Gulf war. It is under the effective control of King Fahd's favourite son Abdulaziz, a figure described by American diplomats as 'the bottom of the barrel in term of probity and decorum' who is heavily involved with the channel's coverage.[2] Saudi Arabia wanted to present the United States with a vision of 'moderation' in the Arab world to counter Al-Jazeera's hip rejectionism at that time when it came to the Western political influence in the region and Al-Jazeera's willingness to treat the ideology of Islamist groups like al-Qa'ida as worthy of debate. Al-Arabiya was part of the wider Saudi response discussed in the previous chapter to the threats the Saudi state faced in the post-9/11 world. It formed a key role in the transformation of Saudi Arabia into the Arab state, in the first years of Abdullah's rule, leading Arab public diplomacy with policies that appeased Western interests in the region and combated Iranian influence.[3]

Today, Saudi Arabia commands an immensely powerful position in the pan-Arab media, encompassing the whole gamut of political, entertainment and religious programming. This media empire seeks to present a specific message that presents itself as 'liberal', 'open-minded', 'moderate' and 'modern'. The message was conspicuously Washington-friendly, soft on Israel and inimical to al-Qa'ida, Hizbullah and Iran, and it became more and more opposed to the Assad regime in time following the assassination of Rafiq al-Hariri. American political and military leaders were given ample airspace to defend their positions in sympathetic interviews with Al-Arabiya, despite the overwhelmingly negative view among the public of the American political and military presence in Iraq, the Gulf, Afghanistan and elsewhere. Saudi media liberally employs entertainment as a means of offsetting political news. Since the late 1990s, MBC, Orbit and ART have saturated Arab viewers in Arab and Western entertainment. Although Al-Arabiya is a bona fide news channel, it carries a large amount of 'light news' to offset the tedium of Arab politics, with sometimes disconcerting results – one news bulletin in June 2007 that was dominated by civil war violence in Iraq included an item about bubblegum Lebanese singer Haifaa Wahbeh surviving an allegedly life-threatening accident while shooting a music video. Orbit shelved a project to carry BBC World Service Arabic television in 1995 after the BBC aired a show on the Saudi justice system; Orbit said it was against 'Arab cultural values'.

There is no evidence of any particular coordination of these positions among these media outlets – in fact they often reflect rivalry between different camps in the regime. But they are all owned by members of the royal family or commoner allies who share the same general outlook on the need to protect the Saudi state from foreign and domestic dangers, and they share ownership in each other's projects. Further, state-controlled media in Arab states friendly to Saudi Arabia filter out criticism of the country, which is particularly significant in the case of Egypt, once the great mobiliser against Western hegemony. Indeed, Egypt's 'media of mobilisation' (*i'lam ta'bawi*) has given way to Saudi Arabia's 'media of pacification', or *i'lam tanwimi* – a new soporific media of as great a reach as that of

Nasser, where entertainment helps put the political mind to sleep and politics is maintained within strict limits. This phenomenon has a long pedigree: Robert Vitalis catalogues in *America's Kingdom* how Saudi Aramco and Saudi authorities cooperated to provide free TV sets in 1955 to provide Western entertainment as an alternative to the nationalist politics finding popularity on radio, and they conducted surveys to see how effective it was.[4]

The effect has been to create a form of *cordon sanitaire* around Saudi Arabia in the Arab media, a sanitised zone where no news inimical to the realm of Al Saud can make its way through the purified information ether. The major threats to this Saudi space have come from Al-Jazeera, and to a much lesser degree Hizbullah's Al-Manar television, the London-based newspaper *Al-Quds al-Arabi*, and a host of opposition and independent newspapers around the region. Indeed, with the advent of Al-Jazeera and Al-Arabiya, Qatar and Saudi Arabia have come to dominate pan-Arab media. By degrees since 2007, Al-Jazeera shifted its ground on Saudi Arabia, as Qatar made peace with Al Saud. Material critical of Saudi Arabia appeared with much less frequency, to the point when hardly any critic of Saudi policy appears on the channel at all, or they are quietened if they start. When the Arab uprisings broke out in 2011, Al-Jazeera became in some respects indistinguishable from Al-Arabiya. Bahrain and other protest movements in the Gulf were roundly ignored, Qatar's project with the United States and Western countries to remove Gaddafi in Libya took centre stage, and the Israeli-Palestinian conflict was relegated to the secondary status the US government always wished it to have.

AL-ARABIYA: THE SAUDI RESPONSE TO AL-JAZEERA

Al-Arabiya's services to the Saudi leadership manifested themselves in the channel's early days through its coverage of Islamist insurgent groups using the name al-Qa'ida as they appeared in Iraq, Saudi Arabia and elsewhere. After the Iraq war, Al-Arabiya ran numerous documentaries and discussion shows about mass graves and other human rights abuses in pre-invasion Iraq in what was presented as an effort to balance the debate about the war. Public opinion was overwhelmingly opposed to the war, and media reflected this, and Al-Arabiya balanced this with a certain focus on the tyrannical regime that the war put an end to. This reflected, however, the conflicted position of the Saudi regime itself. The Saudi leadership was relieved to see the United States rid the region of what they considered another Arab nationalist abhorrence in the form of Saddam Hussein and only feared the potential consequences for its survival and stability. In 2003 the Palestinian uprising that began in 2000 was still a major force in the region's politics and topping the Arab news agenda, and like Al-Jazeera, Al-Arabiya designed powerful montages of Israeli soldiers putting down the intifada, set to a background of stirring music. Al-Arabiya did the same to discredit the activities of the Islamist insurgency movement in Saudi Arabia (while Al-Jazeera gave it oxygen). One of these short pieces referred to a shootout in Mecca between Saudi police and Islamist rebels in June 2003, after which the Saudi authorities made the claim that they had found copies of the Quran rigged with explosives. The words 'holy books booby-trapped with bombs' flicked across the screen, inviting Saudi viewers to consider the heretical violence of al-Qa'ida (though copies of rigged Quran were never produced in evidence).[5]

The Bush administration for some time after the Iraq invasion placed both Al-Jazeera and Al-Arabiya in the same category of Arab 'obstructionism' and 'extremism'. Both were banned for two weeks from covering official activities in Iraq in September 2003. However, by the time President Bush chose Al-Arabiya over Al-Jazeera for an Arab media interview in May 2004 to answer charges of torture of Iraqi detainees at Abu Ghraib prison, Washington had clearly established who was on its side and who was not. When he took office in 2008, US president Barack Obama turned to Al-Arabiya for his first interview with Arab media, since the State Department would have told him it was the moderate Arab channel sympathetic to US interests.[6] Al-Arabiya was promoting the new order in Iraq as early as 2004 with its *Aswaq al-Iraq* (*Iraq Markets*) programme, an effort to promote the economic regeneration that the Bush administration predicted would follow the invasion but which appeared ever more remote as the insurgency and sectarian violence deepened. Al-Arabiya aired some videotaped messages from Iraqi insurgent groups, but never anything from Osama bin Laden or Ayman al-Zawahiri – at most they might get a mention in the news ticker along the bottom of the screen. On Al-Jazeera, by contrast, by September 2003, two years after the attacks in New York and Washington, guests felt sufficiently confident to return to reverential references to bin Laden as 'Sheikh Osama'.[7] Indeed, sensing this pro-Western tilt, Islamist internet users came to brand Al-Arabiya as *al-'Ibriya*, or 'the Hebrew Channel', a taunt used by Hizbullah leader Hassan Nasrallah. The term demonstrated an awareness of the particular alignment of Saudi and Israeli interests in light of 9/11 and the Iraq invasion.

The Gaza war in December 2008 was the last great media event where Saudi Arabia stood apart while Qatar grandstanded alone before Arab public opinion. Days before the Israeli onslaught began, Foreign minister Tzipi Livni announced from Cairo that she would bring Hamas's rule in Gaza to an end, while Egyptian state media, on the defensive after demonstrations in Syria and Iran against Egypt's closure of its border with Gaza, claimed lamely that Mubarak had demanded 'restraint' from Israel. This implied a green light to attack and do to Hamas what the Arab leaders had hoped Israel would do to Hizbullah in 2006. Israeli prime minister Ehud Olmert used the podium of Al-Arabiya to tell Gazans that Hamas was responsible for the impending attack and, by extension, Gazans because they had not turned against their government. Al-Jazeera had heavy coverage of what, by any standards in the region, was a major story, while Al-Arabiya tried to play it down, fitting the carnage (around 192 died in the first set of airstrikes on 27 December) into its routine coverage of Gulf stock markets and global financial crisis. Al-Arabiya also followed the Western media penchant for equating missiles from Gaza with the mass violence of the Israeli army. Saudi website Elaph said Israel was crushing 'Iran's agents' in Gaza, in reference to the Hamas group Riyadh once backed,[8] and *Asharq al-Awsat*'s editor Tareq al-Humayed wrote that Hamas had escalated the situation with Israel as part of an Iranian plan to ruin Israeli-Syrian peace talks.[9] Saudi domination in Arab media meant that street protests against the war by Saudi Shi'ites in the Eastern Province went largely unreported.

Al-Arabiya continued to reflect Saudi irritation with Turkey's championing of Palestinian issues. For example, in 2010 when Turkey's prime minister Recep Tayyip Erdogan again clashed with Israel over aid boats trying to break Israel's siege of Gaza, one lead item on one news bulletin informed viewers that 'the plane of Israeli Prime Minister Benjamin Netanyahu flew threw Turkish airspace on its way to Washington where Netanyahu is due to have talks with US President Barack Obama'.[10] When the Arab uprisings took off in 2011, Al-Arabiya's tone was consistently conservative and behind-the-curve until Libyans rose against Saudi Arabia's *bête noire* Gaddafi. The same kind of enthusiastic coverage Al-Jazeera gave to the fall of Mubarak was accorded to the Libyan uprising in coverage termed 'Libya's revolution'. With Egypt, Al-Arabiya's slogan for its coverage was 'Egypt in crisis'. By the time Syrian demonstrations had morphed into a full-blown armed revolt, the convergence of interests between the two channels was clear as Qatar and Saudi Arabia emerged to lead Arab League efforts to ostracise and oust Assad and his Iranian-allied regime.

Al-Arabiya has used its extensive Gulf stock market coverage to lure viewers in, according to media researcher Jihad Fakhreddine. 'Al-Arabiya is not strong anywhere. It even has a problem in Saudi Arabia. It's viewed because of its business news, not current affairs. Their ratings during the day when business activities take place is higher than during the primetime current affairs viewing period and it has shifted a lot of resources to business coverage', he says.[11] This is not lost on Saudi commentators. The daily *Al-Watan* once ran a cartoon featuring a Saudi glued to the television as a busty presenter discusses stock market news. His angry wife asks, 'How come you've started watching the stock market?', to which he gives the double entendre-laden retort, 'Because the size of trading has significantly increased.' A cat stares at the screen salivating at the sight (*Ish fik, surt tutabi' akhbar al-ashum?? –Li'inno hajm al-tadawul izdad bi-shakl kabir*).[12] The joke reflects the fact that the channel is seen as employing the lurid, the trivial and the financial to deflect the attentions of the masses. Further, its focus on quirky stories about Saudi religion and society reflects that fact that Saudi media have been an important vehicle for promoting the idea since 9/11 that it is towards conservative social mores and religious zealotry one must look to find the source of the dysfunction that the West wants to fix in the country, rather than Al Saud.

MBC1, LBC and Rotana Music serve a repressed Saudi male audience in many of their entertainment shows. The trend began in the late 1990s. One popular show was LBC's *Carla-la-la*, where Scandinavian-looking presenter Carla Haddad received phone calls from viewers who would complement her on her beauty, request a song or offer an opinion on whatever issue the cottequish Carla would raise with them, usually regarding pop trivia and favourite stars. Saudis consistently formed the largest group of callers and some of them would stray into lewd comments or behaviour. The contradiction at the heart of this type of entertainment – a Saudi-Lebanese joint project – was well-demonstrated when a 30-year-old Saudi man appeared on a salacious LBC show called *Ahmar Bil-Khatt al-'Areed* (*Red In Bold Script*) discussing the methods he employed for picking up girls in local supermarkets since he was a teenager and displaying sex toys he said he made use of. Speaking directly to the show from his bedroom in Jeddah,

Mazen Abduljawad seemed to forget what country he was in. In the storm of controversy that followed, he was arrested and LBC offices in Saudi Arabia wereclosed. 'He confessed before the world that he committed fornication and continues to fornicate', an anonymous user wrote on *Al-Medina* newspaper's web forum. 'It is for that reason that he deserves to be stoned to death, as Islamic law stipulates.'[13] The video clips favoured on Prince Alwaleed's Rotana network feature Lebanese singers in sexually provocative outfits and poses, following the trend of bling videos on MTV. They broadcast an array of quiz shows and dramas that Saudi religious scholars consider beyond the pale. Alwaleed is referred to sarcastically on Islamist websites as *al-amir al-majin*, 'the depraved prince'; his brother Khaled attacked him publicly in 2009 for cinema screenings that Rotana organised earlier in that year, accusing him of wanting to 'overturn religious and moral norms'.[14]

Saudi princes think they are promoting openness, reform and keeping up with the West with this media. The agenda favours liberalising socio-religious customs, yet is virtually silent when it comes to promoting popular participation in government, transparency, or open discussion of foreign and economic policy. It is an agenda mainly set by the needs and whims of the key princes involved, not the liberal intellectuals hired to promote it, and in fact these media activities often contradict other policies and positions – for example, Prince Salman presents an image of reform via *Asharq al-Awsat* while having been a key backer of the religious police in Riyadh, when he was governor. In 2007 LBC launched *Imra'a wa Akthar (More Than A Woman)* where Saudi film-maker Haifaa Mansour hosted a discussion of restrictions on women in Saudi Arabia, including gender segregation and the absence of women as Shura Assembly members or judges. To cite another example of this incoherence, Al-Arabiya reported on an incident in Kuwait in June 2008 where Islamist parliamentarians raised public protests over a party in a hospital where men and women were seen dancing in photographs that were publicised. Lebanese presenter Najwa Qassem interviewed one of the Islamists, ridiculing their anger over what she argued was simply a question of 'personal freedom'. 'Is it a crime, or wrong (*mujrim/muznib*)?' she asked incredulously. The intent, again, is to present religious obscurantism as a *sui generis* problem that has Gulf rulers, God bless 'em, just flummoxed.

On state television, the information ministry has been far more cautious in promoting the liberal agenda. There has been a sudden plethora of women presenters on Channel One and the news channel

Al-Ikhbariya, which was intended as a challenge to Al-Jazeera until Al-Arabiya with its private money proved more capable of fulfilling the role. Al-Ikhbariya employees complain of serious underfunding for the channel now that Al-Arabiya has emerged as the number one Saudi alternative to Al-Jazeera. Women present the news, daytime lifestyle shows, and even lead some political discussion programmes. Singing and dancing remain the preserve of the private channels, religious scholars and preachers have ample space on state television to offer guidance on religious affairs, and of course daily news broadcasts devote an inordinate amount of time to royal protocol and visiting dignitaries. The liberals, be they writers, opposition activists or chums of the king, have little space to argue their point on state television. The authorities will argue that though they might agree with the liberal viewpoints, they cannot risk provoking the religious establishment and endangering social peace. Liberal predominance in the media was a complaint of the Sahwa clerics that featured in their Memorandum of Advice in 1991.

State television chose not to air the popular comedy show *Tash Ma Tash* during the month of Ramadan AH 1427 (September/October 2006) because it tried to push boundaries with satire of the religious police and Islamist fighters. Instead the episodes were aired on the Dubai-based pan-Arab alternative, MBC1. In one, would-be revolutionaries attended a school for training and indoctrination named the 'Terrorism Academy' after the popular global TV franchise *Star Academy*. The zealots were depicted as simpletons robotically repeating language about 'infidels', which remains, of course, part of mainstream religious and Islamist discourse. In another episode, a *mutawwa'*, or religious police volunteer, argued at a local council meeting that the town should have separate secondary schools for boys and girls, located so that prevailing winds do not carry the smell of the girls in the direction of the boys. In another, the show satirised the *khususiyya* cited to justify rules of social, religious and political conduct different from the rest of the Arab world, Islamic world or anywhere else. In the season that ran in August 2011, however, the uprisings in Egypt and Tunisia were ridiculed in one episode of *Tash* as the work of children goaded by foreigners and foreign ideology into rebelling against their father.

The arms of Saudi media were set to work in 2006 when Mohammed Hassanein Heikal, a journalist confidant of Nasser accorded enormous respect in the Arab world, attacked the new Saudi public diplomacy in interviews on Al-Jazeera. Heikal said there was no reason why Iran should be considered an Arab enemy, and placed Saudi efforts to resolve the Arab-Israeli conflict within a context of providing Israel or the United States with a fig leaf for future military action against Iran. Saudi and other Arab writers came out with a series of articles in the Saudi pan-Arab papers vilifying Heikal for daring to call Saudi Arabia out in such a manner. Heikal, a former 'state writer', had finally found his chance to write for officialdom once again, wrote the editor of *Al-Riyadh*, Turki al-Sudairy, except this time it was a 'statelet with hardly half a million people'. 'This mole of a country, Qatar, made him its clownish official spokesperson', he said. Al-Arabiya ran a televisual reponse to Heikal's criticisms with its series *Ayyam al-Sayyid al-Arabi (The Era of Mr Arab)*, which sought to discredit Arab nationalism as an ideology of resistance to Western hegemony and to promote the 'moderation' of leaders such as Anwar al-Sadat.

When an Iraqi journalist threw his shoes at George W. Bush in Baghdad, Saudi media writers were on cue again, as if this type of challenge to the order was a threat to the stability of the House of Saud itself. 'Bush on the shoe incident: it was the strangest event. Condoleezza Rice: it's a sign of freedom', the front-page headline of *Asharq al-Awsat* said.[15] In a tone reminiscent of US diplomatic reports filed from Riyadh when opposition figures challenged the Saudi government and Aramco management in the late 1950s, the same edition carried a story that said the thrower, Muntadher al-Zaidi, was 'clearly a leftist' suffering from 'delusions of grandeur' who wanted to gain attention any way he could. One Saudi columnist, a figure in the pro-American liberal camp, wrote:

> What we saw in the press conference was an insult to the journalist profession and a sign of misunderstanding its nature. Journalists are not a *mujahids* or fighters, they are simply people who strive to present information. The journalist does not talk in the name of the nation, or its conscience, as some bankrupt people in this profession claim.[16]

DOMESTIC PRESS

Saudi domestic media is no less dominated by the royal family and its allies. Red lines are shifting constantly and writers and journalists are in then out of favour, facing dismissal, bans and detentions. Sometimes they will find themselves prevented from leaving the country, a practice the Ministry of the Interior has made wide use of over the years – a right that is usually returned after the signing of a pledge not to repeat the offence but sometimes not made clear in advance at all, so that a formerly detained blogger could find himself forbidden from leaving the country, as happened to Fouad Farhan in December 2008.[17] The Committee to Protect Journalists concluded in a report published in 2006 that there is essentially no such thing as an 'opposition press' in Saudi Arabia. It found that government officials order news blackouts on controversial issues, the religious establishment acts as a powerful lobbying force against enterprising coverage of social, cultural and religious matters, and compliant editors generally toe the line and practise self-censorship.[18] Off-limits are criticisms of the royal family, government ministers, friendly foreign governments, corruption, oil policy and major foreign policy stances.

Self-censorship is a major part of this. Information ministry officials often complain that the Saudi press is its own worst enemy and not doing enough to push limits. Iyad Madani, the minister from 2004–09 and a former editor of *Okaz*, was considered to be one of the king's liberal allies among the commoners in government. He was succeeded in 2009 by ambassador to Lebanon Abdulaziz al-Khoja, another liberal Hejazi in the service of Al Saud. But who can be surprised if journalists continue to behave as court poets: senior princes take large contingents of journalists on state visits abroad, giving them free holidays that make Saudi reporters some of the most well-travelled in the world but ensuring obedience from a docile press. Editors and senior journalists included in the royal entourage are given cash gifts for their services to the state on each trip. As in many countries, the media is not fundamentally recognised as an estate with the legitimate right to hold power to account and the media has not been able to win this right for itself. The annual press conference by Prince Nayef at the plain of Arafat outside Mecca days before the hajj pilgrimage was designed to impress upon media the power and prestige of the minister and the subject status of the press. Journalists from around the world are kept waiting for several hours before the prince arrives to take position behind a desk on a raised platform set back at some distance from the gathered assembly. He peers out from beneath his robes and headdress with suspicious eyes scanning the group, offering brief non-answers to the journalists who shuffle one after the other to a microphone at a podium to announce their name, organisation and question. Ministry of Information officials, including the minister himself, are usually in the audience, observing the proceedings. The information ministry plays second fiddle to the interior ministry, which has its own Supreme Information Council. At information/interior ministry prompting, editors will regularly call in staff journalists to inform them that there have been *mulahazat* (observations) made about them concerning the tone of some of their articles, comments they have been overheard making, or the fact that they have frequented foreign embassy receptions, perhaps drinking alcohol. Television presenters are regularly berated for conducting interviews that anger religious or state officials. Journalists and TV presenters are often suspended for some weeks or months, or fired altogether.

The press became the battleground after 9/11 for a new stage of conflict between the liberal intellectuals and religious conservatives. The media took its cue from the reformist dispensation led by the crown prince in the chaos after 9/11 to discuss issues regarding the country's social and political situation in an unprecedented fashion. But the clerics reacted strongly to the muscle-flexing by liberals and found support in the interior ministry, which used the information ministry to rein in writers seen as having gone too far. Many reformist writers found themselves crowded out of the media in a deliberate policy orchestrated by the interior ministry to pressure editors into silencing the critics of Saudi Islam: an estimated 100 writers were effectively banned at this time.[19] Religious scholars or preachers would complain directly to newspaper editors, the interior ministry or the information ministry, which was under the interior ministry's yoke. When a journalist asked Prince Nayef live on state television in May 2003 if the religious police might be disbanded, the minister responded angrily that he could not believe a Saudi national would ask such a question.[20] Mansour al-Nogaidan found himself on an open-ended holiday from *Al-Riyadh* after articles criticising Wahhabism. He was questioned for days by intelligence agents after publishing an article in the *New York Times* in November 2003. Dawood al-Shirian and Khaled al-Dukhayyil were dropped from *Al-Hayat*, and Hussein Shobokshi was stopped from writing in the daily *Okaz* and *Arab News*, and a television programme Shobokshi presented on *Al-Arabiya* was cancelled. Some of these writers later returned to television and the press, enticed by positions, prestige and money. None of them signed the reform petitions that got political activists into trouble.

Jamal Khashoggi was removed from the post of editor-in-chief of *Al-Watan* newspaper in 2003 because of the paper's campaign against the religious police. He was brought back in April 2007 when the political atmosphere was judged to be less tense since Abdullah had become king. He immediately set the paper to giving strenuous support for a campaign to overturn the ban on women driving and reviving the campaign against the vice squad. He refrained from publishing any information in *Al-Watan* about democracy activism and arrests. Asked about the February 2007 petition, which Saudi media uniformly ignored, Khashoggi said: 'If there is a (government) response, then we might cover it, but since it appears as a private dialogue between a number of citizens and His Majesty, we in the media should not get involved in it … I feel encouraged by the changes in Saudi media but I also know my limits.'[21] Khashoggi subsequently moved to London and Washington with Prince Turki al-Faisal in his ambassadorial postings, working as his media advisor.

Around 2009 newspaper editors were noting some changes in how the government was dealing with them. A report from the US embassy in Riyadh noted:

> According to our contacts, however, a more effective system is in place. Instead of being fired or seeing their publications shut down, editors now are fined SR 40,000 ($10,600) out of their own salaries for each objectionable piece that appears in their newspaper. Journalists, too, are held to account. Instead of the Supreme Information Council in Riyadh taking the lead in tracking what journalists write, there are now MOI [Ministry of Interior] committees in each Saudi city that know their community well and have a keen ear for who is talking about what. If these MOI operatives detect a problematic pattern in a journalist's writing (or even hear through channels that he or she is heading down a certain line of inquiry), they will invite the journalist for a chat, during which they will discuss the origin of these perspectives, suggest alternative approaches, ask after the family, etc., … These mechanisms, our contacts say, have been very effective in reining in media opinion that the SAG (Saudi Arabian government) doesn't like.[22]

One notes here a tone of satisfaction at the refined controls the government exerts over media. The United States sees this as an effective way of fighting sympathy for jihad and *takfir* in Saudi Arabia society, notions employed by Islamists to engage in violent actions against the United States and its allies in the region.

Western collaboration in controlling information in the Gulf stretches back to the 1940s. The British Foreign Office was worried about 'rushing' Arabs into modernity, lest that have consequences for political awareness, and Abdulaziz feared that education would lead to the creation of a technocrat intelligentsia as in Egypt and other urban Arab states.[23] In an early experiment in media and information control, preceding the media empire project of the 1990s, Aramco and the Saudi government gave free TV sets to workers in 1955 to provide Western entertainment, with the express intent of seeing whether it kept their minds away from seditious politics. Britain prevented imports of radios lest the population of Dubai listen to the Arab nationalism emanating from Cairo, while worrying that Sheikh Shakhbut in Abu Dhabi was showing such little interest in Arab nationalism that it was risking provoking rebellion among his people.[24] Having secured the removal of Saud in 1964, Faisal only began steps to modernise Saudi education and government once he had crushed the opposition seeking political reforms and an Arab nationalist challenge to the Western powers.

At the same time, the cables reflect a view that US entertainment on Saudi pan-Arab television has increased acceptance of American cultural values and by implication, US policies in the region. Saudi editors feed this fuzzy thinking. Abdulrahman Al-Rashed, the manager of Al-Arabiya and columnist in Asharq al-Awsat, is not just a favoured 'liberal' and 'moderate', he is an apologist for American policies. One unidentified Saudi media figure tells a US diplomat: 'It's still all about the War of Ideas here, and the American programming on MBC and Rotana is winning over ordinary Saudis in a way that "Al Hurra" and other US propaganda never could. Saudis are now very interested in the outside world, and everybody wants to study in the US if they can. They are fascinated by US culture in a way they never were before.'[25] Al-Arabiya is referred to by the author, chargé d'affaires David Rundell, as 'moderate' in relation to Al-Jazeera. A conflation is being made here between a number of separate issues: violent action against Western symbols (be they US government or allied Arab governments); opposition to US policies towards issues of Arab/Muslim concern (such as the Arab-Israeli conflict); the popularity of American television (which the cable describes erroneously as uncensored); the desire to study in American universities. The cables note favourably that the number of Saudis studying in the United States has reached 22,000, above the figure prior to 9/11. It seems quite possible for a Saudi to study in the United States and return with as much of a grudge over American policies as before, which could be made worse by witnessing American culture (via television or otherwise). Is someone really likely to moderate their position on US support for

Israel on the basis of a swell group of American friends? Egyptian Islamist ideologue Sayed Qutb returned from the US in the 1950s so convinced of its infidel nature that he was moved to develop his infamous theories on apostasy. Saudis I met in the country noted anecdotally that the policy of sending students abroad has failed to create a critical mass among the educated young who are capable of changing social values even if they want to. It doesn't help that Saudi students abroad are subject to surveillance to see if they are up to any dissident activities, a well-known secret. The fundamental enmity the Saudi-Wahhabi alliance has for the idea of popular participation in governance offers no avenues for these cultural returnees to effect a new mode of living; as a result, even if they have done in American what Americans do, upon return the *modus operandi* shifts back to 'when in Saudi, do as Saudis do'.

PATROLLING THE INTERNET

Like other countries in the region Saudi Arabia has engaged in massive patrolling of the internet and harassment of bloggers. The King Abdulaziz City for Science and Technology since 1998, an autonomous body presided over by senior officials including the king, the interior ministry and intelligence officials, began internet monitoring in 1998. Control was shifted to the Communications and Information Technology Commission (CITC) in 2007. An estimated 400,000 sites were blocked in 2010, according to the Committee to Protect Journalists. The sites filtered out are mostly pornographic, but extend to politics, Shi'ites and human rights generally. Almost any site can be blocked if influential members of the government, ruling family or senior government clerics complain – the fate of a number of discussion forums (*muntadayat*) and Saudi news and entertainment site Elaph from 2006 to 2008 (owned by another of the liberal media elite, Othman al-Omair). While the system of blocking sites is rather arbitrary and the authorities are quite open about it, the fact is that many people manage to get round the censorship through dialling numbers outside Saudi Arabia, using proxy servers or paying for more expensive DSL services which seem to allow access to some blocked material. Wikileaks, with its moderate stash of material laying bare the extent of connivance between Gulf governments and US administrations in policies against Iran, Hizbullah and Hamas, was blocked in January 2011.

The internet became popular because of the freedom and anonymity it offers to say things that can't be said in the press.

One of the first successful web forums was the Islamist discussion board Al-Saha. By 2006 it had over 100,000 members, many of them sympathisers of al-Qa'ida and other jihadist groups who used the site to publicise activities. The *Sawt al-Jihad* magazine, a Saudi al-Qa'ida mouthpiece, was regularly published in one of its forums in the period 2004–05. However, it was rarely blocked: in once instance in 2006 it was blocked for several weeks because of an article by Mohsen al-Awaji attacking Ghazi al-Gosaibi for using his close relations with the king to promote secularism. According to a US diplomatic report, its owner Tariq Fares may have received an offer of 4 million riyals ($1.1 million) to buy the site.[26] 'Internet is stronger than newspapers, young people are not interested much in print media, and there is more freedom', says Sultan al-Qahtani, managing editor of Elaph. Some 10,000 blogs have been set up in Saudi Arabia, the second largest blogger population in the Arab world, though many sites go inactive after a year or so. A spokesman for social networking and micro-blogging website Twitter estimated in January 2011 that the rate of increase in the daily circulation of Saudi 'tweets' had reached 440 per cent, compared to a global increase of 95 per cent.[27] Some senior princes are active on Twitter, including some such as Prince Talal who are critical of government, while anonymous users such as Mujtahidd have acquired a large following through discussions of political currents and corruption.

Ahmed al-Omran was one of the country's first popular bloggers, discussing social and political issues on his site saudijeans.blogspot. com. At first he kept his name off the site but then took a chance on ditching the anonymity as he attracted more and more readers. 'It's easy to be anonymous. Everyone has his reasons. I used to be afraid', Omran said when I first met him in 2006.[28] 'After a time I was sick of it, so I put my name and photo to see what would happen. I think you have more credibility. But I've become now careful about what I write. I think twice about posting anything.'

The revelation that Saudi Arabia planned to introduced a 'terror law' in 2011 illustrated for the authorities the influence and reach ordinary Saudis could have through the internet, specifically Twitter. A copy of the draft law was leaked to Amnesty International, which subsequently published it on its website and issued a statement to publicise it. Within 24 hours its terms had been thorough bandied around, discussed and roundly attacked by Saudi internet users and others following Middle East political issues on Twitter. The clause that drew particular reactions ran: 'Anyone who doubts the king or crown prince's integrity will face punishment of at least

10 years in jail.' The draft obtained by Amnesty showed that the Shura Assembly had so far made little changes to the draft prepared originally by the interior ministry, which was clearly pushing to have the legislation approved as soon as possible. Amnesty's statement, which asked the king to reconsider the law because it was curtailing his people's legitimate right to freedom of expression in the name of fighting terrorism, provoked a response from the Saudi embassy in London which said Amnesty's concerns were 'baseless and mere assumptions'.

Pro-government writers went on the attack over the 'new activism' whereby activists use the internet to bypass the traditional, controlled media and have a lot more impact for doing so. One homed in on the use of the hashtag, since one had been assigned to the Saudi terror law debate that helped spread word of the issue. Blogger Adhwan al-Ahmari asked: 'What are Saudis doing on Twitter?'[29] In the Saudi edition of *Al-Hayat* newspaper, columnist Saud al-Rayes said the new activism was as dangerous challenge to the state's authority. 'There is no doubt that the new activism has become a dangerous phenomenon because it aims to challenge the state and its organisations', he wrote.[30] Hani al-Dhaheri, a columnist for the same paper, attacked the activists in another column. 'How could a whiner in Twitter, Facebook or YouTube assert that someone is innocent or oppressed unless they have an ulterior motive beyond this cause which they use to cover their agenda?' he said. Dhaheri had actually been a signatory to one of three public petitions for democratic reforms organised earlier in the year after Mubarak was deposed in Egypt. He conformed to the familiar of pattern of activism, a wrap on the knuckles in one form or another, then acting as a loyal policeman of the state by advocating 'limits' to demands.

Media laws were amended twice in the space of a few months in 2011; once in January concerning internet sites, and again in April after the emergence of the protest movements. The Ministry of Information said all Saudi websites, including those run by individual bloggers, must obtain a licence to operate which should be displayed clearly on the site. It also stipulated that they must be over 20 years old, possess a high school or higher qualification, and demonstrate a record of good conduct. The authorities tried to pass the regulations off as an administrative matter. 'It is for organisational supervision and not to supervise or censor. We only need a name and a telephone number if possible', said ministry spokesman Abdulrahman Al-Hazzaa.[31] The intent to censor wasn't lost on anyone though. A user called 'Ali M' wrote on Al-Arabiya's website:

> I believe it is a clear attempt at censorship. Saudis are known to be probably the most conservative and totalitarian of the Middle East countries and Al-Arabiya is owned by the Saudis (I wish you would disclose it when reporting on Saudi Arabia). Just a couple of weeks ago I made a comment on an opinion piece I read in arabnews.com and my comments were edited thoroughly before they were published, turning them into Saudi state propaganda. I have no doubt that Saudis censor the news to their liking. You shouldn't either.

Several months later, a much wider set of regulations were announced that applied to all media, following decrees by the king in March dispensing large amounts of money to various sectors of the population and announcing the intent to outlaw criticism of senior religious scholars. The terms were vague but the punishments were severe – a fine of 500,000 riyals ($133,000) which can be doubled in the case of recurring violations, the closure of outlets that published the violation, and banning the journalist from any work. The acts criminalised were publication of material that contradicts Islamic Sharia, incites to disruption of state security or public order, serves foreign interests or contradicts national interests, slanders the mufti, senior clerics or statesmen, or provokes sectarianism. It also criminalised publication of the results of official investigations without permission from the body of state concerned. But it was clear that a large segment of the Saudi population were blogging and tweeting regardless, and the state could only direct symbolic blows by picking on some as an example.

FOREIGN MEDIA IN SAUDI ARABIA

The 9/11 attacks were the biggest international crisis the Saudi state had faced since the oil embargo of 1973–74, if not since the kingdom's foundation. The project to recover international standing included opening the country's doors to the foreign press. The regime made clear its perception that it had an image problem in the media. Prince Nayef told a Kuwaiti paper in 2002:

> The enmity that we see now in the American media and some European media, especially in Britain, does not frighten us but I

say that it is disturbing because it has no justification and does not serve their interests. The problem is that we tell them 'your position on the Arab world and the Palestinian issue specifically has changed the feelings of the Arab peoples towards you into people who hate you, so what are you waiting for in order to change your image before these peoples, never mind the regimes'.[32]

Word went out that major news outlets were welcome in the kingdom, not just to send correspondents in for reporting stints, but to open offices. The thinking went that the foreigners may not like what they see, but the more familiar they became with Saudi society, the less likely Western decision-makers would be to entertain ideas of changing the regime. During the invasion of Iraq in 2003, foreign media noted a clear change in the government's attitude towards the press. Embassies in Western countries issued visas with more ease to journalists from major news organisations and often stopped the practice of placing limits on which part of the country a journalist could visit. Those who spent time in Saudi Arabia during the Iraq war had the freedom to travel wherever they liked. Information ministry 'guides' were usually attached to a journalist, but their enthusiasm for constantly chaperoning the foreigners usually flagged. There was no comparison to the experience of government minders in Iraq before the Baath regime fell.

However, the opening to foreign media moved at a snail's pace and faced a number of obstacles. Though Reuters established an editorial operation in 2003, the death of a BBC cameraman and injury of a BBC reporter in a shooting incident during the al-Qa'ida insurgency in 2004 caused many media organisations to think twice. It was difficult to find journalists prepared to work in the kingdom, and the costs were prohibitive. When CNN identified an able Saudi in 2006 to establish as their Saudi correspondent, they preferred to send him to Atlanta rather than have him set up an operation inside a country where red tape, invisible lines and suspicious mentality make the journalist's work extremely difficult. To date there is no BBC or CNN office in Saudi Arabia, and the number one Arabic news outlet, Al-Jazeera, spent years shut out of the country because its open editorial line gave no special consideration for Saudi Arabia and its claim of *khususiyya*, though that began to change from 2007. The rapprochement between the Al Thani and Al Saud simply made the rivalry more manageable, rather than end it, and Saudi Arabia is still largely closed to Al-Jazeera, which has to bring Saudis to Doha for studio interviews.

The regulation of the foreign correspondents' presence has also been a discouragement, and as a consequence most of the small number of journalists working full-time in the kingdom are in fact there under 'exceptional' circumstances. Journalists are meant to operate under the 'sponsorship' of the information ministry. This means the ministry retains passports of resident journalists while they are in the country, and the passport has to be requested back when travelling abroad – the system that applies to millions of Asian labourers in the Gulf. White-collar expatriates in Gulf countries usually avoid this system of passport retention, and the demand that journalists surrender their passports is an obvious hurdle to news outlets setting up offices in the country. Some have managed to get round this through obtaining multiple entry visas and avoiding the residency system; some have obtained residency through spouses already resident for business purposes and are thus not required to surrender their passport; others are Saudis or long-time residents who have taken on press work as a secondary interest.

Obtaining information from business leaders and government officials is a challenge. During the stock market crash of 2006, journalists found the pool of analysts prepared to go on the record diminishing for fear of angering the financial market authorities. Some of those analysts admitted they had been 'banned' from appearing on channels such as Al-Arabiya. The officials concerned with economic affairs, such as the finance ministry, central bank, capital markets authority, telecoms authority, large state firms such as SABIC, Maaden and STC, all responded with difficulty to the growth in local and foreign media interest in them and Saudi Arabia since the oil boom from 2002. Local journalists are acutely aware of the restrictions on Saudi media but feel they lack the training to raise the standards of the profession. The Ministry of Information talks about its desire for 'knowledge transfer' to Saudi journalists, and would like the foreign media to employ more Saudis on their teams, but there is little serious effort to make that happen.

Getting information from and access to American diplomats is often no easier than dealing with Saudi government officials. Since the invasion of Iraq, American diplomats have appeared suspicious of foreign journalists and unwilling to offer information and opinions on a country they seem keen to shield from cynical, hostile media as if it was their own. At the same time, they open their doors wide to Saudi journalists in the hope of fostering a team of sympathisers who will write positive stories about the United States in Saudi papers. The presidential election in 2008 was an opportunity to showcase American democracy before Saudi media invited to an election night party in November of that year. But that is about as far as democracy advocacy goes: 'Tonight we celebrate not just a US election but the spirit of democracy and healthy debate that reigns free in an open society that celebrates its diversity of opinion and freedom of expression', the deputy ambassador said in a speech. A series of computers were open on government websites to demonstrate open government in action to journalists who were not really intended to become the vanguard of democratic change in Saudi Arabia – just cheerleaders for American policies in the media. Diplomats from other embassies are generally keen on contact with foreign media because, faced with the opaque political system, they are often as in the dark about what's going on as the journalists. Conversely, the important government departments such as the interior and foreign ministries give privileged access to American media and actively cut out the others. The media audience that matters to the Saudi leadership is that of the Western democracies where public opinion can affect government policy, but especially the United States.

The foreign ministry is generally more media-savvy than the others, but most ministries are secretive and out of bounds, and treat the press as a place for depositing official statements. Saudi journalists are aware of their predicament. At a forum in July 2007 they complained that the country has no journalism courses or colleges, statistics and other information are hard to come by and depend on privileged contacts with ministry officials, and government departments have the irritating tendency to demand questions in advance in writing, slowing up the whole process of getting a story out for days or weeks.[33] The foreign ministry is not above haranguing foreign embassies not to talk to the media. In 2011 a circular was sent out warning them not to speak to foreign correspondents, claiming that protocols ban them from discussing the domestic situation with journalists.

The 'don't-talk-to-diplomats' theme also came up in communications with media after one foreign correspondent was asked to leave Saudi Arabia in March 2011 over coverage of Shi'ite and other protests. One complaint, for example, came from a London law firm acting on behalf of a client registered as a business in the British Virgin Islands 'with Saudi Arabian interests' and apparently bumper-size enthusiasm for media ethics. The last line of the letter explained that it had been prepared 'with the full support of the Culture and Information Minister of Saudi Arabia, who has seen it in draft'. The letter was meant to hint at legal action which could not be pinned as 'Saudi Arabia takes the press to court', though when the government felt it really was on strong ground it did take such action: Nayef accepted undisclosed damages in August 2011 over an article in Britain's *Independent* newspaper by Robert Fisk accusing the prince of ordering police to shoot and kill unarmed protesters. 'Our clients are concerned that reports emanating from your Saudi Arabian offices have recently fallen short of proper standards', it said, claiming no diplomat would have violated protocol to criticise Prince Nayef ('to have a King Nayef is unthinkable for many Saudi Shi'ites', a diplomat had been quoted as saying). Its main complaint was coverage of the attempt to mobilise a protest movement in Saudi Arabia: it was not correct to talk of a 'massive security presence' on 11 March, the day that Facebook activists had set for protests in major cities. Yet the latter included a picture posted on Twitter showing an empty road in central Riyadh that was meant to counter this claim but which on closer inspection showed over a dozen police vehicles parked one after the other along a road. There is a simplistic assumption, it said, that 'any Middle Eastern polity that is not a democracy is necessarily oppressive of its citizens'.

However, on 11 March one Saudi named Khaled al-Juhani, a teacher and father of four, did brave the warnings from just about every arm of the Saudi state that could claim to have a say in the matter and spoke to a group of reporters milling around amidst the full array of Saudi coercive apparatus. Juhani talks to a small group of journalists for some five minutes under a grey sky in the Olaya district outside the Grievances Court, which he describes as another princely institution that does not serve the people. His pleading seems particularly poignant because he subsequently disappeared (he was one of six arrested that day, Amnesty International said) – just as he predicts before he gets into his car and drives off (he was put on trial in February 2012 in a specialised criminal court in Riyadh, established in 2008 to try detainees held on terrorism-related charges). I close the chapter with his words.

'I came to say that we need democracy. We need freedom. We need to speak with absolute freedom. We need to be allowed to speak our minds. Why are all these police here? Why? Is it so that we can't get our voices through to people? No, we will make our voices heard, the government does not own us. We are free and we want to live in freedom. We just want to live in freedom', he says. A reporter asks him why he feels he does not live in freedom:

Because I was driving around and they said if we say you again, we'll put you in jail. Why? Is there a curfew? They didn't announce one. I'm here because I'm a free person and I'm expressing my opinion. You can see all these police around us – why are they here? Are they trying to make the place look better? I came because I heard there would be people gathering here, after the 'Asr prayer. But I don't think they'll gather with all this security around. You can see everyone here in police uniform or plainclothes. They are all police or secret police. There is no free media in the monarchy. Media can't say what it wants. Even media has an agenda. It can only speak with the permission of the Ministry of the Interior. They didn't think we'd speak to the media, they didn't think anyone would dare – because they would go to jail. I want to go to jail. '*The people want to go to jail. The people want to go to jail. The people want to go to jail.*'[34] I was frightened, and continued to be frightened and I shut up, but then something broke: what should I be afraid of? We don't have freedom, we don't have dignity, we don't have justice! … Young people would have been free to come and talk if it were not for this police presence … They will send me to prison, but I'm happy. There's nothing to lose … I'm more worried about the future for my kids, not about this here today. The police will be waiting for me somewhere or other, I'll never get home at all. I'll never get home. But thanks be to God, I expressed my opinion.[35]

8
Controlling Mecca: In the House of God

One of the jewels in the crown of the Saudi-Wahhabi state is its control of the holy cities of Mecca and Medina. When Abdulaziz assumed full sovereignty after his Ikhwan stormed into its cities, he added 'King of the Hejaz' to his list of titles. Pilgrim revenue, mainly from the hajj season, became the major domestic source of income for the nascent Saudi state, though the Najd-run entity still relied on foreign handouts to survive.[1] The state took control of pilgrim tour operations as part of the wider process of severing Hejazi autonomy and tying its political and economic life to Riyadh.[2] As the country moved into the era of modern communications then entered the petrodollar era in the 1970s, significantly larger numbers of pilgrims were able to visit, but the hajj they were to experience was a hajj with a very specific Saudi and Wahhabi stamp. Processing the world's Muslims through Saudi-Wahhabi pilgrimage became a vast industry, a major preoccupation of the state and a key element in its self-legitimising rhetoric. Petrodollars are of vastly greater importance to state and princely finances, but, raking in some $24 billion a year in tourist receipts mainly linked to Mecca and Medina, hajj remains a major earner for Saudi Arabia.[3] It is also a monopolistic practice – there is little Saudi Arabia can do to compete with Shi'ite pilgrimage centres such as Najaf and Kerbala, but Jerusalem, which contains the Al-Aqsa mosque, the site towards which Islamic tradition says the first Muslims turned in prayer, is accorded little significance in Saudi media or Wahhabi religious discourse, whether it was under Jordanian or Israeli control. It is a rival to the prestige and revenue of the Saudi-Wahhabi state.[4]

Yet organising pilgrimage has been a complicated and controversial affair over the years. The event has been marred by a seemingly unending litany of tragedies, from fires, overcrowding, hotel collapses and flooding, to political disputes over demonstrations and granting of hajj visas,[5] to security operations to stop alleged al-Qa'ida attacks or Shi'ite plots, to failure to prevent militant operatives meeting under the guise of hajj to plan ahead. The hajj itself is a media spectacle of great political import for Saudi Arabia, an opportunity to demonstrate to Muslims and Muslim governments around the world its vast resources, its largesse and its leadership of Islam. After the debacle of 9/11, the policy of media openness extended to the pilgrimage: the information ministry invited most of the world's major media outlets to send teams to cover the event, presented as a great feat of organisation despite the fact that millions more take part in several Hindu pilgrimages in India each year. News agencies began referring to the hajj as the world's largest *organised* manifestation of mass religious devotion, a description that suited the Saudi authorities fine.

I visited Mecca twice under the auspices of the Saudi government's invitation to media outlets to send teams to cover the event, in January 2004 and January 2005. Though all of us were there to do a job, the coverage involved going through the rites of pilgrimage: journalists were thrilled to have the chance to perform hajj, not least with someone else arranging it. It's not quite five-star hajj, but it's certainly a lot easier than travelling with many of the large tour groups. It was a thrilling experience on a personal and professional level; a chance to contemplate many issues, both spiritual and political. But I witnessed much that speaks to the criticisms often levelled at Saudi Arabia over its organisation of hajj and which illustrated the many stark differences between the claims of Saudi Islam and the practices of most of the world's Muslims. Hajj is a testament to the diversity of Islam and Muslims, and Saudi Arabia struggles in vain to tame it.

Located in the rough mountains of the Jeddah hinterland, Mecca bears a character that is neither East nor West, Asian nor African, ancient nor modern. A community of believers of diverse origins comes together to seek forgiveness at the place on earth where they believe God will most appreciate their prayers. More a mega-pilgrimage or a number of pilgrimages rolled into one, the hajj consists of a circuit that is well over ten kilometres long, involving three visits to the Grand Mosque in Mecca, a day at the plain of Arafa and three days at Mina where pilgrims must throw stones at three spots known as the Jamarat where the devil is said in Islamic tradition to have appeared to Ibrahim.[6] It is an exhausting schedule, though many try to avoid doing as much as possible of it on foot these days. Muslims implicitly acknowledge the labour involved when they congratulate each other on completing the hajj, one of the five 'pillars' of Islam that God asks able-bodied Muslims to perform.

The complex rituals betray signs of merging a number of Arabian customs into one. Anthropologists see in the individual rites ancient cults connected with the seasons – for example, the day at Arafa was a rain-making cult, stone-throwing at Mina was to cast down the sun god, Muzdalifa where pilgrims spend time after the day at Arafa was associated with the thunder god Quzah (Saudi Arabia often calls for the nationwide 'rain prayer'). Visiting and circum-ambulating the Kaaba is a well-attested pre-Islamic custom, and the idea of Mecca as a sacred precinct may have its origins in a pre-Islamic neutral zone where tribal warfare and bickering was put aside. 'The central ritual of Islam, the Hajj, was arranged out of existing cultic practices. The actions themselves were almost unchanged, but their meaning was transformed to fit a new, vastly expanded, cosmic vision. The result was a religious and ideological *tour de force*', Malise Ruthven writes.[7]

The hajj that fell in January 2004, when I first went, came after the fall of Baghdad and the outbreak of al-Qa'ida insurgency in Saudi Arabia, so media interest was high for material that would indicate responses these events. The teams of journalists, from text, pictures and television, usually gather days in advance in Jeddah, allowing a few days to attend government-arranged events such as the interior minister's regular pre-hajj press conference, or visit the massive hajj terminal of Jeddah airport. While still based in Jeddah, we travelled to Mecca for pre-hajj *'umra*, donning our white robes of *ihram*; on the way we passed through checkpoints where they didn't bother checking our identities since we were Ministry of Information guests. In hindsight, the breezy arrival hinted at the divisions of class and culture that, as I was to discover, continue to lurk beneath the surface. Wealth and privilege help ease your path, and the Saudi authorities frown on those who don't do things their way – in particular, Asians, who are in any case treated with some contempt in Saudi society and especially patronised if they are new converts.[8]

Mecca was a shock. I had expected the pristine, marble sense of space of the main cities. What I got was al-Azhar street in central Cairo. Crowded, polluted, randomly-built housing vying for space around the centre of the town where the Grand Mosque is situated and which brings to mind Prince Charles' famous comment about St Paul's Cathedral and London's financial district: blocking the Mona Lisa with a team of basketball players. Hundreds of thousands of people squeezed into the town and into the mosque, but I suspected it was like this for much of the year. The setting in the mountains was quite stunning, but the position of the town was a heat and dust trap. For sure, before the modern age this was a place of great tranquillity and rough beauty. Now it was New Delhi meets Cairo in the hills. Around the holy mosque the sacred mixes with the profane. Traders cram the streets with shops selling trinkets and American fast food on streets lined with five-star hotels. American fast food – Burger King and KFC. Shops also sold Islamic alternatives to this Americana, drinks like Mecca Cola developed after the Palestinian intifada of 2000 inspired the desire to boycott all things American.

Mecca seems not to have been much known to the literate civilisations before the Islamic period. This has caused some Western historians to treat the centrality of Mecca in the early Arab-Islamic state with some scepticism. The Quran even refers to the place as Bakka – what sort of famed commercial and spiritual centre was that, that the Greeks hadn't heard of it and the revelation gets its name wrong, one scholar infamously asked?![9] Having visited it, I doubt it was ever much of a trading entrepôt myself, but there's plenty to convince that it was a mystical site for the communities of the peninsula, a sheltered sanctuary inland from the hot coastal town of Jeddah, and a site that perhaps had become more important in the centuries preceding the Islamic conquests when Hejazi tribes were part of the Nabataean confederation that was based in modern Jordan. For all that really matters in Mecca is the mosque and its black stone. If all roads lead to Mecca, all roads in Mecca lead down the hill to the Kaaba. French director of Morrocan origin Ismail Ferroukhi captured the spirt of the city well in a ten-minute sequence in his film *Le Grand Voyage*: all cars, crowds and noise. I felt calm and relief when my feet touched the worn white marble of the mosque precinct.

Our driver let us out in an underground underpass with stairs that let up into the mosque complex. The mosque was huge – it has 85 entrances – and because of the stop-start nature of mosque expansions, it lacked a specific form or shape. We walked around it through the crowds interminably it seemed, until we found a fence where we thought we could leave our sandals. When we walked in we still had some way to go before we reached the central space where the black stone, or Kaaba, lay. What we passed through was one mega-mosque or a series of mosques around the central *sahn*. We passed the special section known as Safa and Marwa, a walkway the length of which pilgrims walk seven times after having circled the Kaaba seven times. This sounds straightforward, but as I was to find out, it was gruelling. Eventually we came to the *sahn*. Crowds of people sat on the ground on the outside, making it difficult to get into the mass of people walking round the large cube-shaped edifice.

The closer you get to the Kaaba itself, the less distance you will be walking in all, and in fact many people, including the disabled, choose to walk around the roof of the mosque which, despite the comfort of no crowds and plenty of space, means walking some seven kilometres in all. Down in the square it was a mix of faith and violence, as the pilgrims jostled for space amid their prayers. The basic rule is to just keep moving with the flow. Entering and leaving the ring of circumambulators is the most fraught part of the process.

'Oh Lord, bring us the good in this life and good in the hereafter and save us from hell', pilgrims chant as they circle the Kaaba, the object which Muslims are facing when they pray towards Mecca. The river of people included Turks, Afghans and Indonesians, many in groups, tightly holding onto each other back-to-back to avoid getting lost. Their leader chants verses from the Quran while they repeat after him. Others go around individually saying private prayers. This is your chance to pray for all the things you want from God, from the grand and the political to the mundane and the personal. Friends will ask people to say a prayer for them at the Kaaba, and some were walking around sending and receiving text messages on their mobile phones, which, along with jewellery and the other accoutrements of daily life, should not really be there. The ring of worshippers squeezed ever harder against one another as they tried to near the Kaaba and the frenzy reached its peak at the inner circle closest to the black stone. Some kiss it, but for most the crush is too much to get that near, so they simply hold out their right hand and call out 'in the name of God, God is greater' each time they pass. It's at this point, on one corner of the Kaaba, that the crush is the worst on each circumambulation.

It was the strangest experience. Some of the groups of pilgrims were rough, rude and violent, crushing through the crowd to get to the centre. It seemed the ultimate act of selfishness, the idea that their salvation was so important, and so much more likely, if they could just get closer to the stone. It also seemed singularly un-Muslim. Some nationalities stood out more than others. The movement of people pulled you round in nervous small steps amid the crush, as you grip your garments in case they fall or the pressure of people pulls them away. The prayers, the walking round and round, the crowds, the people all around – it seemed to induce a state of delirium at some level or another for most of the pilgrims. Counting the seven is not so easy, but once it's done one heads to the Safa and Marwa area of the mosque complex. We had lost each other going round the Kaaba and I wasn't clear on the next stage of the ritual, so I was gripped now with a fear of getting lost. It was mid-afternoon prayer time. Once that was over I walked around the outside of the mosque looking for my colleagues. The marble was cold on my bare feet, the distance was huge and the crowds endless. I couldn't find the place where we had left our shoes, the only point where I could be sure of eventually finding them. After about an hour, in late afternoon, I found them by the fence where the sandals were. Now we needed to find the hotel where the other journalists were congregating and our driver. When we did, there was a congratulatory feeling in the air because everyone had performed 'umra. At this point we were able to end our *ihram*, meaning we could don our normal clothes. The TV producer asked me over coffee how I found the going during the *mas'a* at Safa and Marwa. 'What?!' I asked. 'No, I didn't know I should do that. When I was lost I just wanted to find you guys. Will it still count?' He laughed. 'Don't worry about it. It counts. *Yataqabbal* – God will accept your 'umra.' On the final day I had to fit extra time at the *mas'a* to make up for it.

Hajj for all its apparent complexity is in many ways beautifully simple: it revolves around the Kaaba. Simple and unpretentious against the grandiosity of the mosque, the large cube-shaped structure houses this mysterious black stone which centuries of veneration through kissing and touching has worn hollow. The Kaaba and the stone are located at a point which may have been mythologised as the centre of the world in pre-Islamic Arabia. It is regarded by some Muslims as where God's presence is most felt on earth, which is why it's the key place to lodge your prayer requests: here He might listen to you. 'The Kaaba is the heart of Islam and to imagine that you are seeing this place where the Prophet was one day with all his followers touches your heart immediately', an Egyptian colleague said when I asked her to describe her feelings on visiting the site for the first time during that week.

Islamic tradition says the Kaaba was built by Abraham and his son Ismail, who in the Islamic version of Semitic monotheism is regarded as the genealogical father of the Arabs (while Judaism emphasises Isaac as the father of the Jews), as the first temple to the one true God. All the hajj rituals are linked to Abraham. Safa and Marwa are the two points between which Abraham's servant-wife Hagar – the Egyptian mother of Ismail – searched desperately for water and shelter with her young child. The walking between the two points inside the mosque symbolises the search that God brought to a happy end when she miraculously came upon the well of Zamzam. While secular and Muslim historians agree the Kaaba was the centre of pre-Islamic Arabian cults, Muslim tradition notes the obvious point that veneration of the stone is reminiscent of the idolatry Islam stridently opposes. The paradox is solved by the hadith attributed to the caliph Omar: he is said to have addressed the object, saying: 'I know you are only a stone and can do neither good nor ill, and if I had not seen the Prophet kiss you, then I would not do so too.'

Some writers see a reflection of the cosmic order in the spatial movement of hajj. 'The planets revolve around the sun, each in a separate orbit, with specific speed. In the same way, the Kaaba which God made the first sanctuary for mankind is located at the center of the earth', Egyptian scholar Abdulhakam al-Sa'idi wrote on popular Islamic website islamonline. Sami Angawi, the Meccan Sufi scholar and architect, says hajj symbolises the continuity and change in the order of things. 'The constant – the Kaaba – gives you unity and continuity, the variable – walking around it – gives you change and diversity. The two create a balance, an equilibrium', he says. 'The closer we get to the Kaaba the more we are pulled by its gravity. So we do *tawaf*. The Kaaba is a timeless point. All are one at this point, symbolising the house of God and Mecca and the Kaaba are the heart of the Muslim world.' Sufis also see in hajj an act of purification, like the blood flowing around the body before returning to its vital organs. In one hadith the Prophet declares that 'he who performs hajj voluntarily and without moral blemish has gone back to the day his mother gave birth to him'. Hajj is spiritual rebirth.

However, the in-gathering of Muslims in the universal city of Islam also offers a forum for revolutionary action. Saudi riot police are on hand to stop any displays of political activism, no matter how peaceful. The army of some 50,000 police and security force members involved in organising hajj includes a special 'anti-protest' force to stop pilgrims staging protests – Iranians have tried on numerous occasions since the 1979 revolution.[10] In July 1987 up to 400 pilgrims died during shooting and a deadly stampede after Saudi police tried to close part of the route. The booklets the Saudis hand out in various languages to arriving pilgrims stress that the event is simply about doing things as the Prophet said they should be done in order to win God's favour.

This went far beyond politics. For Saudi Arabia to welcome all these people as they are with their different ideas and customs is a major test of nerves for al-Wahhabiyya. In vain would the

Saudi religious police try to force the mass of world Muslims to conform to their view of proper behaviour. The sheer volume of the crowds forces the religious police to take a back seat and let the assorted heretics and newbies be. The authorities 'give general instructions not to interfere too much with pilgrims during the hajj', says Mansour Nogaidan, a former Wahhabi rejectionist who left the country. 'The clerics here need to realise that Islam isn't one form and the world is more diverse than they want to accept. They want to impose their idea of Utopia on us all.' Booklets and signposts in different languages ask pilgrims not to engage in acts which venerate individuals such as the Prophet through excessive interest in certain pilgrimage sites (for example, Mount Hira, off the hajj trail, where the Prophet is said to have received his first revelation). *Mutawwa'een* stood on the side of the Kaaba, sometimes with sticks, in an effort to push away worshippers who were trying to kiss and touch it in veneration, but with little success. As I was walking round the first level of the mosque doing *tawaf*, I found a *mutawwa'* poking me in the back with a stick. 'Lower!' he snapped, because my robe was pulled high, showing my legs. Some of what they do is aimed at maintaining order. While I was going around the Kaaba I saw them shouting in vain at a group of men and women who wanted to pray in organised lines, as hundreds of people pushed their way round in circumambulation. 'Don't pray here, don't pray here!' they shouted.

I came across a Wahhabised American convert in a Jeddah hotel who seemed more preoccupied with the heresies of the masses than anything else. 'Yeah, it's something amazing to see people from different countries of the earth come together for one purpose', he said when I asked him how he felt being on hajj. 'It really touched me to see a long line of people in wheelchairs, the old and the pregnant. But you see inside the mosque people doing *bida'* [unorthodox acts], like clinging on to the Place of Abraham [a point inside the *sahn* several metres from the Kaaba]. There's a lot of innovation, polytheistic practices, Shia, Sufis and other different groups.' Innovators, polytheists, Shi'ites, Sufis. It sounded like a list of crimes in some political show trial. Many pilgrims in turn talked of their distaste for the Saudi Islam. 'Their Islam is very dry, there's something missing. They have such a sense of orthodoxy and control', Sayeed Mohamed, an imam from South Africa, told me.

The next day was the traditional tour of the holy sites made by interior minister Nayef before a news conference in the evening at Arafa, the huge plain in the mountains outside Mecca where the pilgrims spend the first day and night of hajj. First we saw a parade of some 5,000 troops including anti-terrorist forces in black balaclavas, elite special forces and crowd control personnel as they marched past Nayef. He was on his best form – later on we were kept waiting in a large hall for about two hours before he deigned to turn up. He sat alone at a long distance from the press pack on a large podium, so that with his headdress and robes on, we could hardly see him at all – court ceremonial intended to intimidate. His answers to questions, on the dubious theme of al-Qa'ida attacking pilgrims, were gruff and curt. 'We are ready for anything that could happen'; 'We always say there is no guarantee that nothing could happen but we trust the security forces to be able to do their job'; 'All efforts are being made to secure the house of God. In past years and this year we give confidence to the pilgrims so they can safely carry out their rituals.' Afterwards we were allowed to gorge ourselves on a fat buffet dinner in the open air before being taken back to Jeddah.

The real danger, however, was safety. In 1990, 1,426 people were crushed to death in a stampede in a road tunnel in Mecca; in 1998, 2001 and 2003, at least 172 people were killed in various other overcrowding incidents at the Jamarat, three spots where pilgrims gather over a three-day period to throw stones at a spot where the devil is said to have appeared to Abraham. Hajj affairs minister Iyad Madani was asked about Jamarat safety issues at the buffet on the grass after Nayef's priggish performance. 'Any gathering of people of this size in a limited geographical area could lead to problems but we have plans to prevent this', he said. 'We have started to bring pilgrims to the Jamarat on the basis of a specific timetable so that everyone doesn't come at one time to the bridge. The other step is preventing cars completely from entering the Jamarat Bridge so there is no mix of cars and people. We hope these measures together will stop incidents.'

But according to Sami Angawi, the best-laid crowd control plans had been obstructed for years by the reluctance of the authorities to stop pilgrims coming in cars to the Jamarat area as well as the insistence of the Wahhabi religious establishment on everyone performing rites at specific times. Saudi clerics say the stone-throwing should take place in the afternoon of the third day, as booklets handed out to pilgrims advise. Angawi, who set up the kingdom's Hajj Research Centre in 1975, said the problem was that there could be an estimated 50,000 cars at the same time in one location. 'Seventy-five per cent of the pilgrims throw stones in 25 per cent of the available time and that's because of the particular insistence of one school', he said. 'Now they want to increase the capacity of Jamarat, but then you create problems at the next stage. They always work on the space side, expanding roads and tunnels, but there are two factors: space and time.'

The hajj starts with pilgrims streaming out from Mecca on the eighth day of the month to the plain of Arafa where they must spend the ninth day in commemoration of the Prophet Mohammad's farewell sermon 14 centuries ago. Though hundreds of thousands came on around 20,000 buses in a massive logistical operation, many come on foot tracing the Prophet's path through mountain passes to Arafa. Sometimes referred to as Mount Arafat, the plain consists of a massive tented village that the Saudi authorities throw up every year to lodge the pilgrims according to nationality. On the first night there we headed down to the main mosque of Namura to speak to some pilgrims. The act of springing someone for a quote, with editors breathing down your phone, is rarely anything but deeply unsatisfying. Laying in wait for pilgrims was worse. The questions are clichéd and the answers even more so. 'What will you be praying for this year?' which we sometimes followed with, as an encouragement or prod in the right direction, 'what with the war in Iraq and ...'. Rarely would you get anything that veered away from standard responses that people felt obliged to offer. For example, Ribhy Yaseen, a Palestinian: 'I feel like any Muslim who comes to the house of God – we want God to give the Islamic nation success, to liberate our land from the Jews and to return the al-Aqsa mosque to Muslims.' Or Iraqi Qadir Khidr: 'We hope God will give success to the Muslim people around the world and especially in our region.' Some at Namura were not impressed with the media presence: 'May God curse all cameramen!' a Saudi hissed at our Mahmoud. He hit back: 'You're meant to have a pure heart and intent for the days of the hajj, so you shouldn't say things like that.'

The morning of the day at Arafa began with pilgrims heading to a large rocky outcrop in the area called Jabal al-Rahma (Mount Mercy). It was at this spot specifically that the Prophet is said to have given his farewell sermon. This was one of most pleasant and memorable moments of the hajj. We must have risen at five in the morning in our pilgrim towels, then made our way the kilometre or so to the Mount. As the sun rose in the mountains surrounding the plains, it gradually became a blanket of white as pilgrims trekked to the top. Since we had got there early we reached the top without much problem, though getting back down looked like it would be tricky. There was one main path up between the huge boulders and hundreds were now streaming up the outcrop. Many had slept here the night before. People sat around and prayed in groups or alone, or chanted in Arabic the hajj refrain known as the *talbiya*: 'O God, I am in tThy presence again, there is no presence like Thine presence, to You is the praise, the power and domain, there is no equal to You.' The beauty of the scene demanded a prayer, which five of us did, with the cameraman leading our group and us repeating after him, in the Muslim fashion.

Negotiating our way down the mountain as the crowds swarmed upwards, we had the first sense of the kind of chaos that was to come. Down below I noticed huge multilingual signposts from the Saudi authorities warning that the Prophet did not sanction prayer there, but clearly no one was paying any attention to what the Saudis thought. A carnival atmosphere was filling this huge pilgrim city at Arafa, which by mid-morning had come alive. Hawkers by the roadside sold everything from umbrellas to keep off the sun, to prayer mats and prayer beads. Men were offering to take pictures of pilgrim groups for up to $12 a shot and enterprising teenagers were offering camel rides for around $3. 'It's God that gives me my daily sustenance, but I get about 500 pilgrims every day during the hajj season', one camel boy said shyly at being questioned about the time-honoured tradition of making money out of the pilgrims.

By night-time pilgrims began moving on to the next stage – heading back down towards Mecca to an area known as Muzdalifa and the Jamarat at Mina. I really didn't know what was coming next at any stage, something that gave the whole experience a magical aspect. I imagine it was like this for everyone there for the first time. Everyone is in a group and learning as they go along about what hajj entails and the numerous booklets the authorities gave out were in general pretty useful. It was a nice evening, cool and pleasant. We sat around inside a ministry compound at Muzdalifa with waiters serving us big pots of Arabic coffee and tea as we lounged around on cushions and chatted. There were quite a few *khawaga*s (educated Westerners) amongst us, and whilst I was aware of being a European in what some might consider a Third World religious event, the mix of people was too diverse to get lost in that dark alley: if anything, it was Saudi approaches to non-Western non-Arabs that constituted the major fault-line in the proceedings, a divide that involved issues of wealth and culture. The compound was full of small stone chips and people took the chance to gather stones for their trips to the three pillars marking the site of the temptation at Jamarat. Apparently, we would need 49 in all: later that evening we would throw seven at the central pillar, sometime in the 24 hours after that we would throw seven at each of the three pillars, and in the next 24 hours we would do the same again. The size of the stones, and the spirit in which they are thrown, is an issue of some debate. Wahhabi scholars also don't like to see too much passion put into throwing stones at the pillars, which is a good thing, I'd say. Government booklets explained: 'Some believe they are throwing stones at the devil himself, so they do it with anger and insults, but we are only asked to do the Jamarat in order to remember God. Some throw big stones, shoes or pieces of wood, but this is going too far and the Prophet forbade it.'

Later in the evening we drove down to the ministry's lodgings at Mina on the mountainside overlooking the Jamarat, which were accessible via an aerial roadway or bridge which had been constructed around them for pilgrims to walk onto. Or they could throw stones at the pillars from under the bridge at their base. The Jamarat lay in a narrow bottleneck at the end of a deep valley overlooking Mecca and the bridge made the area even narrower. Most of the pilgrims were housed in camps on a wider part of the valley floor before the bridge area. As we drove down we witnessed the stunning site of hundreds of thousands of pilgrims in white moving along the huge night-lit highway the Saudis had built between Arafa and Mina. It must have been around midnight by now. We dumped our stuff in the rooms allocated for us and where we'd spend the next three days and nights, then got on a bus which took us down to the Jamarat bridge.

The pillars were located some 50 metres apart, rising up through the middle of the specially designed roadway to allow access to those who walked over the bridge. We were underneath at the central one and there was a modest crowd of maybe 500 people. It was an odd atmosphere, sort of celebratory but a bit dangerous with stones flying everywhere. Since people are circling the pillar from every side, anyone can easily overthrow and hit those standing opposite. But mostly you wouldn't want to risk getting too close to the inside of the group of pilgrims doing the throwing, and many timidly move up to the outer ring of the circle to throw their seven stones. 'In the name of God, the compassionate, the merciful' is the standard utterance when throwing each one, or 'I seek God's help from the devil.' The occasion seemed disappointingly inauspicious. Perhaps it was the location. It felt like standing at an ugly underpass in central Cairo. Grey concrete, huge pillars, stones, even the grey-brown of the mountainside. Someone had daubed 'USA' at the base of the central pillar in blue paint. 'This country was founded on this faith and, God willing, will stick to it', the mufti said that evening in his Namura sermon.

After that, at around one in the morning, we were taken into the heart of Mecca to the mosque for midnight *tawaf* and the *mas'a* at Safa and Marwa run that I hadn't done before. It was quieter going round the Kaaba, but still there was a huge crowd and one was constantly trying to avoid being jabbed by an arm or rammed by a determined pilgrim heading on a new trajectory, or having one's foot trodden on. In a spirit of martyrdom, perhaps, one utters non-stop praise and prayer to God and does not stop moving until the seventh wave is done. At that point you quickly try to eject yourself from the swirling circle without more violence being done to you. The entering and the leaving are delicate processes involving moving forward with the crowd but gradually moving outwards too. I saw the tall figure of Egyptian cabinet minister Ahmed Nazif moving more gracefully than some others with the crowd: it was a few months before he became prime minister, but seven years later he faced trial for corruption and wasting public money. Once I was out I drank holy Zamzam water at the numerous taps around. Pilgrims would come by and fill whole bottles with the stuff which they would then take home with them to friend and family, believing in its curative powers. Then I went over to the Safa and Marwa circuit. I was with Sohaib, our photographer who was my sheikh for the occasion since he was much more informed about these affairs than I was. There is a special passageway that runs up the middle of the hall which allows those in wheelchairs to move unhindered by the crowds. Some people seemed to think this was a good way to complete each circuit quickly without having to negotiate the crowds all around. I followed, protesting that this wasn't an appropriate thing to do. I did two of the seven this way then decided to suffer with the other pilgrims. *Tawaf* in the cool of the night, on the eve of Eid al-Adha, was a blessing.

At some time around eight in the morning I collapsed onto the floor mattress at the ministry's retreat on the mountainside. We had been up for 24 hours and had only slept four hours the night before that. No one had had a proper shower in two days and we were wearing these white robes. Then at 9.30am my colleague's phone rang. There had been some accident down at the Jamarat, he said. I called the office then ran down the mountain steps to the Jamarat as fast as I could with my notebook, pen and phone. It was packed with people and I couldn't get to the upper level of the bridge overlooking the Jamarat pillars because security police had blocked access. I asked a policeman what happened. Absolutely nothing, he said. I asked one of the medics at one of the portable clinics around the area. At least 100 people died in a crush on the bridge earlier, he said. My God, I thought. But he wasn't going to give me his name. I asked another one. At least 200, he said. All I could do was tell the office what I had and try and find people who might have been there or in the vicinity when it happened. Our cameraman, meanwhile, had got onto the roof of the ministry lodge where he had a clear shot of dozens of bodies laid out on the ground on the bridge. When I'd done as much as I could do, I headed back up the steps and the road. The information ministry officials were furious that we had run a story saying the numbers of dead were in the dozens before the state news agency had made its official pronouncement.

Two hours later we were bussed to a press conference in Mecca with Madani. The minister's revelation was that 244 people had died (the figure rose later to 251) and 244 were injured. 'There were more than 400 metres of people pushing in the same direction [which] resulted in the collapse of those next to the stoning area and those behind. That led to panic', he said. But he gave some odd comments suggesting a certain resignedness to casualties and even nonchalance. The deaths represented 'less than 1 per cent of 1 per cent of the pilgrims', and 'no matter what research work we do, incidents do happen', 'it's bad luck rather than any lack of follow-up'. 'I confirm that all preparations were made, but God's intentions are sometimes unknowable', he added. The problem, he said, was pilgrims who had not come on organised trips, but rather were ex-pat labour in the kingdom who had come on their own steam – illegally, since hajj requires special visas and permits. Many may have done hajj last year and stayed on in the kingdom illegally, he said: these people were moving around the pilgrimage carrying all their gear with them and that gear had got in the way of other pilgrims on the top of the bridge as hundreds of thousands surged ahead. Most of the dead were Indonesians, Pakistanis and other Asian nationalities.

No one ever produced statistics then or since to prove the dead were all illegal hajjis. There was clearly another problem: pilgrims knew how to get onto the bridge but there was no clear process for getting off. The bridge filled up with more and more people at a far faster rate than they were able, willing or encouraged to get off. Most pilgrims seemed largely unperturbed, though people were a bit wary during the stoning rituals on the rest of Sunday and on Monday. 'I'm not frightened, but you have to be careful', said Indian pilgrim Mohammed Seif later that day, complaining that some pilgrims were still aggressively pushing their way to the pillars. 'You can stone any time, you don't have to do it all at once', he said, which was the view that some Saudi clerics were finally prepared to endorse in subsequent statements. 'In the end it's fate', said Saudi pilgrim Hussein Ahmed. 'What can you do with millions of people in the same spot?' said Ilhami Osman, an Egyptian pilgrim, angry at fielding such questions from a foreigner. The government was still more concerned with terrorism, after Saudis had turned against the regime under the al-Qa'ida banner. 'Terrorism is corruption on earth', a joint statement from King Fahd and his crown prince Abdullah said. 'Such acts must be confronted and their falseness exposed so they do not sway the ignorant. They are the result of sick minds and deviant ideologies alien to Islam's laws and principles.' The imam leading the Eid al-Adha prayer in Mecca attacked *takfir* itself. 'This phenomenon has expanded so much that scholars must confront it with concrete proof from Islam to protect our youth from its stench and putridness', Abdulrahman al-Sudais said. Western fears of Islamic fundamentalism had reached Mecca itself: this could have been Bush speaking, though for sure Bush would have used less colourful language.

At the Jamarat, meanwhile, security police had gone from nonchalant to aggressive. Crowd control warnings were blared via megaphones and helicopters hovered in the sky monitoring the situation. In the evening I went down there with a colleague to do another round of stone-throwing. The crush was as bad as ever. It was astounding. Tens of thousands of pilgrims had crowded under around and under the Jamarat bridge. The problem was that a huge portion of the available ground was taken up by pilgrims camped on the ground. We headed for underneath the bridge where there was a bit more space. A bulldozer had found its way through and was clearing away a mountain of small stones around the base of one of the pillars, dredging up dozens of plastic sandals and slippers apparently thrown by some who got a bit carried away with the 'let-it-all-out' vibe of the ritual. 'USA' had been removed from the central pillar, though the clearing of the stones had revealed 'Bush' written at the base of another. Men crowded in to get a good shot at the pillar while women strained at the back to hit the target. Stones clattered down through the hole through which the pillar reached up to the upper floor of the bridge where the pilgrims above were chucking their stones too. Though we moved away quickly once we'd finished, we weren't in safety yet. The way back to the steps that take you up to the road on the mountain side was completely packed with the squatters. Police on the other side did nothing about it. 'What can we do?' one smirked like it was a comedy when we asked him about the chaos. A few children, some with deformities or missing limbs, sat on the road begging. 'Something given for the sake of God!' they shouted, pointlessly. No one was giving.

Despite everyone's best efforts to maintain good spirits, tempers fray during hajj. With these increasingly large numbers of people 'processed' through narrow mountain passes since the early 1980s, it has become a severe stretch on even the good manners of even the most pious or good-natured. It is amazing to think there were only 20,000 people or so who attended during some hajj years in the early 1930s. That evening at the Jamarat some people's behaviour was hard to excuse. A Yemeni man charged from the front with a woman in a wheelchair gasping for breath. An Egyptian came from behind on a motorbike. 'I didn't think there would be crowds here', he announced with an inane grin on his face. 'Is there anywhere here that isn't crowded?' I barked back. Men from Gulf countries tried to protect their fully-veiled wives, though the smells, the pushing and the shoving had all but left their modesty in shreds. The standard call for making your way through the crowds was 'Tareeg, Ya Hajj!' – 'Please pilgrims, clear the way!' – but it was useless in a situation like this.

As we eventually neared the stairway the ground was covered in compressed garbage – two days' worth of plastic cups, bits of fruits, wrapping papers, and hair cut by an army of on-site barbers once pilgrims have made their first *tawaf* on Eid al-Adha. 'These are people who don't have homes in the first place', I heard one person mutter. He touched on a very real point. Our complaints were the complaints of the relatively prosperous about the ways of the Asian poor who could not easily communicate with the Saudis or the other Arabs in Arabic. It was such an odd sight: the campers, who were mainly Indonesian, sat there silently staring at the mass of people before them. A policeman finally erupted at them. 'Get out! Go!' he screamed in Arabic at the front row. They scurried away without so much as a whimper, gathering up their mats, pots and pans and small parcels of food. In an instant the ideal of a microcosmic world without social or cultural distinctions or a word raised in anger was exposed for the lie, even if a beautiful lie, that it essentially was.

The authorities effected a radical renovation of the Jamarat for the hajj of 1425, which fell in January 2005. The pillars which rise from under the bridge and peak through the upper level on the bridge were transformed into a long wall and the barriers around them had been brought closer to the walls so there would be less of a crush of people trying to throw stones from a distance as in previous years. There were many more exits on the bridge, as well as large electronic signposts telling pilgrims in Arabic, English, French Bahasa Malay and Urdu not to push their way among the crowds. In fact, compared to before, this was so much easier that one wondered why they had only thought of it now. As one pilgrim told me: 'For the first time it feels like it's really organised. Everyone is saying it's much better.' I did wonder whether some sacrilegious act had been inflicted on the pillars through turning them into walls of stone, but then again one had to remember that the pillars themselves are neither sacred nor ancient – they simply represent a site and have been altered throughout the centuries. Since then, the last time I visited Mecca, the Jamarat bridge has morphed into a four-storey structure resembling a car park, with extended walls, to allow far more access to the walls, though the authorities see this as a means to bring even more pilgrims to perform hajj rather than purely a means of making the rites safer. With so many people – the authorities like to cite a figure of 3 million now – there is a danger that the hajj is being reduced to simply a set of actions emptied of any meaning at all, an empty shell, as tired pilgrims are herded from one point to the next and blamed for their own travails whenever disaster strikes, while the affluent live in the lap of luxury in Disneyland-in-the-sky hotel towers bearing down on the Kaaba. Mass transport is being introduced to the pilgrimage sites, but even that project betrays signs of tokenism: it's a high-speed rail link between Mecca and Medina.

Though the 'hajj overstayer' is one of those great fears of Saudi bureaucracy that slips inexorably into racism, there are many Asians who find lives in Mecca, happy to make a humble living in the shadow of the mosque. For some it was what America was for the human surplus produced by the Industrial Revolution in nineteenth-century Europe – sanctuary. Like all those who find their sanctuary in a far-off land, they want to belong and to assimilate. They speak Arabic, and if they've been there long enough will play down their foreign origins if they possibly can. Mecca has absorbed many in this manner over the ages, from West Africa and from East Asia. Many Saudis in Jeddah and Mecca betray a certain Malaysian or

Indonesian look. At Mount Arafat I came across two men from Burma whose parents had settled in Mecca in the 1950s. 'We have lived here all our lives, we have become part of the country', they said. 'But we don't have nationality.' I didn't ask why or ask more. They sat quietly and motionless, keeping warm in their robes on simple plastic sheets by the side of the road, part of the half a million Saudi residents who had slipped into the pilgrimage on their own, confounding the efforts to control the hajj. I met a Bangladeshi working in a shop selling religious books and tapes who gave his name as Abd al-Tahar Mohammed. The name alone reveals only that he is a Muslim, and leaves no trace of his ethnic origin. 'My life is working here in this shop and then going down to the Grand Mosque to pray. God be praised', he beamed, clasping my hand. He had been here four years now, living within a stone's throw of the Kaaba. As far as he was concerned, God had truly smiled on him. Another shop-worker I spoke to gave him name as Nour. He had an Indonesian or Malaysian look, and was coy on giving details about his origins. 'From here', he would just say. I didn't press the point. He was pleasant with me, more so than his Egyptian boss who was rude and suspicious about the *khawaga* reporter asking all the questions.

Editors often wanted quotes from pilgrims that would provoke irritation from those questioned; for example, the CNN-esque 'what do the pillars represent for *you*??' Some said they were Bush, the Israeli leader Ariel Sharon or British prime minister Tony Blair. I'm not sure that any of them really meant it, with the possible exception of Yvonne Ridley, a British journalist and one-time captive with the Taliban who converted to Islam. I came across her on the chaotic road outside the government encampments on the mountainside. I had seen her earlier in the day speaking on Saudi TV from the rooftop studio inside our residence, though in her black robes and hijab she would pass for any other Muslim woman. She was on her first pilgrimage and was happy to talk. 'During the stoning I couldn't help thinking of Bush, Blair and Sharon', she said. 'It's the greatest show on earth. There is nothing to compare anywhere on the planet. It shows how Islam transcends nationalisms, colours and cultures. We are all one – there is no rich, no poor, we are all just Muslims', she said. I loved her next comment, so *Nuevo Christiano*: 'In a way, it's a shame that non-Muslims can't come to witness this sort of unity.' If women can pray alongside men in Mecca, why can't they do it elsewhere, she asked? 'Perhaps some mosque leaders should pay attention to this and promote this sort of unity.' Her minder, who had the appearance of a *mutawwa'*, just smiled politely.

There was a similar media circus in January 2005 during the hajj of Islamic year 1425, which took place after the massive tsunami that hit countries of the southern Asian seaboard on 16 December 2004. Searching for a story in which to frame the hajj for audiences, editors wanted to know how the tsunami had lowered pilgrim numbers from Asia or cast a shadow over the rituals. Around 230,000 people died in 14 countries, 130,000 of them in Indonesia and thus Muslim. Some scholars in Saudi Arabia had suggested the tragedy was to punish Indonesia for welcoming Western tourists with mixed-sex beaches, bars and nightclubs. The Egyptian cleric Yousef al-Qaradawi suggested the same. We set up the equipment on a raised platform outside a KFC branch near the mosque in Mecca and hoisted those ready to speak onto the platform away from the crowd. It was all rather contrived in that I don't think the tsunami was on so many people's minds, unless they actually came from the afflicted areas in South Asia. Also, how much they are troubled by the opinions of a particular religious leader is open to question. Islam is full of muftis, imams and sheikhs, and Muslims can take their pick about whose opinions they want to follow; it's not like there is a Pope. Even Sistani in Iraq is only 'pope' for those Shi'ites who choose to make him their *marja'*. 'How can it be our fault? This tragedy was too big. There was an earthquake and a wave at the same time. I don't think we could be so bad as that" one young Indonesian said. A Pakistani man in his fifties, who I think offered the opinion he did because he thought it was the answer we were looking for, said: 'There is drinking and other things which go on in places in the West but which Muslims don't expect to happen in their own countries.' Perhaps the most thoughtful response came from the South African imam Sayeed Mohamed. 'Although the Quran does talk about God using natural phenomenon to punish people who have gone astray, it is not for us to say or to know', he said.

English is probably the most widely understood language of all among all the pilgrims at hajj, which might seem odd or even ironic, given the sentiments of Salafism in its various forms, but it's not ultimately a surprise. Arabic-speakers, on the other hand, are the elite; they speak not just the language of God's revelation, but that of His bureaucracy. Arabs share culture and understanding with the Saudis that make their life easier during hajj. Asian pilgrims dominate numerically, but must put up with the disdain of their hosts and many of the other Arabs towards them. Ultimately, however, the ingathering of peoples from all four corners of the globe to perform these ancient rites around the Kaaba was the humbling experience it should be; for all the complexities of movement and logistic, there was beauty in the simplicity of hajj, and it was comforting to stare afterwards at those stunning images the photographers managed to get – I'm sure not without some manipulation – of hundreds of thousands of people moving through the night-ether of the mosque, condensed into a mass of white-in-motion around a symmetrical black box, and to know that you were nothing but a pixel in the Meccan dream of one common humanity.

Conclusion

This book has tried to mix some of my own experience of the country with thoughts on religious discourse, media manipulation, domestic repression and foreign policy acrobatics in the era of 9/11, Abdullah and reform. Saudi Arabia is hardly the only contested nation-state established on religious bases in the world – there's Israel and Pakistan for a start – but it's one that I have had extensive contact with over the past decade. Saudi Arabia has always claimed its identity as the true Sharia state makes it 'different', and thus immune to the kind of protest movements that spread through the region in 2011. The popular representation demanded by ordinary people is outside the regime's epistemological framework, as is its mode of expression: protests are un-Islamic and so is democracy. These arguments are nothing but the manipulations of the regime. There is no such thing as an Islamic or un-Islamic protest, or Islamic or un-Islamic democracy, for that matter. The discourse might convince some of this particular generation since Islamic sentiments dominate the political sphere – a social and political development that can ultimately be traced back to the Arab defeat against Israel in 1967 – but in earlier times neither Islamic politics nor social conservatism were as prevalent as they are now in Saudi Arabia, or in certain regions of Saudi Arabia, or elsewhere in the Gulf. The cultural specificity claimed by the state's backers is as 'created in time' as the Mu'tazila regarded the Quran, not in existence since the beginning of time. With its Medinan obsessions, the Saudi-Wahhabi state remains 'a mechanism for reproduction of circumstances that existed before the state itself was established', in Fouad Ibrahim's words.[1] So while the country advances in historical time, it experiences the constant pull of the past. This state of idealised stagnation is assigned a supreme value: it is natural conservatism, authenticity, the spirit of the true Islam. Yet the Sharia state, as scholars of Islamic law have realised, is a caricature whose compromises to the demands of the ruler, his foreign policy and his expanding agencies of coercion have twisted the Utopia into a shape few religious scholars of previous ages would recognise. The *ulama* have become partners in the police state's surveillance and intimidation. They may be the 'clerics of darkness', in the view of some Arab intellectuals, but their rule is 'divine', as the late interior minister Prince Nayef once said. They have established a particular cognitive framework for the subject/believer, one that holds a gang-rape victim to be a prostitute and deserving of flogging for the crime of being alone with an unrelated man.

The number one priority of the ruling family and the *ulama* is maintaining their power in the spheres designated to them through their historical alliance. Despite the periodic temptation of the one to encroach on the territory of the other, coexistence is their best guarantee of survival. Both parties display the occasional caliphal instinct: Abdulaziz is eulogised as father of the nation and possessed of extraordinary abilities, and the real age of King Abdullah is left as some kind of esoteric mystery to mesmerise the masses. At the same time, some religious scholars harbour the desire to achieve the final realisation of clerical supremacy in all sovereign matters of state, fulfilling the historic logic of Sunni legalism: surely the best safeguard for the Sharia state is for the guardians of God's law to assume the highest positions. But both king and cleric, warrior and priest know their place. Thus, the scope for 'reform' is rather limited: allowing women to drive, as will happen sooner or later, is a basic right that has no impact on citizens of the state's basic right to a serious stake in governance. Foreign governments who share Al Saud's concern for survival have every interest in promoting the empty discourse of reform, with its essentially limited gains and ambitions, in order to maintain the stability of a state that offers considerable services to Western governments. The United States was not interested in popular enfranchisement in the 1960s and it is not interested now. Then it feared Arab nationalists would benefit, now it fears Islamists – some of them lay, some of them clergy, and a relatively new phenomenon in the Saudi context – will benefit.

Safe in this knowledge, Saudi leaders used a range of arguments to deflect Western criticism after the 9/11 attacks and took a series of policy stances to demonstrate they are on the same page as the Western powers with the ability to threaten their grip on power. Developing the idea of *al-Wasatiyya*, Saudi Arabia has claimed to lead the fight against jihadist Islam, resurgent Iranian nationalism and Palestinian radicalism. All three positions are tendentious: its public position on Iran has been loud but claiming concern for the greater good of Muslims and Arabs, yet US diplomatic documents reveal bellicosity and panic over Al Saud's standing; its position on the Israeli-Palestinian conflict has required cover-up and obfuscation and caused public discomfort; its war with jihadist Salafism is opportunistic and piecemeal – Saudi Salafis who found themselves in Nahr al-Barid in 2007 lost their lives for being on the wrong side of Al Saud's politicking, not because the princes had ditched al-Salafiyya al-Jihadiyya, but because they continually hedge their bets and play both sides. The interior ministry was once a fortified citadel of rejection for Western political, security and intelligence circles, now the officials in charge so value their close cooperation with American officials that Saudi authorities have the leverage to do much what they want on the domestic front.[2] In the Wahhabi context, the reformist project precludes meaningful participation, or a serious challenge to tribalism, or the entrenched position of al-Wahhabiyya, but it does plan to codify law and entrench a juridical system that sees fit to decapitate for engaging in sorcery.

Al Saud laud the unity that their state project has brought to much of the peninsula as an *ipso facto* good, but it remains the case that, in the words of London-based dissident Hamza Hassan, 'a minority rules a nation of minorities'.[3] It has involved suppressing the capacities of vibrant metropolitan centres such as the Hejazi milieu or that of the Shi'ite Eastern Province, imposing the princely oligarchy's control over key political and administrative positions, melding co-opted families to that order and filling out the lower ranks of the structure with commoners. Saudi princes have extended political and economic domination wherever possible, stifling creativity and production. Saudi Arabia's economy is full of distortions: the pegging of its currency to the US dollar is purely for political reasons;[4] billions are spent on oil production while Washington shifts to a focus on alternative energy and ending reliance on Middle East oil;[5] cities expand horizontally, stretching resources to the limit; ordinary Saudis have difficulty obtaining loans for housing or business start-ups, while untold sums are off-budget for defence, mosque expansion and princely usage.[6] The Saudi-Wahhabi state has consistently striven to introduce scientific/industrial civilisation only on its own terms. Reactionary throughout its history, it has never been on the cusp of change; rather, it is always obliged eventually to acquiesce in it.

Though it is heavily wedded to strict unitarianism, puritan scripturalism and sober religiosity – a protestant ethic, if you will – al-Wahhabiyya remains at heart what sociologists might call a hegemonic magic system. Despite gimmicks like the King Abdullah Economic City or KAUST, the society it seeks to create is pre-modern, pre-science and pre-rationalism (where segregation of women makes no economic sense), a divinely-ordained order in which the *ulama* have their place, Al Saud have theirs, and the people have their fair price inscribed in the nature of things. Women are legal minors, tribes are ranged in pecking order, blue-collar workers whose governments are in need of the remittances (and perhaps in India and Pakistan's case, Saudi investments too) possess utility rather than rights.[7] The system is maintained by voodoo and coercion, and those who challenge the Utopian order face exclusion, marginalisation and jail.

In one of the American diplomatic reports made public by Wikileaks, Sheikh Nimr al-Nimr, the well-known Shi'ite religious scholar (who once said Eastern Province Shi'ites could one day try to secede and was arrested for 'sedition' in 2012), outlined his beliefs candidly to a US diplomat. Two things jump out, two elements in his approach which run counter to that of Western governments and media discourse in general on Saudi Arabia. Nimr 'does not distinguish between different members of the al-Saud, but only judges the government by its actions within the Kingdom, which he feels belie any sign of greater moderation or openness', the report says.[8] This is an attractive approach. Al Saud are happy to entrap all those who will expend mental energy on their realm in the intricacies of internal debates, Islamists versus liberals, progressive princes versus retrograde clerics and hawks, the Kremlinology of who's in and who's out, who's up and who's down. But it's largely a ruse to distract attention from the more fundamental issue of the arbitrary and massive powers of a hyper-dynasty haunted by fear of losing it all. Secondly, Nimr outlines his belief that it is only a policy of action, campaigning and mobilisation that will bring any meaningful change to the country. 'It would seem his plan will be to continue forcefully calling for reform and creating unrest, endearing him to the disaffected, and fitting with his vision of instability as being the only catalyst for real change in the Kingdom', the report concludes. Nimr tells his own story of beatings in detention in 2006 which only ended when his town of Awamiya threatened to stage street protests, since letters from his followers to Prince Mohammed bin Fahd – the Eastern Province son of Fahd whom Abdullah placed on his Allegiance Council – produced no results. Nimr's approach is striking because it is framed in such positive, activist terms.

This book did not set out with the aim of being prescriptive, but in light of the historical movement of dissent that rumbled throughout countries of the Middle East and North Africa in 2011 it would be appropriate to consider what avenues for change exist in Saudi Arabia. The Saudi-Wahhabi state has considerable financial, coercive and discursive tools at its disposal and will continue to employ them with force to maintain the status quo. It will assume the good will of its foreign friends in this endeavour. Indeed, the account of Nimr's statement of purpose contains numerous subtle put-downs; he is 'controversial', has gained 'notoriety', and is obliged to explain his feelings about Iran. This should be no surprise. The kind of philosophy he outlines for dealing with the state, which critics of many ideological backgrounds would subscribe to, rejects rule by sometime handouts and the empty discourse of reform; it is unflinchingly critical of the Utopia and refuses to give it the benefit of the doubt. It reserves the right to say no, to resist, to fight for justice: to take action to change the allegedly perennial state of things.

Notes

INTRODUCTION

1. Even John Burgess, a former US diplomat whom I got to know during my first visit in 2003, set aside his usual positive spirit, decrying a 'retreat on reform' and appeasement of clerics in his Crossroads Arabia blog.
2. Aziz Al-Azmeh, *Muslim Kingship: Power and the Sacred in Muslim, Christian and Pagan Polities*. London: I.B. Tauris, 2001, p. 76.
3. Wael Hallaq, *Sharia: Theory, Practice and Transformations*. Cambridge: Cambridge University Press, 2009, p. 309.
4. A US diplomatic cable from 15 July 2006 discussing view on the war between Israel and Hizbullah notes bluntly, 'the continuing divide between the government and the views of the general Saudi populace'; released by Wikileaks on 15 March 2011, http://wikileaks.org/cable/2006/07/06JEDDAH478.html.
5. Abdel-Rahman Munif, *Mudun al-Malh (Cities of Salt, Part One)*. Beirut: Arab Institute for Studies and Publishing, 1992, pp. 33–4.
6. Abdel-Rahman Munif, *Bayn al-Thaqafa wal-Siyasa*. Arab Organisation for Studies and Publishing. Beirut: al-Markaz al-Thaqafi al-Arabia, 2003, p. 26.
7. Fouad Ibrahim, *Al-Salafiyya al-Jihadiyya fi al-Saudiyya*. Beirut: Dar al-Saqi, 2009, p. 60.

CHAPTER 1

1. Interview with author, June 2007.
2. 'Family members bury Al-Huraisi in Riyadh', *Arab News*, 31 July 2007; also interview with author, June 2007.
3. 'Saudi lawyer to appeal in morals squad death case', Reuters, 15 June 2007.
4. Mamoun Fandy, *Saudi Arabia and the Politics of Dissent*. London: Palgrave Macmillan, 2001, p. 247.
5. Saudi Press Agency report, 23 September 2008, www.spa.gov.sa/print. php?id=592596.
6. Ibid.
7. 'Saudi Arabia goes into overdrive for Ramadan', Reuters, 10 October 2006.
8. Interview with author, October 2006.
9. Ayedh al-Qarni, *La Tahzan*. Riyadh: Obeikan, 2007, p. 35.
10. Interview with author, December 2007.
11. http://wikileaks.ch/cable/2009/11/09JEDDAH443.html.
12. 'Saudi Arabia launches campaign to combat drug use', Reuters, 24 June 2007.
13. Patricia Crone and Martin Hinds, *God's Caliph: Religious Authority in the First Centuries of Islam*. Cambridge: Cambridge University Press, 2003 (reprint).
14. Aziz Al-Azmeh, *Muslim Kingship*. London: I.B. Tauris, 1997.

15. Though Wahhabis reject the term 'Wahhabism' itself, since it conflicts with the principle of unity of God and fighting idolatry, the modern Saudi state has not shrunk from idolising the person of Abdulaziz bin Saud.

16. See the sailor's account in 'Sailor was the piper of history', St Petersburg Times, 2 December 2005.

17. '1945 U.S.-Saudi meeting to be marked', Associated Press, 12 February 2005.

18. Nawaf Obaid, 'The power of Saudi Arabia's Islamic leaders', Middle East Quarterly, September 1999, pp. 51–8.

19. Interview with author, March 2003.

20. Anthony Cordesman, Saudi Arabia: Guarding the Desert Kingdom. Boulder, CO: Westview, 1997, p. 37.

21. As'ad AbuKhalil dubs them the 'Wahhabi liberals'.

22. 'Adonis: I hope to visit Saudi Arabia and visit the places where the Companions of the Prophet were', Elaph, 6 August 2009.

23. 'All Foreign Gifts Report: U.S. Department of Education', available at National Review Online: www.nationalreview.com/kurtz/allforeigngiftsreport.html.

24. Natana Delong-Bas, Wahhabi Islam: From Revival and Reform to Global Jihad. Oxford: Oxford University Press, 2004.

25. The phrase is Azmeh's; see his Islams and Modernities, London: Verso, 1993, p. 112.

26. Mai Yamani, Cradle of Islam: The Hijaz and the Quest for Identity in Saudi Arabia. London: I.B. Tauris, 2009, pp. 14–16.

27. And not fascist: Saudi Arabia lacks the populist politics, the mass political organisation and the full employment goals of classical European fascism. The rentier economy, rather, maintains the people in a submissive condition of permanent expectation of economic improvement from the patriarchal state.

28. 16 September 2009, released 26 June 2011 by Wikileaks, http://wikileaks.org/cable/2009/11/09BAKU915.html.

29. Comments to author.

30. 'Mecca goes upmarket but commercialism unnerves some', Reuters, 12 November 2010.

31. Ibid.

32. Abdo Khal, Fusouq. Beirut: Dar al-Saqi, 2005, p. 54.

33. Ibid., p. 60.

34. Note the fate of writer Hamza Kashgari, deported from Malaysia in 2012 after Saudi pressure because of comments critical of the Prophet on Twitter.

35. Sheikh Saleh al-Haseen, Al-Madina, March 2003.

36. 'Saudis hit back over Mecca castle', BBC, 9 January 2002; http://news.bbc.co.uk/2/hi/middle_east/1748711.stm

37. See YouTube: www.youtube.com/watch?v=lZJpscw0_qE&feature=related.

38. See YouTube: www.youtube.com/watch?v=PporVs3DZjA&eurl=http%3A%2F%2Fwww.architectsjournal.co.uk%2Fnews%2Fdaily-news%2Fvideo-atkins-plans-to-redesign-mecca%2F5202301.article&feature=player_embedded; see also www.architectsjournal.co.uk/foster-and-hadid-to-redesign-mecca/1935469.article.

39. 'Ruling on the mas'a and running there', Islamlight website, 23 July 2008, www.islamlight.net/index.php?option=content&task=view&id=10541ltemid=.

40. Interview with author, May 2006.

41. Interview with author, May 2007.

42. 'Saudi utility needs Aramco help to avoid power cuts', Reuters, 29 May 2007.

43. Abdullah al-Ghaddami, *Hikayat al-Hadatha*. Casablanca: al-Markaz al-Thaqafi al-Arabia, 2004, p. 177.

44. Ibid., p. 164.

45. Ibid., p. 5.

46. Rabbi Marc Schneier, North American chairman of the World Jewish Congress, quoted in 'Saudi king shuns extremism as faiths gather', Reuters, 16 July 2008.

47. See Nina Shea, 'A medal for brass', *Weekly Standard*, 26 May 2008.

48. Something akin to Saudi Arabia's eye-on-the-Brotherhood, Khashoggi maintains ties with its cadres, while there are indications that Saudi Arabia gives backing to Egypt's Salafi movement as a counterweight to the group.

49. 'Ghadr al-Khawarij fi Ramadan: Kulluna Muhammad bin Nayef', *Al-Watan*, 29 August 2009.

50. 'Hal hiya azmatu nizam wahdahu?', 29 January 2011; 'Al-ru'asa' al-'arab wa tasfir al-'addad', 3 February 2011; 'Li jumhouriyyaat-na: hadha 'ilaj al-thawraat',' 14 February 2011.

51. 'Hukmuna al-saleh badil al-dimuqratiyya', *Al-Eqtisadiah*, 11 February 2011.

52. *Al-Watan*, 20 June 2011, www.alwatan.com.sa/Local/News_Detail.aspx?Arti cleID=59034&CategoryID=5.

53. Interview with Saudi Press Agency, 1 July 2008.

54. Ibid.

55. To Saudi television, 2008; the text can be accessed at www.saaid.net/arabic/209. htm#5.

56. 'Saudi king says keeping some oil finds for future', Reuters, 13 April 2008.

57. Comments to author, April 2010.

58. Interview with author, August 2007.

59. Mohammed Ibn Abdulwahhab, *Kashf al-Shubuhat*. Riyadh: Tiba Publishing, 2005, pp. 13, 69.

CHAPTER 2

1. Prince Alwaleed bin Talal said in 1996 that revenues of 1 million barrels of oil a day went to five or six princes, but it is not known if Abdullah ever managed to change that; see diplomatic cable 30 November 1996, released by Wikileaks 30 August 2011, http://wikileaks.org/cable/1996/11/96RIYADH4784.html.

2. Nayef is 'our Saddam', a Jeddan youth tells US diplomats in a cable, 8 February 2006, released by Wikileaks 30 August 2011, http://wikileaks.org/cable/2006/02/06JEDDAH128.html.

3. See Gilles Kepel, *Muslim Extremism in Egypt: The Prophet and the Pharaoh*. Berkeley: University of California Press, 1985; pp. 194–7.

4. Interview with author, November 2008.

5. Interview with author, August 2008.

6. See Thomas Hegghammer and Stephane Lacroix, 'Rejectionist Islamism in Saudi Arabia: the story of Juhayman al-'Utaybi revisited', *International Journal of Middle East Studies*, vol. 39, no. 1, 2007, pp. 103–33.

7. See Hamadi Redissi, 'The refutation of Wahhabism in Arabic sources, 1745–1932', in Madawi Al-Rasheed, ed., *Kingdom Without Borders*. London: Hurst, 2008, pp. 157–81.

8. Walid Saleh, 'The politics of Quranic hermeneutics: royalties on interpretation', public lecture, www.international.ucla.edu/cnes/podcasts/article.asp?parentid=

110233; also see payments by the Saudi embassy in Washington to PR agencies in the United States, http://www.foreignlobbying.org/.

9. See Khaled Abou El-Fadl's story in Franklin Foer, 'Moral Hazard', *New Republic*, 18 November 2002, www.tnr.com/article/moral-hazard.

10. Yousef al-Qaradawi told *Al-Masry al-Youm* of 9 September 2008, 'Wahhabi thought's problem is fanaticism against other ways of thinking', yet he is the preacher of a Doha mosque bearing Ibn Abdulwahhab's name.

11. See US diplomatic cable 10 February 2008, released by Wikileaks 30 August 2011, http://wikileaks.org/cable/2008/02/08RIYADH190.html.

12. Since the 9/11 attacks, Qatar has made efforts to send religious scholars to Al-Azhar for training instead of Saudi Arabia's Wahhabi centres of learning: this trend is expected to continue as Al-Azhar is reformed.

13. See the following cables from 6 July 2009 released by Wikileaks: http://wikileaks.org/cable/2009/07/09RIYADH887.html, http://wikileaks.org/cable/2009/07/09RIYADH888.html. The US embassy has tried to reach out to some scholars there, helping some to obtain Fulbright scholarships.

14. Wael Hallaq, *Sharia: Theory, Practice, Transformations*. Cambridge: Cambridge University Press, 2009, p. 439.

15. Human Rights Watch, *Precarious Justice: Arbitrary Detention and Unfair Trials in the Deficient Criminal Justice System of Saudi Arabia*, 2008, pp. 25–7, www.hrw.org/fr/node/62305.

16. See website: www.moj.gov.sa/layout/NewsDetails.asp?ArticleID=782. However, it began with the Grievance Court, a traditionally separate judicial track under the jurisdiction of the king: it is caliphal, not Sharia, justice.

17. Diplomatic cable 22 August 2009, http://wikileaks.org/cable/2009/08/09RIYADH1084.html.

18. Abdullahi Ahmed an-Na'im, *Islam and the Secular State: Negotiating the Future of Sharia*. Cambridge, MA: Harvard University Press, 2008, p. 28.

19. The Saudi government says families of murder victims have the right to waive death sentences, thus it is not the state itself that is claiming a life. The rare sentences against adulterers involve decapitation, not stoning.

20. Hallaq, *Sharia*, pp. 361–2.

21. And the coercion restricts creative capacities, as tends to happen 'when backward societies are dominated by states which borrow techniques of coercion from outside', as Ernest Gellner noted of the agricultural and industrial revolutions in his *Plough, Sword and Book: The Structure of Human History*. London: Paladin, 1991, p. 162.

22. Amnesty International, 'Affront to justice: death penalty in Saudi Arabia', October 2008, www.amnesty.org/en/library/info/MDE23/027/2008/en.

23. Khaled Abou El Fadl, *Speaking in God's Name: Islamic Law, Authority and Women*. Oxford: One World Books, 2008, pp. 171–2.

24. Ibid., pp. 209–63.

25. Khaled Abou El Fadl, 'Islam and the theology of power', *Middle East Report*, issue 221, vol. 31, winter 2001, www.merip.org/mer/mer221/.

26. Statement signed by 100 Arab intellectuals in 2008 after Saudi clerics demanded a trial for two newspaper columnists they denounced as 'infidels': '(They are) clerics of darkness, fooled through their arrogance and inflated by their status into thinking that they speak in the name of God.'

27. See Nathan Brown, 'Arab judicial structures', 2001, www.pogar.org/publications/judiciary/nbrown/.

28. See www.pakistani.org/pakistan/constitution.
29. Martin Lau, *The Role of Islam in the Legal System of Pakistan*. Leiden: Brill Academic, 2005.
30. See English translation at www.servat.unibe.ch/law/icl/ir00000_.html.
31. Published on Islamist websites in August 2009: see http://www.muslm.net/vb/showthread.php?t=356769.
32. Abdullahi Gallab, 'The insecure rendezvous between Islam and totalitarianism: the failure of the Islamist state in the Sudan', *Arab Studies Quarterly*, spring 2001, p. 1, http://findarticles.com/p/articles/mi_m2501/is_2_23/ai_77384492/?tag=content;col1.
33. Hallaq, *Sharia*, p. 476.
34. Gallab, 'The insecure rendezvous between Islam and totalitarianism', p. 5.

CHAPTER 3

1. Abdulaziz Al-Fahad, 'From exclusivism to accommodation: doctrinal and legal evolution of Wahhabism', *New York University Law Review*, vol. 79, 2004.
2. The incident is detailed in Guido Steinberg, 'The Wahhabi ulama and the Saudi state', in Paul Aarts and Gerd Nonneman, eds, *Saudi Arabia in the Balance*. London: Hurst, 2005.
3. 13 December 2006, released by Wikileaks 30 August 2011, http://wikileaks.org/cable/2006/12/06RIYADH9068.html.
4. Saif al-Islam bin Saud bin Abdulaziz Al Saud, *Qalb Min Banqalan*. Beirut: Dar al-Farabi, 2004, p. 265.
5. Ibid., p. 326.
6. Ibid., p. 384.
7. The term 'Surouriyyun' is sometimes used to refer to Sahwa figures Salman al-Odah, Safar al-Hawali and Ayed al-Qarni, who fell under the influence of Syrian Brotherhood figure Mohammed Surour Zain al-Abideen.
8. Stephane Lacroix, 'Islamo-liberal politics in Saudi Arabia', in Aarts and Nonneman, *Saudi Arabia in the Balance*, pp. 39–40.
9. Scene described in Yaroslav Trofimov, *The Siege of Mecca*. New York: Doubleday, 2007.
10. Ibid., p. 52.
11. Ibid., p. 91.
12. Abdulrahman Munif's *Cities of Salt* quintet, written in the 1980s, depicts Salafism as the only trend in Saudi politics capable of mobilising the people to overthrow Al Saud; see Elias Nasrallah, *Al-Saudiyya wa bid'at al-ta'rikh al-badil: qira'a naqdiyya li-khumasiyyat Abdulrahman Munif*. Damascus: Dar al-Mada, 2010.
13. Steinberg, 'The Wahhabi ulama and the Saudi state', p. 29.
14. Interview with author, July 2008.
15. Fawziah al-Bakr, *Madrasati Sunduq Mughlaq*. Riyadh: Dar al-Rushd, 2005.
16. First-hand account offered in Carmen Bin Laden, *The Veiled Kingdom*. London: Virago, 2004.
17. Abdel Bari Atwan, *The Secret History of al-Qa'ida*. London: Abacus, 2007, p. 154.
18. Madawi al-Rasheed, *A History of Saudi Arabia*. Cambridge: Cambridge University Press, 2002, p. 163.
19. Atwan, *The Secret History of al-Qa'ida*, p. 157.

20. The early Islamic states also relied on foreigners, but they were Muslims. The caliphs of the Abbasid state in Baghdad were obliged to man the bureaucracy with Persians and turned to Turkish tribes to form an army they could trust, though it ultimately turned against them.

21. See 'Young Osama', *New Yorker*, 12 December 2005, and Jonathan Randal, *Osama*. London: I.B. Tauris, 2005.

22. See Mamoun Fandy, *Saudi Arabia and the Politics of Dissent* (London: Palgrave Macmillan, 2001) for an in-depth discussion of the sermons.

23. The Sahwa may have brought Brotherhood political activism to Saudi Arabia, but Wahhabism thinks the Brotherhood is soft on issues such as gender segregation. King Abdullah's projects such as the King Abdullah University of Science and Technology, with its co-ed classes, are demonised as Egyptian Islam-lite – see this posting on Nasser al-Omar's website forum: http://www.muslm.net/vb/showthread.php?t=360708.

24. Al-Rasheed, *A History of Saudi Arabia*, p. 174.

25. 'Ru'ya li-hadir al-watan wa-mustaqbil-hi', January 2003; 'Nidaa' watani lil-qiyada wal-sha'b ma'an: al-Islah al-dusturi awwalan', 16 December 2003, http://www.saihat.net/vb/showthread.php?t=56827.

26. Lacroix, 'Islamo-liberal politics in Saudi Arabia', pp. 52–4.

27. Fandy, *Saudi Arabia and the Politics of Dissent*, p. 99.

28. 'Risalat al-shabab fi-l-sa'udiyya ila al-malik Abdullah', 23 February 2011; see text at http://hasantalk.com/?p=492.

29. 'I'lan watani lil-islah', 23 February 2011, http://www.saudireform.com/; English translation available at http://Saudijeans.org/2011/02/28/Saudi-reform-petitions/.

30. 'Nahwa dawlat al-huquq wa-l-mu'assasaat', February 2011; www.facebook.com/dawlaty?sk=app_4949752878.

31. See Sheikh Mohsen al-Obaidan, 'Political and administrative reform is possible without having to resort to the ways of the Muslim Brotherhood', *Asharq al-Awsat*, 24 May 2005, http://awsat.com/english/print.asp?artid=id85.

32. Sami Moubayed, 'Loose Saudi cannons in Lebanon,' *Asia Times*, 19 July 2007.

33. 'Saudis fighting in Iraq, Lebanon, embarrass homeland', Reuters, 19 July 2007.

34. Seymour Hersh, 'The Redirection: is the Administration's new policy benefitting our enemies in the war on terrorism?', *New Yorker*, 5 March 2007.

35. 14 November 2008, released by Wikileaks 28 May 2011, http://wikileaks.org/cable/2008/11/08STATE121325.html.

36. US diplomats feared that shortsighted funding could again backfire in 2009: Saudi Arabia and the UAE provided a 'tidal wave' of arms to President Ali Abdullah Saleh against the Houthi movement, who senior princes were convinced had backing from Iran; 11 November 2009, http://wikileaks.org/cable/2009/11/09SANAA2052.html.

37. 'Saudis warn clerics over militants in Iraq', Reuters, 20 June 2007.

38. 'Saudi cleric issues warning over Saudi militants,' Reuters, 1 October 2007.

39. 'Leading Saudi cleric publicly denounces bin Laden', Reuters, 18 September 2007.

40. 30 December 2009, released by Wikileaks 16 June 2011; http://wikileaks.org/cable/2009/12/09STATE131801.html.

41. Statement, Saudi Press Agency, 6 March 2011.

42. 30 July 2006, released 15 March 2011, http://wikileaks.org/cable/2006/07/06JEDDAH511.html.

43. 'Saudi clerics torn between hatred for Israel and Hizbollah', Reuters, 27 July 2006.
44. Ibid.
45. 9 February 2009, released 26 June 2011, http://wikileaks.org/cable/2009/02/09RIYADH346.html.
46. 9 September 2009, released 26 June 2011, http://wikileaks.org/cable/2009/09/09DHAHRAN246.html.
47. Saffar's mentor Shirazi was partial to Khomeini's idea that Shi'ite communities should be ruled by a supreme jurisprudent, but preferred rule by committee. After Shirazi's death in 2001, most of Saffar's group chose to follow Ali al-Sistani as their religious *marja'*, though some looked to Hussein Fadlallah in Lebanon, or al-Shirazi's successors, Ayatollah Sadeq al-Shirazi in Qom or Grand Ayatollah Mohammed Taqi al-Mudarrasi in Kerbala.
48. 22 March 2009, released 2 July 2011, http://wikileaks.org/cable/2009/03/09DHAHRAN40.html.
49. 16 December 2006, released 5 December 2010, http://wikileaks.org/cable/2006/12/06RIYADH9095.html.
50. 11 February 2010, released 20 August 2011, http://wikileaks.org/cable/2010/02/10RIYADH178.html.
51. 11 August 2008, released 26 June 2011, http://wikileaks.org/cable/2008/08/08RIYADH1230.html.
52. 'Qaeda video berates Saudi king over faith dialogue', Reuters, 23 May 2008.
53. Interview with author, October 2008.
54. See Fandy, *Saudi Arabia and the Politics of Dissent*, chapter 1.
55. Article on website, 'Waliyy al-amr, bayn al-hakim wa-l-'alim, waliyy al-amr huwa al-hakim la il-alim', 29 January 2002, www.princetalal.net/post.php?id=484&partid=17.
56. *Al-Jazeera*, 30 May 2006, www.suhuf.net.sa/2006jaz/may/30/ar3.htm.
57. 'Reviving the message of the clerics and their role in life', *Asharq al-Awsat*, 29 August 2009, www.aawsat.com/details.asp?section=44&article=533714&feature=1&issueno=11232.

CHAPTER 4

1. See Joseph Massad, *Desiring Arabs*. Chicago: University of Chicago Press, 2007, and 'The kingdom in the coset', *Atlantic Monthly*, May 2007.
2. Satirised in the popular TV show *Tash Ma Tash* in October 2006; see 'Saudis push anti-militant line in Ramadan TV shows', Reuters, 3 October 2006.
3. Madawi Al-Rasheed, *Politics in an Arabian Oasis*. London: I.B. Tauris, 1997, p. 101.
4. For a recent review of clerical debates on segregation, see Roel Meijer, 'Reform in Saudi Arabia: the gender-segregation debate', Middle East Policy Council, 2011.
5. For example, Ahlam Mostaghanemi's *Dhakirat al-Jasad*; see Abdullah al-Ghaddami, *Al-Mar'a wal-Lugha*. Casablanca: al-Markaz al-Arabi al-Thaqafi, 2006, p. 142.
6. Saudi diplomatic source.
7. The conclusion of a European diplomat who follows Islamic issues in Saudi Arabia.
8. 'Itlaq awwal markaz riyadi wa tarfihi hukumi lil-nisaa' fil-riyadh', *Al-Riyadh*, 23 November 2008.

9. Naomi Wolf, 'Behind the veil lives a thriving Muslim sexuality', *Sydney Morning Herald*, 30 August 2008.

10. While Saudi money abroad collaborates with right-wing Western media: Alwaleed has his stake in News Corp., the Rupert Murdoch conglomerate that owns Fox News.

11. As'ad AbuKhalil, "Asruka Bin Baz', *Al-Akhbar*, 21 September 2008.

12. Prince Nayef also talks of his affection for Bin Baz in Yaroslav Trofimov, *Siege of Mecca*. New York: Doubleday, 2007.

13. Khaled Abou El Fadl, *Speaking in God's Name*. Oxford: One World, 2008, p. 236.

14. Official website: www.binbaz.org.sa/mat/9372.

15. Official website: www.binbaz.org.sa/mat/331.

16. Official website: www.binbaz.org.sa/mat/77.

17. Official website: www.binbaz.org.sa/mat/1660.

18. See http://hadith.al-islam.com/Display/Display.asp?hnum=2091&doc=2&IMAGE.

19. Official website: www.binbaz.org.sa/mat/18194.

20. Human Rights Watch, *Perpetual Minors: Human Rights Abuses Stemming from Male Guardianship and Sex Segregation in Saudi Arabia*, 2008. The report can be accessed at www.hrw.org/en/reports/2008/04/19/perpetual-minors.

21. Ibid., p. 27.

22. 'Saudi "guardianship" said key to women's rights abuse', Reuters, 21 April 2008.

23. Ali al-Qahtani, 'Al-da'wa ila ta'ziz al-musa'ala fil-ajhiza al-hukumiyya wa man' isa'at istikhdam al-sulta', *Al-Watan*, 21 May 2007, www.alwatan.com.sa/news/newsdetail.asp?issueno=2425&id=6259.

24. Human Rights Watch, *Perpetual Minors*, pp. 25–6.

25. Statistics from UNESCO, www.uis.unesco.org/en/stats/statistics/literacy2000.htm.

26. Abou El Fadl, *Speaking in God's Name*, p. 192.

27. Ibid., p. 288.

28. Labour Code, Part IX, Article 149.

29. Interview with author; see 'Economic fears forcing Saudi women into workplace', Reuters, 5 May 2008.

30. From an email exchange with Husseiny in 2008.

31. US diplomatic cable 30 November 1996, released by Wikileaks 30 August 2011, http://wikileaks.org/cable/1996/11/96RIYADH4784.html.

32. UNDP, *Millennium Development Goals Report on the Kingdom of Saudi Arabia, 2005*.

33. 'Al-kitab al-ihsa'i al-sanawi li-wizarat al-'amal', 2006, www.mol.gov.sa/mol_site/1428_BB.pdf.

34. See 'Quand le rigorisme religieux fait fuir la jeunesse', *Courrier International*, 24 September 2009.

35. As'ad AbuKhalil, *The Battle for Saudi Arabia*. New York: Seven Stories Press, 2003, p. 123.

36. Official website: www.binbaz.org.sa/mat/8566.

37. See '50-year-old divorces child bride?', Reuters, 30 April 2009.

38. A Dosari tribal leader confesses that princely favour allows him to play the role of community intermediator in a US diplomat cable from 26 June 2006, http://wikileaks.org/cable/2006/06/06RIYADH5111.html.

39. Interview with author; 'Saudi woman just wants family back', Reuters, 30 January 2008.
40. Abdo Khal, *Fusouq*. Beirut: Dar al-Saqi, 2005, p. 94.
41. Ibid., p. 159.
42. 'Saudi Arabia says Games team will not include women', Reuters, 30 July 2008.
43. 'Saudi Arabia clamps down on unlicensed female gyms', Reuters, 30 April 2009.
44. 'Saudi wants to trim waists of overweight population', Reuters, 5 March 2006.
45. 'Put breaks on osteoporosis', *Arab News*, 2 August 2007.
46. 'Al-Manie says diabetes reaching epidemic proportions', *Arab News*, 28 May 2007.
47. 'Commentary: suspend Saudi Arabia's Olympic team', 8 August 2008, Investigative Project on Terrorism, www.investigativeproject.org/article/745.
48. 'Saudi official criticizes ruling on rape victim', Reuters, 27 November 2007.
49. 'Bush avoids criticism of Saudi king on rape case', Reuters, 4 December 2007.
50. 'U.S. offers mild criticism in Saudi rape case', Reuters, 19 November 2007.
51. 'Saudi king pardons rape victim', Reuters, 18 December 2007.
52. Ibid.
53. Comments to author, December 2007.
54. 'Saudi clerics want to restrict women praying at Mecca', Reuters, 28 August 2006.
55. Ibid.
56. See 'Girls of Riyadh spurs rush of Saudi novels', Reuters, 23 July 2007.
57. Badriya Al-Bisher, *Hind wal-'Askar*. Beirut: Dar al-Adab, 2006, p. 123.
58. Ibid., p. 124.
59. Siba al-Harz, *al-Akharun*. Beirut: Dar al-Saqi, 2006, p. xx.
60. Ibid., p. 189.
61. The Saudi Shi'ite community has sought to place itself to the left of al-Wahhabiyya on the issue of women. See Sheikh Hassan al-Saffar, *Shakhsiyyat al-Mar'a*. Casablanca: al-Markaz al-Thaqafi al-Arabi, 2003. Saffar and the group of exiles who returned to work within the Saudi system are often referred to as Shirazis since they were influenced by Ayatollah Muhammad al-Hussayni al-Shirazi after Shirazi moved to Kuwait in the 1970s.
62. Ayedh al-Qarni, *La Tahzan*. Riyadh: Obeikan, 2007, p. 376.
63. Ayedh al-Qarni, *As'ad Imra'a fil-'Alam*. Riyadh: Maktabat al-Obeikan, 2004, p. 6.
64. Ibid., p. 148.
65. Ibid., p. 177.
66. See Ghaddami, *Al-Mar'a wal-Lugha*, p. 115, on street parades in Mecca.
67. See Fred Halliday, *Arabia Without Sultans*. London: Saqi Books, 2002, p. 241.
68. Ibid., p. 246.
69. Asef Bayat, *Life as Politics: How Ordinary People Change the Middle East*. Cairo: American University in Cairo Press, 2009, p. 97.

CHAPTER 5

1. Interview with author, June 2008.
2. Abdullah al-Ghaddami, *Hikayat al-Hadatha*. Beirut: al-Markaz al-Arabi al-Thaqafi, 2004, p. 164.
3. Published in *Al-Jazeera*, 12 January 2009.

4. Interview with Aramco employee Wajiha Huweidar.
5. Abdelbari Atwan, *The Secret History of al-Qa'ida*. London: Abacus, 2007, p. 154; David Ottaway, *The King's Messenger: Prince Bandar bin Sultan and America's Tangled Relationship with Saudi Arabia*. New York: Walker & Company, 2008.
6. Interview on al-Arabiya.net, 10 August 2009.
7. Fatwa on official website: www.binbaz.org.sa/mat/8340.
8. 'Al-Bayan al-Khitami al-Sadir 'an al-Dawra al-Thalitha li-Mu'tamar al-Qimma al-Islami al-Istithna'i', 8 December 2005, www.islamicsummit.org.sa/9-5.aspx.
9. *Al-Riyadh*, 15 January 2004, http://www.alriyadh.com/Contents/15-01-2004/Mainpage/LOCAL1_13526.php.
10. US diplomatic report 10 February 2008, http://wikileaks.org/cable/2008/02/08RIYADH190.html.
11. Samia Nakhoul, 'Saudi schoolbooks under spotlight', Reuters, 15 October 2003.
12. 'Saudi textbooks still preach hatred-report', Reuters, 24 May 2006.
13. Interview with author, September 2008.
14. Interview with author, July 2008.
15. 'Ma'alim fi tariq al-malikiyya al-dusturiyya', 1 April 2007; for text see www.alonysolidarity.net/alonyWEB2007/golfrights/matrouk.htm.
16. *Asharq al-Awsat*, 13 July 2011, www.aawsat.com//details.asp?section=4&article=630876&issueno=11915.
17. The US State Department accepted the Saudi government's argument that Hashemi and some others were 'terror funders', though it acquiesced in a Saudi request to keep Sheikh Safar al-Hawali and Salman al-Odah's names off the UN Sanctions Committee's list of militant suspects. See diplomatic cables 10 September 2007, http://wikileaks.org/cable/2007/09/07RIYADH1891.html, and 11 September 2007, http://wikileaks.org/cable/2007/09/07RIYADH1894.html, both released by Wikileaks 30 August 2011.
18. Rima al-Juraish to author, July 2007.
19. 21 October 2009, released 8 May 2011, http://wikileaks.org/cable/2009/10/09RIYADH1396.html, and 24 February 2007, released 5 December 2011, http://wikileaks.org/cable/2007/02/07RIYADH367.html.
20. Conversation with author, July 2011.
21. 5 May 2008, released 30 August 2011, http://wikileaks.org/cable/2008/05/08RIYADH720.html.
22. Sandy Mitchell, *Saudi Babylon: Torture, Corruption and Cover-up Inside the House of Saud*. London: Mainstream Publishing, 2005; William Sampson, *Confessions of an Innocent Man: Torture and Survival in a Saudi Prison*. Toronto: McClelland & Stewart, 2006.
23. Saudi Civil and Political Rights Association, 'The Systematic Human Rights Violations by the Directorate of General Investigation (The Ministry of Interior) in the Kingdom of Saudi Arabia', 13 August 2011, www.acpra1.net/news.php?action=view&id=140.
24. Ibid.
25. Abdo Khal, *Fusouq*. Beirut: Dar al-Saqi, 2005, p. 93.
26. Asef Bayat, *Life as Politics: How Ordinary People Change the Middle East*. Cairo: American University in Cairo Press, 2009, chapter 13.
27. Interview with author, July 2008.

28. 'Saudi to get $26 bln makeover with tourism project', Reuters, 20 December, 2005.
29. 'The king versus the radicals', *Newsweek*, 17 May 2008.
30. Discussed in US diplomatic cable 23 August 2006, http://wikileaks.org/cable/2006/08/06JEDDAH557.html, and again 1 August 2009, http://wikileaks.org/cable/2009/08/09JEDDAH288.html.
31. For example, 'Sahafi ruwaiterz hammond yuwasil talfiq al-akhbar 'an al-saudiyya'; note the comments that followed in the web forum: www.sabq.org/inf/news-action-show-id-8281.htm.
32. Interview with author, September 2008.
33. Interview with author, September 2008.
34. 'Wafd min wizarat al-'adl yazur al-wilayat al-muttahida al-amrikiyya', Saudi Press Agency, 20 October 2008.
35. Interview with author, October 2008.
36. 'Hay'at kibar al-ulama tujiz al-taqnin', *Al-Hayat*, 18 March 2010, citing arguments from a study by Abdulrahman bin Ahmed al-Jar'i, 'Taqnin al-ahkam al-shar'iyya bayn al-mumani'een wa-l-mujizeen'.
37. See Human Rights Watch, *Precarious Justice: Arbitrary Detention and Unfair Trials in the Deficient Criminal Justice System of Saudi Arabia*, March 2008, pp. 33–5.
38. 'Saudi displays Sri Lankan bodies to deter crime', Reuters, 20 February 2007.
39. Interview with author; 'Saudi appeals court upholds flogging researchers', Reuters, 30 July 2008.
40. Interview with author, June 2006.
41. Identified as a problem by US diplomats in 1996: see http://wikileaks.org/cable/1996/11/96RIYADH4784.html; see also 12 February 2007, http://wikileaks.org/cable/2007/02/07RIYADH296.html.
42. Contact by email, June 2008.
43. Interview with author, October 2008.
44. A transcript is at Islamlight: www.islamlight.net/index.php?option=content&task=view&id=11118&Itemid=23; a recording can be heard at the Saudi Quran Station website: www.liveislam.net/browsearchive.php?sid=&id=54389.
45. His response is documented at www.saaid.net/arabic/209.htm#5.
46. Ibid.
47. An excerpt of this incident is available on YouTube, www.youtube.com/watch?v=QrVXTHD7O-8.
48. 'Saudi king's interfaith call faces Muslim divisions', Reuters, 4 June 2008.
49. From a conversation with a diplomat who described the Madrid meeting as 'an international event with no potential for domestic reverberations'.
50. 'Saudi clerics attack Shi'ites, Hezbollah', Reuters, 1 June 2008.
51. See www.imamu.edu.sa/news/p515.htm.
52. Interview with author, October 2008.
53. For a review of sibling rivalries among the senior princes, see Simon Henderson, 'After King Abdullah: succession in Saudi Arabia', Washington Institute for Near East Policy, August 2009. See also US diplomatic cable 28 October 2009, released by Wikileaks 30 August 2011, http://wikileaks.org/cable/2009/10/09RIYADH1434.html.
54. 'The king versus the radicals', *Newsweek*, 17 May 2008.
55. 'A black imam breaks ground in Mecca', *New York Times*, 12 April 2009.

56. 'Rebellious girl band breaks Saudi taboos', *New York Times*, 25 November 2008.
57. Afshin Molavi, 'Saudi Arabia's moment of redemption?', *International Herald Tribune*, 3 September 2006.
58. Stephane Lacroix, 'Vers un nouveau printemps de Riyad?', *Alternatives Internationales*, September 2005, p. 18.
59. Robert Lacey, *Inside the Kingdom: Kings, Clerics, Terrorists, Modernists, and the Struggle for Saudi Arabia*. Viking Adult, 2009.
60. Thomas Carothers, 'Think again: Arab democracy', Carnegie Endowment for International Peace, 10 March 2011.
61. Statement, 28 February 2011, by ambassador Tom Phillips.
62. Mark Weston, *Prophets and Prince: Saudi Arabia from Muhammad to the Present*. Hoboken, NJ: Wiley, 2008.
63. Ibid.
64. Comments bin Nayef made to a blogger; name withheld.
65. But he did fiddle with Saudi ceremonials: Abdullah banned the custom of kissing the king's hand.
66. Fatwa no. 5845, 'The greatest pride and dignity is in belonging to Islam', at www.alifta.com.
67. Joseph Massad, *Colonial Effects: The Making of National Identity in Jordan*. New York: Columbia University Press, 2001, p. 217.

CHAPTER 6

1. 20 April 2008, released 28 November 2010, http://wikileaks.ch/cable/2008/04/08RIYADH649.html.
2. Recounting another discussion with Jubair, one states: 'The King rejects the argument that military action against Iran will coalesce popular support around President Ahmadinejad. "He believes that the opposite will happen," the Saudi ambassador said', 20 November 2007, http://wikileaks.org/cable/2007/11/07RIYADH2322.html.
3. Saudi ambassador to Lebanon Abdulaziz al-Khoja, 19 Febuary 2008, released by Wikileaks 21 July 2011, http://wikileaks.org/cable/2008/02/08BEIRUT271.html.
4. Diplomatic cable from US embassy in Sanaa, 11 November 2009, released by Wikileaks 4 May 2011, http://wikileaks.org/cable/2009/11/09SANAA2052.html.
5. King Abdullah's son Prince Mutib, head of National Guard: 'It is time for you ... to understand that the Iranians are supporting them ... The sooner that Yemen finishes the Houthi, the better it will be for them', in cable 10 November 2009, released April 2011, http://wikileaks.org/cable/2009/11/09RIYADH1502.html.
6. Prince Turki bin Saud Al-Kabeer, Under Secretary for Multilateral Affairs at the Saudi Ministry of Foreign Affairs, in cable 10 November 2009, released 8 April 2011, http://wikileaks.org/cable/2009/11/09RIYADH1501.html.
7. Diplomatic cable from Riyadh embassy, 30 July 2006, released 15 March 2011, http://wikileaks.org/cable/2006/07/06JEDDAH511.html.
8. 1 November 2009, released 2 July 2011;, http://wikileaks.org/cable/2009/11/09DHAHRAN266.html.
9. Fred Halliday, *Arabia Without Sultans*. London: Saqi Books, 2002, p. 61.

10. Halliday, *Arabia Without Sultans*, citing SAMA estimate in *The Times* of London, 30 January 1974.

11. David Ottaway, *The King's Messenger: Prince Bandar bin Sultan and America's Tangled Relationship With Saudi Arabia*. New York: Walker & Company, 2008. Ottaway pins the arms sales to the cavalier politicking of Prince Bandar bin Sultan, the Saudi ambassador to Washington at the time.

12. 'Saudi offers Russia arms deal to curb Iran ties-paper', Reuters, 15 July 2008.

13. King Abdullah wanted a state-of-the-art upgrade to his personal jet thrown into one arms deal he discussed with the United States. 'Diplomats help push sales of jetliners on the global market', *New York Times*, 3 January 2011.

14. One 'strongly advised against taking military action to neutralize Iran's program', 22 July 2008, released 28 November 2010, http://wikileaks.org/cable/2008/07/08RIYADH1134.html.

15. Cable from December 2009 written by Secretary of State Clinton, released 26 June 2011: 'While the Kingdom of Saudi Arabia (KSA) takes seriously the threat of terrorism within Saudi Arabia, it has been an ongoing challenge to persuade Saudi officials to treat terrorist financing emanating from Saudi Arabia as a strategic priority', http://wikileaks.org/cable/2009/12/09STATE131801.html#.

16. 15 May 2008, released 6 May 2011, http://wikileaks.org/cable/2008/05/08BEIRUT698.html.

17. Ibid., sourced to a British diplomat.

18. Ibid.; the same report describes Saudi Arabia in a continuing losing battle with the Yemenis over illegal immigration. In 2007, some 400,000 Yemenis were deported, a huge figure, many of them on Saudi Airlines flights to Sanaa.

19. 11 November 2009, released 4 May 2011, http://wikileaks.org/cable/2009/11/09SANAA2052.html.

20. For example, the National Guard run by Abdullah's son Miteb is interested in acquiring its own air force.

21. 12 July 2006, released 30 August 2011, http://wikileaks.org/cable/2006/07/06RIYADH5546.html.

22. 22 March 2009, released 27 March 2011, http://wikileaks.org/cable/2009/03/09RIYADH447.html.

23. Ibid.

24. 'People will no longer speak to American diplomats frankly', *Der Spiegel International*, 5 December 2011.

25. Clerics sometimes acknowledge this point. Sheikh Abdulaziz al-Fawzan said in 2009: 'Islamic governments have renounced the resistance, forcing Palestinian resistance movements to resort to Iran and others', Dalil TV, 10 February 2009, on www.muslm.net/vb/showthread.php?t=332762.

26. 'Mufti al-mamlaka li-Hamas', *Okaz*, 10 January 2009.

27. Saudi Press Agency, 27 November 2002, text available at: www.arabiyat.com/forums/showthread.php?t=49498.

28. Robert Lacey, *Inside the Kingdom: Kings, Clerics, Modernists, Terrorists and the Struggle for Saudi Arabia*. London: Hutchinson, 2009, p. 232.

29. See 'Biladna mustahdafa wa aydun sahyuniyya wara ma hadath', *Al-Riyadh*, 2 May 2004, www.alriyadh.com/Contents/02-05-2004/Mainpage/LOCAL1_16360.php.

30. Ambassador James Oberwetter met with foreign minister Saud al-Faisal for clarification. 'Terror watch: a new rift?', *Newsweek*, 4 May 2004.

31. *Asharq al-Awsat*, November 2002.

32. 'Fi risala lil-wazir al-saudi: al-Hudaibi yastankir hujum al-amir Nayef 'ala al-Ikhwan al-Muslimin', *Al-Hadath*, 3 December 2002, www.mafhoum.com/press4/131S23.htm.
33. This has produced an interesting concurrence of opinion: US embassy officials concurred at a dinner with clerics of the Imam University in 2009 that the Brotherhood was largely to blame for increased conservatism and militancy in Saudi Arabia since the 1970s. 6 July 2009, http://wikileaks.org/cable/2009/07/09RIYADH887.html.
34. Maher al-Abdullah, *Al-Saudiyya wal-khalij wa mutatallabat al-taghyir*, chapter 6, Rasid.com, 21 November 2007, www.rasid.com/artc.php?id=19240.
35. Jack Shafer, 'The PowerPoint that rocked the Pentagon', 7 August 2002, www.slate.com/id/2069199.
36. 'Top US commander visits Saudi Arabia', AFP, 18 July 2004; 'Middle East to 2020', National Intelligence Council, www.dni.gov/nic/NIC_2020_2003_12_08_intro.html.
37. Editorial, *Al-Watan*, 21 March 2003.
38. Commentary, *Al-Hayat*, 25 June 2003.
39. 'Prince Turki accuses US government of doublespeak', *Arab News*, 2 November 2008. Turki was on a tour of the United States to promote the kingdom as a new US administration was set to replace that of Bush.
40. Al-Abdullah, *Al-Saudiyya wal-khalij wa mutatallabat al-taghyir*, chapter 6.
41. Ibid.
42. Thomas L. Friedman, 'An Intriguing signal from the Saudi Crown Prince', *New York Times*, 17 February 2002. Abdullah's comments read like a prepared text, not least for a man of little words with a speech defect. Friedman said Abdullah's office called him the next day to review and approve the quotes for publication.
43. *Okaz*, 15 May 2002.
44. Ottaway, *The King's Messenger*, p. 235.
45. Lacey, *Inside the Kingdom*, p. 284.
46. For example, a US diplomatic cable from Beirut on 15 May 2008, released 6 May 2011, shows that Bandar was still actively involved in Saudi Arabia's Lebanon policy, http://wikileaks.org/cable/2008/05/08BEIRUT698.html.
47. Jawad al-Hamad, *The GCC and Resolving the Arab-Israeli Conflict: A Reading of Gulf Summit Statements* (Arabic); www.mesc.com.jo/OurVision/2008/5.html.
48. Ibid.
49. *Okaz*, 15 May 2002.
50. See Bob Woodward, *Plan of Attack*. New York: Simon & Schuster, 2004.
51. Lacey, *Inside the Kingdom*, p. 290.
52. 'Bush moves to ease tensions with Saudis', *Washington Post*, 28 August 2002.
53. Saud al-Faisal blatantly lied on this point in a meeting I attended with foreign journalists in Riyadh.
54. Lacey, *Inside the Kingdom*, p. 291, 'The US could go on using al-Kharj and some other bases for the duration of the war, it was agreed, on a basis of strict military secrecy.'
55. US diplomatic cable 20 July 2008, released by Wikileaks 30 August 2011, http://wikileaks.org/cable/2008/07/08RIYADH1137.html.
56. 'Saudi Arabia blames Hizbollah in Lebanon crisis', Reuters, 14 July 2006.
57. Ottaway, *The King's Messenger*, p. 250.

58. 15 July 2006, released 15 March 2011, http://wikileaks.org/cable/2006/07/06JEDDAH478.html.

59. 29 July 2006, released 15 March 2011, http://wikileaks.org/cable/2006/07/06JEDDAH505.html.

60. The *Memoirs of Elias Shufani*, a PLO official, accuse al-Faisal of misleading Arafat into believing that a full-scale Israeli invasion of Lebanon was not on the cards in 1982. Elias Shufani, *Memoirs of Elias Shufani*. Beirut: Institute of Palestine Studies, 2010.

61. 30 July 2006, released 15 March 2011, http://wikileaks.org/cable/2006/07/06JEDDAH511.html.

62. 'The Arabs alone should solve the issue of Palestine ... We don't want anyone to trade in our issues and become stronger through them', he told Kuwait's *Al-Seyassah*, 27 January 2007.

63. Saudi Press Agency, 4 June 2008, www.spa.gov.sa/print.php?id=562083.

64. 4 September 2006, released 30 August 2011, http://wikileaks.org/cable/2006/09/06RIYADH6976.html.

65. 19 June 1996, released by Wikileaks 30 August 2011, http://wikileaks.org/cable/1996/06/96RIYADH2406.html.

66. Comments to author, November 2009.

67. 'Ambush kills 15 Iraqi troops north of Baghdad', Reuters, 3 December 2005.

68. *Liqaa Khaass* programme, Al-Jazeera, 4 October 2005.

69. 'Saudi says U.S. policy handing Iraq over to Iran', Reuters, 21 September 2005.

70. 'Iraq blasts Saudi Arabia for anti-Shi'ite remarks', Reuters, 2 October 2005. Syria's UN ambassador Bashar Jaafari used the same argument regarding Saudi Arabia's naming after its ruling dynasty in March 2012.

71. 'Egypt's head questions Shi'ites loyalty', Associated Press, 10 April 2006.

72. 'Saddam death raises tribal, religious ire in Saudi', Reuters, 4 January 2007.

73. *Al-Masry al-Youm*, 9 September 2008.

74. www.imamu.edu.sa/news/p515.htm.

75. As'ad AbuKhalil, *The Battle for Saudi Arabia*. New York: Seven Stories Press, 2003, p. 87.

76. Osama bin Laden said the mufti had 'given legitimacy to documents of surrender signed by traitors and cowards among the Arab tyrants'; see www.muslm.net/vb/showthread.php?t=77064.

77. Emad Mekay, 'Iraq was invaded "to protect Israel" – US official', *Asia Times*, 31 March 2004. Mekay told me the story of the decision at *Asharq al-Awsat*, where he worked, not to run the piece.

78. 'Saudi Arabia says Israel meeting report fabricated', Reuters, 26 September 2006.

79. 'Riyadh seen trying to wean Russia away from Iran', Reuters, 16 July 2008.

80. 'Saudi king promotes tolerance at U.N. forum', Reuters, 13 November 2007.

81. Robert Lacey, comment to author.

82. Recounted by German diplomat, October 2008.

CHAPTER 7

1. http://wikileaks.ch/cable/2009/05/09RIYADH651.html.

2. See cable 27 June 2001, released by Wikileaks 30 August 2011, http://wikileaks.org/cable/2001/06/01RIYADH1771.html. Also, an employee of the channel comments on this in a US diplomatic cable from Riyadh in 2009: 'When asked

if the thirty-something prince was interested only in the profits of the station, or if he also took an active role in the ideological direction of Al-Arabiya, XXXXXXXXXXXX whispered with a grimace, "Both"', 11 May 2009, released 7 December 2010, http://wikileaks.org/cable/2009/05/09RIYADH651. html.

3. It is not above making 'mistakes': A heavily-promoted series about King Abdullah was pulled in October 2007 after Prince Bandar suggested in the first episode that 9/11 could have been prevented if the US had just consulted more with Riyadh.

4. Robert Vitalis, *America's Kingdom: Mythmaking on the Saudi Oil Frontier.* Stanford: Stanford University Press, 2007, p. 184.

5. 'Saudi militants rigged Koran with explosives: report', Reuters, 13 November 2003.

6. See this US diplomatic report from May 2009: http://wikileaks.ch/cable/2009/05/09RIYADH651.html.

7. Noted on 10 September 2003 in comments by London-based Islamist Hani Sibai and *Al-Quds al-Arabi* editor Abdelbari Atwan, who would never say that in his regular appearances on BBC television.

8. Khudair Taher, 'Al-jaysh al-isra'ili yashaq umala' iran fi ghazza', *Elaph*, 28 December 2008.

9. 'Damaa Ghazza mashru' tijari', *Asharq al-Awsat*, 28 December 2008.

10. News bulletin, Al-Arabiya, 5 July 2010.

11. Interview with author at Pan-Arab Research Centre in Dubai, June 2007.

12. *Al-Watan*, 6 December 2008, p. 26.

13. 'Man scandalises Saudi Arabia with TV sex confession', Reuters, 30 July 2009.

14. 'Shaqiq al-Waleed yunadi bil-hajr 'ala amwal akhih', www.bbc.co.uk, 29 June 2009.

15. 'Bush 'an waqi'at al-hadhaa': aghrab haadith. Wa Rice: dalil hurriyya', 17 December 2008.

16. 'Sahafat dimuqratiyyat al-ahdhiya', *Asharq al-Awsat*, 17 December 2008.

17. Farhan was harassed by state security to prevent him setting up a Huffington Post-type website. See US diplomatic report 19 March 2009, http://wikileaks.org/cable/2009/03/09JEDDAH119.html.

18. 'Princes, clerics and censors', Committee to Protect Journalists, 9 May 2006.

19. Ali Al-Ahmed, Institute for Gulf Affairs in Washington; see 'Saudi reformers face media shut-out, death threats', Reuters, 10 October 2003.

20. Ahmed Yousef of the *Saudi Gazette* at a press conference on 19 May 2003.

21. 'Saudi liberal reappointed as newspaper editor', Reuters, 17 April 2007.

22. 11 May 2009, released 7 December 2010, http://wikileaks.ch/cable/2009/05/09RIYADH651.html.

23. See Vitalis, *America's Kingdom*; pp. 80, 111.

24. Christopher Davidson, *Dubai: The Vulnerability of Success.* London: Hurst & Co., 2008, pp.23/81.

25. http://wikileaks.ch/cable/2009/05/09RIYADH651.html.

26. http://wikileaks.org/cable/2006/05/06JEDDAH374.html.

27. 'Saudis must apply for govt license to start blogging', Al-Arabiya, 3 January 2011, www.alarabiya.net/articles/2011/01/03/132053.html.

28. Interview with author; see article 'Saudi youth bored in model Islamic state: blogger', Reuters, 26 October 2006.

29. 3 August 2011, http://adhwan.com.

30. Translations by Ahmed al-Omran; see his blog entry: 'The New Activism', *Saudi Jeans*, 2 August 2011;, http://saudijeans.org/2011/08/02/saudi-new-activism.
31. Ibid.
32. *Al-Seyassah*, 28 November 2002, www.arabiyat.com/forums/showthread.php?t=49498.
33. 'Saudi media discuss creation of second MSI', *Arab News*, 27 July 2007.
34. A play on the slogan of the Arab uprisings: 'The people want to bring down the regime.'
35. The footage can be seen on YouTube: www.youtube.com/watch?v=mxinAxWxXo8.

CHAPTER 8

1. Fred Halliday, *Arabia Without Sultans*. London: Saqi Books, 2002, p. 49.
2. Mai Yamani, *Cradle of Islam: The Hijaz and the Quest for Identity in Saudi Arabia*. London: I.B. Tauris, 2009, pp. 43–4.
3. Fahd al-Jarboa, Assistant Deputy Secretary General of Saudi Commission for Tourism and Antiquities: 'Tourism Commission develops new strategies to attract international tourists', Reuters Television, 31 October 2008.
4. King Abdullah often cites the location of the Mecca and Medina sacred zones in discussions of rivalry with Iran over Muslim leadership. See US diplomatic report 12 July 2006, http://wikileaks.org/cable/2006/07/06RIYADH5546.html.
5. Abdullah confesses that visas have been withheld from Iraqis for 'political reasons' in his US diplomatic cable of 16 September 2006, http://wikileaks.org/cable/2006/09/06RIYADH7211.html. Madawi Al-Rasheed says hajj visas are withheld from Saudi dissidents in Britain: 'Al-hajj: siyasat al-sa'udiyya al-ma'zuma', *Al-Quds al-Arabi*, 9 December 2008.
6. The precise order of rites can differ according to when and where you enter the state of *ihram* and the sacred zone.
7. Malise Ruthven, *Islam in the World*. London: Penguin, 2000, p. 48.
8. Religious bodies including the Ministry of Islamic Affairs offer money to converts, as this US diplomatic report notes: 25 August 2007, http://wikileaks.org/cable/2007/08/07RIYADH1776.html.
9. Patricia Crone, *Meccan Trade and the Rise of Islam*. New Jersey: Gorgias Press, 2004.
10. In 2009, Iranian president Mahmoud Ahmadinejad talked of 'immoral and inhuman treatment' of Iranian pilgrims and the mufti denounced attempts to stage political demonstrations. See US diplomatic cable 10 November 2009, http://wikileaks.org/cable/2009/11/09RIYADH1507.html.

CONCLUSION

1. Fouad Ibrahim, *Al-Salafiyya al-Jihadiyya fi al-Sa'udiyya*. Beirut: Saqi Books, 2009, p. 299.
2. 10 August 2008, released by Wikileaks 30 August 2011, http://wikileaks.org/cable/2008/08/08RIYADH1218.html.
3. BBC Arabic Television, 6 October 2011.
4. Media still took seriously the possibility of a shift away from a weakened dollar from 2007 onwards, though finance minister Ibrahim al-Assaf could not have

been blunter: 'We will not drop it. That's it', he said. See 'Saudi Arabia says will not drop dollar peg', Reuters, 2 December 2007.

5. See Aramco's anxiety in this US diplomatic cable from 21 February 2010, http://wikileaks.org/cable/2010/02/10RIYADH213.html 21.

6. Abdullah has tried to scale back unpopular royal abuse: see US diplomatic cable of 12 February 2007, http://wikileaks.org/cable/2007/02/07RIYADH296.html; for a good overview of princely wealth in the 1990s see Wikileaks cable, http://wikileaks.org/cable/1996/11/96RIYADH4784.html.

7. The Saudi government refused 'out of hand' Indian requests for a bilateral labour agreement to protect Indian workers: see US diplomatic cable 9 September 2009, http://wikileaks.org/cable/2009/09/09RIYADH1170.html.

8. 23 August 2008, released 30 August 2011, http://wikileaks.org/cable/2008/08/08RIYADH1283.html.

Bibliography

Interviews and conversations with the family of Salman al-Huraisy, Ramzi al-Ghanem, Hassan al-Buluwi, Mohsin al-Awaji, Abdulrahman Said, Irfan Al-Alawi, Saad al-Sowayan, Sami Angawi, Sami Nawwar, Abdullah al-Ghaddami, Hamad Alisa, Mansour Nogaidan, Taleb Alrefai, Yousef al-Mohaimeed, Muffid Abo Khamseen, Hassan al-Saffar, Shaheed Quraish, Wajiha Huweidar, Faisal bin Muammar, Fatima Azzaz, Jamila al-Ukla, Hassan al-Maliki, Mohamed Said Tayeb, Fouad Farhan, Mohammed al-Askar, Ibrahim al-Mugaiteeb, Rima al-Juraish, Abdullah al-Hamed, Ahmed Turki al-Saab, Fahd Al-Rasheed, Abdullah al-Alami, Majed Garoub, Samar Fatany, Khaled al-Zahrani, Suleiman al-Sharif, Abdulaziz al-Gasim, Turki al-Rashid, Jamal Khashoggi, Jihad Fakhreddine, Ahmed al-Omran, and many diplomats and others whose names are withheld.

Aarts, Paul, and Gerd Nonneman, eds, *Saudi Arabia in the Balance*. London, Hurst & Company, 2005.
Abou El Fadl, Khaled, 'Islam and the theology of power', *Middle East Report*, issue 221, vol. 31, winter 2001, www.merip.org/mer/mer221/
——, *Speaking in God's Name: Islamic Law, Authority and Women*. Oxford: One World Books, 2008.
AbuKhalil, As'ad, 'Methods of Saudi media', Angry Arab blog, 23 December 2008.
——, *The Battle for Saudi Arabia*. New York: Seven Stories Press, 2003.
——, '"Asruka Bin Baz', *Al-Akhbar*, 21 September 2008.
——, 'Methods of Saudi media', Angry Arab blog, 23 December 2008.
Aburish, Said, *The Rise, Corruption, and Coming Fall of the House of Saud*. London: Palgrave Macmillan, 1996.
Agence France Presse, 'Top US commander visits Saudi Arabia', 18 July 2004.
——, 'Rice hopes to see Saudi women at Olympic Games', 18 August 2008.
Ahmad, Atif, *Women's Freedom and Limitations of Guardians' Authority: Based on the Sources of Hanbali Law and Other Sources of Islamic Law*, Human Rights Watch, 2008.
Al-Abdullah, Maher, *Al-Saudiyya wal-khalij wa mutatallabat al-taghyir*. Published online by Rasid.com, 2007.
Al Ahmad, Ali, 'Bar countries that ban women athletes', *International Herald Tribune*, 19 May 2008.
Al-Akhbar (Lebanon), 'Zaven wa-l-Mustaqbal bi-ri'ayat al-CIA', 27 December 2008.
Al al-Sheikh, Mohammed bin Abdullatif, Column, *Al-Jazeera*, 30 May 2006.
Al al-Sheikh, Mufti Abdulaziz, Comments on Hizbullah: www.imamu.edu.sa/news/p515.htm.
Al-Arabiya.net, 'Al-Qaradawi yuhadhdhir min ikhtiraq shi'i li-misr 'abra bawwabat al-mutasawwifa', 2 September 2006.
——, 'Saudis must apply for govt license to start blogging', 3 January 2011.
Al-Awaji, Mohsin, Twitter comments; appearance on *Al-Ittijah al-Mu'akis*, Al-Jazeera, 5 May 2008.
Al-Azmeh, Aziz, *Islams and Modernities*. London: Verso, 1993.

——, *Muslim Kingship: Power and the Sacred in Muslim, Christian and Pagan Polities*. London: I.B. Tauris, 2001.

Al-Bakr, Fawziah, *Madrasati Sunduq Mughlaq*. Riyadh: Sar al-Rushd, 2005.

Al-Barrak, Abdulrahman, 'Ruling on the *mas'a* and running there', Islamlight website, 23 July 2008.

Al-Bisher, Badriya, *Hind wal-'Askar*. Beirut: Dar al-Adab, 2006.

Al-Fahad, Abdulaziz, 'From exclusivism to accomodation: doctrinal and legal evolution of Wahhabism', *New York University Law Review*, vol. 79, 2004.

Al-Ghaddami, Abdullah, *Al-Mar'a wal-Lugha*. Casablanca: al-Markaz al-Arabi al-Thaqafi, 2006.

Al-Hadath, 'Fi risala lil-wazir al-saudi: al-Hudaibi yastankir hujum al-amir Nayef 'ala al-Ikhwan al-Muslimin', 3 December 2002.

——, *Hikayat al-Hadatha*. Casablanca: al-Markaz al-Thaqafi al-Arabi, 2004.

Al-Hamad, Jawad, *The GCC and resolving the Arab-Israeli Conflict: A Reading of Gulf Summit Statements* (Arabic). Amman: Middle East Studies Centre.

Al-Hamad, Turki, *Sharq al-Wadi (East of the Valley)*. London: Saqi Books, 2000.

Al-Harz, Siba, *Al-Akharun*. Beirut: Dar al-Saqi, 2006.

Al-Hayat, 'Hay'at kibar al-ulama tujiz al-taqnin', 18 March 2010.

Al-Humayed, Tareq, 'Damaa Ghazza mashru' tijari', *Asharq al-Awsat*, 28 December 2008.

——, 'Hal hiya azmatu nizam wahdahu?', *Asharq al-Awsat*, 29 January 2011.

——, 'Al-ru'asa' al-'arab wa tasfir al-'addad', *Asharq al-Awsat*, 3 February 2011.

——, 'Li jumhouriyyaat-na: hadha 'ilaj al-thawraat', *Asharq al-Awsat*, 14 February 2011.

Al-Huzayem, Othman, 'Hukmuna al-saleh badil al-dimuqratiyya', *Al-Eqtisadiah*, 11 February 2011.

Al-Jabri, Mohammed 'Abed, *Arab-Islamic Philosophy: A Contemporary Critique*. Austin: University of Texas Press, 1999.

Al-Jawziyya, Ibn Qayyim, *Al-turuq al-hukmiyya fi al-siyasa al-shar'iyya*. Cairo: Dar al-madani, 1985.

Al-Jazeera, Decree banning gender mixing, 1983, republished in *Al-Jazeera* 12 January 2009.

Al-Khamis, Abdulaziz, 'The future of the Muslim Brotherhood in the Arabian Gulf', *Middle East* Online, 8 May 2011.

Al-Luhaidan, Saleh, interview on Saudi radio show *Noor 'ala al-Darb*, Saudi TV, September 2008; transcript at Islamlight: www.islamlight.net/index.php?option =content&task=view&id=11118&Itemid=23.

——, Transcript of interview on Saudi TV, September 2008: www.saaid.net/ arabic/209.htm#5.

Al-Mohaimeed, Yousef, *Fikhakh al-Ra'iha*. Beirut: Riad al-Rayyes, 2003.

Al-Mozainy, Abdulrahman, Muslim.net website, August 2009, www.muslm.net/vb/ showthread.php?t=356769

Al-Obaidan, Mohsen, 'Political and administrative reform is possible without having to resort to the ways of the Muslim Brotherhood', *Asharq al-Awsat*, 24 May 2005.

Al-Qahtani, Ali, 'Al-da'wa ila ta'ziz al-musa'ala fil-ajhiza al-hukumiyya wa man' isa'at istikhdam al-sulta', *Al-Watan*, 21 May 2007.

Al-Qaradawi, Yousef, interview, *Al-Masry al-Youm*, 9 September 2008.

Al-Qarni, Ayedh, *As'ad Imra'a fil-'Alam*. Riyadh: Maktabat al-Obeikan, 2004.

——, *La Tahzan*. Riyadh: Obeikan, 2007.

——, interview, Al-Arabiya.net, 10 August 2009.

——, 'Reviving the message of the clerics and their role in life', *Asharq al-Awsat*, 29 August 2009.

Al-Rashed, Abdulrahman, 'Tadamanu ma'ahu khawfan 'ala anfusihim', *Asharq al-Awsat*, 1 July 2008.

Al-Rasheed, Madawi, *Politics in an Arabian Oasis*. London: I.B. Tauris, 1997.

——, *A History of Saudi Arabia*. Cambridge: Cambridge University Press, 2002.

——, 'al-hajj: siyasat al-sa'udiyya al-ma'zuma', *Al-Quds al-Arabi*, 9 December 2008.

——, ed., *Kingdom Without Borders*. London: Hurst, 2008.

Al-Riyadh, televised speech by King Abdullah, 14 January 2004, printed in *Al-Riyadh*, 15 January 2004.

——, 'Biladna mustahdafa wa aydun sahyuniyya wara ma hadath', 2 May 2004.

——, 'Itlaq awwal markaz riyadi wa tarfihi hukumi lil-nisaa' fil-riyadh', 23 November 2008.

——, Government statement recalling ambassador to Syria, reprinted in *Al-Riyadh*, 7 August 2011.

Al-Saffar, Hassan. *Shakhsiyyat al-Mar'a*. Casablanca: al-Markaz al-Thaqafi al-Arabi, 2003.

Alsanea, Rajaa, *Banat al-Riyadh*.Beirut: Saqi Books, 2005.

Al Saud, Saif al-Islam bin Saud bin Abdulaziz, *Qalb Min Banqalan*. Beirut: Dar al-Farabi, 2004.

Al-Shirian, Dawoud, 'Ad'af al-iman: al-wada' bil-kaffayn', *Al-Hayat*, 16 December 2008.

Al-Seyassah, interview with King Abdullah, 27 January 2007.

Al-Sudairy, Turki, 'Ajir li-ajir', *Al-Riyadh*, 29 April 2007.

Al-Watan, editorial, 21 March 2003.

——, 'Qass sha'ir wa jald al-shabab mu'akisi al-fatayat bil-jawf', 26 April 2008.

——, 'Al-Amir Nayef: Inna hukmuna laysa wad'an bashariyyan', 20 June 2011.

Alyami, Ali, 'Commentary: suspend Saudi Arabia's Olympic team'. Investigative Project on Terrorism, 8 August 2008.

Ambah, Faiza, 'A drive toward the goal of greater freedom', *Washington Post*, 15 April 2008.

Amnesty International, 'Affront to justice: death penalty in Saudi Arabia', October 2008, www.amnesty.org/en/library/info/MDE23/027/2008/en.

An-Na'im, Abdullahi Ahmed, *Islam and the Secular State: Negotiating the Future of Shari'a*. Cambridge, MA: Harvard University Press, 2008.

Arab News, 'Civic polls seen as stepping stones to major elections', 5 December 2004.

——, 'Al-Manie says diabetes reaching epidemic proportions', 28 May 2007.

——, 'Saudi media discuss creation of second MSI', 27 July 2007.

——, 'Family Members Bury Al-Huraisi in Riyadh', 31 July 2007.

——, 'Put breaks on osteoporosis', 2 August 2007.

——, 'Qutb books banned in school libraries', 26 November 2008.

Arendt, Hannah, *The Origins of Totalitarianism*. New York: Schocken Books, 2004.

Asharq al-Awsat, 'Leading Arab television stations reject Zogby Report', 2 January 2006.

——, 'Na'ib wa da'iya maghrabi: adwa al-tashayyu' tajtah mudun shimal al-maghrib', 12 July 2008.

——, 'Bush 'an waqi'at al-hadhaa': aghrab haadith. Wa Rice: dalil hurriyya', 17 December 2008.

——, 'Sahafat dimuqratiyyat al-ahdhiya,' 17 December 2008.

——, 'Muhakamat munadhdhama sirriyya', 13 July 2011.

Associated Press, '1945 U.S.-Saudi meeting to be marked', 12 February 2005.
——, 'Egypt's head questions Shi'ites loyalty', 10 April 2006.
Attallah, Samir, 'Kitabatu l-tarikh masalatun mawdu'iyyatun', *Asharq al-Awsat*, 30 April 2007.
Atwan, Abdelbari, *The Secret History of al-Qa'ida*. London: Abacus, 2007.
Bayat, Asef, *Life as Politics: How Ordinary People Change the Middle East*. Cairo: American University in Cairo Press, 2009.
BBC Arabic online, 'Shaqiq al-Waleed yunadi bil-hajr 'ala amwal akhih', 29 June 2009.
BBC online, 'Saudis hit back over Mecca castle', 9 January 2002.
Bin Baz, Abdulaziz, *Collected fatwas*, on website: www.binbaz.org.sa/mat/331.
Bin Laden, Carmen, *The Veiled Kingdom*. London: Virago, 2004.
Bloomberg, 'Court jails Emirati woman in gang rape case', 14 July 2010.
Bradley, John, *Saudi Arabia Exposed: Inside a Kingdom in Crisis*. New York: Palgrave Macmillan, 2005.
Brown, Nathan, 'Arab Judicial Structures'. UNDP Programme on Governance on the Arab Region, 2001.
Carothers, Thomas, 'Think again: Arab democracy'. Carnegie Endowment for International Peace, 10 March 2011.
Cole, Juan, *Sacred Space and Holy War: The Politics, Culture, and History of Sh"ite Islam*. London: I.B. Tauris, 2002.
Coll, Steve, *Ghost Wars: The Secret History of the CIA, Afghanistan and Bin Laden*. Penguin, 2005.
Committee to Protect Journalists, 1997 regional press freedom report, www.cpj.org/attacks97/mideast/saudiarabia.html.
——, 'Princes, clerics and censors', 9 May 2006.
Cordesman, Anthony, *Saudi Arabia: Guarding the Desert Kingdom*. Boulder, CO: Westview, 1997.
Courrier international, 'Quand le rigorisme religieux fait fuir la jeunesse', 24 September 2009.
Crone, Patricia, *Meccan Trade and the Rise of Islam*. New Jersey: Gorgias Press, 2004.
Crone, Patricia, and Martin Hinds, *God's Caliph: Religious Authority in the First Centuries of Islam*. Cambridge: Cambridge University Press, 1986.
Daily Times, 'Muqrin, Hariri urge Nawaz to honour agreement', 9 September 2007.
Davidson, Christopher, *Dubai: The Vulnerability of Success*. London: Hurst & Co., 2008.
Dawisha, Adeed, *Arab Nationalism in the Twentieth Century: From Triumph to Despair*. Princeton, NJ: Princeton University Press, 2003.
Delong-Bas, Natana, *Wahhabi Islam: From Revival and Reform to Global Jihad*. Cairo: The American University in Cairo, 2005.
Der Spiegel International, 'Turki al-Faisal: people will no longer speak to American diplomats frankly', 5 December 2011.
Dirgham, Raghida, Commentary, *Al-Hayat*, 25 June 2003.
Elaph, 'Al-jaysh al-isra'ili yashaq umala' iran fi ghazza', 28 December 2008.
——, 'Adonis: I hope to visit Saudi Arabia and visit the places where the Companions of the Prophet were', 6 August 2009.
Fandy, Mamoun, *Saudi Arabia and the Politics of Dissent*. London: Palgrave Macmillan, 2001.
——, 'Wa-khitamuhu Fisk', *Asharq al-Awsat*, 30 April 2007.

Fanon, Frantz, *The Wretched of the Earth*. Penguin, 2001 (first published 1961).

Feldman, Noah, *The Fall and Rise of the Islamic State*. Princeton, NJ: Princeton University Press, 2008.

Fisk, Robert, 'Mohamed Hassanein Heikal: the wise man of the Middle East,' *Independent*, 9 April 2007.

Foer, Franklin, 'Moral hazard', *New Republic*, 18 November 2002.

Friedman, Thomas L., op. ed, 'The real war', *New York Times*, 27 November 2001.

——, 'An intriguing signal from the Saudi Crown Prince', *New York Times*, 17 February 2002.

FrontPageMagazine.com, 'The Future of US-Saudi relations', 11 June 2003.

Gallab, Abdullahi, 'The insecure rendezvous between Islam and totalitarianism: the failure of the Islamist state in the Sudan', *Arab Studies Quarterly (ASQ)*, spring 2001.

Gellner, Ernest, *Plough, Sword and Book: The Structure of Human History*. London: Paladin, 1991.

Guardian, 'UK feared Americans would invade Gulf during 1973 oil crisis', 1 January 2004.

Ha'aretz, 'The peace process: only Saudi Arabia can do it', 12 March 2007.

Haim, Sylvia, ed., *Arab Nationalism: An Anthology*. Berkeley: University of California Press, 1976.

Hallaq, Wael, *Sharia: Theory, Practice and Transformations*. Cambridge: Cambridge University Press, 2009.

Halliday, Fred, *Arabia Without Sultans*. London: Saqi Books, 2002.

Hammond, Andrew, 'Maintaining Saudi Arabia's *cordon sanitaire* in the Arab media', in Madawi Al-Rasheed, ed., *Kingdom Without Borders*. London: Hurst & Co., 2008.

——, 'Reading Lohaidan in Riyadh: media and the struggle for judicial power in Saudi Arabia', *Arab Media & Society*, issue 7, 2009.

——, 'Liberal enclaves: a royal attempt to bypass clerical power', in *The Kingdom of Saudi Arabia, 1979–2009: Evolution of a Pivotal State*. Washington: The Middle East Institute, October 2009.

Hegghammer, Thomas, and Stephane Lacroix, 'Rejectionist Islamism in Saudi Arabia: the story of Juhayman al-'Utaybi revisited', *International Journal of Middle East Studies*, vol. 39, no. 1, 2007, pp. 103–33.

Henderson, Simon, 'After King Abdullah: succession in Saudi Arabia'. Washington Institute for Near East Policy, August 2009.

Hersh, Seymour, 'The redirection: is the administration's new policy benefiting our enemies in the war on terrorism?', *New Yorker*, 5 March 2007.

Hourani, Albert, *History of the Arab Peoples*. London: Faber and Faber, 1992.

——, *Arabic Thought in the Liberal Age 1798–1939*. Cambridge: Cambridge University Press, 1993.

Human Rights Watch, *Perpetual Minors: Human Rights Abuses Stemming from Male Guardianship and Sex Segregation in Saudi Arabia*, 2008.

——, *Precarious Justice: Arbitrary Detention and Unfair Trials in the Deficient Criminal Justice System of Saudi Arabia*, 2008, www.hrw.org/fr/node/62305.

Ibn Abdulwahhab, Mohammed, *Kashf al-Shubuhat*, Riyadh: Tiba Publishing, 2005.

——, *Al-Usul al-Thalatha*. Riyadh: al-Mu'tamin Publishing (n.d.).

——, *Kitab al-Tawhid*. Riyadh: al-Juraisy Distribution (n.d.).

Ibn al-Shaikh, Mohammed ibn Khalaf, Letters section, *Al-Hayat*, 28 September 2008.

Ibn Taimiyya, Ahmed, *Al-Siyasa al-Shar'iyya fi islah al-ra'I wa al-ra'iyya*. Beirut: Dar al-Afaq al-Jadida, 1983.

Ibrahim, Fouad, *Al-Salafiyya al-Jihadiyya fi al-Sa'udiyya*. Beirut: Saqi Books, 2009.

International Herald Tribune, 'American invasion plan stirs fierce Saudi debate: echoes of 1973', 9 January 2004.

Kepel, Gilles. *Muslim Extremism in Egypt: The Prophet and the Pharaoh*. Berkeley: University of California Press, 1985.

Khal, Abdo. *Fusouq*. Beirut: Dar al-Saqi, 2005.

——, *Tarmi bi-Sharar*. Freiberg: Al-Kamel Verlag, 2010.

Khashoggi, Jamal, 'Ghadr al-Khawarij fi Ramadan: Kulluna Mohammed bin Nayef', *Al-Watan*, 29 August 2009.

Lacey, Robert, *Inside the Kingdom: Kings, Clerics, Terrorists, Modernists, and the Struggle for Saudi Arabia*. Viking Adult, 2009.

Lacroix, Stephane, 'Islamo-liberal politics in Saudi Arabia', in Paul Aarts and Gerd Nonneman, eds, *Saudi Arabia in the Balance*. London, Hurst & Company, 2005, pp. 35–56.

——, 'Vers un nouveau printemps de Riyad?', *Alternatives Internationales*, September 2005.

Lau, Martin, *The Role of Islam in the Legal System of Pakistan*. Leiden: Brill Academic, 2005.

Lawrence, T.E., *Seven Pillars of Wisdom*. London: Penguin Books, 2000.

Massad, Joseph, *Colonial Effects: The Making of National Identity in Jordan*. New York: Columbia University Press, 2001.

Roel Meijer, 'Reform in Saudi Arabia: the gender-segregation debate'. Middle East Policy Council, 2011.

Mekay, Emad, 'Iraq was invaded "to protect Israel" – US official', *Asia Times*, 31 March 2004.

Mitchell, Sandy, *Saudi Babylon: Torture, Corruption and Cover-up Inside the House of Saud*. London: Mainstream Publishing, 2005.

Molavi, Afshin, 'Saudi Arabia's moment of redemption?', *International Herald Tribune*, 3 September 2006.

More, Thomas, *Utopia*. Penguin, 2004.

Moubayed, Sami, 'Loose Saudi cannons in Lebanon', *Asia Times*, 19 July 2007.

Munif, Abdel-Rahman, *Mudun al-Malh (Cities of Salt, Part One)*. Beirut: Arab Institute for Studies and Publishing, 1992.

——, *Bayn al-Thaqafa wal-Siyasa*. Beirut: al-Markaz al-Thaqafi al-Arabia, 2003.

Nakhoul, Samia, 'Saudi schoolbooks under spotlight', Reuters, 15 October 2003.

Nasrallah, Elias, *Al-Saudiyya wa bid'at al-ta'rikh al-badil: qira'a naqdiyya li-khumasiyyat Abdulrahman Munif*. Damascus: Dar al-Mada, 2010.

National Defence Council, *Middle East to 2020*, 8 December 2003, www.dni.gov/nic/NIC_2020_2003_12_08_intro.html.

National Review Online, 'All foreign gifts report: US Department of Education', www.nationalreview.com/kurtz/allforeigngiftsreport.html.

Obaid, Nawaf, 'The power of Saudi Arabia's Islamic leaders', *Middle East Quarterly*, September 1999, pp. 51–8.

Okaz, Report on Abdullah's talsk with Bush, 15 May 2002.

——, 'Mufti al-mamlaka li-Hamas', 10 January 2009.

Organisation of the Islamic Summit meeting in Mecca, Closing statement, 8 December 2005.

Newsweek, interview with Shah of Iran, 21 May 1973.

——, 'Terror watch: a new rift?,' 4 May 2004.

——, 'The King versus the radicals,' 17 May 2008.

New York Times, 'Rebellious girl band breaks Saudi taboos', 25 November 2008.

——, 'A black Imam breaks ground in Mecca', 12 April 2009.

Ottaway, David, *The King's Messenger: Prince Bandar bin Sultan and America's Tangled Relationship with Saudi Arabia.* New York: Walker & Company, 2008.

Pappe, Ilan, ed., *The Israel/Palestine Question.* London: Routledge, 1999.

Perkins, John, *Confessions of an Economic Hitman.* San Francisco: Berrett-Koehler Publishers, 2004.

Petition to the royal family, 'Ru'ya li-hadir al-watan wa-mustaqbil-hi', January 2003.

——, 'Nidaa' watani lil-qiyada wal-sha'b ma'an: al-Islah al-dusturi awwalan', 16 December 2003.

——, 'Ma'alim fi tariq al-malikiyya al-dusturiyya', 1 April 2007.

——, 'Nutalib bi-fath malaff huquq al-insan wa-muqadat wizarat al-dakhiliyya', 18 April 2007.

——, 'I'lan watani lil-islah', 23 February 2011.

——, 'Risalat al-shabab fi-l-sa'udiyya ila al-malik Abdullah', 23 February 2011.

——, 'Nahwa dawlat al-huquq wa-l-mu'assasaat', February 2011.

Phillips, Tom (British ambassador in Riyadh), Statement, 28 February 2011.

Qusti, Raid, 'Fixing the problem of extremism', *Arab News*, 21 July 2004.

Qutb, Sayed, *Ma'alim Fil-Tareeq (Milestones).* Beirut: Dar al-Shurouq, 1979 (first published 1965).

Randal, Jonathan, *Osama.* London: I.B. Tauris, 2005.

Reuters, 'Lebanon restores opposition TV foreign broadcasts', 5 January 2003.

——, 'Saudi reformers face media shut-out, death threats', 10 October 2003.

——, 'Saudi militants rigged Koran with explosives: report', 13 November 2003.

——, 'Saudi Shi'ite clerics slam remarks by Mubarak', 10 April 2005.

——, 'Iraq blasts Saudi Arabia for anti-Shi'ite remarks', 2 October 2005.

——, 'Saudi says U.S. policy handing Iraq over to Iran', 21 September 2005.

——, 'Ambush kills 15 Iraqi troops north of Baghdad', 3 December 2005.

——, 'Saudi to get $26 bln makeover with tourism project', 20 December, 2005.

——, 'Saudi wants to trim waists of overweight population', 5 March 2006.

——, 'Saudi clerics fete Hamas delegation', 13 March 2006.

——, 'Saudi textbooks still preach hatred', 24 May 2006.

——, 'Saudi Arabia blames Hizbollah in Lebanon crisis', 14 July 2006.

——, 'Saudi clerics torn between hatred for Israel and Hizbollah', 27 July 2006.

——, 'Saudi clerics want to restrict women praying at Mecca', 28 August 2006.

——, 'Saudi minister defends policies on unemployment', 10 September 2006.

——, 'Saudi Arabia says Israel meeting report fabricated', 26 September 2006.

——, 'Saudis push anti-militant line in Ramadan TV shows', 3 October 2006.

——, 'Saudi Arabia goes into overdrive for Ramadan', 10 October 2006.

——, 'Saudi youth bored in model Islamic state: blogger', 26 October 2006.

——, 'Saudi clerics call for help for Sunnis in Iraq', 11 December 2006.

——, 'Saddam death raises tribal, religious ire in Saudi', 4 January 2007.

——, 'Saudi displays Sri Lankan bodies to deter crime', 20 February 2007.

——, 'Saudi liberal reappointed as newspaper editor', 17 April 2007.

——, 'Saudi utility needs Aramco help to avoid power cuts', 29 May 2007.

——, 'Saudi lawyer to appeal in morals squad death case', 15 June 2007.

——, 'Saudis warn clerics over militants in Iraq', 20 June 2007.

——, 'Saudi Arabia launches campaign to combat drug use', 24 June 2007.

——, 'Saudis fighting in Iraq, Lebanon, embarrass homeland', 19 July 2007.
——, 'Girls of Riyadh spurs rush of Saudi novels', 23 July 2007.
——, 'Leading Saudi clerics publicly denounces bin Laden', 18 September 2007.
——, 'Saudi cleric issues warning over Saudi militants', 1 October 2007.
——, 'Saudi king promotes tolerance at UN forum', 13 November 2007.
——, 'US offers mild criticism in Saudi rape case', 19 November 2007.
——, 'Saudi official criticizes ruling on rape victim', 27 November 2007.
——, 'Bush avoids criticism of Saudi king on rape case', 4 December 2007.
——, 'Qaeda's Zawahri calls Annapolis meeting a sellout', 14 December 2007.
——, 'Saudi king pardons rape victim', 18 December 2007.
——, 'Saudi woman just wants family back', 30 January 2008.
——, 'Saudi king calls for new interfaith dialogue', 25 March 2008.
——, 'Saudi king says keeping some oil finds for future', 13 April 2008.
——, 'Saudi "guardianship" said key to women's rights abuse', 21 April 2008.
——, 'Economic fears forcing Saudi women into workplace', 5 May 2008.
——, 'Qaeda video berates Saudi king over faith dialogue', 23 May 2008.
——, 'Saudi clerics attack Shi'ites, Hezbollah', 1 June 2008.
——, 'Saudi king's interfaith call faces Muslim divisions', 4 June 2008.
——, 'Saudi Shi'ites hit back at Sunni critics', 2 July 2008.
——, 'Saudi Arabia to announce "openness" at Spain forum', 15 July 2008.
——, 'Saudi offers Russia arms deal to curb Iran ties', 15 July 2008.
——, 'Riyadh seen trying to wean Russia away from Iran', 16 July 2008.
——, 'Saudi king shuns extremism as faiths gather', 16 July 2008.
——, 'Saudi appeals court upholds flogging researchers', 30 July 2008.
——, 'Saudi Arabia says Games team will not include women', 30 July 2008.
——, 'Saudi cleric wants death for TV astrologers', 14 September 2008.
——, 'Saudi Arabia clamps down on unlicensed female gyms', 30 April 2009.
——, '50-year-old divorces child bride?', 30 April 2009.
——, 'Kuwait's democracy troubles Gulf Arab rulers', 24 June 2009.
——, 'Man scandalises Saudi Arabia with TV sex confession', 30 July 2009.
——, 'Mecca goes upmarket but commercialism unnerves some', 12 November 2010.
Reuters Television, 'Tourism Commission develops new strategies to attract international tourists', 31 October 2008.
Rodgers, Peter, *Herzl's Nightmare: One Land, Two Peoples*. New York: Nation Books, 2005.
Ruthven, Malise, *Islam in the World*. London: Penguin, 2000.
Saleh, Walid, 'The politics of Quranic hermeneutics: royalties on interpretation', public lecture at UCLA Center for Near Eastern Studies, 6 July 2009.
Said, Edward. *Orientalism*. Princeton, NJ: Princeton University Press, 1979.
Sampson, William, *Confessions of an Innocent Man: Torture and Survival in a Saudi Prison*. Toronto: McClelland & Stewart, 2006.
Saudi Civil and Political Rights Association, 'The Systematic Human Rights Violations by the Directorate of General Investigation (The Ministry of Interior) in the Kingdom of Saudi Arabia', 13 August 2011, www.acpra1.net/news.php?action=view&id=140.
Saudi Gazette, 'Girl gets a year in jail, 100 lashes for adultery', 12 January 2011.
——, 'Long coats and scarfs now obligated by ministry', 20 July 2008.
Saudi Jeans website, 'The New Activism', 2 August 2011.
——, 'Saudi reform petitions', Saudijeans.org/2011/02/28/Saudi-reform-petitions.
Saudi Press Agency, 'Comments from the Interior Minister', 27 November 2002.

——, interview with Crown Prince Sultan, 4 June 2008.

——, interview with King Abdullah, 1 July 2008.

——, 'Wafd min wizarat al-'adl yazur al-wilayat al-muttahida al-amrikiyya', 20 October 2008.

——, statement by clerics against protests and petitions, 6 March 2011.

Shea, Nina, 'A medal for brass', *Weekly Standard*, 26 May 2008.

Shafer, Jack, 'The PowerPoint that rocked the Pentagon', Slate.com, 7 Aug 2002.

Shafir, Gershon, 'Zionism and colonialism: a comparative approach', in Ilan Pappe, ed., *The Israel/Palestine Question*. London: Routledge, 1999, pp. 86–90.

Shufani, Elias, *Memoirs of Elias Shufani*. Beirut: Institute of Palestine Studies, 2010.

Soage, Ana Belen, 'Shaykh Yusuf Al-Qaradawi: portrait of a leading Islamist cleric', *Middle East Review of International Affairs (MERIA)*, vol. 12, no. 1, March 2008.

St Petersburg Times, 'Sailor was the piper of history', 2 December 2005.

Steinberg, Guido, 'The Wahhabi ulama and the Saudi state', in Paul Aarts and Gerd Nonneman, eds, *Saudi Arabia in the Balance*. London, Hurst & Company, 2005.

Trofimov, Yaroslav, *The Siege of Mecca*. New York: Doubleday, 2007.

UNDP, *Millenium Development Goals Report on the Kingdom of Saudi Arabia, 2005*.

UNHCR, Press Release, 'United Nations rights expert on violence against women concludes visit to Saudi Arabia,' 13 February 2008.

Vitalis, Robert, *America's Kingdom: Mythmaking on the Saudi Oil Frontier*. Stanford, CA: Stanford University Press, 2007.

Washington Post, 'Bush moves to ease tensions with Saudis', 28 August 2002.

Weston, Mark, *Prophets and Prince: Saudi Arabia from Muhammad to the Present*. Hoboken, NJ: Wiley, 2008.

Wikileaks cables, Saudi Arabia, pp. 1–47, http://wikileaks.org/tag/SA_0.html.

Wolf, Naomi. 'Behind the veil lives a thriving Muslim sexuality', *Sydney Morning Herald*, 30 August 2008.

Woodward, Bob, *Plan of Attack*. New York: Simon & Schuster, 2004.

Wright, Lawrence, *The Looming Tower: Al Qaeda's Road to 9/11*. London: Allen Lane, 2006.

Yamani, Mai, *Cradle of Islam: The Hijaz and the Quest for Identity in Saudi Arabia*. London: I.B. Tauris, 2009.

Yapp, M.E., *The Near East since the First World War*. New York: Longman, 1991.

Ynetnews, 'Olmert urges Gazans to stop Hamas', 25 December 2008.

Zakaria, Fareed, 'The politics of rage: why do they hate us?', *Newsweek*, 1 October 2001.

Index